Sweet Land of Liberty

Sweet Land of Liberty

AMERICA IN THE MIND
OF THE FRENCH LEFT, 1848–1871

Tom Sancton

LOUISIANA STATE UNIVERSITY PRESS
BATON ROUGE

Published by Louisiana State University Press
www.lsupress.org

Manufactured in the United States of America
First printing

DESIGNER: Michelle A. Neustrom
TYPEFACE: Garamond Premier Pro

JACKET ILLUSTRATION: *The Statue of Liberty by Bartholdi in the Workshop
of Gaget-Gauthier, Rue de Chazelles, Paris,* ca. 1884, by Victor Dargaud.
Courtesy Alamy Limited.

LIBRARY OF CONGRESS CATALOGING-IN-PUBLICATION DATA
Names: Sancton, Thomas (Thomas Alexander), 1949– author.
Title: Sweet land of liberty : the French left looks at America, 1848–1871 / Tom Sancton.
Description: Baton Rouge : Louisiana State University Press, 2021. | Includes bibliographical
    references and index.
Identifiers: LCCN 2020028670 (print) | LCCN 2020028671 (ebook) | ISBN 978-0-8071-
    7430-2 (cloth) | ISBN 978-0-8071-7498-2 (pdf) | ISBN 978-0-8071-7499-9 (epub)
Subjects: LCSH: United States—History—Civil War, 1861–1865—Foreign public opinion,
    French. | United States—History—1849–1877—Foreign public opinion, French. | France—
    History—1848–1870. | France—Civilization—American influences. | Public opinion—
    France—History—19th century.
Classification: LCC E469.8 .S26 2021 (print) | LCC E469.8 (ebook) | DDC 973.7/1—dc23
LC record available at https://lccn.loc.gov/2020028670
LC ebook record available at https://lccn.loc.gov/2020028671

For Theodore Zeldin,
Historian, teacher, mentor, friend

CONTENTS

PART IV   L'Année Terrible and Beyond

PREFACE

S
ince the Revolutionary era, the French left has included many diverse ideologies beneath its standard. The present study uses the term in a broad
sense: it examines the views of people who considered themselves left wing
and were so considered by their contemporaries, who accepted the tradition of
the French Revolution, and who believed in democratic ideas and hoped for
their triumph in France. They described themselves variously as liberals, republicans, democrats, radicals, socialists, or anarchists.

Among them was Alexis de Tocqueville, who had explained American democracy to his compatriots with two landmark volumes, then went on to serve as
a deputy and, briefly, as foreign minister. The novelist George Sand (Amandine
Aurore Lucile, baronne Dudevant, née Dupin), who shocked contemporaries
with her baggy men's clothing and sexual mores, was a romantic socialist and fervent supporter of the Second Republic. Victor Hugo, a towering literary figure
and ardent republican, stood on flaming barricades to oppose Louis Napoleon's
1851 coup d'état, then fled to the rocky Channel Islands to spend the next two
decades as France's most famous and impassioned exile. The socialist Louis Blanc,
who played a major role in shaping the idealistic Second Republic, escaped to
England after the Bonapartist coup and completed a monumental twelve-volume
history of the French Revolution. The visionary Fourierist Victor Considérant,
another post-1851 exile, preached salvation through emigration to America and
lured hundreds of followers into the arid wilderness of Texas in a disastrous attempt to set up a utopian community. The anarchist Pierre-Joseph Proudhon—
author of the famous formula "Property is theft!"—commanded a large working-
class following and wound up an improbable supporter of the Confederacy. The
eminent geographer Elisée Reclus, another anarchist, had observed American
slavery firsthand while working as a tutor on a Louisiana plantation in the 1850s

and would later fight for the Paris Commune of 1871. The Commune's military commander, the radical socialist Gustave Cluseret,[1] had fought as a volunteer in the Union army during the American Civil War before returning to Europe to serve various and sundry revolutionary causes with his sword and pen. On the more moderate end of the political spectrum, the republican jurist Edouard Laboulaye, an authority on the U.S. Constitution, emerged during the Civil War as the most ardent champion of the Union cause and later launched a subscription to place the Statue of Liberty in New York harbor. The republican and future prime minister Georges Clemenceau thrilled to the news of Abraham Lincoln's Emancipation Proclamation and reported on American Reconstruction as a journalist.

These prominent figures on the French left were keen observers and commentators on American events. Alongside them were hundreds of others—journalists, lawyers, professors, politicians, and workers—who looked at the United States during these tumultuous years with an eye on events in their own country. Ever since the American War of Independence, liberal-minded Frenchmen had felt a special, often paternal, sense of kinship with the United States.[2] Both historically and ideologically, America had ties with the French Revolutionary tradition, and those in France who were sympathetic toward democracy were often drawn to the American republic as a source of inspiration and propaganda. In the nineteenth century, as Sigmund Skard has written, "the United States became the arsenal of French democratic idealism."[3] Like the Soviet Union in the first part of the twentieth century, America was seen by many on the left as the "wave of the future."

Similar ideological considerations often led opponents of political liberty to denigrate the United States and predict its ruin. But it would be a gross oversimplification to say that the left was pro-American and the right anti-American. Numerous individual exceptions can be found on both sides. The left's enthusiasm for the United States, moreover, varied in intensity at different periods, depending both on political circumstances in France and events in America.

This book seeks to show how the image of the United States was perceived and used by the French left during the years between the Revolution of 1848 and the Paris Commune of 1871. For most of this period, the left stood in opposition to the authoritarian government of Napoleon III. Since it was difficult and often dangerous to promote democratic ideas at this time, there was a natural tendency to extol the American republic as the living symbol of political liberty. Thus, to a great extent, the left's image of the United States was a product of their own propaganda needs. But this admiration was not blind or unconditional: their opinion was also influenced by America's own political and social development during these eventful years.

It happened that the United States faced one of its greatest national crises during the period under consideration. The 1850s witnessed an eruption of expansionist fever, the exacerbation of the slavery controversy, and the rise of sectional passions. The 1860s saw the disintegration of the Union, the American Civil War, the emancipation of the slaves, the assassination of President Lincoln, and the beginnings of Reconstruction. One of the main objects of this study is to determine the extent to which these events affected the left's image of America and the use they made of that image in pursuing their own goals in France.

As useful as the U.S. example was to those who promoted democratic ideas in France, American political, social, and economic realities were not always well understood. Viewed through French lenses, America might seem like a repository of the same values and republican ideologies that emerged from the French Revolution. In fact, as Tocqueville well knew, American democracy was a very different expression of political liberty. The United States that emerged from the Civil War—capitalist, assertive, flawed by the excesses and corruption of the Gilded Age—could hardly be a positive model for the French left that had earlier extolled the country. Moreover, America's pro-German sentiments in the Franco-Prussian War (1870–71) and hostility to the Paris Commune further tarnished the U.S. image in the eyes of the French left. The resulting sense of disappointment and betrayal nourished the deep-seated anti-Americanism that pervaded the French left's thinking into the twentieth century and beyond. It is hoped that the present study can also illuminate patterns that are commonly found in other times and places whenever a domestic political faction perceives a foreign power in the light of its own culture and ideology.

PART I

The Rise and Fall of the American Image, 1848–1861

I confess that in America I saw much more than America; I sought the image of democracy itself, its inclinations, its character, its prejudices and its passions; I wanted to understand it in order to learn what we should hope or fear from it.
—ALEXIS DE TOCQUEVILLE, *Democracy in America*

O n May 9, 1831, a young French jurist landed in Newport, Rhode Island. His goal was to study the workings of the world's only major democracy in order to prepare his compatriots for the time when political liberty would come to France. Neither Tocqueville nor any of his contemporaries expected that moment to arrive so swiftly. In February 1848, in the space of several hours, the July Monarchy suddenly fell amid the flames and clamor of a popular uprising. As the country's new leaders struggled to improvise their own republic, American democracy became their central reference, and giddy incantations of Franco-American friendship rivaled the days of Rochambeau and Lafayette. But this fascination with the United States would soon fade.

CHAPTER I

America and the Second Republic

Every Frenchman has for Americans the heart of Lafayette.
—ALPHONSE DE LAMARTINE, April 1848

Don't you see how much the latest revolution has brought France and America together, and how much the experience of one is made to enlighten the endeavors of the other?
—EDOUARD LABOULAYE, 1849

F rance is no stranger to revolutions. The first one beheaded Louis XVI, ushered in the Reign of Terror, and ended with an empire. The second, in 1830, sent Louis's younger brother, Charles X, into exile and put his cousin Louis-Philippe on the throne of a constitutional monarchy. By the late 1840s, the winds of revolution were starting to blow again. Against the backdrop of economic distress, social discontent, and high unemployment, the pear-shaped "bourgeois king" faced rising opposition from the disenfranchised workers and middle classes. Their central demand was expansion of the right to vote, then enjoyed by only the top tier of taxpayers, composing about 1 percent of the population.[1]

Electoral reform was the focus of the political banquets that, starting in July 1847, served as vehicles for the opposition views of liberals, republicans, and socialists and enjoyed broad popular support. Meanwhile, the toiling classes and their defenders demanded a "right to work" and a reorganization of the labor system. Members of revolutionary secret societies called for insurrection. "We are sleeping on a volcano," warned Alexis de Tocqueville, who had taken a seat in the Chamber of Deputies in 1839 and was a close observer of the events that followed.[2]

The banning of a major Paris banquet on February 22, 1848—the anniversary of George Washington's birthday, as it happened—was the spark that set off the conflagration. By noon of that day, angry Parisians flooded the streets of the capital and began to erect barricades. The next day soldiers fixed bayonets to their rifles and fired into the crowd on the Place Vendôme, killing twenty people and wounding more than fifty. At that point, what had been a popular protest turned into a violent uprising as angry Parisians, largely supported by the Garde nationale citizens' militia, paraded the bodies of their martyrs through the streets, overturned omnibuses, set fires throughout the capital, and surged toward the royal residence in the Tuileries palace. Fearing for his life, Louis-Philippe abdicated on February 24 and fled to England in disguise—he had shaved off his famous muttonchop sideburns and donned an oversized pair of glasses—escaping by ferry from Le Havre under the rather unconvincing alias of "Mr. Smith."[3]

On February 26 the Chamber of Deputies named a provisional government with Jacques-Charles Dupont de l'Eure, an octogenarian veteran of the original Revolution, as its president. Meeting at the Hôtel de Ville, Paris's ornate sixteenth-century city hall, this impromptu eleven-member body proclaimed the Second Republic. For those on the French left, it was a long-awaited moment of triumph. After years of ineffectual opposition, advocates of democratic ideas— men like Alphonse de Lamartine, Alexandre Ledru-Rollin, and Louis Blanc— were suddenly thrust into positions of power and influence. The revolutionary slogan "liberty, equality, fraternity" was once again the official motto of the government. The new regime immediately decreed universal male suffrage, proclaimed a guaranteed right to work, and launched an ambitious state-supported jobs program known as National Workshops, an idea Blanc had proposed in his influential book *L'Organisation du travail* in 1841. Among the popular masses, democratic aspirations rose to new heights, along with hopes for a rapid improvement of their material condition.[4]

It was not only the Parisian masses who rejoiced. The novelist George Sand, a onetime lover of Louis Blanc who embraced his socialist ideals, rushed to Paris from her country home in Nohant to witness the heady events firsthand. "Vive la République!" she gushed to a friend upon her return. "I saw the people, the grand, sublime, naïve, generous French people, gathered together in the heart of France, in the heart of the world; the most admirable people in the universe. . . . We are crazy, we are drunk, we are happy to have gone to sleep in the mire only to awaken in the heavens."[5] Sand's euphoria reflects what Louis Girard has called the "social romanticism" of the Second Republic's early days.[6] It would not last.

But in the meantime, friends of liberty and democracy around the world applauded the revolution and encouraged the leaders of the fledgling republic.

Unlike his more cautious colleagues of the diplomatic corps in Paris, American minister Richard Rush hastened to recognize the new regime on February 26, acting on his own authority in the absence of instructions from Washington. A former U.S. attorney general and secretary of state, Rush had maintained cordial relations with the king and his prime minister, François Guizot, and was stunned by their sudden downfall. Though he had refrained from taking sides in the heated political debates that preceded the revolution, he considered the French people "the sole judges of what form of government they would have."[7] It was his duty to respect their choice.

On February 28, decked out in formal diplomatic attire, Rush left his office in the Rue de Lille and headed across the river to the Hôtel de Ville, where the provisional government had set up its headquarters. After shouldering his way through the excited throngs gathered outside, Rush was presented to the government. He then read a short address offering his congratulations and recalling "the alliance and ancient friendship which have joined together France and the United States [and] is still living and in full force among us." Spontaneous shouts of "Vive la République des Etats-Unis!" rang out from the government members and the crowd outside.[8] Dupont de l'Eure, the provisional president, grasped Rush's hand and told him, "The French people shakes the hand of the American nation." Thus began a resurgence of "Americanophilia" that marked, along with the ritual incantations to universal brotherhood and the planting of liberty trees, the period of "lyrical illusions" that followed the February Revolution.[9]

Displays of mutual friendship and esteem were numerous during the early days of the Second Republic. In Paris, delegations of American citizens paraded to the Hôtel de Ville to congratulate the provisional government. French expressions of sympathy and gratitude flooded into the American legation, and the United States was widely praised by French statesmen and journalists. In America the first reactions were no less enthusiastic. Large pro-French rallies were held in many U.S. cities, and the American press, with very few exceptions, cheered the downfall of the monarchy and the founding of a new republic in France.[10]

Amid these popular demonstrations, the government in Washington approved Rush's recognition and instructed him to give all possible assistance to the new regime. On April 6 the U.S. Senate took the unprecedented step of adopting a resolution "tendering the congratulations of the American to the French people."[11] When Rush officially communicated this resolution to the provisional government on May 22, Foreign Minister Lamartine, the government's most gifted orator, declared his nation's faith in the example and principles of the American republic. "The names of Washington, Jefferson and Jakson [*sic*] are inscribed on the banner of the New Republic," he said, "and if France is fortunate enough in the future to find men worthy of these great names, liberty will assume her true character on the old continent as she has done on the other side of the Atlantic."[12] These expressions of reciprocal goodwill surpassed the courtesies of formal diplomacy. At no other time during the nineteenth century, in fact, did the French and American nations enjoy such cordial relations as in the spring of 1848.

Once the dust of the February Revolution had settled, the country's new leaders faced the problem of drafting a constitution amid a power struggle between partisans of an idealistic "social" republic and those who favored a more conservative regime based on order. This was a critical process, for the form in which this document would be cast would determine the nature and the destiny of the Second Republic. At that point, the vague admiration for their "Sister Republic" gave way to more critical evaluations as the French began to examine the American political system in detail.

The American example seemed to impose itself on all discussions of the new constitution. References to it—pro and con—abounded in the press, in electoral manifestos and pamphlets, and in the debates of the Constituent Assembly, which convened in May. Michel Chevalier, an authority on America, wrote a long series of articles on the United States in the *Journal des Débats*.[13] The legal scholar Edouard Laboulaye published his *Considérations sur la constitution* shortly after the revolution and launched a course on the U.S. Constitution at the Collège de France the following year.[14] Another noted Americanophile, Alexis de Tocqueville, brought out a new edition of his *De la Démocratie en Amérique* and frequently cited U.S. precedents as a member of the commission that drafted the new constitution.

But the French were not unanimous in embracing American political doctrines. The most enthusiastic partisans of the American model in 1848 were the liberals, who saw the United States as an example of a moderate, orderly republic that provided the best arguments against their enemies on both extremes. The liberals had long admired Anglo-Saxon institutions, with their traditions of representative government, checks and balances, and individual liberty. Most of them would have preferred an English-style parliamentary monarchy, but since the republic seemed to be a fait accompli, many now looked to the American system as an effective bulwark against the dangers of extreme democracy.[15]

But if the American model seemed made to order for the liberals in 1848, it clashed with many of the basic ideas and prejudices of those further to the left. In the first place, the left did not generally share the liberals' admiration for the Anglo-Saxon people or their institutions. Democrats of the Jacobin school tended to look on the English with an "age-old hatred" as the historic enemies of the French Revolution.[16] The Anglo-Saxons, moreover, were seen as the champions of laissez-faire capitalism, individualism, and private property, all of which further condemned them in the eyes of many French democrats and socialists.[17]

No one voiced this view more forcefully than Victor Hugo, whose scorn for the English *esprit de commerce* was coupled with a deep skepticism about American society. In an 1840 poem he had bewailed the rising influence of American materialism at the expense of the spiritual values symbolized by Italy:

America rises up and Rome dies . . .
Thus matter steals the world from thought!
Italy was art, faith, heart, fire.
America is soulless. A frigid worker.
An ardent star is fading, a cold star is ascending.
Seigneur! Philadelphia, a merchant's counter,
Will replace the city where Michelangelo dreamed."[18]

When Hugo wrote those words, he was not yet the ardent republican he was to become. He had begun his political life as an ultraroyalist under the Bourbon Restoration. He later supported Louis-Philippe, who named him to France's upper legislative house, the Chamber of Peers. It was only in the wake of the 1848 revolution that he finally gravitated into the republican camp, which did not prevent him from supporting Louis Napoleon Bonaparte in the presidential election.[19] By that time, Hugo was already an esteemed literary figure and a member of the Académie française, having published numerous poetic and dramatic works in addition to his monumental *Notre Dame de Paris* (1831). Elected to the Constituent Assembly in June 1848, he finally emerged as one of the most ardent exponents of a generous and humanist republican ideal. Though he never achieved a position of political power as a minister or party leader, no one was more influential than Hugo in the realm of words and ideas. From that time on, he was a leading light on the French left and would remain so until his death in 1885.

Not surprisingly, given his jaundiced views on Anglo-Saxon materialism, Hugo ignored the American example in his public speeches. While others on the left extolled or criticized the U.S. model, Hugo held up France itself as the world's shining light of liberty. "For three centuries the world has imitated France," he declared in March 1848 while planting a liberty tree in the Place des Vosges. "For three centuries, France is the first among nations. . . . Let us establish throughout the world, by the force of our examples, the empire of our ideas. Every nation should be happy and proud to resemble France!"[20]

As Jean-Noël Jeanneney has noted, Hugo's words ring with "an excess of national self-satisfaction."[21] And yet they were typical of a certain view on the left that hailed the French Revolution as the true fount of human liberty and democracy, even though the American Revolution had predated it by more than a decade. Hugo, for his part, could never embrace America as a model for the "universal republic" that he envisioned, even though events would lead him on occasion to praise the United States.

Hugo's uneasy ambivalence was shared by many others on the French left. Their misgivings about the American model were reinforced when they saw it invoked against the ideal of social democracy in 1848. Moderates and conservatives preached the American virtues of individualism, saving, and self-help as the proper code of behavior for workingmen in a "true democracy." Benjamin Franklin's maxims celebrating thrift and deferred gratification were widely used to combat the spread of socialist doctrines among the workers.[22] At the same time, attempts to alter the conditions of labor through government intervention were systematically opposed in the name of liberty. Projects like the nationalization of the railroads and the establishment of the National Workshops were denounced by moderates like Tocqueville and the Catholic activist Charles de Montalembert, who cited the American example in asserting that political liberty and laissez-faire economics went hand in hand. Mocking the idea that the state should guarantee employment, Tocqueville declared before the Constituent Assembly, "Democratic America is today that country in all the world where the socialist doctrines you pretend accord so well with democracy have the least circulation."[23]

Tocqueville's admonition reflected the struggle that had emerged between the defenders of a social republic and the partisans of order. The main target of the conservatives was the National Workshops, established in the euphoric early days of the republic to provide government jobs for the masses of unemployed workers. In the conception of Blanc, who initiated the idea, it was both a vehicle for social justice and a solution to the problem of unemployment. In practice, however, it was a shambles: some 115,000 workers were assigned to useless ground-leveling projects at a cost to the state of 2,000 francs a day.

The government's decision to close the workshops on June 21 triggered the "June Days" uprising (June 23–26), which was brutally repressed by the army under the command of General Louis Cavaignac. The scale of the bloodshed was horrendous: between 3,000 and 5,000 insurgents were killed during the fighting, while another 1,500 died in summary executions. On the other side of the barricades, some 1,200 soldiers were killed, including four generals. The violence left Hugo, an eyewitness, with a sense of disgust and despair. "What remains," he wrote in his journal, "of all we have accomplished, desired, strived for, constructed, built, founded over the past sixty years [since the first Revolution]? Ruins above us, the void beneath us. We are trapped between a ceiling that is falling over our heads and a floor that is collapsing under our feet."[24] The republic did not collapse in the wake of the June Days, but the horrific clash marked the end of its social orientation and consolidated the political control of the forces of order.

It was against this backdrop that the Constituent Assembly pursued its work on the new constitution, a crucial task that had begun a month before the insurrection and terminated in November 1848. As noted, the American example was often cited during the debates, but that model proved more useful to moderates and conservatives than to partisans of more advanced democratic ideals. The basic features of the U.S. Constitution—federalism, bicameralism, and an independent executive—ran counter to the ideas and traditions of the French left.

Their main constitutional model was the revolutionary National Convention, in which the will of the people fused with the centralized power of the state in a single legislative chamber. Their political models were the Jacobin Montagnards, whose name and style were adopted by the radical deputies of 1848. There was little in America's political institutions that fit this pattern.

The federal basis of the U.S. Constitution was one of the main reasons for the left's coolness toward the American model in 1848. Federalism was out of harmony with the French political experience and was especially repugnant to the left. Tainted by its historical association with the Girondists, federalism conflicted with the ideal of centralization, to which the left had been passionately devoted since 1793. The far left of that era had looked scornfully on the federalism of the Americans as a vestige of aristocratic and feudal institutions.[25] The prejudice against federalism remained a part of the revolutionary ideology into the nineteenth century and continued to color the left's view of the United States.[26] Tocqueville, who was a member of the eighteen-man constitutional commission that drafted the document, noted sardonically in his memoirs, "In France there is only one thing we cannot create: that is a free government, and there is only one institution we cannot destroy: centralization."[27]

Bicameralism, with its elitist upper chamber, was associated in the French mind with aristocratic and monarchical institutions. In European governments the upper legislative chamber had traditionally served to control and restrain the lower chamber elected by popular vote. It seemed antidemocratic to many Frenchmen and was strongly opposed by public opinion.[28] Only two other members of the constitutional commission joined Tocqueville in supporting the idea of a bicameral legislature.[29] But the question of bicameralism was revived when the draft constitution came before the full assembly in September. At that time the Orleanist Prosper Duvergier de Hauranne, a journalist and member of the antirepublican right, proposed an amendment calling for an upper chamber, basing his arguments largely on the American precedent. Praising the United States as a republic founded on order and moderation, he asked his colleagues: "Is it not strange that the example of the American republic, that example so often cited by republicans, should become today, because it bothers them, the object of their sarcasms and their disdain?"[30] After a heated debate, the partisans of the single chamber prevailed and Duvergier's amendment was defeated by a large majority.

The question of the presidency found republicans divided. Moderates like

Tocqueville and Laboulaye recommended an American-style presidency to counterbalance the power of the legislative assembly. But the more advanced republicans and socialists tended to see an independent president as a "potential despot" and a "permanent-danger to order and liberty."[31] Those who looked to the Convention of 1793 as their model wanted no head of state and no external check on the power of the National Assembly. A presidency, warned the socialist Louis Blanc, would lead to "a parliamentary revolution or another 18 Brumaire. . . . I predict that, within a month, the president will be everything and the Assembly nothing."[32]

But the American example seems to have been more persuasive on this point than on any other. No member of the constitutional commission even questioned the idea of an independent president. After a brief discussion concerning the means of choosing the executive—Tocqueville argued in vain for indirect election by an electoral college—the commissioners decided on direct election by universal suffrage.[33] In contrast with the American practice, however, they decided to limit the president's mandate to a single four-year term.

When the constitutional project came up for debate before the assembly, the republican deputy Jules Grévy, a lawyer from the eastern Jura region, proposed that the presidency be abolished. Recalling the precedent of Napoleon I, he warned that an ambitious and popular leader might once again attempt to seize absolute power in a coup d'état. But Lamartine (who had his own eye on the presidency) brushed aside these objections in an eloquent and famous speech. He foresaw all the dangers Grévy pointed to but maintained that the republic had to remain true to the democratic principle by letting the people choose their own leader. "We must leave something to Providence !" he declared. "Whatever may happen, it will be beautiful in the eyes of history to have attempted the Republic . . . of enthusiasm, of moderation, of peace, of protection for society, property, religion, the family, the Republic of Washington! (Applause.) Perhaps it is a dream, but it will have been a beautiful dream for France and the human race!"[34] Following Lamartine's oration—which makes a fitting epitaph for the Second Republic—the Grévy amendment was roundly defeated.

With the aid of hindsight, it is easy to see that the arguments of men like Grévy and Blanc were well founded: lacking those traditions of decentralization, local liberties, and checks and balances that made a strong executive tolerable in the United States, it was a fatal mistake for France to adopt an American-style presidency—especially with a Bonapartist pretender waiting in the wings. Tocqueville later expressed bitter regrets over his support for a popularly elected president. "Any way you look at it," he wrote, "the Republic became impossible once we decided to give a president the powers of a king and have him chosen by the people."[35] Elected by a landslide on December 10, 1848, with 74.31 percent of the vote and supported by a rural public voting mainly on the basis of name recognition, Louis Napoleon Bonaparte seized absolute power with the coup d'état of December 2, 1851. One year later he proclaimed the Second Empire and took the name Napoleon III.

Though Louis Napoleon had always considered it his destiny to restore the French Empire, the coup's timing was precipitated by the approaching end of his term, revealing another flaw in the 1848 Constitution: the nonrenewable four-year mandate. Indeed, as Robert Badinter has observed, it was a "political aberration" to decide "that the president of the Republic would be elected by universal suffrage and, at the same time, that his term could not be renewed.... They had adopted the thing that would lead to the destruction of the constitution: a limited and distorted projection of the American institution."[36]

Louis Napoleon's power grab should have surprised no one. A nephew of Napoleon I and a grandson of Josephine, he openly trumpeted himself as the legitimate Bonapartist heir—"My power is an immortal name," he was fond of saying.[37] He had already staged two ill-prepared and abortive coups—one in Strasbourg in 1836, the other in Boulogne-sur-Mer in 1840. Following the Boulogne debacle, he was arrested for treason and imprisoned for six years behind the grim stone walls of the Château de Ham in northern France before escaping in the borrowed clothes of a workman and fleeing to England. He returned to France after the fall of Louis-Philippe and, financed by his wealthy English mistress, launched a campaign to seize power.[38] Anyone who sincerely thought Louis Napoleon intended to serve as a loyal republican president after winning election in 1848 was either naïve or deluded. As Samuel Johnson said of second marriages, it was a "triumph of hope over experience."

The coup d'état began in the early morning of December 2, 1851, with the posting of printed proclamations dissolving the National Assembly and the occupation of the Palais Bourbon by armed troops. Sixteen deputies and several dozen others who might have organized an opposition were immediately arrested. By midday, the situation seemed calm enough for the self-proclaimed "prince-president" to take a triumphal carriage ride through the streets of Paris. The coup seemed like a fait accompli at that point, but by the next morning, barricades began to appear around the capital after a group of republican deputies, led by Hugo, formed a *comité de résistance* in opposition to the takeover.[39] Over the next twenty-four hours, the resistance was brutally repressed by some 30,000 army troops armed with rifles and bayonets and backed by artillery. According to official figures, 215 insurgents were killed, though the actual number was probably twice that. For good measure, Bonaparte ordered the arrest of some 27,000 republicans and socialists and expelled more than 1,500 from the country.[40]

Prominent among the exiles was Hugo, who fled first to Brussels, then to the Channel Island of Jersey, and finally to Guernsey, where he remained a vocal opponent of the man he called "Napoléon le petit" for the next two decades. Unlike many French refugees, Hugo lived a rather comfortable life abroad. With his substantial publishing royalties, he bought an imposing four-story house on Guernsey, with a landscaped park and view of the port.[41] In that roomy mansion, grandly named Hauteville House, he lived with his wife, his two grown sons, and his daughter; Hugo's longtime mistress, Juliette Drouet, was housed in a rental down the street. In between visits to Juliette (who dutifully copied all of his manuscripts), Hugo explored every nook and cranny of the island during his long walks through the countryside and swam in the bracing channel waters almost daily. In the evenings after dinner, the family often engaged in table-turning séances, during which Hugo bizarrely attempted to communicate with the ghosts of departed literary giants like Chateaubriand, Dante, and Shakespeare. (His son François-Victor actually translated the Bard's complete works into French, but Hugo himself never learned English.) Interestingly, Hugo's exile was one of the most prolific periods of his writing life. Standing at his writing desk on the top floor, the so-called "crystal room," with its panoramic view of the sea, he penned some of his greatest works, including *Les Misérables, Les Travailleurs de la mer,* and *Les Chatiments.* Proudly spurning the emperor's offer of amnesty in 1859, Hugo vowed to return to France only when liberty was restored. "If only one remains," he famously declared, "I will be that one."[42]

But in the wake of the coup d'état, the principled opposition of republican exiles like Hugo, Ledru-Rollin, and Blanc, passionate though it was, proved powerless to overcome Bonaparte's popular support. In the plebiscite of December 20, 1851, according to the official figures, some 90 percent of the eight million voters approved his seizure of power. On December 2, 1852, exactly one year after the coup, 97 percent supported his restoration of the empire.[43] Despite the implausibility of these Soviet-style election results, Louis Napoleon claimed an overwhelming popular mandate that legitimized his rule.

The coup d'état reinforced the left's hostility to a strong presidency and seemed to vindicate their resistance to the American model. Looking back in 1870, Blanc blamed the fall of the Second Republic largely on the Constituent Assembly's imitation of the U.S. presidency. "The majority found it difficult to conceive of a republic without a president," he wrote. "So much did the example of the United States blind them! So little did they comprehend the necessity of entirely subordinating the executive to the legislative power everywhere that an immense standing army exists."[44] For many of those on the left, suspicion of the American political model was one of the legacies of 1848.

For all their initial rejoicing over the events of 1848, many Americans nurtured the underlying belief that "no one else could make a proper revolution."[45] The fact that France had changed its form of government four times since 1789 caused many Americans to wonder whether its people had enough political wisdom and maturity to make self-government work.[46] These doubts increased as the year wore on. The ardor for a "Sister Republic" first began to cool when Americans learned of the sweeping social and economic reforms envisaged by the Provisional Government. Southerners were alarmed by the March 4 decree abolishing slavery in the French colonies, while property-minded citizens throughout the country looked askance at the new government's moves to limit the workday, establish the National Workshops, and guarantee employment to all.[47] The June Days insurrection and the repression that followed seemed to confirm the most pessimistic predictions, and few Americans retained much faith in French republicanism in the wake of these events. But the troubles of the Second Republic seem to have aroused more contempt than sympathy among American observers and tended to reinforce their own sense of political superiority.[48]

The election of Louis Napoleon to the presidency was widely viewed as the death knell of the republic and the prelude to an imperial restoration. Both the

Bonapartist pretender and the people who had elected him were blasted by the American press at that time.[49] The prince-president, for his part, had no particular love for the United States. During his brief American exile following the 1836 Strasbourg affair, Louis had expressed a strong personal distaste for the materialistic, Protestant, and democratic society he had observed there—even though he was impressed by the dynamism of the Americans.[50] He also resented the abuse that was heaped on him by the American press once he had come to power.

Franco-American relations, so cordial after the February Revolution, deteriorated rapidly during Bonaparte's presidency. In September 1849 a series of trivial incidents led to the recall of the French ambassador from Washington and an angry exchange of letters between Secretary of State John Clayton and Foreign Minister Tocqueville.[51] This minor crisis was smoothed over, and Louis Napoleon consistently strove afterward to avoid open conflict with the United States. But his personal anti-American sentiments—and the contempt that Americans felt for him—would strain Franco-American relations for the next two decades.[52]

The coup d'état of December 2, 1851, severed the remaining ties of friendship between the "Sister Republics" of 1848. Although American opinion was unanimous in its condemnation of the usurper, its disapproval extended beyond the person of Louis Napoleon. The coup and its subsequent ratification by a large majority were taken by many Americans as final proof that the French people were unfit for liberty and deserved despotism.[53] John W. De Forest, an American novelist residing in France at this time, wrote home in December 1851: "Did you ever see anything in your life so ridiculous, so contemptible, as the conduct of this great and civilized nation in this emergency?" He saw the results of the December 21 plebiscite, which overwhelmingly approved the coup d'état, as "a disgrace to the sense & courage of the nation, a dark fact showing how little the French people as yet understand and prize liberty, & how little consequently they deserve it."[54]

This tendency to blame the republican leaders and the French masses for the return of despotism was shared by many Americans, including those in the highest circles of government. The future president James Buchanan, who as American minister to England had met many of the French exiles in London, expressed this disdainful opinion of them in an 1854 letter to the State Department: "I have strong sympathies for the Poles, Hungarians and Italians, but none at all for the French. They have chosen Louis Napoleon, and let them have him. *De gustibus non disputandum.* I am not partial to him, neither to Ledru-Rollin, Louis Blanc, Victor Hugo, or any Red Republicans or Socialists."[55]

The official American response to the coup d'état was similarly discouraging for the defeated French republicans. While protesting the brutal measures of the coup, the U.S. government took no strong action against it. The American minister to France made the gesture of boycotting official receptions until the plebiscite was held, but he extended official recognition to the new regime once it had been sanctioned by popular vote.[56] Secretary of State Daniel Webster approved this action, saying that the "overthrow had become necessary," although it was "deeply to be deplored." While he regretted the failure of the Second Republic, he noted that "every nation possesses a right to govern itself according to its own will and change its institutions at discretion."[57] This apparent acquiescence in despotism greatly disappointed the French left, which had looked to the United States for more active support. "We expected a greater solidarity from this powerful republican family . . . which has not made any great efforts so far for the cause of humanity in the world," wrote Hugo's friend Charles Ribeyrolles, editor of *L'Homme,* the Jersey-based organ of the republican exiles.[58]

Shortly after the coup d'état, Pierre-Joseph Proudhon lashed out against "those who do not know us, who judge our affairs by their institutions and their prejudices," caustically remarking that "the American, like any parvenu, spits in our faces."[59] Writing from London in 1854, the American consul, George N. Sanders, described the bitterness of the French exiles, with whom he had close contacts and strong personal sympathies:

> They accuse America of indifference towards the shame and sufferings of this people to whom we are so obliged for our national independence,—of accepting the slanders adroitly hurled against their most honorable and purest patriots,—of morally helping Napoleon III to smother the voice of the French press,—of uniting with him in declaring that the French people deserve their lot, being capable only of anarchy and fit only for despotism; finally, they feel that Americans prefer and have more confidence in all other republicans than in those of France.[60]

This resentment continued long afterward to color the left's attitude toward America. Not only were U.S. political doctrines cited by the left's adversaries in France, but the opinions, the esteem, and the good wishes of the American people themselves also seemed to be arrayed against them. Although Americans had decried the forces of despotism and reaction in Europe, they often expressed an even greater contempt for the irresponsible French masses and the demagogic republican leaders who had allegedly duped them. These attitudes—voiced by American statesmen, American travelers, and the American press—did much to damage the image of the United States in the eyes of the French left at this time.

A merican prestige in France had reached new heights with the coming of the Second Republic in February 1848. But with enhanced prestige came rising expectations that the United States would not, and could not, satisfy. The way was thus prepared for a drastic falling off of French sympathies after Louis Napoleon's coup d'état. The United States was widely viewed with disfavor in France during the following decade, not only by partisans of Napoleon III's antidemocratic government but also by many of those who had supported the republic and were disappointed by its failure. Tocqueville summed up this double reaction in an 1852 letter to his American friend Theodore Sedgwick: "I hardly need tell you that you are not in good odor on our continent. The governments despise you. They consider the United States as a bottomless pit, from which nothing but a pestilence emerges; and the peoples blame you for having made them believe in a democratic republic."[61]

CHAPTER 2

Manifest Destiny and Revolution

The French papers . . . all see & lament that a new race of statesmen has now
succeeded to power among us,—the men of "progress"—the annexationists,
the demagogues. It is true.

—JOHN W. DE FOREST, 1852

uropean observers were often alarmed at the rapaciousness of American
expansionism during the 1850s. This was the heyday of "Manifest Destiny," when the urge for territorial aggrandizement became a consuming
national passion. The expansionist fever had actually erupted during the previous decade with the agitation over the Oregon boundary and the annexation
of Texas. The Oregon question was settled through peaceful negotiations with
the British, but the 1845 annexation of Texas led to a brief one-sided war with
Mexico that brought the immense territories of New Mexico and California into
the U.S. fold. Flushed with victory, Americans next began to cast a covetous eye
on Cuba. When Spain rebuffed offers to buy the island, expansionists began calling for more direct means of acquiring it. In 1850 and 1851 the Venezuelan-born
adventurer Narciso Lopez led two filibustering raids on the island, funded largely
by American contributions and manned by American volunteers. Officially condemned but secretly winked at by the U.S. government, these raids attracted
much sympathy throughout the country—especially among Southerners, who
were eager to add a new slave state to the Union to compensate for California's
recent admission as a free state. In 1852 the Democrat Franklin Pierce was elected
president on an expansionist platform that openly called for the acquisition
of Cuba.

Europeans looked on these developments with apprehension. Frenchmen of
all political colors joined in criticizing America's predatory impulses, and many
warned that the seizure of Cuba would lead to a confrontation with Europe.[1]

The recklessness of American expansionism during these years naturally alarmed European governments already concerned about the growth of U.S. power and influence. Conservative propagandists attributed America's invasiveness to the excesses of democracy and warned of the need to curb its voracious appetite in order to protect European interests in the Western Hemisphere.[2]

But even those who were in sympathy with America's political institutions often voiced similar criticisms. Writing to an American friend in 1852, Tocqueville declared: "It is not without apprehension that I see this spirit of conquest, and even plunder, which has appeared among you in the past few years. It is not a sign of good health in a people which already has more territory than it can fill. I admit that I would be grieved to learn that the nation had embarked on a campaign against Cuba, or worse, allowed this to be done by her bastard children."[3]

The republican Victor Schoelcher, a prominent French abolitionist, charged that American designs on Cuba were really aimed at the extension of slavery. "The aggrandizement of the United States is an evil," he wrote, "for by tolerating slavery at home, they fortify it elsewhere. . . . As long as their Constitution, otherwise so admirable, remains stained by slavery, they can do nothing to promote the happy destiny of the world. . . . That is why we do not favor the annexation of Cuba by the Union at this time."[4]

These reservations were shared by an array of Schoelcher's fellow republicans. For them, however, the situation was complicated by the fact that their strongest supporters in the United States were also the most ardent promoters of expansionism. Since 1845 there had grown up within the Democratic Party a movement known as "Young America," whose program called for an aggressive foreign policy based on territorial expansion in the New World and active support for the revolutionary movements in Europe.[5] Ideologically, Young America represented a curious mixture of chauvinism, imperialism, and democratic idealism. As Yonatan Eyal has shown, the movement served as a progressive vanguard within the party of Andrew Jackson and Martin Van Buren, promoting an active reform agenda and new economic thinking in addition to its expansionist goals.[6] Young America had played an active role in the 1852 presidential campaign, and its adherents' support had helped put Pierce in the White House. In addition to embracing their expansionist ideals, the new president rewarded the Young Americans with a number of diplomatic appointments, naming (among others) Sanders as U.S. consul in London and the eccentric Pierre Soulé as minister to Spain.

Sanders, a seasoned political wire-puller from Kentucky, was simultaneously devoted to the causes of European revolution, Yankee capitalism, and Southern slavery.[7] Even before his appointment as consul, he had been in touch with the Hungarian revolutionary Lajos (or Louis) Kossuth, with whom he had concocted an abortive scheme to buy up 144,000 obsolete muskets from the War Department for distribution among the republicans of Europe. After his arrival in London in November 1853, Sanders maintained close relations with the republican exiles there, and his home on Weymouth Street soon became their main rendezvous. One memorable dinner in February 1854 included a veritable Pantheon of revolutionary leaders among the guests: Kossuth, Giuseppe Mazzini, Ledru-Rollin, Giuseppe Garibaldi, Alexander Herzen, and Felice Orsini (the man who later threw a bomb at Napoleon III and missed). Also present was the American minister, James Buchanan, who did not share Sanders's ardor for revolution. Sitting next to Mrs. Sanders at the table, the ambassador jokingly asked "if she was not afraid all the combustible materials about her would explode and blow us all up."[8] (Wit was not lacking on the part of the revolutionaries either: Herzen referred to this occasion as "the red dinner, given by the defender of black slavery.")[9]

During his stay in London, Sanders seems to have spent more time promoting revolution than attending to his consular duties. He published a number of incendiary manifestos calling for the assassination of Napoleon III and the overthrow of the Continental monarchies. He allowed the exiles to smuggle out their correspondence and revolutionary propaganda in the dispatch bags of the U.S. legation. He even attempted to put a merchant steamer at Kossuth's disposal so the Hungarian could round up an army of exiles and unleash pandemonium in Europe. But Sanders was light years ahead of most of his countrymen in his sympathy for the European revolutionaries. His activities on their behalf were loudly decried in Congress and in the American press. When his appointment came up for Senate confirmation in February 1854, it was flatly rejected.[10]

Meanwhile, as Sanders was hobnobbing with the revolutionary exiles in London, an equally subversive Young American diplomat was conspiring in Madrid. The son of a Napoleonic army officer, Pierre Soulé had been forced to leave his native France in 1825, when his republican activities had gotten him in trouble with the government of the last Bourbon king, Charles X. Settling in Louisiana, he had prospered as a lawyer and worked his way up to become a member

of the U.S. Senate, where he was known as an acclaimed orator, a leading defender of states' rights and expansionism, and a fanatical advocate of Cuban annexation.[11] His appointment to the Madrid mission in April 1853 was generally
taken as a sign of the Pierce administration's desire to "detach" Cuba from Spain.
Such, indeed, were the State Department's instructions to Soulé before his departure.[12] On his way to Madrid, the minister stopped off in London, where he met
with Sanders, Ledru-Rollin, Mazzini, and Kossuth. There, according to certain
reports, these American diplomats and revolutionary exiles discussed plans to
embroil the United States, Spain, England, and France in a war over Cuba, with
the double objective of destroying European monarchy and bringing Cuba under
American control.[13]

If starting a war with Spain was indeed his goal, Soulé pursued it with admirable diligence: he insulted Queen Isabella at his first audience, wounded the
French ambassador Turgot in a duel, encouraged republican insurrections in Madrid, and attempted to provoke a conflict over the *Black Warrior* affair, a minor
naval incident involving the detention of an American frigate by Spanish authorities in Cuba. According to Turgot, Soulé was also involved in a republican plot
to smuggle 100,000 guns into Spain for use by Continental revolutionaries.[14]
In October 1854 he arranged the famous Ostend Conference, at which the U.S.
ministers to England and France joined him in recommending that the U.S. government try to buy Cuba from Spain. In the event of a Spanish refusal, it was
suggested that the Americans would be justified in "wresting" the island from the
mother country.[15] For political reasons, the State Department repudiated the Ostend Manifesto and attempted to soft-pedal the Cuban question for the time being, yet it was only a frank statement of America's longstanding attitude toward
Cuba.[16] Ostracized at the Spanish court and repudiated by his own government,
Soulé resigned his post and returned to New Orleans. By 1855, the influence of
Young America, both at home and abroad, had declined drastically.

For all its brevity, the presence of these and other Young Americans in Europe
had a significant effect on their country's image. Among conservative Europeans,
they encouraged visions of America as a dangerous source of revolutionary ideas
and suggested the possibility of active U.S. intervention on behalf of republican
movements. (Such fears were fed by fantastic rumors: Soulé, for example, was
said to have used his Yankee ingenuity to invent a steam-driven guillotine for
chopping off the crowned heads of Europe!)[17] Much as America was gripped

by fears of a vast communist conspiracy in the 1950s, so European governments a century earlier were alarmed by these subversive American agents who were preaching assassination and revolution on their very doorstep. But such fears were highly exaggerated. The revolutionary zeal of Young America was out of harmony with U.S. government policy and public opinion. The Senate refused to confirm Sanders's appointment because of his red republican sympathies, as we have seen, and when Napoleon III complained about Sanders's activities in October 1854, the emperor received the State Department's assurance that the United States had no intention of exporting its political doctrines.[18]

The Young American interlude also affected the American image in the eyes of European republicans. Many of the exiles were personally grateful to them for their help and sympathy. "When you write, Monsieur, it is your lofty and free soul which writes," declared Hugo in a typically effusive letter thanking Sanders for his activities on behalf of the French republicans. "My admiration for you rises to affection. . . . Continue your good and sound work of propaganda."[19] Soulé, too, enjoyed the esteem of many French republicans, especially after his famous duel with the Bonapartist ambassador in Madrid.[20]

But it soon became apparent that the U.S. government and the American people did not share the radical views of the Young Americans. The republican exiles saw the rejection of Sanders's appointment as an ominous sign that the United States had turned its back on their cause—and they were not wholly mistaken. In March 1854 Ledru-Rollin, Mazzini, and Kossuth voiced this alarm in a joint letter to Sanders. They had expected America "to lend, if not more, at least her moral aid to the Republicans in Europe." But so far there had been painfully little evidence of such encouragement, "a fact certainly neither advantageous to the interest of republicanism in general nor adding to the consideration abroad of Republican America." The fact that the Senate had rejected Sanders "precisely on account of the marked sympathy that you have shown to the democracy in Europe" was "a hard and mischievous blow at the prospects of democracy."[21]

The case of the Young Americans also illustrates another problem that the United States posed for European republicans: many of these activists defended slavery at home while advocating revolution abroad. (Both Sanders and Soulé, in fact, would later put their revolutionary talents at the service of the proslavery cause as agents of the Confederacy.) In their dealings with such men, how were European republicans to resolve their own commitment to liberty with their abhorrence of slavery? Some of the more opportunistic exiles were willing to gloss over this paradox in the interest of promoting their own cause. During his 1851–52 tour of the United States, for example, Kossuth had refused to discuss the slavery issue for fear of losing Southern contributions—a fact that won him the lasting enmity of the American abolitionists.[22] Ledru-Rollin also downplayed the slavery question and even seems to have encouraged Southern expansionism as long as it was accompanied by a commitment to European republican movements. In an August 1854 letter to Sanders, he suggested that the United States "take advantage of the internal broils of [Spain] . . . to excite an insurrection in which Cuba should proclaim its independence and place itself under the protection of America."[23]

But most French republicans were bothered by the marriage of democratic principles with slavery and expansionism in the Young American ideology. Writing at the outset of the Civil War, Louis Blanc recalled that both Sanders and Soulé had expressed "scandalous opinions on the legitimacy of slavery" when he had known them in London. Charles Ribeyrolles, like his friend Schoelcher, denounced the Americans' attempt to use the cause of European republicanism as a smokescreen for the southward expansion of slavery. "If by aiding the Revolution in Europe, the United States sought only to create a favorable diversion for their covetous designs on Cuba," he wrote, "they would be betraying the politics of brotherhood, and they would find no accomplices among us. The republicans of Europe have no intention of serving the South's exploitation."[24] Coming shortly after the Ostend Manifesto, Ribeyrolles's outburst was obviously aimed at the revolutionary Machiavellianism of Sanders, Soulé, and company.

Other republican voices rose to denounce the invasive tendencies of the Americans during these years. Writing in 1859, the historian Jules Michelet issued a rather wacky call for a hybrid nation formed of Spanish, Indian, and Black stock to create a South American buffer against the Anglo-Saxon "invasion" from the United States. "In the face of this torrent . . . which descends under the false banner of the United States," he wrote, "a powerful mulatto world must form a barrier. This North [America] of immigrants, shopkeepers and pirates will only bring you violence and sterility."[25] Michelet's friend Edgar Quinet, while also denouncing American "aggression," warned against being overly critical of the Americans, for the despots of the Old World were only "waiting for the chance . . . to crush the United States by which liberty is saved, and with it, the hope and the honor of the human race! . . . You may be sure that the sound of American liberty is intolerable to our old enslaved societies. They will unite [against America] as soon as they see the chance."[26]

Quinet's words illustrate the problem that the United States posed for many European republicans at this time: while its conduct was far from exemplary, it remained the only bastion of democracy in a reactionary world. Although many republicans were reluctant to associate their cause with the United States, they could not condemn it without implicitly discrediting their own principles.

One way out of this dilemma was simply to ignore the American example, as many republicans did. But even those who were tempted to cite it at this time were obliged to qualify their praise. The liberal philosopher Etienne Vacherot, for example, wrote in 1860: "The United States, in spite of all its imperfections, is surely the society which best satisfies the democratic principle. . . . But how imperfect this democracy still is." Pointing to the existence of slavery in the South and pauperism in the cities of the North, Vacherot warned his compatriots to "beware of taking the republic of the United States as the ideal of democracy."[27]

These cautious allusions to the American example suggest that it was as much of an embarrassment as an encouragement to French republicans during the 1850s. This ambivalence would remain until the Civil War forced the slavery issue to a head and rallied European partisans of liberty to the Union cause.

CHAPTER 3

Slavery and Democracy

I don't see how the Americans can reconcile slavery with their professed
love of democracy.

—PAUL BÉRANGER

I never would have drawn my sword in the cause of America if I could have
conceived that thereby I was helping to found a NATION OF SLAVES.

—LAFAYETTE

N othing did more to damage the American image in European eyes than
the institution of slavery. This was especially true of France, whose abolitionist tradition went all the way back to the Enlightenment. From
the philosophes down to the "forty-eighters," antislavery sentiments had gone
hand in hand with the idea of political liberty in the French mind. Following the
1848 Revolution, one of the first acts of the provisional government had been to
abolish slavery in all the French colonies. Great Britain having banned slavery
from its colonies in 1833, the United States and Spain now remained the last great
Western nations to retain this barbarous institution. With their own hands clean,
the French began to take an even harsher view of American slavery after 1848.
In the wake of English and French emancipation, as Edouard Laboulaye later
remarked, "America was blocked by public opinion. When an American arrived
in Europe, if he spoke of his country with a justifiable pride, he was told: 'Do not
speak to us of your liberty, you are the land of slavery!'"[1]

It happened that the French had solved their slavery problem at the very moment when slavery was becoming the main preoccupation of U.S. politics. America's 1848 victory over Mexico had brought vast western lands under U.S. control, thus rekindling the debate over slavery in the territories. Sectional tensions
mounted rapidly and rumblings of secession were heard from Southern extrem-

ists until an uneasy truce was struck by the Compromise of 1850. In addition to regulating the status of slavery in the new territories—California was admitted as a free state; Utah and New Mexico would decide the slavery question by popular sovereignty—the compromise gave the South an enormous concession: the stringent new Fugitive Slave Law that required federal authorities to hunt down escaped slaves in the free states and return them to their masters. This law contained the germs of future conflict, for it infuriated the abolitionists and caused them to redouble their agitation. From that time until the end of the Civil War, there would be no lasting peace between the sections.

French republicans observing these developments were shocked by the U.S. government's repeated efforts to accommodate itself to slavery. Instead of acting on pure republican principles, as the French had done in 1848, American statesmen seemed to have embarked on a policy of permanent compromise, subordinating all moral considerations to the goals of national prosperity and selfish material interests.

One of the sharpest critics during these years was the republican abolitionist Victor Schoelcher, who had witnessed American slavery firsthand during an 1830 visit to Louisiana and Florida.[2] Having led the movement for French emancipation in 1848, Schoelcher was indignant over the passage of the Fugitive Slave Act two years later. At a time when all of Europe was "marching at a rapid pace towards liberty," said Schoelcher, "the Republic of the United States . . . stops, turns back and retrogresses!" Instead of declaring its "sympathy with the nations of the old world in their work of regeneration," Congress had "tightened the chains of slavery which still shame its institutions. . . . The country which adds this new sanction to slavery, to this outrage against humanity, does not know what liberty is; no, a thousand times no, this country is not worthy of the title republican." Schoelcher declared that it was "an immense danger for democratic ideas—at present and in the future—that the people which is par excellence democratic possesses slaves."[3] Forced into exile after the coup d'état, he continued to denounce American slavery from his refuge in London.

Schoelcher was not wrong in seeing American slavery as a danger for the cause of liberty everywhere, for it gave European conservatives an easy target for their antidemocratic propaganda. The comte de Bastérot, for example, severely criticized the slavery and racial prejudice he observed during his 1858 tour of the United States. Drawing a pointed political lesson from these facts, he remarked:

"When one thinks that this takes place under a democratic government in a country which calls itself free . . . , the villainies and betrayals of old Europe seem less grievous, and one realizes that nothing can equal the power and intelligence of an aristocracy."[4] Such observations were common during these years, making partisans of democracy all the more reluctant to claim the United States as their model.

But just as the right could use the example of American slavery to discredit the idea of political liberty, so the far left could use it to criticize a republican model judged insufficiently democratic.[5] During the constitutional debates of 1848, radicals had often cited the existence of slavery to underscore their objections to various features of the American political system. In subsequent years many of them continued to criticize such a model that lent itself so well to the principle of involuntary servitude. American society, wrote Ribeyrolles, still reflected the "tainted ideals" of "the feudal monarchy of old England. . . . In slavery, which remains today the living scandal of this *new society,* we find a decisive proof of the profound influence exerted by the institutions, principles and memories of the lost homeland."[6]

From his Jersey exile, Victor Hugo declared that the Anglo-Saxons were incapable of grasping the revolutionary French ideals of liberty, equality, fraternity, and solidarity. The Americans' hypocritical toleration of slavery was glaring proof of this failing:

> The American republican is free to sell, buy, resell, bargain and barter old men, women, virgins and children. He imprisons those who teach little negroes to read, he fires his rifle at a fugitive slave in the middle of a so-called free city, he trains dogs to hunt men: he finds all that quite normal. He is both slave-dealer and citizen. He is a democrat and a slave-trader. He has the Rights of Man under his right arm and the Black Code under the left. That doesn't bother him a bit. He smokes his pipe over it.[7]

The publication of Harriet Beecher Stowe's *Uncle Tom's Cabin* in 1852 threw a harsh spotlight on American slavery. The book became an instant best seller in France, running through eleven translations in one year, so that Stowe surpassed James Fenimore Cooper as the most popular American author in France.[8] Men and women of all ages and political persuasions were deeply moved by this abolitionist melodrama, but it had a particular appeal to the republicans: with its emphasis on brotherhood and equality, the book struck a resonant chord with the humanitarian sentiments of the whole *quarante-huitard* generation. "All honor and glory to you, Mrs. Stowe!" wrote George Sand in a preface to one of the translations. "One day your reward which is graven on heavenly records will also be of this world."[9] Michelet called the book "the Gospel of freedom" for the Black race.[10] The book also stirred the consciousness of future republican generations, for it appeared in several illustrated children's versions and stage adaptations.[11] It seems likely that the republican *jeunesse* of the 1860s got some of their first vivid notions of America from *Uncle Tom's Cabin*. One of the most illustrious members of that generation, Georges Clemenceau, was moved to tears upon seeing a stage version of *Uncle Tom's Cabin* at the Théâtre de Nantes when he was eleven years old.[12] Stowe herself described the touching reception she received from the working-class children of the Faubourg Saint-Antoine during her 1857 visit to Paris. Upon learning that the author was to visit their school, the students pooled their lunch money "to send to the poor slaves."[13]

While *Uncle Tom's Cabin* aroused French sympathies for the enslaved Blacks, it also painted an unflattering picture of American society. Old Tom was admired for his Christian sentiments and heroic martyrdom, but the image of white Americans was mainly associated with the whips and bloodhounds of the slaveholders in the popular mind. Howard Jones notes that French readers across the political spectrum tended to see the book as "an accurate portrayal of slavery's inhumanity in the South and a sure stimulus to servile war."[14] But it should not be assumed that foreign readers made a clear-cut distinction between North and South in their reactions to Stowe's book. For one thing, as Halvdan Koht has suggested, the specific issues of the sectional controversy went over the heads of most European readers. They were universally appalled by slavery, writes Koht, but "they did not for that reason imagine that Southerners were more cruel than other people."[15] Furthermore, Stowe's declared intention was not to denounce the South, but to show how slavery degraded the whole American nation.[16] On the whole *Uncle Tom's Cabin* probably helped tarnish the American image while stirring Europe's indignation over slavery.

While Stowe's tale was bringing tears to millions of French eyes, the writings and actions of other American abolitionists were also being followed with great interest. In 1855 Laboulaye translated William Ellery Channing's *On Slavery* and wrote an introductory essay on the American antislavery movement.[17] Channing's works were widely read in France during the Second Empire, and his ideas, both political and philosophical, had a certain vogue among republicans.[18] A number of French liberals and republicans also corresponded with William Lloyd Garrison's American Anti-Slavery Society and other abolitionist groups.

Citing articles from the American antislavery press and the reports of his U.S. correspondents, Schoelcher regularly publicized the details of atrocities committed against Blacks and abolitionists all over the United States. He declared it the "imperative duty of the whole French press to raise its voice against such monstrosities. . . . The more the Republic of the United States serves as a model in certain respects for European democrats, the less we should tolerate the most frightful exploitation of man by man that has ever existed."[19]

In an 1855 letter to the American Anti-Slavery Society, Tocqueville declared himself "pained and astonished by the fact that the freest people in the world is, at the present time, almost the only one among civilized and Christian nations which yet maintains personal servitude." America's continued toleration of slavery, he noted, served to "retard her progress, tarnish her glory, furnish arms to her detractors, and compromise the future career of the Union."[20] Shortly after the passage of the Fugitive Slave Act, Hugo wrote to the abolitionist Maria Weston Chapman that he was horrified at seeing "the collar of a negro chained to the pedestal of Washington! . . . It is the duty of this republic to set such an example no longer. It is a shame, and she was never born to bow her head. It is not when Slavery is taking leave of the old nations that it should be received by the new."[21]

As with *Uncle Tom's Cabin,* the republicans' interest in the abolitionist movement did not necessarily uplift the American image in their eyes. On the contrary, those who had studied the question knew that the true reformers and humanitarians were only a small minority in the United States and that they were denounced and intimidated by their countrymen in the North as well as the South. The abolitionists, moreover, were not without their detractors on the French left. Some radicals found their methods too tame and their ideology too evangelical to suit their own revolutionary temper. The socialist Sainte-Suzanne Melvil-Bloncourt sharply criticized the pacifism of the abolitionists and the docility of the Blacks themselves. "You don't need a Bible to break chains," he wrote. "All Spartacus needed was his gladiator's sword. . . . I prefer [Haitian liberator] Jacques Dessalines to Uncle Tom. Enough of this resignation!"[22]

Without a doubt, slavery was the darkest stain on the American image at this time, the most troubling shortcoming to French partisans of liberty. North and South were condemned in their eyes for continuing to tolerate human bondage within the borders of the United States. But slavery was not the only cause for the decline of U.S. prestige during these years. Many other aspects of American politics, manners, and society were also distasteful to French observers. And some of the harshest judgments were pronounced by French travelers and emigrants who saw the United States firsthand during this period.

CHAPTER 4

French Travelers and Emigrants in Judgment

Some go to America in search of money, and if they succeed, they tell us it
is the most beautiful and enlightened of all countries; if they fail, it is the
opposite. Others go in search of liberty and progress. If they are men
of progress themselves, they come back angry and outraged.

—GEORGE SAND, 1843

The French came to the United States in unprecedented numbers during
the fifteen years preceding the Civil War. Between 1845 and 1860, a
variety of economic and political circumstances sent French emigration to its highest levels of the nineteenth century. More than 120,000 French
immigrants arrived in the United States during this period, including 20,126 in
the peak year, 1851.[1] In addition to those seeking permanent residence, many visitors traveled to the country as well, some of whom produced books and articles
on their American experiences. It was also during this period that major Parisian newspapers began to send correspondents to the United States and to give
greater attention to U.S. news in general.[2] As a result of these increased contacts,
the French public had access to a greater volume of firsthand information on
America than ever before.

But if great numbers of citizens were attracted to the United States during
these years, they were not always enthusiastic about what they found there. In
fact, the overall image of American society that emerged from the travel accounts
of the 1850s was decidedly unfavorable. In his bibliographical study of French
travelers in America, Frank Monaghan has observed that "hostile literature
reached a flood-stage" after 1850.[3]

Almost all French tourists, regardless of their political orientation, commented on the same unattractive aspects of American civilization: vulgarity of manners, racism, xenophobia, and the universal obsession with making money. It was the "bluff" and "humbug" of P. T. Barnum, rather than the wisdom of Washington and Franklin, that seemed to typify the American character in the eyes of most French observers of this period. On the whole, French travelers of the fifties seemed disinclined to take the United States seriously, concentrating on the burlesque and eccentric aspects of American life in contrast with the more sober analyses of predecessors like Tocqueville and Chevalier.[4]

Such unflattering views of American manners and society were not devoid of political implications. Conservative French writers, still shaken by the experience of 1848, naturally exploited the foibles of Americans in order to discredit liberal ideas. Like the British Tory writers of the 1830s, many Frenchmen now crossed the Atlantic with the express purpose of attacking democracy.[5] One such traveler frankly declared that his aim was to debunk "democratic idylls, sung in every key by certain self-interested republicans who straight-facedly cite the political mores of the Americans as a perfect model for civilization."[6]

It is no surprise to find French conservatives attacking the United States; the French right had been doing that since the days of Joseph de Maistre. But in contrast to earlier periods, America now found few champions on the left to refute those hostile views. Those "who would be tempted to exalt the United States in order to oppose Imperial power remained silent in general," writes Simon Jeune. "Their apologies pale not only before the existence of slavery, but also before the crude and eccentric manners" of the Americans themselves.[7] Among all travelers, as a British journalist observed in 1851, French liberals and republicans were the ones likely to experience the greatest disillusionment, having been led to expect too much from this "democratic Utopia."[8]

This observation is borne out by many of the French travelers who went to the United States during the 1850s. Liberals like Alfred Assollant, Xavier Eyma, and Oscar Comettant often tended to be skeptical about American manners and society, occasionally outdoing the conservatives in their criticisms.[9] The country seemed to have little more appeal for those of advanced democratic and socialist opinion who went there at this time. This group was well represented, for in addition to those who arrived as visitors or ordinary immigrants, the United States also received a number of exiles who had been forced to leave France for political reasons.[10] This exodus had started after the June Days repression in 1848 and reached its peak following Louis Napoleon's coup d'état, which sent thousands more into exile. Most of these refugees settled in Belgium, Switzerland, or England, but a number of them also emigrated to the United States.[11]

The decision to come to America was not always a happy one or even voluntary. According to Amedée de Saint-Ferréol, most of his fellow exiles would have preferred to remain in Europe, but the governments of neighboring countries often harassed and expelled the French refugees, forcing them to leave for the United States, "where assistance, subsidies, resources, work, everything was lacking. . . . [T]hey were lost amidst a crowd speaking a different language and having different customs."[12] Under such circumstances, America could appear more like a land of banishment than a haven for the oppressed.

Emigration to America was viewed by many proscribed Frenchmen as a last resort, reluctantly adopted by those who were unable to establish a base in Europe. Even before 1848, in fact, it had been frowned upon by many republicans who felt, with Michelet, that France was "the beacon of the future."[13] During the severe economic depression of 1846, Michelet had complained that many impoverished French peasants, in "the credulity of their misfortune," believed the "fables" about the United States and left their homes and families, thinking "that the Ocean is hardly wider than the Rhine."[14] "To emigrate is to lower oneself," he later wrote; in America the Frenchman "loses his soul, his self."[15]

Republicans redoubled their hostility to emigration in the wake of the February Revolution. In an 1848 article criticizing Etienne Cabet's project for a communist colony in America, Charles Delescluze wrote, "France is big enough to feed all her children, and the founding of the true republic requires the help of all good citizens."[16] Forced to flee to England himself in 1849, Delescluze continued to dissuade his comrades from going to America. Writing in the *Voix du proscrit* in 1851, this future Communard declared it "the firm duty of democrats of all nations not to leave the theater where the supreme battle between past and future, justice and privilege, will soon be fought." Those exiles who sought comfort and refuge in the United States were guilty of "desertion before the enemy," charged Delescluze:

> It is not shelter that we must ask of republican America; revolutionary Europe is looking for more effective evidence of her respect for the solidarity of nations. Let her remember that . . . our fathers mingled their blood with the blood of

Washington's warriors. Free and prosperous today, the time has come for her to pay her debt to the sons of those 18th-century crusaders.

If America, disclaiming this imperative and sacred obligation, refused to risk anything to help Europe reconquer her liberty, who would want to ask this selfish and indifferent nation for a refuge on its immense territory? In the midst of its crowded cities, our exiles would find themselves more abandoned than anywhere else, for the ingratitude of this free people would be more unbearable than the severity of the monarchical nations of Europe.[17]

After the coup d'état, those who were committed to the overthrow of Napoleon III were all the more opposed to the idea of American emigration, regarding it as an abandonment of their cause. France was the focal point of all their actions and, to their minds, the key to the republican triumph throughout Europe. This view was often expressed by *L'Homme*'s editor Charles Ribeyrolles, who had settled on the windy Channel Island of Jersey along with Victor Hugo and a number of other French expatriates. In one 1854 article, for instance, Ribeyrolles bewailed the fact that the hardships of European exile were forcing many of his fellow republicans to emigrate to America: "Death is decimating us here at Jersey.... In Switzerland, in Belgium, even in Spain, allied police hunt our men down day and night, and in England—the land of fraternal solidarity ... for dogs and horses—we enjoy the great liberty of starvation. Under overwhelming necessity, therefore, the departures for America are more and more frequent."[18] Citing dismal reports from French exiles who had gone to the United States, he warned his readers that "the New World might be just as hard on the poor as the Old World!.... Young America has many of the vices of her mother." He advised his fellow exiles to forget about going to the United States, relying instead on mutual aid and cooperation to help one another endure the difficulties of European exile. "That way we will keep our dignity and our strength for the struggle!"[19]

In 1852 Proudhon turned down an offer by the American socialist Albert Brisbane to set him up as a journalist in New York, saying that it was "too far away for men of action" and that "only in the most desperate case" would he consider going to the United States.[20] When Victor Considérant announced his plans to establish a Fourierist colony in Texas in 1854, he was bitterly criticized by those who felt that "it was not the moment to go and found a new society in America when it was first necessary to topple the government in France."[21] Such sentiments were widespread among the exiles: it is a significant fact that—with the exceptions of Cabet and Considérant—not one of the major republican or socialist figures emigrated to America during these years.

Many of those exiles who did go to the United States regretted their decision and warned others to stay in Europe. The Fourierist Auguste Savardan, who participated in Considérant's colonization experiment in Texas, returned totally disillusioned with the United States. Describing the situation of French immigrants there, he said that most of them lamented leaving France and longed to return. "For every family whose lot has been at all favorable," observed Savardan, "there are ten who vegetate, and to vegetate far from France is to perish twice."[22] The same judgment was passed by the workers Lacour and Crétinon, who had emigrated to Cabet's Icarian community at Nauvoo, Illinois, in 1855. They returned to France eight months later disenchanted, both with Icary and with "this land of which we had dreamed so before our departure, that we had gone to see with such enthusiasm, hope and joy, and that we leave without regret." In one particularly harsh comment on American life, they remarked that those immigrants who died in steerage during the Atlantic crossing were "often not the most unfortunate of the lot, and more than one of those who survived them in the New World would prefer such a fate, for all is not rosy in this land of liberty."[23]

Few French travelers expressed more contempt for American society during these years than the young geographer and anarchist intellectual Elisée Reclus, who would later fight for the Paris Commune.[24] The son of a Calvinist minister and an in-law of Michelet, Reclus had abandoned his theological studies at Montauban Seminary to devote himself to scientific pursuits and radical politics. After traveling extensively in Europe, he went to America in 1855 with the vague intention of setting up an agricultural community along socialist lines. Instead, he wound up working as a tutor on the Fortier plantation in Louisiana. Reclus gained an intimate knowledge of the South's "peculiar institution" during his year's residence among this slaveholding Creole family. He eventually became one of the foremost French authorities on the subject of American slavery. In an 1860 article he recalled the horror and indignation he felt as he wandered through the streets of New Orleans and saw the open-air slave market for the first time:

On this fatal platform pass all the negroes of Louisiana, one by one: children who have finished their seventh year, and whom the law, in its solicitude, judges old enough to go without a mother; young girls, offered up to the stares of two thousand spectators, and sold for so much per pound; mothers who have just given up their children, and who must be gay under the threat of the whip; doddering old men, auctioned off many times before, who must appear one last time before these pale-faced men, who scorn them and laugh at their white hair.... According to the slaveholders, all this is commanded by the very cause of progress, the doctrines of our holy religion, the most sacred laws of family and property.[25]

As a socialist, Reclus saw slavery not as an isolated Southern phenomenon but as merely one form of the exploitation and injustice inherent in all existing societies. In America exploitation followed racial lines, while in France it followed class lines, but Reclus saw "a perfect parallel between the two continents."[26] He also felt that the debates and struggles over the slavery question in America were part of an irresistible movement toward universal brotherhood and solidarity. "Here the givens of the problem are so clear and so numerous that no one can mistake them," he wrote to his brother Elie, "everyone knows that the slaves will disappear, along with the gods, the kings, the executioners, the savants, the men, the women, all which has gone before.... It is wonderful to see this fierce battle in the press, in conversation, in the incessant harangues . . . against this elusive phantom of human liberty . . . which threatens to sweep before it all that has hitherto existed."[27]

It was Reclus's abhorrence of slavery—and his guilty sense of "robbing the negroes, who earn by their sweat and blood the money that goes into my pocket"—that ultimately caused him to give up his comfortable job on the Fortier plantation. (Another reason for his abrupt departure was somewhat less noble: he had seduced the planter's daughter, Eléanor, and the family was pressing him to marry the girl.)[28] But slavery was only one of his many grievances against this flawed republic. Almost everything about the American character and society seems to have touched a raw nerve. Shortly after his arrival in New Orleans, he wrote to his brother that America was "a great auction hall where everything is for sale, the slaves, and the master as well, their votes and their honor, the Bible and the conscience. Everything to the highest bidder."[29] His loathing for Americans seems to have been something almost visceral. "What you say about the *vomito-yankee* is very true," he wrote to Elie. "In this *vomito,* one does not vomit his entrails, he vomits his spirit, his heart, his self."[30]

To Reclus, America's reputation as a land of freedom and human progress was a fraud. "I have often asked myself, dumbfounded before this America so respected abroad . . . and so little respectable at home, where is that progress that each people must accomplish in its evolution," he wrote. So far the Yankee's only progress was a physical "development in space," as American civilization spread over the continent, and an improvement in "the vegetative life of man, since they all seem to have a piece of bread between their teeth." The American's only contribution to "the age of social reconstruction in which we live" was that of "exploring human nature . . . to its lowest . . . depths. This is what the Americans are doing for certain vices with a rare joy; they delve into lies and impudence with an indomitable energy, they move mountains by the force of mendacity, for now that faith is tottering, it is up to hypocrisy to accomplish miracles."[31]

The riotous riverfront neighborhoods of New Orleans provided Reclus with all he might wish to find in the way of vices. The city was terrorized by "incendiaries, murderers and thieves" who "commit their crimes without fear." Its population was infected by "the national vice of drunkenness" that fed "the most violent passions." Its politicians were corrupt. Even its air was polluted with the deadly vapors of yellow fever.[32] "No other city in the world, except perhaps Mexico City and the capital of California, disgorges such torrents of iniquity," said Reclus.[33]

Based on his experiences in Louisiana, Reclus concluded that American society was torn by racial and class hatreds that were even more severe than the class conflicts of Europe. He compared the vices of European society to "a hidden ailment that gnaws at the individual under his clothing, while the vices of American society appear in all their hideous brutality. The most violent hatred separates the parties and races: the slaveocrat abhors the abolitionist, the white hates the negro, the native detests the foreigner, the rich planter disdains the small farmer and the rivalry of interests creates an insurmountable barrier of mistrust even within families."[34] Such a republic could be no model for a man like Reclus, for whom universal solidarity and brotherhood were the ultimate goals of human progress.

Another hostile traveler was the concert violinist Dominique Tajan-Rogé. A veteran of the Saint-Simonian "church" at Ménilmontant and a devout socialist, Tajan-Rogé visited the United States in 1856, experiencing "nothing but disillusionment," as he told his friend Proudhon upon his return to France.[35] His tour took him from Boston to New Orleans, but his impressions were no more favorable than those Reclus had garnered in the Deep South. Although a believer in democratic principles, he had only contempt for this republic "nourishing slavery in its breast and adoring the book of antiquated societies [the Bible]." Tajan-Rogé felt that the democratic spirit of American institutions was subverted by the "mores and prejudices . . . and religious ideas" of the American people. "The human race," he wrote, "must necessarily and fatally appear to them in terms of two separate categories: the Jew and the Gentile, the Elect and the Damned, the Conqueror and the Conquered, the Master and the Pariah, the Native and the Foreigner." These attitudes were just as strong in the "free abolitionist states" as in the slave South. Because of their nativist prejudices, their puritan traditions, and their indifference to everything but "the golden calf," Americans were doomed to cultural mediocrity, declared Tajan-Rogé. "Great art, serious and civilizing art" was not possible in a society "where one passion reigns exclusively, . . . business, the counting-table, figures and lucre."[36]

For all the hostility they expressed, the degree of disillusionment felt by sophisticated radicals like Reclus and Tajan-Rogé was comparatively mild, for they were doubtless prepared for many of America's shortcomings before they arrived. A greater disappointment was in store for those who had looked on the United States as a "Promised Land" and sought to regenerate mankind by the successful demonstration of their utopian social theories on American soil. One such experiment was launched in 1848 by the utopian communist Etienne Cabet, whose *Voyage en Icarie* (1839) had won him a large following among French workers. Though Cabet's utopian novel was not primarily concerned with the United States—it is set on an imaginary island off the coast of East Africa—it did show a great admiration for the democratic and egalitarian ideas that reigned in Jacksonian America. He described the United States as "the nation that perhaps resembles Icary the most" and asserted that "nothing would be easier" than to propagate the doctrines of Icarian communism there.[37]

America took on a special importance for the Icarians in 1847, when Cabet decided to found an experimental communist colony in the uninhabited wilds of Texas. His call for emigration was enthusiastically received by his followers, many of whom seem to have been attracted as much by the utopian image of America itself as by their hopes of creating their own communist utopia. "New Moses," wrote one Icarian to Cabet, "you are delivering millions of modern slaves from the servitude of industrialism to take them to another promised land."[38]

In spite of all their sanguine hopes, these Utopian emigrants were headed for a rude shock once their expectations gave way to American experience. The first little band of sixty-nine Icarians arrived on the Texas site in the summer of 1848, only to be decimated by heat, cholera, malaria, and yellow fever. Retreating to the turbulent city of New Orleans, they found themselves engulfed in what one unhappy pilgrim called "this agglomeration of so many people in a city where selfishness and individualism have reached their apogee."[39] Their numbers swollen by the arrival of several hundred new colonists, the group fell to quarrelling, and half of them returned to France in anger and disgust. Cabet led the remaining Icarians to Nauvoo, Illinois, where they built a settlement on lands purchased from the Mormons. But the dissensions continued. Cabet himself was ousted from Nauvoo in 1856 and died shortly afterward in Saint Louis. After his death, Icarian splinter groups formed new colonies in Kansas and Missouri. But though their various settlements continued to vegetate for many years after Cabet's death (the last one was dissolved only in 1898), they never achieved the success that he had dreamed of and upon which humanity's hopes were said to have rested.[40]

Several years after the Icarians had gone to America, the Fourierist Victor Considérant made a similar attempt to establish a utopian colony in Texas. Described by Tocqueville as a "chimerical dreamer" who deserved to be locked away, Considérant had been one of the leaders of the democratic and socialist left during the Second Republic.[41] Exiled after the coup d'état, he had sailed to the United States in 1852 to scout out the possibility of planting a "phalanstery" on American soil. Upon arriving in New York, he made contact with a group of prominent American Fourierists, including Albert Brisbane, Charles Dana, and Horace Greeley, whose New York Tribune extolled Considérant as France's "most eloquent expounder of Associative Life and Industry" who had come "to observe here the results of self-government and industrial freedom."[42]

After a six-week trip to Texas in the company of Brisbane, America's foremost champion of Fourierism, Considérant returned to Europe and published a zealous appeal on behalf of socialist colonization in the United States. "What fields of action!" he wrote. "What opportunities for a great socialist experiment. . . . I have seen the Burning Bush. . . . Friends, I tell you that the Promised Land is a reality. . . . One strong resolution; one act of collective faith, and this Land is conquered."[43] Considérant was convinced that America held the key to the triumph of socialism in the world. Since the beginning of history, he noted, progress and civilization had spread westward from Asia, therefore the ultimate perfection of human society was destined to take place in America, which was "the *West of the World*."[44] Considérant declared that the successful demonstration of socialist principles there would "prepare the salvation" of all humanity.[45]

Considérant's effervescent enthusiasm for America stands out as an exception to the generally hostile view of the French left during these years, and many of his fellow exiles resented his attempt to encourage emigration. Yet the evangelistic appeal of *Au Texas* attracted many Fourierists to his colonization project. By September 1854, his Brussels-based Société de Colonisation had raised some 1,800,000 francs. The first group of 120 colonists sailed for New Orleans in December.

Considérant's "Réunion" fared little better than Cabet's Icary. The region's climate and soil were poorly suited to agriculture (as the Icarians' experience had already shown). The motley band of colonists, which included many opinionated windbags but no skilled farmers, was torn by quarrels and jealousies. Their American neighbors proved hostile to the very presence of these foreign socialists and abolitionists. Promised land grants did not materialize, and confidence men swindled them out of thousands of dollars. On top of these formidable obstacles, Considérant himself proved to be an atrocious administrator.[46] Driven to near-madness by the debacle, he ungallantly abandoned his followers and moved to San Antonio, where he remained until his return to France in 1869. Less than a year after his defection, the rest of the group disbanded, and the short-lived experiment was at an end.[47]

Whatever ideas individual participants in these experiments may have gathered about the United States are difficult to discern. Apart from the fact that they were isolated from American society, most of them were obscure, semiliterate workers—not the sort of people to go publishing memoirs. Judging from the rare sources that are available, they seem to have shared the generally low opinion that other French travelers and emigrants expressed during the 1850s.[48] But it is doubtful that the ideas of such individuals had much effect on the left's overall view of America, for they received little or no publicity outside their own narrow circles.

In the eyes of the left, the main significance of these American experiments was that they were dismal failures. This fact contributed to the general disillusionment with utopian ideas that had been going on since 1848, when utopianism was given full reign and crashed spectacularly. Coming in the wake of that experience, the failure of these projects helped clear the way for the more "scientific" theories that were gaining ascendancy among French socialists during the 1850s and 1860s. Rival socialist schools had predicted the collapse of these American experiments and pointed to them as proof of the superiority of their own systems.[49] As for their effect on the American image itself, these experiments served to discredit the idea that the United States held the key to "the destinies of collective humanity," as Considérant had claimed.[50] Most French republicans and socialists were probably glad to see such notions exploded, for the hope of finding collective or individual salvation in America was widely viewed as a diversion from their struggles in Europe.

CHAPTER 5

The Impending Crisis

For over half a century, everything that Europe heard about America showed
that there existed, across the Atlantic, a free and tranquil nation, dedicated
exclusively to the arts of peace, growing at a wondrous rate, presenting the
spectacle of unexampled prosperity. . . . Today, everything we hear from America
bears the echo of desperate quarrels, like a distant rumbling of civil war.

—ATHANASE CUCHÉVAL-CLARIGNY, 1856

French partisans of liberty looked on in sorrow and dismay as the rising violence of sectional passions in the United States announced the final crisis
of disunion. The 1854 Kansas-Nebraska Act turned Kansas Territory into
a bloody battleground where proslavery men and free-soilers fought to establish
their supremacy. The fragile sectional truce of 1850 was sundered by "Bleeding
Kansas." Nor was strife limited to the territories. In Northern cities antislavery
leaders were attacked by mobs, their presses were destroyed, and their headquarters sacked. Abolitionist bands went South, liberated slaves, and spirited them
northward via the famous "Underground Railroad." Outraged Southerners per-
secuted, brutalized, and occasionally lynched those among them suspected of
abolitionism. As these acts of violence multiplied, the entire political life of the
nation was gradually sucked into the vortex of this storm.

Slavery had become the central issue of American politics by the time of the
1856 presidential election, in which the abolitionist-friendly Republican Party
made its first appearance on the national scene. Momentarily appeased by the
election of the Democrat James Buchanan, the South scored a great legal victory
with the U.S. Supreme Court's 1857 *Dred Scott* decision, which denied Congress
the right to exclude slavery from any part of the territories and disallowed citizenship for Blacks. But Southerners' complacency was shattered in 1859 when

the militant abolitionist John Brown led a desperate raid on the U.S. arsenal at Harpers Ferry, Virginia, hoping to incite a widespread slave revolt.

Regardless of their political tendencies, French observers generally agreed that America was becoming engulfed in a perilous—possibly fatal—crisis during these years. But if the gravity of the situation was apparent to all, it was most disconcerting to those who wished for the triumph of republican ideas in the world. Twenty years earlier, the young traveler Alexis de Tocqueville had taught a whole generation of liberal-minded Frenchmen to admire American democracy. Now in failing health, suffering from the tuberculosis that would strike him down in 1859, Tocqueville sadly contemplated the moral and political decadence into which the United States was sinking during the 1850s. In his correspondence with American friends, Tocqueville described Europe's dwindling faith in their country and warned that the cause of European liberty was being compromised by the deepening crisis. "You have just given in the West [Kansas] spectacles of popular disorder which do not uplift the ailing cause of liberty in Europe," he wrote to Theodore Sedgwick in September 1855. The Americans were damaging that cause, noted Tocqueville, "by the violent, intolerant, and lawless spirit which seems to be spreading over a part of the Union."[1] A year later he informed Sedgwick that "Europe is beginning to think that the time is not far off when you [North and South] will split apart." For the past several years, observed Tocqueville sadly, the United States had "inspired throughout Europe a combination of low esteem for your wisdom and fear of your force. . . . You disappoint the friends of democratic liberty and you make all its adversaries rejoice. . . . [Europeans] are becoming more and more hostile towards you and the number of those who would gladly see you fall into great difficulty and disgrace grows daily."[2] Just a year before his death, the Frenchman wrote to Senator Charles Sumner of Massachusetts that America's destiny seemed to have "fallen into the hands of a race of political adventurers, an energetic, intelligent race, but violent, crude and unprincipled."[3]

Tocqueville's bleak view was shared by many of his countrymen in the face of the growing American crisis. In 1858 the liberal writer Emile de Montégut sadly described America's declining prestige in the world:

The great republic is far from keeping all its promises. Shameful compromises between the parties; guilty complacency on the part of those in power; an unscrupulous audacity among the citizens; principles sacrificed to the most unworthy interests, justice each day put off until the morrow, everywhere transactions without dignity where honor is lost and peace is not won: such is the record of the republic for the past few years. And yet this is the country upon which humanity fondly gazed, full of hope, and to which she entrusted the glorious mission of continuing her destinies. Alas! Hope itself seems banished from the world today.[4]

Reflecting the general pessimism that had enshrouded the American image by the end of the decade, Jules Michelet declared in 1859: "We once admired the United States and her destruction would cause us pain. But what good are all her conquests if mongrel hordes, slavery, alcohol and money annihilate what was once her life and her soul?"[5]

During the closing months of 1859, Europe was electrified by the news of John Brown's daring raid. With money and support obtained from various New England abolitionists, this gray-bearded, half-mad Connecticut farmer had led a guerilla attack on the arsenal at Harpers Ferry in order to foment slave rebellions all over the South. Surrounded and captured by U.S. Marines after a two-day shootout, Brown and seven other survivors of his band were summarily sentenced to death before a slaveholding judge, jury, and prosecutor in Charlestown, Virginia, on October 31.[6]

These events caused a sensation in France. The details of the raid and trial received extensive coverage in the French press, and Brown's blow for freedom was widely praised by liberals and republicans.[7] No Frenchman was more thrilled by the news than Victor Hugo, who saw the raid as a sublime act of revolutionary heroism. On December 2, 1859, the date scheduled for Brown's hanging, Hugo heard a false rumor of its postponement. He immediately wrote an impassioned letter to President Buchanan calling for Brown's pardon in the name of humanity. Widely reproduced in the French and European press, his plea reached a large audience and was later republished in pamphlet form.

In addition to pleading for Brown's life, Hugo issued a stern warning to the American people, reminding them that their honor and credibility before the world were at stake. Denouncing the iniquities of slavery and the mock justice of Brown's summary trial, he wrote: "You cannot do such things with impunity in the face of the civilized world. . . . The eyes of Europe are fixed on America at this moment." The North as well as the South would be disgraced by Brown's death, said Hugo, for "the whole American Republic" would be his "hangman." Expressing the disillusionment felt by his fellow republicans in Europe, he wrote, "we who hold this democratic symbol as our common homeland feel wounded and in a sense compromised." If Brown were executed, "from then on, before incorruptible history, the great federation of the new world would add a bloody crime to all its lofty deeds." Hugo predicted that Brown's execution would provoke the destruction of the Union and the dissipation of that moral force that the United States had hitherto exerted throughout the world in favor of human liberty: "From the moral point of view, it seems that a part of human enlightenment would be eclipsed, that the very notion of the just and the unjust would be obscured on the day when we should see Deliverance assassinated by Liberty. . . . Yes, let America know this and ponder it well, there is something more horrifying than Cain killing Abel, it is Washington killing Spartacus."[8]

It was several weeks before Europe learned that Brown had actually been executed on December 2 (which by a grim irony was also the eighth anniversary of Louis Bonaparte's coup d'état). Upon hearing this news, Hugo, a longtime opponent of the death penalty, bitterly commented in his diary: "A free people kills a liberator, and thus commits suicide. . . . From now on, the New World, like the Old, will be stained by a December 2nd."[9] In March 1860 he wrote to a Haitian journalist: "The American Union . . . may henceforth be considered dead. . . . [B]etween the South and the North stands Brown's gallows: Solidarity is no longer possible."[10] Later that year Hugo produced a lugubrious engraving depicting the martyred Brown on the gallows and bearing the inscription "Pro Christo, Sicut Christus."[11] Copies of this engraving were sold in newsstands all over Europe. Brown remained one of Hugo's all-time heroes and became a symbol of human liberation for many other republicans and radicals in subsequent years.[12] But Hugo's eloquent words, in addition to popularizing Brown's legend, had also reinforced Europe's moral condemnation of slavery and of the republic that continued to tolerate and protect it.

French liberals and republicans were initially encouraged by the election of Abraham Lincoln in November 1860.[13] Here at last was a sign of America's resolution to end its shameful compromise with slavery. But these initial rejoicings were soon followed by more somber views. Friends of liberty were perplexed by Lincoln's failure to make a strong antislavery statement following his election and by his repeated pledges to leave the institution alone where it already existed. The secession of the Southern states seemed to many observers to be the death knell for the American Union, while Lincoln's vacillating attitude in the face of the crisis puzzled and disappointed those on the left. By the end of 1860, secession had become an accepted fact in the eyes of most French observers, and postmortems on the United States could be heard on all sides.[14]

In December 1860, as war clouds gathered over North America, the radical polemicist Pierre-Joseph Proudhon pronounced a thorough condemnation of the United States and almost gleefully predicted its ruin. Proudhon, a former typographer turned economist and philosopher, was an anarchist who preached a brand of "mutualism" based on workers' federations. As a relentless critic of bourgeois capitalism, he had never had much liking for the Americans. As far back as 1840, in his *Qu'est-ce que la propriété?*, he had expressed doubts about the ability of American-style democracy to promote real liberty.[15] His anti-Americanism came out strongly in 1848, when he railed against the American constitutional model in the pages of his newspaper, *Le Représentant du peuple.*[16] Following the collapse of the Second Republic, as we have seen, he particularly resented the scorn that Americans expressed for the French left. Now the shoe seemed to be on the other foot, as the American Union was itself in the process of disintegration. It was at this juncture that Proudhon vented his anti-American sentiments in a lengthy letter to the Belgian writer Joseph Dulieu, who had just published an admiring book on the United States.

While he claimed to share Dulieu's overall admiration for the democratic principle represented by the United States, Proudhon had only contempt for the Americans as a people. Their country was supposedly an "incarnation of liberty," said Proudhon, but the Americans themselves did not "sense the grandeur of such a role." Having "no clear consciousness of their position," they indulged in a totally unwarranted sense of superiority. Of what were the Americans so proud after all, he demanded. They had not produced "a shadow of philosophical thought"; they understood nothing of the "march of history"; they had never examined "the great problems of Economics, object of the great nurturing of our century." In their ignorance of these matters, the Americans now found themselves amid a great crisis: "Half the nation biblically cultivates slavery, and the other is already creating a proletariat."[17] The Americans' unique circumstances—

offering space, isolation, and independence—had made them prosperous and temporarily spared them the worst of Europe's social ills.[18] But the same isolated circumstances had also made the American "a stranger . . . to the moral, philosophical and political development of the Old World," which was working toward the definitive solution of the social problem.

Not only were Americans unable to contribute anything useful to this movement, they were also unprepared to deal with social crises when they appeared in their own country—witness the present muddle over slavery and secession. Proudhon thus predicted that the United States would sooner or later succumb to the same social maladies that troubled European nations: "The American is currently recontracting all the vices that devour us, and he will finish by falling into the ancient quagmire if . . . he does not elaborate the civilizing idea in the cesspool of servitudes from which he is only halfway emancipated." Because of their exclusive preoccupation with material interests and their total indifference to culture and philosophy, Proudhon declared, the Americans occupied "the lowest rank of civilized nations."[19]

If others on the French left did not share Proudhon's fundamental aversion for America, few would have disputed his pessimistic view of its future at that moment. On the eve of the American Civil War, French observers generally felt that the United States was sinking into a moral and political abyss that could prove fatal to its own institutions and weaken the democratic cause worldwide. The evolution of the slavery controversy during the 1850s had largely contributed to this impression, but many observers also felt that the crisis was one of values, morals, and character as well as politics. Under the leadership of mediocrities like Pierce and Buchanan, the nation bore little resemblance to the republic of Washington and Franklin that the French had traditionally admired. The American people, in their relentless pursuit of selfish material interests, seemed to have lost the sense of moral unity and transcendent national purpose that had motivated their ancestors. The disintegration of the Union seemed to be the logical conclusion of that moral decline. By the end of 1860, American prestige in France had reached its lowest ebb. Far from inspiring the French left, America's identification with the democratic principle actually appeared now to be a liability. It would take the "fiery trial" of civil war and emancipation to redeem the American image in their eyes.

PART II

The Resurrection
of the American Image,
1861–1865

In order to know what sacrifices democratic nations can endure, we must wait
until the American people are obliged to put half of their entire income in the
hands of the government, as England has done, or put the twentieth part of the
population on the battlefield, as was done by France.

—ALEXIS DE TOCQUEVILLE, *Democracy in America*

Now we are engaged in a great civil war, testing whether that nation, or any
nation, so conceived, and so dedicated, can long endure.

—ABRAHAM LINCOLN, 1863

T
he election of the "Black Republican" Abraham Lincoln in 1860 triggered the secession of seven Southern states and set the stage for the
American Civil War, which erupted on April 12, 1861, when Confederate shore batteries in Charleston, South Carolina, fired on Fort Sumter. Since the
War of Independence, no American event had aroused more interest in France.
For four years, discussions of the war filled French newspapers, books, and pamphlets. Stocks on the Paris Bourse rose and fell with the news of each battle.
Thousands of unemployed French workers suffered from the economic effects
of the conflict. Military men studied the technological innovations produced by
the world's first "modern" war. Diplomats pondered its implications for the European balance of power and for the fortunes of the Mexican expedition, which
would never have been undertaken had the United States not been absorbed

in its own life-or-death struggle. Several hundred French observers even had a chance to watch a Civil War naval battle off the coast of Cherbourg, when the USS *Kearsarge* engaged and sank the Confederate commerce raider *Alabama* in June 1864—a combat painted by Edouard Manet and sensationally recounted in the French press. Rarely has a domestic upheaval in one country had so great an effect on the political and economic life of another nation.

CHAPTER 6

Early French Reactions to the American Civil War

What an immense step America has just taken! Between the presidency of Mr. Buchanan and that of Mr. Lincoln, there is the distance of a social revolution. The sons of the Puritans are slow to move; but once set in motion, they go forward and nothing stops them.
—AGÉNOR DE GASPARIN, March 1862

It seems that God has abandoned them to punish them for the sin of slavery, which lives on in their prejudices and customs.
—GEORGE SAND, January 1862

Like the Dreyfus affair three decades later, the American Civil War split French opinion into two rival camps, dividing along ideological lines.[1] As the republican historian Henri Martin put it in a letter to Senator Charles Sumner, "all who are liberal are for the North; all who are anti-liberal are for the South."[2] Like most generalizations, this one is subject to exceptions, but on the whole it was an accurate assessment. The Confederacy found its warmest sympathizers among those who feared the spread of democratic ideas and the growth of American power: Bonapartists, legitimists, aristocrats, and the bulk of the Roman Catholic clergy. Support for the Union came mostly from those who believed in the principle of political liberty and hoped to see it reestablished in France. The ensuing debate between these two camps was motivated as much by their clashing ideas over French government and society as by the events that were taking place on the battlefields across the sea. Looking back in 1869, Edouard Laboulaye gave this description of the ideological alignment that took place in France following the outbreak of the Civil War:

[T]he upper classes in France, as in England, had only contempt for this nation of farmers, workers and lawyers, who did not even understand the art of war. . . . They joyfully contemplated the fall of this republic that set such a bad example for Europe. . . . It was at this moment that all the friends of liberty in France recognized one another. All the newspapers that defended French liberty defended American liberty. . . . Regardless of their political color, all partisans of freedom met on this common ground. . . . With one voice, they rose to support America.[3]

Seeing the possibility of weakening a powerful rival and deflating the prestige of democratic ideas, Napoleon III and his entourage made no secret of their pro-South sympathies. Shortly after the outbreak of the war, the emperor told British ambassador Lord Cowley that "he could not forget the overbearing insolence of the United States government in its days of prosperity and hoped that they might receive a lesson."[4] In his first meeting with Confederate commissioner John Slidell in July 1862, he stated flatly that his sympathies had "always been with the South."[5]

In a strict sense the emperor never wavered from the neutrality that he declared in June 1861. But he nevertheless aided and encouraged the South in various ways. Like the English, he officially accorded belligerent status to the Confederacy. He secretly facilitated the building of Confederate ironclads in French shipyards and allowed for a Confederate loan to be arranged in France. Through the official and semiofficial press, he encouraged the diffusion of pro-South propaganda. He twice proposed mediation in the conflict and came dangerously close to intervention and recognition of the Confederacy on several occasions.

Meanwhile, as Laboulaye observed, most partisans of liberty threw in their lot with the Union, regardless of their own political shading. So united was this pro-North front, in fact, that it is difficult to distinguish between liberal, republican, and radical views of the war. As far as the American question was concerned, these ideological lines tended to blur. In August 1861 the duc d'Aumale, the Orleanist pretender to the throne, wrote to Senator Sumner to pledge his support for the American Union, "to which we are attached by the traditions of our family and by our liberal opinions."[6] In keeping with those traditions, two young Orleanist princes—the comte de Paris and the duc de Chartres—served as volunteers in the Union army, seeking to aid "a young and liberal nation defending its institutions and its very existence."[7]

From the outset, prominent liberal publicists like L.-A. Prévost-Paradol, Eugène Forcade, Agénor de Gasparin, and Auguste Laugel emerged as champions of the Union cause. These men were joined by liberal Catholics like Henri Lacordaire, Charles de Montalembert, and Augustin Cochin, who defended the Union both in the name of liberalism and Christian humanitarianism. In the republican camp Laboulaye, Eugène Pelletan, Henri Martin, and Elisée Reclus were among the most ardent defenders of the North, as were republican exiles like Edgar Quinet, Louis Blanc, Alexandre Ledru-Rollin, and Victor Hugo.

Naturally hostile to slavery, republicans and liberals alike felt that a setback for the Union would weaken the cause of political liberty everywhere. They also saw that an outspoken defense of the Union could be an effective means of voicing their common opposition to the authoritarian regime of Napoleon III. The tight press censorship of this period made it difficult to openly criticize government policies or advocate liberal reforms. But the expression of pro-Union sentiments was an oblique means of attacking the empire.[8] Not only was their praise of American democracy in itself an indirect condemnation of the imperial regime, but the government's visible preference for the Southern slaveholders also made the pro-North position all the more effective as opposition propaganda. In their discussions of the Union war effort, critics of the empire could advance their own cause without making any direct reference to French politics.

In linking their cause to that of American democracy, liberals and republicans were departing from the skeptical view of the United States that had prevailed during the 1850s. In a sense it seems paradoxical that they should find renewed respect for the United States just when the country seemed to be falling to pieces—as conservatives had long predicted it would. Yet the coming of the war seems to have sparked a resurrection of the American image in the eyes of the left. This was partly due to the fact that it suited their propaganda needs to champion American democracy at this time. But many of them also believed that the United States was in the process of rehabilitating itself, that the war would purify and regenerate the American republic so that it could once again assume its natural role as a beacon of liberty for the rest of the world.

Gasparin developed this theme in his influential 1861 book, *The Uprising of a Great People,* whose title became a rallying cry for all French partisans of the Union. During the 1850s, observed Gasparin, "the whole nation was, in effect, yoked to the cause of slavery. . . . The policy of the Government, under its slaveholding inspiration, was a policy of adventure, without principle as without scruple; a policy which was bent on triumph, even at the expense of all the freedom and morality of the nation."[9] But the election of an abolitionist president in 1860 had marked a turning point and signaled America's determination to end its shameful compromise with slavery. Far from announcing its forthcoming destruction, Gasparin argued, the war that had just erupted would lead to "a purer and greater" era for the United States.[10] Early the following year, he published a book on the war's European repercussions, declaring that "The whole world . . . is involved in the struggle. In raising themselves up, this people uplifts us as well."[11]

This belief in America's regeneration was shared by the anarchist savant Elisée Reclus, who had bitterly criticized the United States during his sojourn in Louisiana. In December 1860 and January 1861, when war seemed imminent, Reclus published two major articles on slavery in the *Revue des deux mondes,* describing its well-known horrors for the slaves themselves and examining its effect on American society.[12] Tracing the slavery issue through American history, he saw it as the main source of contention in U.S. politics. It was also the cause—directly or indirectly—of much that Europeans found objectionable about the United States. As for its effects on Southern society, Reclus found slavery responsible for the violence and narrow-mindedness of the South's population as well as for the region's intellectual and economic backwardness. But the gathering crisis, believed Reclus, would eventually bring about the demise of slavery, and the true republican spirit would spread across the continent: "Once slavery is defeated, it will leave an open field for the intrepid and victorious spirit that has justly made the states of New England so dear to the friends of civilization. Then the tree of liberty will bear fruit, and the world will see what can be realized by a truly democratic republic, undertaking improvements of every sort with the characteristic zeal of the American spirit."[13]

Across the Atlantic, the Union cause was actively defended by the Icarians, that band of French utopian communists who in 1848 had been led to America by Etienne Cabet. Like most European immigrants in the Northern states, they unhesitatingly rallied around the Union: within a few months of the war's commencement, some twenty-seven Icarian men were serving as volunteers in the Union army, temporarily laying aside their pacifist creed in order to serve the cause of "Progress." They also aided the Northern propaganda effort by publishing enthusiastic accounts of the war in their *Lettres Icariennes,* which were read by thousands of workers back in France. One of their soldiers, a certain Mercadier, described the war as a cleansing crisis that would redeem and strengthen the American nation as the French Revolution had done for France: "If some alarmist says that the hour of decline has sounded for the United States, do not believe it. The revolution that has just erupted is a revolution that will make the Union progress materially and morally. . . . Has France ever known a more painful and fruitful upheaval than '89 or '92? . . . No, America is not weak; nor is she declining: she will surprise Europe by the marvels of moral force and power that she will display."[14] The Icarians' support of the Union was more than a patriotic gesture toward their adopted homeland. They also felt that a Northern victory would advance the cause human freedom, brotherhood, and equality everywhere, thus their own ideals were at stake in the conflict: "The American question is one of Icarian doctrine . . . concerning the great cause to which we have devoted our lives. . . . Wherever the wind of progress blows, we are ready to lend a sympathetic ear and a helping hand."[15]

But it would be a mistake to suppose that the French left was unanimous in identifying "the wind of progress" with the Union cause. The contempt that some had felt for the United States during the preceding years was not necessarily dissipated by the outbreak of the war. Some even felt a secret satisfaction at the humbling of this "false democracy." Upon learning of the disastrous Union defeat at the First Battle of Bull Run, for example, Proudhon fairly gloated. "In America, the puritans of the North are beaten by the slave-traders of the South, which does not displease me," he wrote. "Although I do not like the commerce of human flesh, the men of the North needed a lesson."[16]

A similar attitude colored the impressions of George Sand's son, Maurice, who toured the United States with the entourage of Prince Jerome-Napoleon during the summer of 1861.[17] Sand, who had inherited his mother's socialist opinions (if not her literary talents), painted a derisive picture of the North at war in a series of hastily written letters that his illustrious parent got published in the *Revue des deux mondes.*[18] Arriving in New York shortly after the Bull Run debacle, the moment when Northern fortunes and morale were at their lowest ebb, Sand observed that the Yankees had no "real soldiers" and that they had "lost all idea of the discipline necessary in wartime."[19] His opinion of the Union's political leaders was little better than his assessment of the army. At a White House dinner for Prince Jerome, Sand was put off by Lincoln's frontier crudeness. In

General George B. McClellan, who sat across the table from him, he saw a future military dictator.[20] Northern society—or what little he saw of it on a fleeting visit—inspired his contempt. He repeated the usual snobbish remarks that European travelers were wont to make about whiskey, violence, materialism, crude manners, bad taste, and P. T. Barnum. As for the Southerners, whom he observed during a quick jaunt to General Jeb Stuart's cavalry camp near Fairfax, Virginia, Sand admiringly described them as "supple, hardy cavaliers. . . . At least these men are not playing soldier."[21] Although he criticized their arguments in favor of slavery and secession, Sand's undisguised admiration for the rebels' military capacities—and his scorn for those of the North—probably contributed to the widespread belief that the South could not be beaten.

George Sand, who had never been a wholehearted admirer of American democracy, was not inclined to modify her judgment after hearing her son's impressions.[22] In a January 1862 letter to the socialist exile Armand Barbès, she said that Maurice had

> quickly and clearly judged this false democracy that, while proclaiming equality and liberty, has forgotten only one thing: fraternity, without which the other two principles are sterile or even harmful. . . . It seems that the level of [American] hearts and minds is even lower than our own. They even lack the military instinct, which in our country can work wonders for good causes under any banner. It seems that God has abandoned them to punish them for the sin of slavery, which lives on in their prejudices and customs.[23]

As these skeptical views suggest, the coming of the war had not entirely dispelled the clouds under which the American image had fallen during the preceding decade. The left had often judged the United States severely before the war, and their criticisms had been leveled at the foibles of Northern society as well as at the institution of slavery. Although they perceived slavery as the country's greatest single vice—and sincerely hoped for its abolition—there was little concrete evidence of the North's commitment to antislavery during the eighteen months between the opening salvo on Fort Sumter and the Emancipation Proclamation. Indeed, there were some alarming signs to the contrary.

For the first eighteen months of the struggle, Lincoln's stated war aim was reunion, not abolition. Concerned with retaining the loyalty of the so-called border states (the slave states of Kentucky, Maryland, Missouri, and West Virginia,[24] which remained in the Union), Lincoln moved much more slowly on the slavery question than the majority of his party would have liked—certainly more slowly than Europeans expected. When in August 1861 the abolitionist General John C. Frémont emancipated the slaves of disloyal masters in Missouri, Lincoln revoked the order and relieved Frémont of his command. A later order by General David Hunter freeing the slaves in the occupied coastal areas of Georgia and South Carolina was similarly repudiated by the president. In July 1862 Congress passed the Confiscation Act, freeing the slaves of treasonous masters. Lincoln reluctantly signed the bill but neglected to enforce it.[25] As late as August 1862—only a month before he issued the Preliminary Emancipation Proclamation—Lincoln declared in a highly publicized letter to Horace Greeley, "My paramount object in this struggle *is* to save the Union, and is *not* either to save or destroy slavery."[26]

With Lincoln repeatedly asserting that reunion was the North's only war aim, it had to be taken on faith that a Union victory would lead to emancipation. Most of the French left did take it on faith, but the North's ambiguity on the question clearly bothered them. Without a moral commitment to abolition, the purely constitutional and political questions raised by secession could not guarantee European support for the North. "It is of great importance to all mankind that slavery cease to dishonor civilization," wrote Louis Blanc from his London exile in September 1861. "It is of less importance to mankind that the Northern and Southern United States form one or two nations." If the North was really fighting against slavery, said Blanc, "why hasn't the Federal government openly declared this? Why has it informed one and all that its only goal was the preservation of the Union?" If the North wanted to rally European sympathy, it must first "proclaim its resolution to end this scandalous marriage between slavery and the republican principle . . . and raise the war to the heroic proportions of a social crusade."[27]

Blanc's impatience to see the war put on a humanitarian basis was shared by the revolutionary Auguste Blanqui, who followed these events attentively from his cell at Sainte-Pélagie Prison. Blanqui had no sympathy for the slaveholders, but he could only give lukewarm support to the Union, which he identified with capitalism, materialism, and Anglo-Saxon individualism. In a letter of February 1862, he criticized the North's failure to "say a single word in favor of the blacks." Instead of fighting for human liberation, Blanqui feared that the North would seek "a reconciliation at any cost, in order to restore the United States and their external power." Such a course would result in "some contemptible, patched-up peace . . . at the expense of the principles of justice."[28] Two weeks later Blanqui again expressed his impatience to see the war develop into a revolutionary crusade: "The Negroes have not yet made their entrance on stage," he wrote. "This play will not become truly dramatic until they arrive in the theater. Up till now, we have only seen the prologue."[29]

Even Elisée Reclus, who never wavered in his sympathy for the Union, impatiently noted in 1862 that "the Negro slaves . . . are still waiting for the justice and sympathy that their white countrymen owe them. As long as the Northern cause, unassailable from a constitutional point of view, is not reinforced by a principle of human and universal truth, that cause will not be assured of victory."[30]

In sum, while the Union enjoyed the support of the vast majority of the French left, that support was not unanimous or unqualified, especially during the first year and a half of the struggle. The Emancipation Proclamation would do much to solidify the left's support after 1863. In the meantime, three developments intervened that gave Frenchmen a more direct interest in the struggle and had a profound influence on public opinion: the *Trent* crisis, the Mexican expedition, and the cotton famine.

CHAPTER 7

The *Trent* Crisis

There was a time within the three days which immediately followed the news
of the seizure when one would have counted on his fingers about all the people
in Europe not Americans who still retained any hope or expectation of the
perpetuity of our Union.
—JOHN BIGELOW, U.S. consul general in Paris

On the Morning of November 8, 1861, the USS *San Jacinto* intercepted
the British mail packet RMS *Trent* in the choppy waters of the Ba-
hama Straits.[1] On board the British ship were two former U.S. senators, James Mason of Virginia and John Slidell of Louisiana, who were headed
to Europe as Confederate envoys. The commander of the *San Jacinto*, Captain
Charles Wilkes, sent aboard an armed party with instructions to arrest the two
rebels and take them back to the United States as prisoners. In a scene that could
have been ripped from the pages of *Gone with the Wind,* Slidell's daughter, à
la Scarlett O'Hara, blocked the door to her father's cabin and—"with flashing
eyes and quivering lips," according to one witness—cursed the Yankees as "spies
and traitors."[2] Ordered to advance, the marines fixed their bayonets and pointed
them at the defenseless demoiselle. At that point Slidell, who had taken refuge
in his stateroom along with his wife, climbed out of a window and was arrested
on deck. He was removed from the ship along with Mason and taken to a fort
in Boston.

Behind that narrative of maritime seizure lies a more complicated story. In
fact, it had been publicly announced weeks earlier that Mason and Slidell were
being sent respectively to London and Paris. Their avowed mission was to seek
British and French recognition of the Confederacy. On October 11 they ran the
Union blockade at Charleston on a chartered ship bound for Havana. While

awaiting the arrival of the *Trent* from England, they made no secret of their travel plans. The *San Jacinto* had also put into port in Havana, apparently intending to seize the two diplomats once they headed out to sea. According to some accounts, Mason and Slidell fraternized with the Yankee sailors, inviting the *San Jacinto*'s officers to lunch and announcing their intention to take the British steamer to Europe. When they left Havana aboard the *Trent* on November 7, Captain Wilkes was in their wake and arrested them the following day. It seems plausible that the diplomats were actively seeking that outcome, hoping the seizure would spark a war between England and the United States and prompt recognition of the Confederacy.[3]

If that was indeed their scheme, it nearly worked. The British immediately denounced this action on the high seas as an insult to their flag and a violation of neutral rights. For the next six weeks, the two nations tottered on the brink of war. The event also caused a sensation in France. To that point, the French had taken a more-or-less sporting interest in the American war. Now that the possibility of a direct European involvement seemed imminent, they were forced to evaluate the situation in the light of their own national interests.

The incident put the French government in a delicate situation. Having agreed at the outset of the conflict to coordinate his American policy with England's, Napoleon III now faced the prospect of entanglement in an Anglo-American war. Although he personally wanted to see the United States humbled and was hoping to recognize the South at the first opportune moment, the emperor was not anxious to join in a struggle that might destroy the only effective rival to British seapower. He therefore had Foreign Minister Edouard Thouvenel dispatch a carefully worded note to Washington that supported the British insistence on the prisoners' release but was nevertheless conciliatory in tone. Thouvenel's note, which arrived in the middle of a crucial December 25 cabinet meeting on the *Trent* question, appears to have been the decisive factor in persuading Lincoln to comply with the British demands.[4] The liberation of the prisoners and Secretary of State William H. Seward's qualified apology brought the affair to a peaceful conclusion.[5] The French emperor had ironically helped the United States avoid a disastrous war with Great Britain on this occasion.

Public opinion on the *Trent* affair was initially severe toward the United States. While the French did not contract the acute war fever of their English neighbors, the seizure was widely condemned, even by those liberal and republican journals that had hitherto supported the Union. The news bred consternation among the friends of the Union and encouraged pro-Southern papers to redouble their demands for recognition.[6] But the month of December brought a significant change in French opinion. John Bigelow, the American consul general, and other Northern diplomatic agents in Paris published documents indicating that Captain Wilkes had acted on his own authority and that Lincoln's government was innocent of any intentional provocation.[7] Furthermore, England's bellicose attitude caused the French to step back and consider the consequences of an Anglo-American war. Here, the traditional French distrust of John Bull worked in favor of the United States.

Writing in the *Journal des débats,* the liberal journalist L.-A. Prévost-Paradol stressed the divergence between British and French interests. As a major industrial and maritime power, England had everything to gain by the independence of the agricultural South and the destruction of the Northern navy. France, with much less commercial interest in an independent South, had a vital interest, however, in the maintenance of Northern seapower as a counterbalance to England's formidable fleet. Thus it would be a great mistake for France to join England in a war against the United States.[8]

On the far left, where anti-English feeling was especially strong, the *Trent* affair actually helped rally sympathy for the North. As soon as the controversy exploded, the socialist Louis Blanc dropped his earlier reservations and became one of the most ardent supporters of the Union. On December 2, 1861, contradicting the views he had expressed just two months earlier, he declared the North to be, "despite its own proclamations, the armed enemy of the principle of slavery. And it is against this armed enemy of the principle of slavery that England would fight." The *Trent* affair would have a "monstrous result" if it led Britain to "crush North America for the benefit of the South, thus preparing the triumph of the fatal principle which she formerly condemned."[9] A week later Blanc cried out against those Frenchmen who were urging their government to join England in a war against the United States. Whatever pretexts might be advanced to support such an act, said Blanc, France would stand condemned forever "in the eyes of history" if the country "deliberately put herself in the same camp . . . with the institution of slavery."[10] How could French democrats think of supporting an anti-American action that was so obviously dictated by the desire of the English aristocracy to destroy a powerful democratic rival?[11]

Pierre-Joseph Proudhon, like Blanc, was also concerned by the prospect of an Anglo-American war growing out of the *Trent* affair. While he was no admirer of American society, his combined hatred of England and slavery led him to defend the North on this occasion. Shortly after the publication of Foreign Minister Thouvenel's note, Proudhon wrote to his friend Gustave Chaudey, criticizing French efforts to "hinder our former protégés and espouse the quarrel of our eternal rivals." The emperor's "too-visible preference for the South over the North," he declared, "oversteps the bounds of impartiality and puts France in a dangerous position." [12] Several days before the news of Mason and Slidell's release reached Europe, Proudhon expressed his alarm over rumors of a "secret treaty" whereby France and England had agreed to recognize the Confederacy and destroy the North's naval blockade. "So we are to undo in 1862 what we helped create in 1775 [*sic*]; after proclaiming the freedom of the slaves in Saint-Domingue, we defend slavery in Virginia, Louisiana, etc.; and, desiring the destruction of England, we remain her ally and work for her benefit." [13]

The *Trent* episode also prompted Auguste Blanqui to vent his anti-English sentiments. The affair had betrayed Britain's desire to intervene in the American war at any price, said Blanqui. In addition to the cotton famine—which was only a short-term cause of economic disorder—England feared that the abolition of slavery would cause a permanent decrease in American cotton production, thereby raising the price of the raw material for Britain's textile industry. This, charged Blanqui, was the real reason for England's belligerent attitude toward the North. "The American war," he wrote, "will be a fatal blow [to England]. It has shown her the bottom of the barrel and tested the limits of her humanitarian sentiments. She would give all the negroes in the universe for one bale of cotton." [14]

Thus the *Trent* affair, which had at first provoked widespread criticism of the North, ultimately helped turn French opinion in its favor—or at least to dampen sentiment in favor of pro-South intervention. During the six weeks that the crisis lasted, the French were forced to take a closer look at the American war. Many of them then realized that their country's own long-range interests and security required a strong United States to counterbalance the power of their English rivals. By their peaceful resolution of the affair, moreover, Lincoln and Seward showed themselves to be prudent and conciliatory statesmen, thereby winning increased respect in the eyes of the French. Summing up the French reaction in a letter to Charles Sumner, Henri Martin wrote that "the explanations given in the *Mason and Slidell* affair, showing on which side moderation and sincerity lay, have produced a bad effect for [England] and a good one for you . . . [reviving] the passions always ready to flare up among us against our *old rival.*" [15]

Just as the excitement over the *Trent* affair was subsiding, two other situations were developing that threatened to provoke a direct French involvement in the American war: the Mexican expedition, which nearly caused a Franco-American war over the emperor's flouting of the Monroe Doctrine, and the cotton crisis, which ravaged the French textile industry and caused severe suffering among the working classes.

CHAPTER 8

The Mexican Expedition

It has taken eleven years for December Second to cross the Ocean.
Now [Napoleon III] is seeking to implant it in America. He wants to
exterminate the hope and future . . . of the whole world.

—EDGAR QUINET, 1862

Few of Napoleon III's policies aroused as much domestic discontent as his ill-fated Mexican expedition. A military and diplomatic disaster abroad, it also turned into a political liability at home, greatly contributing to the growing unpopularity of the empire.[1] The Mexican debacle quickly became a rallying point for the opposition and even caused grumbling within Bonapartist ranks. As the imperial minister of education, Victor Duruy, noted in his memoirs, the government's Mexican policy provided its critics with "the occasion to pronounce violent words that began the popular disaffection for the Emperor in France and sustained the courage of our enemies in Mexico."[2] For liberals and republicans, the venture seemed to be a direct challenge to the principle of democratic liberty represented by the embattled American Union. Linking the American and Mexican questions, they launched an energetic and effective attack on the emperor's foreign policy.

The idea behind the Mexican expedition was the foundation of a Latin, Catholic monarchy to block the southward expansion of the United States and provide France with a foothold in the Western Hemisphere. The ultimate aim, writes Howard Jones, was to "reestablish French influence in the New World and tip the world balance of power toward Paris."[3] That the mission sought to hinder the growth of American power and influence was frankly admitted by the emperor in an 1862 letter to the expedition's first commander, General Élie Frédéric Forey. "It is to our interest that the Republic of the United States be strong and prosperous," he wrote, "but it is not at all to our interest that she control the whole

Gulf of Mexico, dominate the Antilles and South America, and act as the unique distributor of the products of the New World."[4] Napoleon III seems to have been toying with the idea of a Mexican intervention during the 1850s, but America's jealous defense of the Monroe Doctrine was a constant deterrent to such projects. The outbreak of the American Civil War gave the emperor his long-awaited chance. "The American war," he wrote to his ambassador to London in October 1861, "has made it impossible for the United States to interfere."[5]

The Mexican expedition ostensibly began as a debt-collecting mission undertaken jointly by England, France, and Spain at the urging of Napoleon III. When it became apparent that French objectives went beyond the terms of their original agreement, England and Spain withdrew in April 1862, leaving France to go it alone. The emperor had expected an easy victory over President Benito Juarez's republican forces, but French troops, decimated by heat and yellow fever, did not take Puebla and Mexico City until the summer of 1863. These costly victories led to the proclamation of a French-backed Mexican Empire. Archduke Maximilian of Austria, Napoleon III's handpicked candidate, accepted the crown in April 1864.

The French emperor's Mexican policy was clearly connected to American events. He based it upon the double assumption that disunion was permanent and that the South would be more kindly disposed than the North toward the French presence in Mexico. Thus the expedition increased his stake in a Southern victory and raised much speculation about French recognition or intervention on behalf of the Confederacy.[6] This idea was developed at length by the economist Michel Chevalier in an anonymously published 1863 pamphlet entitled *La France, le Mexique et les Etats confédérés.* Praising the Mexican venture as a legitimate assertion of French "national interests," Chevalier argues that its success required immediate recognition of the Confederacy followed by a Franco-Confederate alliance. "The French navy," he concludes, "is an argument that would back up these diplomatic acts if necessary."[7] Chevalier, an authority on the United States, was close to imperial circles at this time, and it is possible that this pamphlet was inspired by Napoleon III himself. The emperor certainly concurred in its views, although he was too shrewd to commit himself to recognition without considering all the other factors involved.

One of those factors was the fear of Northern reprisals in Mexico in the event of a French recognition of the Confederacy. The truth is that while the Mexican expedition increased the emperor's stake in a Southern victory, it also restricted his freedom to actively aid the South. Mexico was an exposed and vulnerable flank, almost a hostage. For the duration of the Civil War, France and the United States shared a situation of dual belligerency that effectively guaranteed American neutrality in Mexico in exchange for French neutrality in the Civil War.[8] Though the Lincoln administration had its hands full with the rebellion, it did not conceal its discontent over the French presence in Mexico. Secretary of State William Seward, hostile to the expedition but anxious to avoid open conflict, consistently put Napoleon III on his guard.

In July 1863, shortly after the fall of Mexico City, Seward sternly warned France not to "raise up in Mexico an anti-republican and anti-American government or to maintain such a government there."[9] The following year he refused to recognize Maximilian and declared Juarez to be the legitimate representative of the Mexican people in the eyes of the United States. Northern opinion generally was a few steps ahead of Seward's diplomatic restraint. While the press bristled with bellicose language, Congress passed a joint resolution in April 1864 calling for the enforcement of the Monroe Doctrine in Mexico. The Republican Party platform, upon which Lincoln was reelected in 1864, stated menacingly that the administration would "view with extreme jealousy . . . the efforts of any . . . power to obtain footholds for Monarchical Government sustained by foreign military force, in near proximity to the United States."[10] As long as the Civil War lasted, there was little chance that these implied threats would be carried out, but the stage was set for a showdown following the defeat of the Confederacy.

In France the Mexican expedition never aroused much popular enthusiasm, and opinion grew increasingly hostile to the venture as time passed. Liberals and republicans did not hesitate to exploit this widespread hostility to oppose the emperor's policies regarding the Civil War. The American connection, in fact, seems to have been the primary concern of many on the left. From his Swiss exile, the intransigent democrat Edgar Quinet published a widely read pamphlet in which he denounced the Mexican expedition as an attempt to destroy American democracy itself. "In order for the *Napoleonic Ideas* to succeed," wrote Quinet,

> it is absolutely indispensible that this vast Republic disappear from the Earth. . . .
> As long as it exists and shines brilliantly, it attracts the admiration and maintains
> the hopes of all those who have not given up on freedom! . . . It is the absolute ref-
> utation, contradiction and condemnation of *Caesarism*. . . . Thus, in the mind of

its perpetrator, the Mexican expedition was conceived as a charged mine placed beneath the feet of the United States. . . . In this war between slavery and emancipation, the choice was never in doubt for the Bonapartist spirit.[11]

Sounding a theme that was often repeated over the next four years, Quinet pointed to the threat of a Franco-American war over the Mexican question: "If the Union emerges victorious from the Civil War, do you believe that she will look on indifferently while this monster of an absolute monarchy raises its head over the two Americas? These millions of men, armed, battle-ready, educated by victory, do you think they will silently accept this servitude that they have never known?"[12]

Quinet's indignation was widely echoed by others on the left. His close friend Jules Michelet concurred in his opinion and particularly regretted that "Mexico and the slavery that we defend will prevent us from acting on behalf of Poland."[13] The revolutionary Pierre Vésinier railed against the government's Mexican policy in the same terms as Quinet, calling it a treacherous attack on the democratic ideal represented by America.[14] Proudhon likewise decried the Mexican venture at the outset as a dangerous provocation hurled at the United States. "What are we going to do in *Mexico,* especially now that England and Spain are leaving?" he wrote in April 1862. "Try to found a monarchy to check the republic of the *United States* whose godfathers we were in 1783 . . . and make an enemy of this republic which in ten years' time will be stronger than us from every point of view!"[15]

In the Corps législatif, the lower parliamentary body of the Second Empire, the Mexican question provided the liberal and republican opposition deputies with the chance to launch an oblique attack on the government's American policy, a subject that had been systematically avoided in the parliamentary debates. The attack was led by the republican Jules Favre, one of the original five opposition deputies elected in 1857. Having first denounced the Mexican policy in June 1862, Favre returned to the charge in February of the following year, declaring in an emotional speech: "You are going to create a place in South America that will become the battlefield upon which the United States and Europe will meet. . . . Shall we find ourselves at war against the North and fight alongside the South? . . . Is that your policy? As for me, I renounce it in the name of my principles and the rights of man."[16]

Emboldened by the growing unpopularity of the expedition and by their electoral successes of the previous year, the small group of opposition deputies intensified their criticism of the Mexican policy. In May 1864 Favre again blasted the venture from the tribune of the Corps législatif. The government's conduct, he declared, had "sowed the seeds of defiance and hostility" between France and the United States. The end of the Civil War would "leave adventurers on the deserted battlefields who will sooner or later carry their swords wherever their passions lead them." This danger could have been avoided had the government acted in accordance with "the secret sympathies which, I do not doubt, are in the hearts [of the French people] for the triumph of human liberty and for the definitive suppression of slavery." Instead, Favre charged, the government had consistently encouraged the South and hindered the North.[17]

Warnings of American reprisals in Mexico multiplied as the end of the Civil War approached. From the final months of that struggle until January 1866, when Napoleon III promised to withdraw his troops, a very real war scare existed. The French government was sufficiently alarmed in the spring of 1865 to order a secret report on the feasibility of carrying on a naval war with the United States in the Gulf of Mexico; it conceded a considerable advantage to the Americans.[18] But if the prospect of such a conflict was disturbing to most French citizens, some of those on the left actually welcomed this eventuality as a means of bringing down the empire and ushering in a new republic, as we shall see in a later chapter.

CHAPTER 9

The French Economic Crisis and the Threat of Intervention

Do those who speak in ironical terms of calico and cotton forget that behind cotton are men, women and children—miseries already great, and which will go on increasing?

—AGÉNOR DE GASPARIN, 1862

Under other skies a barbarous struggle
Fixes the gaze of a horrified world
Which darkly awaits the verdict
For slavery or for freedom.
Even at our walls this fratricidal war
Strikes the heart of the valorous worker;
Its sword, alas, is called destitution.
Give, give: the people are suffering.

—FORTUNÉ HENRY, song dedicated "to the poor workers
of Lyons and Saint-Etienne," 1862

France faced one of the worst economic depressions of the nineteenth century during the American Civil War. The Union's naval blockade and a Confederate embargo had cut the exportation of Southern cotton to a trickle by the end of 1861. As a result, the French textile industry, which had depended on this source for about 90 percent of its raw material before the war, faced a potentially disastrous situation.[1] Other industries were hard hit by the reduction of American markets, which in 1860 had absorbed 367 million francs' worth of exports and accounted for over 10 percent of France's total international trade.[2] Since the United States was a major outlet for French luxury items like silk, lace, ribbon, porcelain, and perfume, these industries were bound to suffer severely during the long struggle. Whatever its political and ideological aspects, it was in the economic sphere that the Civil War had its greatest effect on the daily lives of French citizens. These economic consequences, in turn, influenced the way the French thought and felt about America. As the procureur général at Colmar noted in an 1862 report, the rapid shifts of public opinion on the American war showed "how large a role personal interest has in shaping men's judgments of events."[3]

The cotton industry did not suffer from the blockade immediately. Large stockpiles resulting from the American bumper crops of 1859 and 1860 permitted production to continue normally for many months before any shortages occurred. The first acute effects of the war were felt in those sectors that were heavily dependent on the U.S. export market, particularly the silk industry of Lyons and the ribbon industry of Saint-Etienne.[4] These were affected even before the war broke out, for the uncertainties of the secession crisis had interrupted the American orders that formed the main basis of their operations.[5] By July 1861, the procureur at Lyons reported more than 20,000 indigent persons in that city and estimated that two-thirds of the 50,000 workers employed by the Saint-Etienne ribbon industry were jobless. At the peak of the crisis, some 80,000 workers and dependents faced unemployment in the region of Lyons alone.[6] The value of French silk exports plummeted from 103,638,000 francs in 1860 to 25,346,000 in 1861 and 23,714,000 in 1862.[7] The Lyons delegates to the 1862 London Exhibition complained bitterly of the "distress this deplorable war has brought to our workshops" and warned that "even darker days lie before us."[8]

The crisis in the cotton industry developed somewhat later but was even more devastating. Modern studies have shown that the Civil War was only one of several factors contributing to the cotton crisis of 1862–63. For one thing, the American bumper crops of 1859 and 1860 had led to overproduction and gluts in the cotton markets. Another factor was the Anglo-French Commercial Treaty of 1860, which abruptly abandoned the protectionist system and exposed French manufacturers to English competition. In order to increase production in the face of this challenge, many textile firms had invested heavily in modernization of their machines, and so the subsequent cotton shortages caught them at the worst possible moment. Meanwhile, a poor 1861 wheat harvest had sent the price of bread soaring, directly aggravating working-class suffering. All of these factors contributed to the crisis, and it is probable that the French textile industry was in for trouble even if the American war had not occurred.[9] Yet there is little doubt that the Civil War was "the essential agent" of the French cotton crisis, as Claude Fohlen has observed.[10]

In terms of public opinion, the American war was widely considered to be at the bottom of all the economic disorders. This conclusion was encouraged by the government, for it was politically useful to ascribe to external causes a situation for which Napoleon III might ordinarily be held responsible. This was an important consideration in view of the hostility that the Cobden Treaty had aroused among French manufacturers.[11] By keeping the focus on the cotton famine as the cause of industrial distress, Napoleon III also had an additional pretext for mediation or direct intervention on behalf of the South. This is precisely what the rebels were counting on, convinced that "King Cotton" would oblige England and France to break the blockade and recognize the Confederacy in order to feed their factories. To increase the pressure on the Europeans, the Confederate Congress imposed an embargo on cotton exports in late 1861. The gambit almost worked: it was not by chance that the emperor's mediation offensives of October 1862 and January 1863 coincided with the most acute phase of French industrial distress.[12]

Whatever its causes, no one could deny that working-class misery was real and acute. All the textile regions were affected, but Normandy suffered the most. In December 1862 *Le Temps* reported 21,000 persons unemployed in Rouen.[13] A prefect's report of the same month counted 96,679 out of work in the whole department of the Seine-Inférieure, including 52,545 in the weaving town of Yvetot alone.[14] In March 1863 distress reached a peak in this department, with the total number of unemployed workers and dependents reaching 121,562. On a nationwide level some 223,336 French workers were unemployed as of April 1863.[15]

These figures tell a grim story. But no statistics can adequately express the degree of human suffering wrought by the crisis. Some of the most vivid firsthand descriptions of the disaster were provided by the journalist Hector Pessard, sent by *Le Temps* in December 1862 to report on the situation in Normandy. "At dusk," he wrote during a visit to Rouen, "the dark streets are invaded by emaciated shadows. . . . Children wander into the countryside to beg a bit of soup or a few potatoes from the farmers. . . . [T]here are thousands of individuals here who succumb silently in an impossible struggle whose end is not even foreseeable.

There are women who cry, naked children who huddle together at night, seeking in sleep a refuge against hunger."[16]

Another sympathetic witness was Eugène Noël, editor of the *Journal de Rouen* and a close friend of Michelet's. A socialist and freethinker, Noël was moved to rage and pity by the plight of the workers starving before his eyes. "You cannot imagine how painful it is to live in Rouen at this time," he wrote to Michelet in January 1863. "Part of the population is dying of starvation," Noël declared, "not only in the streets, but also in miserable hovels where the most desperate cases are to be found. A merchant who recently saw the weavers of Yvetot tells me: it is impossible for them ever to recover. Such a situation puts horror and dismay in one's soul. Do not come to Normandy, dear friends; it is a wretched country that seems to be struck by a curse."[17]

In February 1863 Noël wrote a caustic article in the *Opinion nationale,* blaming the manufacturers themselves for much of the misery caused by the cotton crisis. It was not the American war alone that had caused this suffering, he argued, but instead a system of production that systematically exploited workers and kept them in a permanent state of physical and moral abasement—even in the best of times. "The war and the crisis were born of a common cause," wrote Noël. "Cotton, which is cultivated in slavery, is spun amidst tears and sickness." His article concluded with this poignant description of working-class distress in Normandy: "Cauchois weavers now eat colza leaves; in Rouen, the parish of Saint-Vivien alone counts 1,170 destitute families, who have a hundred thousand francs' worth of indispensable belongings in the pawn shops. Mothers register their daughters as prostitutes; when the registrar tries to dissuade them from taking this horrible step, they reply: *'we have no bread.'*"[18]

Noël's outburst caused quite a stir, infuriating Rouen manufacturers and bringing the wrath of the government down on his head. Imperial police seized the issue of the newspaper in which his article had appeared and hauled its author into court for "inciting the citizens to hatred and scorn for one another."[19] Noël got off with a warning, but the affair shows both how sensitive the government was on this question and how difficult it was to discuss the real facts of the cotton crisis.

The economic situation represented a serious political liability for the emperor. Pondering the political consequences of the crisis, the procureur général at Paris gloomily observed in June 1862 that "the masses . . . almost always hold the governmental powers responsible for their suffering, and their loyalty [to the government] can be measured by the amount of material prosperity they enjoy."[20] The truth of this observation was demonstrated by the 1863 legislative elections, in which urban workers voted heavily against the government, increasing the number of opposition deputies from five to thirty-five.[21] More worrisome than this electoral setback, the government faced a potentially revolutionary situation growing out of working-class discontent. A number of strikes occurred in Alsace in 1863 and 1864, triggered by reduced salaries, shortened hours, and rising unemployment in the cotton industry. The alarmed prefect at Colmar warned in April 1863 that "such occurrences might become general with the spread of the economic crisis."[22] In Roanne some four hundred workers demonstrated before the Hôtel de Ville in June 1862, placarding the city with posters proclaiming "Republic, employment, or the pillage of Roanne."[23] These were isolated and relatively minor disturbances, but they underscored the threat of a major upheaval if the crisis were to continue indefinitely.

Seeking to defuse the situation, the government gave active aid and encouragement to the nationwide relief effort. The first such initiatives had been local and spontaneous. Private charities, church congregations, and citizens' committees had begun collecting money for needy workers and their families. As the crisis grew in proportion, major newspapers like Le Siècle and Le Temps launched national fundraising drives, while Parisian workers organized subscriptions for their brothers and sisters in the stricken areas. In February 1863 the local Rouen relief group was transformed into a "national benevolent committee," which raised some 2 million francs in donations.[24] But these private efforts proved inadequate to deal with the situation, and the government finally had to pump large sums into the relief effort. Two million francs were appropriated in March 1862, 5 million in January 1863, and 1.2 million in July 1863.[25]

These stopgap measures barely sufficed to keep the workers' heads above water. The only hope for a real recovery seemed to lie in the pacification of America and the reopening of its ports to French commerce. Napoleon III sought to achieve this end through diplomacy. Encouraged by Southern military successes in the summer of 1862, the French and British governments seriously considered issuing a joint recognition of the Confederacy in the autumn of that year. But McClellan's victory at Antietam in September 1862, halting the Confederate advance into Maryland, caused the British cabinet to hold up on recognition until military events took a more decisive turn.[26]

Napoleon III then tried to force the issue. In October he invited England and Russia to join with him in proposing a six-month truce to the American belligerents. According to this plan, the truce would be followed by a reopening of the blockaded ports, negotiations between North and South, and, possibly, a mediation by the European powers. Judging the moment inopportune, the British cabinet politely declined the offer but left the door open for future action along these lines. Russia, openly friendly toward the North, flatly rejected the idea.[27] Undaunted by this failure, the emperor unilaterally offered Washington his good offices in January 1863. His proposal drew a predictably frosty response from Seward, and there the matter ended.[28] Coming in the wake of the foiled October offer, the latest initiative had little chance for success. The emperor's real motivation, it seems, was to convince the French public that he was doing all he could to relieve the economic suffering caused by the conflict.[29]

The French economic situation began to improve dramatically by the second half of 1863. Cotton from India, Egypt, and Algeria was partially compensating for the shortage of the Southern staple. The wool and linen textile industries, which had in fact benefited from the situation, were able to absorb great numbers of cotton operatives. Other affected industries developed new markets to offset the decline in exports to America. Good wheat harvests in 1863 made bread cheaper and more plentiful. By February 1864, the total number of unemployed had dropped to 174,052 from a peak of 223,036 ten months earlier.[30] Although cotton prices continued to fluctuate, causing a certain amount of economic disturbance until the end of the war, the situation had ceased to be critical by the end of 1863. Thereafter, pressures in favor of intervention subsided, and Napoleon III made no further attempt to act directly on the American question. With the improvement of the economic situation, this issue lost much of its urgency. The government's concerns now focused increasingly on Europe, where events in Poland, Denmark, Italy, and elsewhere demanded its attention. Leaving America to its destiny, the emperor remarked to his ministers in 1863: "If the North is victorious, I shall be happy; if the South is victorious, I shall be enchanted."[31]

CHAPTER 10

French Workers and the Civil War

If [the Americans] are suffering at this moment, it is because they did not want liberty for all! Woe to him who succumbs to the vile stupidity of selfishness! He is inviting disaster.

—AGRICOL PERDIGUIER, worker from Avignon, 1864

W hat was the attitude of the workers themselves toward the apparent source of all their suffering? This is one of the most interesting questions concerning the French response to the American Civil War, but it is also one of the most difficult to answer. Workers had little means of expressing their views under the Second Empire: they published no newspapers; trade unions were illegal; and unauthorized meetings of more than twenty persons were forbidden, as were marches and public demonstrations. Strikes and workers' "coalitions" were outlawed until 1864. The resulting scarcity of documentary evidence makes it almost impossible to know what workers really did think about the American war.

The generally accepted idea on this subject is that French workers overwhelmingly supported the Union cause and opposed intervention. Henry Blumenthal, for example, writes that "French workers, like those of England, decided they would rather tighten their belts than lend support to the American slave owners."[1] Donaldson Jordan and Edwin J. Pratt similarly state that "the working classes, in France as in England, steadfastly upheld the Northern cause."[2] Samuel Bernstein asserts: "Though they [French workers] were without jobs or food, they did not call for intervention on the side of the South. Like the workers of England, they preferred to suffer rather than to be the allies of the slave owners."[3]

Such confident declarations suggest that the question is settled once and for all. Yet none of these statements is backed up by any concrete evidence. The reaction of the French workers almost seems to have been extrapolated from the English response. To some extent, these historians are justified in looking to the English example, for British workers also suffered severely during the Civil War. Furthermore, their greater freedom of expression allowed them to voice their opinions on the American question in various ways. If one assumes that similar circumstances prompted similar responses in both countries, one might also suppose that the views of British laborers were shared by their French brethren.

Since historians have leaned so heavily on the English reaction, that example is worth examining more closely. For over a century, it has been a cliché of Civil War historiography to praise the Lancashire cotton operatives for refusing to support British intervention on behalf of the Southern slaveholders. Their faith in democracy, their belief in free labor, and their sense of solidarity with the oppressed slaves, this argument goes, turned them into unshakable supporters of the Union, even at the price of their own continued suffering. In support of this view, historians have cited various pro-North meetings, petitions, articles in the workingmen's press, and especially the declarations of contemporaries like John Bright and Richard Cobden, who were the foremost British propagandists for the Northern cause.

But this long-established view has been questioned by several British writers. Among the first scholars to challenge it was Royden Harrison, a leading labor historian, who in 1959 and 1961 devoted two important articles to the question of British workers and the Civil War.[4] Harrison argues that British antislavery had always been a middle-class liberal cause and that only a small minority of labor leaders actively supported it. When the Civil War broke out, moreover, the anticapitalist sentiments of many British workers made them hostile to the Yankee capitalists. This hostility was reinforced by the fact that the North's most ardent champions were liberal free traders like Bright, who represented the manufacturing classes of northern England and were detested by the average British trade unionist. Supporting his argument with a wealth of documentation, Harrison concludes: "It is a problem to find a single influential working class paper which consistently favoured Lincoln and opposed intervention. The predominant tendency was decidedly the other way. . . . Famous and respected leaders of the working people sided with the Confederacy."[5]

Following Harrison's lead, Mary Ellison delved into the archives and libraries of Lancashire and discovered ample evidence that the workers there strongly favored both Southern independence and British intervention. They did so, says Ellison, not only for obvious economic reasons but also because they saw the Southern cause as one of national self-determination—like the causes of Greece, Poland, and Italy. Such sentiments were not incompatible with antislavery beliefs since it was commonly argued that an independent South, under the influence of enlightened European opinion, would carry out emancipation in a more humane and practical way than the North.[6] In an epilogue to Ellison's study, Peter d'A. Jones traces the fallacy of the workers' pro-North stand back to contemporary propagandists like Cobden, Bright, and Karl Marx. "The myth was born in propaganda," writes Jones, "and was sustained because, like all myths that endure, it told people what they wanted to believe."[7]

If historians were wrong about British workers, it is quite possible that they have been wrong about their French counterparts as well. The scarcity of first-hand documents makes it difficult to explode the French myth (if myth it be) as convincingly as Harrison and Ellison have done for England. But a close look at the available sources might throw new light on the question. It is a remarkable reflection on the paucity of hard evidence that one single paragraph, written by the liberal journalist Eugène Forcade in 1863, has been cited by at least half a dozen writers as their sole illustration of French working-class opinion:

> [W]hile the Imperial government . . . shows a certain partiality for the South in hopes . . . of insuring employment for our workers, the workers themselves have taken a very different attitude. If they were asked: "Which do you prefer? The triumph of the South and the return of cotton with the continuation of slavery, or the emancipation of the slaves and the continuation of unemployment and misery?"—we are certain that they would reply: "It is a thousand times better for us to remain in misery than to pay for our well-being with the continued bondage of four million souls."[8]

It is easy to see why so many historians have seized upon this passage: it corresponds exactly to the accepted version of the story. It is unfortunately a weak source. Though Forcade was a contemporary observer, his claim to speak for the starving workers of Normandy is dubious. Like Cobden and Bright, Forcade was himself a pro-North propagandist, anxious to convince himself and others that the workers were behaving in the proper way. The opinions he ascribed to them may or may not be true, but the statement of one bourgeois journalist is an insufficient barometer of working-class opinion. More conclusive evidence is called for.

One attempt to deal with this question in depth is Samuel Bernstein's 1955 essay "French Democracy and the American Civil War."[9] Bernstein does come up with some authentic expressions of working-class sympathy for the Union at the time of Lincoln's assassination. By that time, however, the war had become a moot question: the Confederacy was defeated, slavery was abolished, and the economic distress caused by the conflict had largely subsided. One cannot extrapolate back from that cathartic moment and assume that workers felt the same sympathy for the Yankees during the first phase of the conflict, when Lincoln was firmly denying abolition as a war aim, Northern armies were floundering in the field, and the cotton crisis was raging in Europe. It cannot be denied that many French workers grieved over Lincoln's death in April 1865—but then, so too did Napoleon III and the notoriously pro-South London *Times*.[10]

For all the years preceding Lincoln's assassination, Bernstein fails to produce a single overt expression of working-class sympathy for the North. In attempting to account for this silence, he writes: "If they did not publicly demonstrate their stand with free labor, as their English brethren did, the reason lay in the political restrictions. . . . French workers were silent; but theirs was the silence of the penitentiary."[11] This argument is unconvincing as well: silence—even when imposed—does not give us the right to impute unexpressed opinions.

In the absence of hardcore evidence, Bernstein attempts to tease out the workers' opinion through indirect clues. He suggests, for example, that their manifest hostility to the Mexican venture was actually a secret expression of pro-North sentiments, "a less suspect way of opposing intervention on behalf of the slave owners."[12] But why should it be less suspect to attack the Mexican policy—to which the prestige and fortunes of the empire were heavily committed—than to express an opinion on a foreign war toward which the French government was officially neutral?

Bernstein similarly cites the opposition's 1863 electoral gains as an indirect expression of the workers' pro-North sentiments. "Circumspect, even devious, in their sympathy with the North," he writes, "French workers nevertheless exhibited it in every available way."[13] Here again, the reasoning is shaky. For one thing, workers were far from unanimous in voting for opposition candidates in 1863. Furthermore, there is scant basis for attributing the opposition gains to the

American question: to a great extent they reflect Catholic dissatisfaction with the emperor's Italian policy and the Commercial Treaty of 1860 with England.[14] Such roundabout evidence is not persuasive.

The idea that French workers supported the North seems to rest on two basic assumptions: first, that they accepted their hardships with calm resignation; second, that their resignation somehow implied sympathy for the Union. As Bernstein puts it: "Their grim, silent suffering had a power and eloquence all its own. It helped stay the hand of the pro-Confederate party in France."[15]

In fact, the workers were not all that passive. Readers of contemporary newspapers get the idea that a perfect calm reigned among the laboring classes. This impression was actively fostered by the government, which saw to it that the press printed nothing to the contrary. But the internal reports of government officials describe the deep dissatisfaction that actually existed in many of the affected areas. Although there was no major uprising, diverse demonstrations of popular discontent took place throughout the Civil War period. In the textile industry alone, there were more than fifty strikes during these years.[16] This is a significant number given that strikes were illegal until May 1864.

These incidents were most frequent in the département du Nord, a major textile center in the north of France and one of the regions that suffered most severely from the cotton crisis.[17] During the Civil War years, workers in various branches of the textile industry participated in more than thirty strikes and "coalitions." Most of them were quickly suppressed by authorities, but the department's prefect described several incidents as having "a certain gravity."[18] In March 1862, for example, angry workers in Caudry attacked the home of Charles Decaudin, a cotton manufacturer who had laid off his weavers. After breaking his windows and roof slates with stones, they burned their former employer in effigy before a crowd of a thousand approving onlookers.[19] At Roubaix an unemployed cotton-mill foreman was arrested in March 1862 for saying, "For sure, we will break the machinery on Tuesday." The prefect warned, "In five or six days, things can turn bad if there is no change in our commercial situation."[20] In May 1864 an unemployed Lille weaver was arrested for shouting, "The workers are not happy!"[21]

The cotton districts of Alsace witnessed a number of similar incidents during the Civil War years. In May 1862 a series of strikes broke out in the cotton mills of Sainte-Marie-aux-Mines. Imperial police had to arrest ten strike leaders in order to "stop the effervescence that was spreading to other workshops and could have produced a general strike." Shortly afterward, weavers from a nearby town invaded Sainte-Marie and staged a demonstration to demand higher salaries. It took the combined efforts of police and gendarmes to clear them out.[22] In July 1862 posters proclaiming "Bread or death" and "Vive la République" appeared in Mulhouse, along with anonymous letters threatening to burn down the city. In reporting these incidents, the prefect could not conceal his alarm over the increasing agitation of the workers:

> These manifestations . . . do not appear to me to be isolated events, but seem to result from a plan aimed at upsetting the working class. . . .
>
> Although the [economic] situation in Mulhouse is not as bad as some would have us believe, nevertheless the administration of this town is worried for the future, and the situation is worse in other parts of the [Haut-Rhin] Department. . . . That's where the real danger lies, as these workers could form a dangerous group in Mulhouse. In the arrondissement of Belfort, the industrial crisis is becoming increasingly grave, and the language of the workers betrays a certain agitation. . . . In sum, the situation . . . could become very grave in the near future.[23]

The simmering unrest prompted this prefect to request a reinforcement of the military garrison at Mulhouse. In April 1863 the same official reported a fresh series of strikes in the cotton industry. These events, he wrote, were "symptomatic of the workers' mood, & I fear that their disposition might spread and worsen with the prolongation of the industrial crisis."[24]

Nor was working-class discontent limited to these two regions. At Rouen, an important textile center in Normandy (département de la Seine-Inférieure), a large number of weavers sent a petition to Napoleon III in April 1862, bitterly protesting the 10-percent salary cuts decreed by their employers.[25] In January 1862, anonymous handbills at Origny (département de l'Aisne) warned employers that if they reduced wages any further, "we will turn your homes into butcheries, & we will soak our hands, withered by hunger, in your blood. Yes, before dying, I will kill."[26] In May 1864 Limoges (département de la Haute-Vienne) witnessed a chain reaction of strikes affecting, among others, the textile and porcelain industries that were still suffering from the effects of the American war.[27]

It would be a mistake to exaggerate the significance of these incidents, but it would be a greater mistake to ignore them. Considering the degree of political repression that existed in France at this time, such overt signs of discontent might be likened to the visible tip of the iceberg. In any event, these facts belie the notion that French workers patiently suffered in support of saving the American Union.

The claim that political repression alone prevented the workers from speaking up for the North is likewise questionable. Despite the restrictions placed on their political activities, workers did have some rudimentary form of organization and some means of expressing their views. For example, they elected a two-hundred-man delegation to attend the 1862 London Exhibition. Upon their return, these delegates published reports totaling over a thousand pages, touching on a great variety of subjects and putting forward a number of social and political demands. If French workers were indeed anxious to express their pro-North sympathies "in every available way," as Bernstein has suggested, here was a good opportunity to do so. Yet in all those pages, only two incidental allusions to the American question appear. Lyon silk weavers complained of "the distress that this deplorable war has caused in our workshops" and said that its prolongation "will show us an even bleaker future."[28] In another passing reference to the Civil War, bronze workers compared the laissez-faire philosophy of free traders like Bright to the Southerners' defense of slavery.[29] Though this was an implied criticism of the slaveholders, it was accompanied by no statement in favor of the North. This allusion is actually rather ambiguous, for the main target of the bronze workers' criticism here, John Bright, was the foremost champion of the Northern cause in England. Royden Harrison has shown that many British trade unionists opposed the Union cause precisely because it was identified in their eyes with the sort of laissez-faire liberalism represented by Bright and Cobden.[30] We also know that many French workers, particularly in the textile industry, were hostile to the free-trade principles of the 1860 Commercial Treaty. This alone would give them sufficient reason to dislike its coauthor Cobden. Now, if French workers were opposed to the economic principles of Cobden and Bright, might they not—like many of their British brothers—be suspicious of the Yankee capitalists whom these celebrated free traders were supporting with such ardor? All this is pure conjecture, of course, but it is no less plausible than the claim that contacts and parallels between English and French workers forcibly bred pro-North sentiments.

That the French delegates to the London Exhibition were acutely aware of the suffering caused by the cotton famine is evident from the relief activities they organized shortly after their return. In January 1863 the officers of the London delegation launched a nationwide workers' subscription on behalf of the suffering cotton operatives of Normandy. This, they declared, was a fraternal response "to the cries of distress and despair uttered by thousands of half extinct voices of our brothers in the valley of the Seine-Inférieure."[31] A second committee of Parisian workers was formed by Henri Tolain, J.-J. Blanc, Blaise Perrachon, and other future members of the first International.[32] Both of these groups organized collections in the workshops and factories and published regular appeals in the press.

Had they chosen to speak up for the North on this occasion, these organizations could have found the means of doing so. Their published appeals on the economic distress felt in their industries contain many ringing phrases about solidarity and fraternity among French workers but not a word on the American war that was causing this suffering. Of course, their silence on this question cannot be taken for opposition to the North—they may have feared that an overt political statement would compromise their humanitarian appeal. Still, it is worth noting that opportunities for expressing pro-North sentiments did exist and that these groups chose not to use them.

The more sophisticated and articulate elements of the Parisian working classes—those who helped create the International, for example—did take stands on some political issues. Officially known as the International Workingmen's Association, the International was in fact born of an 1864 Anglo-French workers' meeting on the Polish question (the abortive 1863–64 uprising against Russian domination). Parisian workers likewise spoke out on the Mexican and Italian questions. In general, as Lynn M. Case has noted, they "sympathized with every revolutionary movement, be it republican, socialistic, or nationalistic."[33] (Such sentiments might have led them to sympathize with the South's revolution, especially during the first eighteen months, when Lincoln's declared war aim was reunion rather than the abolition of slavery.)

Urban workers also issued statements on certain internal political issues. In 1864 a group of Parisian workers published the *Manifeste des Soixante,* which demanded parliamentary representation for the working classes and a greater measure of democracy. So the question is not so much whether they had a voice, but rather what issues they chose to address. Apparently, support for Lincoln's government was not among those issues. Even at the time of Lincoln's assassination, the Parisian section of the International abstained from drafting a message of condolence. Bernstein attributes this conspicuous silence to the fact that, as devout Proudhonists, these Parisians eschewed political action.[34]

Bernstein is correct in claiming that Proudhon had a powerful influence on the French labor movement at this time. But Proudhon also had strong opinions on the American war, and his views presumably affected the way his working-class followers judged the conflict. Thus it is worthwhile to take a close look at his various statements on this subject.

An authentic proletarian by birth and temperament, Proudhon addressed a lengthy response to the authors of the *Manifeste des Soixante* entitled *De la capacité politique des classes ouvrières* (On the political capacity of the working classes). Published shortly after his death in January 1865, it was his last testament to the workers. This book contains a very explicit reference to the Civil War:

> At the time of this writing . . . the United States of the North are attempting, by force, to retain the United States of the South in their Union, calling [the Confederates] *traitors* and rebels, as if the former Union was a monarchy and Mr. Lincoln was an emperor. However, it is clear that . . . leaving aside the question of slavery, the war waged against the South by the North is unjust. . . . [I]n this case the Americans would do well in the future to strike from their manifesto the words of political liberty, republic, democracy, confederation, and even Union. Already, on the other side of the Atlantic, they are starting to deny states' rights, which embodies the federal principle.[35]

This was no isolated reference. In fact, Proudhon's correspondence and writings of the Civil War period abound with anti-Yankee sentiments. In September 1862, for instance, he wrote to Gustave Chaudey: "I have no faith in the North's philanthropy; nor do I admit that the federal Constitution prevents separation. . . . The armies of the North go from defeat to defeat; England, Belgium and France, devoured by pauperism, cry out for cotton; and if the imperial government, felicitously linking the two questions of Mexico and the Confederates, reestablished relations with New Orleans, would you still attack it for that?"[36] In a letter of August 1863, Proudhon declared: "You know I have never had a weakness for Lincoln and his people; if the others are brazen slaveholders, [the Northerners] are hypocritical exploiters."[37] Lamenting over the inevitable Northern victory in October 1864, he wrote to a Belgian correspondent: "I admit that I am no friend of the Anglo-Saxons, and I think that few people like them. Thus I deplore the policy of our Emperor, who, had he chosen to, could have obtained from the South a promise to emancipate the blacks, and could then have intervened as an interested party in the current war and . . . brought the North to reason."[38]

Proudhon did not speak for the entire French working class, of course. But it is possible that many of those workers who espoused his mutualist and federalist doctrines also shared his belief that the North was violating those very principles by attempting to force central control on the South. It is also possible that their hostility to capitalist exploitation made them dislike the Yankees a priori, as was clearly the case with Proudhon.

Proudhon was not the only working-class writer to publish books during these years, nor was he the only one to comment on the American war in print. While none of the others seem to have shared his visceral contempt for the Yankees, not a single enthusiastic pro-North statement appears in any of them. Even while denouncing the institution of slavery, none of these writers attack the South outright. Instead, they tend to blame all Americans for having tolerated slavery for so long, thereby making this disastrous war inevitable.

Writing at the outset of the conflict, the typographer Henri Leneveux, a former editor of L'Atelier, alluded to "this grave question of race that is currently disrupting the United States over the maintenance of this atrocity called slavery; a question that has been decided a thousand times over for us French democrats, who in 1848 had the honor of breaking the last link of this ignominious chain."[39] Another veteran of L'Atelier, Anthime Corbon, similarly criticized the Americans for failing to abolish slavery long before the 1860s. Writing in 1863, Corbon declared:

> The United States of America contained within itself the cause of the terrible and inevitable conflict that is upsetting the whole world. . . . [S]ooner or later slavery had to produce the bloody crisis from which the old world, like the new, is now suffering. At the present hour, all human societies are receiving a frightful lesson! They all bear a responsibility for the crime committed by one of their number. . . . Unfortunately, it is those populations that could do the least about that crime who are now suffering the most![40]

If these writers showed no sympathy for the slaveholders, they had surprisingly little to say in favor of the North.

Like the writings of Proudhon, the views of these proletarian journalists provide some useful insights into working-class opinion. But the really significant question concerns the views of those who were most directly affected by the American war: the hungry masses of Normandy, Alsace, the north, and other distressed areas. Here the task is especially difficult, for the workers of these regions—unlike their more sophisticated Parisian brothers—were largely unorganized, unpoliticized, and in many cases illiterate. Not only did they lack means of expressing political opinions, but a large number of them probably also had no clear-cut political opinions at all. The attitude of many of these provincial workers may be summed up in the words of a popular 1861 song, written in the Lille patois:

> Above all, don't listen to politics
> All those words drive me crazy
> China, Syria and Africa
> Whenever they talk about all that
> It bores me and I yawn.[41]

This indifference to politics is confirmed by a procureur général's observation concerning the attitudes of the working classes in the north of France: "They only pay attention [to politics] . . . to the extent that this situation can affect their own immediate interests, that is, by raising workers' salaries or facilitating sales of their bosses' merchandise."[42] If this was so, then they must have been more concerned with the return of prosperity to their own region than with the political aspects of the American war.

In the absence of any deep political ideas, many provincial workers seem to have placed their confidence in the paternal care of the imperial government. One Lille cotton worker, for example, lamenting over the misery caused by the crisis in 1863, consoled himself with the thought that the government was doing all it could to relieve the suffering:

> Stay calm, my children,
> Worry no more;
> The Government is working hard

To give us bread. . . .
In spite of all our suffering, We can only repeat
That the necessary aid
is bringing relief to our workers.[43]

The same filial trust in the government seems to have characterized the workers of Normandy. In January 1862 the procureur at Rouen noted, "the great majority [of workers] go about their business and trust the task of running the government to the wisdom of the Emperor." The working classes, he added, "like the Emperor, who has restored France's power and grandeur; they feel that he looks after them, that he works to improve their situation and they are devoted to him as they were from the first days [of his reign]."[44] The procureur at Colmar similarly remarked in July 1861 that the emperor was the object of "the warmest sympathies" in Alsace, adding, "this is the general feeling in this region, especially among the popular classes."[45]

As far as the American question is concerned, the main factor affecting working-class opinion was not politics but economics. For those reduced to misery and indigence by the cotton shortage, the vital issue was work and bread. The political questions involved in a foreign war—even the question of slavery—were far less important to a starving worker than his or her own existence. To claim the contrary is to fly in the face, not only of human nature, but also of basic animal survival instinct. That instinct produced a marked increase in prostitution among working-class women during the Civil War.[46] It seems highly implausible that people who were forced to sacrifice their own human dignity in this way would choose to continue suffering because of a political struggle on the other side of the ocean. Surely their main desire was for the return of employment and prosperity.

This would logically lead them to support the idea of mediation or intervention to bring the hostilities to a close. While support for such measures did not necessarily imply a preference for either side, the practical effect would have favored the Confederacy and possibly led to some form of Southern independence. During the first two years of the war, moreover, it was commonly believed that the South could never be forced back into the Union. Thus the North's acceptance of the fait accompli of separation seemed to be the only path to peace and the only hope for economic recovery in France.

That was apparently the prevalent opinion in those regions most affected by the crisis. While the cotton shortage persisted, the imperial government was besieged by calls for intervention coming from local officials, industrialists, chambers of commerce, and newspapers in the stricken areas. These pleas, many tinged with Southern sympathies, were most often voiced in the name of the suffering workers.

As early as October 1861, the procureur at Colmar reported that Alsatian textile manufacturers were shuddering at the prospect of a prolonged cotton famine that would condemn millions of French and English workers to starvation. Many of them consequently felt "that France and England should intervene in the American conflict, even if this intervention might lead to a recognition of the Southern Confederacy."[47] In July 1862 the same procureur wrote, "[public] opinion increasingly favors either a mediation by the European powers, or a prompt recognition of the Confederate States of the South."[48] That same month the prefect of the Haut-Rhin described widespread agitation among the workers in his district and ended his report with this observation: "I can tell your Excellency that the unanimously expressed desire of the industrialists and the population would be a mediation by Europe to terminate this conflict, whose end we have awaited for 18 months with little hope."[49] In January 1863 the procureur at Colmar reported, "sympathies in favor of the Confederation of the South grow stronger each day." Regretting the failure of the emperor's second mediation proposal, he remarked that "the renewal of this proposal, even if it were presented in stronger terms and backed up by warships, would be enthusiastically applauded by the industrial sector of Mulhouse."[50]

A look at the local press confirms the claim that the cotton centers of Alsace overwhelmingly favored the South. Mulhouse's major daily, *L'Industriel Alsacien,* was an enthusiastic supporter of Southern independence and French intervention. "How long will you be duped by the Northern States?" thundered a typical editorial jab at the liberal journals of Paris. "And when will you finally admit that the slavery question has nothing to do with the excesses of the American dictatorship?"[51] Another editorial in this paper proclaimed, "The Southern States are fighting to win their autonomy and not for the perpetual maintenance of slavery."[52] For the South, "it is a question of their most vital interests, their possessions and their independence."[53] Colmar's *Journal du Haut-Rhin,* though somewhat less fanatical, likewise favored Southern independence and French mediation.[54] In January 1863 the procureur at Colmar reported that the *Courrier du Bas-Rhin* was the only paper in all Alsace that remained sympathetic to the North.[55] It is true that these were bourgeois papers, but the workers who read them were likely to be influenced by their editorial policies to some extent.

Leading Alsatian industrialists also spoke out publicly in favor of Southern independence. Gustave Imbert-Koechlin, a Mulhouse cotton broker, expressed "hopes in the name of all humanity, and in the name of the working populations that are most directly affected, . . . for peace to reign *between the two States of America.*"[56] (This obviously implied that Southern independence was a necessary condition to any peace settlement.) Considering the strong tradition of paternalism that existed in the Alsatian textile industry, it is not implausible that workers shared their employers' views on the American war, just as they did on matters like free trade.

The distressed cotton districts of northern France also seem to have favored mediation and Southern independence.[57] In October 1861 the prefect in Lille reported that the textile manufacturers of his department unanimously called for "the pacification of America" in order to "remedy a situation that is as prejudicial to the industrialists as it is to their workers."[58] In July 1863 the procureur in Douai observed, "the opinion of the working classes, like that of the big manufacturers, is grateful to the Emperor who sought to end [the American conflict] and resentful towards England for not supporting this humanitarian and loyal intervention."[59] Three months later another report from Douai declared: "The civil dissensions in America . . . are reducing the workers of several regions to indigence. For this reason, the people want [the war] to end, but most of them would not want to end with the defeat of the South, whose courage could not fail to win the sympathies of a country like ours."[60]

From Cambrai, a weaving center that was severely affected by the war, the local chamber of commerce issued repeated pleas for intervention. The only hope for economic recovery, its members wrote in December 1861, was "for the European powers to secure, by whatever means, an end to the blockade of the Confederate ports in order to enter into a relationship with the Southern planters who would provide raw cotton in exchange for finished fabric."[61]

Such hopes found a resonant echo in the departmental press. *Le Mémorial de Lille,* an important mouthpiece for the region's industrial interests, editorialized in January 1863: "Napoleon III is right to ask why Europe must remain calm and

make no effort to save our Christian society from the hardships it is now suffering. The Emperor would perform a great service if he persuaded the federals to
abandon their insane enterprise."[62] These sentiments were shared by the *Echo du
Nord,* and even the *Journal populaire de Lille,* read mainly by workers, showed a
certain sympathy for the Confederates.[63]

In Normandy, hardest hit of all the cotton districts, opinion also seems to have
favored a pro-South intervention. According to a procureur's report of July 1862:

> The big industrialists, and along with them, nearly the whole mass of the popu-
> lation, would like to see us intervene in the American conflict.... [T]hey would
> like the governments of France and England to propose their mediation with a
> view to organizing the separation that has become inevitable; if the Northern
> states refuse, we should solemnly recognize the Southern states, with all the polit-
> ical consequences that this recognition would entail. That is the dominant opin-
> ion in Rouen among the entire industrial class.... [I]n Le Havre, as in Rouen, all
> the sympathies are for the Southern cause.[64]

Another revealing indication of opinion in Normandy is provided by Monseigneur Marie-Gaston de Bonnechose, the respected cardinal-archbishop of
Rouen. As head of the Catholic relief activities in his diocese, Bonnechose took
a personal interest in the condition of the distressed workers. He visited their
homes, distributed alms to them, heard their complaints, and tried to comfort
them.[65] Few outside observers were in a better position to know what the workers thought about the situation. One may assume, then, that this prelate was
speaking for workers as well as industrialists when he discussed the situation of
Rouen with British journalist Nassau W. Senior in April 1863. "The commercial
treaty and the American war have ruined us," he told Senior. "We accuse you [the
English] of depriving us of cotton by preventing the Emperor from recognising
the South and breaking the blockade, and we accuse you of having entrapped us
into free trade."[66]

From other affected areas came similar expressions of sympathy for the South
and calls for intervention. In July 1862 the chamber of commerce of Cholet reported: "The position of our working populations is deplorable; this winter, if
the situation does not improve, [will be] frightening. If the Government can
hasten a solution to these American questions . . . God grant that it come as

soon as possible."[67] The procureur at Nancy reported in April 1863 that the local population deplored "the obstinacy and blindness that leads the Federal Government to reject the French overtures. . . . Nonetheless, we have to applaud the good sense of the working populations who, grateful for the aid and sympathy occasioned by their sufferings, are equally grateful to the Emperor for the double proposal [of mediation] of which he alone took the initiative in the interest of both hemispheres."[68] In an 1864 report, the chamber of commerce of Poitiers similarly encouraged French intervention—and did so in the name of the workers themselves:

> After serving as a feeble echo to the great sufferings [of the workers], we feel the need to express the desire that is on everyone's lips. . . . In the name of humanity and in the name of all our workers who often lack the bare necessities. In the name of our industrial, commercial and agricultural interests who are suffering! We implore the Emperor, with the deepest respect, to seek, by all means in his power, and as rapidly as possible, to put an end to the war that is desolating the united States of America.[69]

The above sources indicate that public opinion in the stricken areas was strongly in favor of French intervention in the American war and almost as strongly in favor of Southern independence. Thus it seems that Napoleon III's diplomatic efforts to end the conflict were more a reflection of popular demand than a purely personal initiative. This suggests a different explanation for the fact that there was no major uprising by French workers during the cotton crisis: perhaps they felt that the government was doing all it could to remedy the situation, not only through its relief efforts, but also through its repeated attempts to stop the American war. In both these ways it might be said, in the words of our Lillois songster, that "the Government is working hard to give us bread."[70]

There is no indication that the workers formed an exception to the views expressed in these reports. On the contrary, most of the documents cite the workers' sufferings as a major argument in favor of intervention, and many specifically include the working classes in their assessments of public opinion. Thus they flatly contradict the notion that French workers preferred to continue suffering rather than lend their support to a pro-South intervention. It is true that these are secondhand sources of working-class opinion, but they come from observers who were in a far better position to know what such people actually thought than Parisian journalists like Forcade.

Of course, these indirect sources do not tell the whole story of French worker opinion on the Civil War. But one may safely say that there was no unanimity among the workers: if some of them supported the North and believed that their own suffering was serving the causes of humanity and democracy, there were doubtless others who supported Southern independence, and there were still others who were indifferent to the outcome of the war and only wished for the return of prosperity and employment. It does not appear, on the basis of available evidence, that the attitude of the workers was an important factor in preventing French intervention in the conflict, as has often been claimed. That myth, at least, may be laid to rest.

CHAPTER 11

Emancipation

Things had gone from bad to worse, until I felt that we had reached the end of
our rope on the plan of operations we had been pursuing; that we had about
played our last card, and must change our tactics, or lose the game!
—ABRAHAM LINCOLN, 1862

President Lincoln's failure to acknowledge an antislavery purpose during
the first eighteen months of the American Civil War greatly damaged the
Northern cause in the eyes of Europe. This failure not only demoralized
the North's defenders but also allowed its opponents to portray secession as a
legitimate independence movement. They furthermore urged intervention as a
"humanitarian" measure designed to end the bloodshed and bring relief to the
cotton-starved workers.

The president had originally hoped to crush the rebellion and bring the
Southern states back into the Union without dealing directly with the question
of slavery. But by mid-1862, the hope of a quick Union victory had evaporated.
The Northern military situation at that time was far from brilliant. The cotton
crisis was nearing a critical point in Europe. The governments of England and
France were under increasing pressure to recognize the Confederacy and break
the blockade. At this juncture Lincoln decided on a new tactic: he would save
the Union by freeing the slaves.

Lincoln had prepared a draft of the Preliminary Emancipation Proclamation
by mid-summer 1862 but had refrained from making it public until the North
was in a more favorable military situation. When General McClellan checked
Robert E. Lee's invasion of Maryland at the Battle of Antietam in September
1862, Lincoln seized the long-awaited opportunity to announce his plan to free
the slaves. The Preliminary Emancipation Proclamation, published on September 22, 1862, declared, "That on the first day of January in the year of our Lord,

one thousand eight hundred and sixty-three, all persons held as slaves within any state . . . the people whereof shall be in rebellion against the United States shall be then, thenceforward, and forever free."[1] The loyal slave states—Delaware, Maryland, Kentucky, Missouri, and what would become West Virginia—were specifically excluded from the proclamation, although the president recommended congressional action providing for voluntary, compensated emancipation in these border regions. He also stated that "the effort to colonize persons of African descent" outside the United States would continue.[2]

In his December 1862 message to Congress, Lincoln outlined a detailed plan calling for gradual, compensated emancipation. According to this program, the process would last until 1900 and would be followed by "deportation" of the freedmen to "congenial climes" populated by "people of their own blood and race."[3] Offered as an alternative to the more drastic measures prescribed by the proclamation, this plan drew no response from Congress. On January 1, 1863, therefore, Lincoln issued the definitive Emancipation Proclamation, invoking his military authority as commander in chief to decree this "fit and necessary war measure for suppressing the rebellion."[4]

One of the president's main objectives in issuing the proclamation, of course, was to demoralize and weaken the South. Another was to quiet his abolitionist critics at home. But the proclamation was also motivated to a great extent by the fear of European intervention in the war. This threat had never appeared more imminent than in the summer and early autumn of 1862, when the Northern armies were foundering on the battlefield and the cotton famine was tightening its grip on European manufacturing. Lincoln hoped that his emancipation policy would generate enough popular support in Europe to forestall any moves toward recognition or intervention. But the initial overseas response to the proclamation was generally unenthusiastic.

In France the South's sympathizers were in no way deterred by it. On the contrary, they used it as additional ammunition with which to attack the North. Many critics claimed that the act was hypocritical and unenforceable since it freed slaves only in the states where Lincoln had no authority and left them in chains in areas under Union control. Others argued that it was not dictated by humanitarian considerations but was rather a desperate war measure aimed at fomenting slave rebellions and massacres throughout the South. Such cynical responses from Southern sympathizers were predictable, but even among the

North's supporters, there was a certain disappointment over the limited and ineffectual nature of the act. While approving of the antislavery sentiment behind the proclamation, leading democratic papers like the *Siècle* and the *Phare de la Loire* hoped that it would be followed by more radical measures, leading to the complete abolition of slavery.[5]

Though the immediate French response lacked enthusiasm, the proclamation nonetheless constituted a crucial turning point for the Northern cause. However limited its scope, it gave the Union the moral edge of an antislavery commitment. To this extent, it helped underpin the position of those in France whose support for the North had rested on the unconfirmed assumption that its true cause was abolition. Now they had proof. Writing from his London exile in February 1863, Louis Blanc declared that "the arguments advanced by the partisans of the South can have no meaning since the recent proclamation of M. Lincoln, which, at last, solemnly adopts the principle of the emancipation of the blacks."[6] Not only did the proclamation establish slavery as the central issue of the war, but it also cleansed the North of its long and shameful association with that institution. As Elisée Reclus observed in November 1862, "the word *Union* formerly signified the maintenance of slavery; today it signifies the advent of liberty. Of course much remains to be done; but it is precisely because we are conscious of the greatness of this work that we joyfully hail each small victory."[7] To many of those on the French left, it seemed that America had at last taken it rightful place in the march of progress.

One prominent French republican, the immensely popular novelist Alexandre Dumas, was so encouraged by the proclamation and by Lincoln's recent recognition of the Haitian Republic that he immediately began planning a grand tour of the United States. The mixed-race grandson of an impoverished French nobleman and a slave woman from Saint-Domingue, Dumas was a fierce critic of the slave trade and, by some accounts, even contemplated volunteering to fight for the Union as he had earlier supported Garibaldi in Italy. He was talked out of the idea of a U.S. tour by friends who convinced him that Americans who did not know his racial background might be surprised by his "café au lait" complexion and kinky hair and give him a less-than-enthusiastic reception. Dumas finally had to face the fact that the announced abolition of slavery in no way eliminated the deep-seated racial prejudices of many Americans.[8]

As the war advanced, it became increasingly difficult to doubt the North's

antislavery commitment. Shortly after the Emancipation Proclamation was issued, the Union army began to enroll Black troops on a large scale, which not
only contributed materially to the Northern war effort but also reinforced its image as a liberating crusade.[9] Thousands of escaped slaves flocked to Union lines,
while Northern schoolteachers, nurses, and missionaries followed the armies into
the South to help prepare the slaves for freedom. Congressional adoption of the
Thirteenth Amendment (January 31, 1865), which categorically abolished slavery
throughout the United States, was the logical consummation of the policy that
Lincoln had announced two years earlier.

Once the Emancipation Proclamation had unambiguously linked the North's
cause with antislavery, its French supporters redoubled their efforts. In February
1863 Eugène Pelletan published his *Adresse au roi Coton,* an almost Whitman-
esque hymn to the genius of the American republic. A devout Protestant, Pelletan traced the spirit of American liberty to "that heroic race" of New England
Puritans, who by "prayer and work" had created "something more marvelous
than More's *Utopia.*"[10] After winning their independence and establishing "the
most perfect form of government," these Yankees had seen their nation grow and
prosper at a dazzling rate. Pelletan glorified Yankee civilization as the highest embodiment of freedom, justice, and progress. "If ever there was a nation that honors the human race," he wrote, "surely it is North America, which . . . has given
the world the spectacle of man in all his power and splendor."[11] Southern society,
on the other hand, he viewed as the incarnation of all the Old World vices: aristocracy, privilege, intolerance, idleness, and despotism. Like the French aristocrats of the ancien régime, the Southern slaveholders were consigned by Pelletan
to the ash heap of history for having refused progress. Lincoln's proclamation, he
said, had already inflicted "the death blow upon the rebellion."[12] Shortly after the
publication of this pamphlet, Pelletan expressed his renewed faith in America in
a letter to Gustave Cluseret. "America is undergoing a moral resurrection at this
moment," he wrote. "At bottom, there is only one cause in the world: liberty."[13]

In the optimistic climate that followed the proclamation, pro-American
books like Edouard Laboulaye's *Paris en Amérique* won an enthusiastic reception. Cast in the form of a novel, this panegyric appeared in the spring of 1863
and was an instant popular success.[14] Writing under the pseudonym "Dr. René
Lefebvre," Laboulaye describes the imaginary voyage of a Parisian bourgeois to
the New England town of "Paris," Massachusetts, where he becomes initiated to

the American Way of Life. Hostile at first to this unfamiliar society, the Parisian is finally converted by his Yankee cicerones into a fanatical believer in American democracy. Awaking from his dream to find himself back in Paris, France, he vainly attempts to proselytize his countrymen, but they view his talk of liberty as the ravings of a madman.

While lauding diverse aspects of American life—republican institutions, freedom of the press, the work ethic, individual initiative, the independence of women, the spirit of equality, the separation of church and state, and public education—Laboulaye also criticizes the defects of French politics and society. His near-utopian portrait of America would have seemed sadly out of place had it appeared a year earlier, when the Union's detractors were loudly trumpeting its demise and even its friends were wondering if the country would survive the war with its liberties intact. But the new mood created by emancipation and by the improvement of the North's military fortunes was apparently well suited to Laboulaye's optimistic affirmation.

Elisée Reclus also voiced the theme of redemption by emancipation in two major articles on the slavery question in the spring of 1863.[15] Examining the experiences of fugitive slaves, "contrabands," and Black soldiers, he drew the most optimistic conclusions concerning both the future of the freedmen and the triumph of justice and equality in American society. The "liberating word" of the Emancipation Proclamation, said Reclus, had "signaled the accomplishment of an immense revolution in the life of the American people.... Once it has rid itself of the heavy burden of slavery, American society will march rapidly towards progress."[16] He rejoiced in America's redemption, not only for its own sake but also for the momentum he felt it would give to the cause of liberty throughout the world. Having been an embarrassment and a liability to that cause before the war, America would reemerge from the struggle as liberty's foremost champion. "Let it not be forgotten," wrote Reclus, "that when the planters instigated the rebellion, the United States was the land of slavery, and all the friends of liberty blushed when they spoke of the American Republic; at the end of the struggle, four million blacks will have been liberated, the land of Washington will no longer be dishonored by the spectacle of servitude, and throughout the world the force of democratic ideas will have doubled by this triumph of justice."[17] Thanks to Lincoln's emancipation policy, he declared, the Northern cause had ceased to be purely national; it had now become "the cause of humanity."[18]

Another socialist whose faith in America was revived by emancipation was Sainte-Suzanne Melvil-Bloncourt, a mixed-race West Indian who had taken an active part in the revolutionary movement of 1848 and would later fight for the Commune. An ardent abolitionist, Melvil-Bloncourt wrote a monthly column on American affairs for Adolphe Noirot's *Revue du monde colonial* during the Civil War. He corresponded regularly with members of the educated creole community of New Orleans, who kept him informed with firsthand accounts of American political and racial developments. As an *homme de couleur* and a native of the West Indies, he was especially sensitive to the questions of race and slavery, understanding them better than most of his French contemporaries.

From the outset of the war, Melvil-Bloncourt denounced the Southern slave-holders and called for immediate emancipation. To him, the granting of true freedom and equality to Blacks was the only issue that mattered.[19] But while he supported the Union, he incessantly demanded that Lincoln declare abolition a war aim. Even after the Emancipation Proclamation, Melvil-Bloncourt criticized the act's limited scope and decried the persistence of racist attitudes among the Yankees. Mocking Laboulaye's idealized *Paris en Amérique,* he wrote in August 1863, "as long as a single slave remains on the vast territory of the Union; as long as the Africans and their descendants are excluded from American citizenship, the Republic of the United States will count for less in the moral balance of the world than the tiny Republic of San Marino."[20] But the subsequent enrollment of Black troops, the rising influence of true abolitionists like Charles Sumner, and the congressional adoption of the Thirteenth Amendment convinced him that the North's antislavery commitment was genuine. During the last two years of the war, Melvil-Bloncourt emerged as an ardent defender of the Union cause. "Since the revolt of Spartacus," he wrote in June 1864, "no war . . . except per-haps the holy war of the French Revolution, was more just than the one that has armed the Federals against the slaveholders. It has taken a river of blood to cleanse this powerful Republic of the stain of slavery."[21] Melvil-Bloncourt hailed the passage of the Thirteenth Amendment as "one of the most memorable events in the history of Humanity."[22]

Reclus and Melvil-Bloncourt were not alone in attributing universal signifi-cance to these American events. To all those who believed in liberty of whatever degree or form, the tendency to see American abolition in terms of universal progress seems to have been almost irresistible. This was to be expected from those liberals and republicans like Henri Martin, Pelletan, and Laboulaye who had long looked on the United States as a model. More remarkable was the effect emancipation had on the thinking of the far left, which had shown little enthusiasm for America in the years before the war. Elisée Reclus, bitterly critical of the United States in the 1850s, became a warm partisan of American democracy. Louis Blanc, who had opposed the American influence in 1848, similarly emerged as one of the Union's strongest supporters during the war. Félix Pyat, another radical who had scoffed at the "Girondist" American republic in 1848, now called the United States the protector of "liberty in the New World and . . . a model for the Old."[23] Emancipation seems to have redeemed America in the eyes of these and many other French radicals, who now extolled it as the embodiment of the most progressive political and social ideas. It was as though the amputation of what was most reactionary about American society had suddenly radicalized the rest.

Pierre Vésinier's 1864 biography of John Brown gives an idea of just how revolutionary the American image could appear in the wake of emancipation. A grotesque, hunchbacked exile who was forever calling for the assassination of Napoleon III, Vésinier portrayed Brown as a model of revolutionary heroism. His book assimilated the 1859 Harpers Ferry raid—and by extension the whole emancipation movement in America—into the universal struggle of the exploited against the exploiters. The supreme lesson taught at Harpers Ferry and on the Civil War battlefields, said Vésinier, was the moral imperative of armed insurrection against exploiters and masters everywhere. "John Brown, man of faith and action, knew by experience that liberty is only conquered . . . at the price of blood, by *insurrection.*" By acting on that faith, Brown had struck a major blow in the battle for universal freedom. His martyr's blood had sown "the seeds of the future victory."[24] In claiming Brown as a fellow traveler of European revolutionaries, Vésinier was not content merely to point out the general similarities of action and purpose. He asserted that "if John Brown had been in Europe, he would have fought for the white slaves just as he fought for the black slaves in America; the proletarians would have aroused in him the same sympathies as the negro slaves. . . . If this old pilgrim father of Massachusetts had been on our continent, he would certainly have counted among the ranks of the most illustrious defenders of new ideas."[25]

Vésinier's view of the Union was no less radical than his image of John Brown. This future Communard depicted the North as an immense democratic republic, composed largely of workers and farmers, which had proven its devotion to "the principles of equality . . . and free labor" by electing the "proletarian worker" Abraham Lincoln as president.[26] In his eyes the North's abolitionist war was part of a worldwide struggle for the emancipation of labor: "This great question of the abolition of slavery is not only a question of justice and humanity; it is above all a question of progress, containing the solution to the great social problem of our age, that of labor, upon which hinge all the progressive evolutions of human history."[27] The destruction of slavery in America would promote the demise of capitalist exploitation in Europe, affirmed Vésinier, for "the disinherited of the old and new worlds are linked by solidarity, one cannot be emancipated without emancipating the others."[28] Once their "shackles and chains" had been broken, the American slaves would join arms with the Russian serfs and the European proletarians to smash the exploiters and initiate the era of human equality and "universal happiness."[29] Viewed in this way, the American Civil War appears as a direct precursor of the Bolshevik Revolution (as Vladimir Lenin himself would claim in 1918).[30]

Vésinier's identification of the Northern cause with that of the European proletariat was shared by many other radicals. This included Karl Marx, whose articles on the Civil War, appearing in the *New York Tribune* and the *Vienna Presse,* depicted the Northern cause as that of "popular self-government" and "free labor" against "the most shameless form of man's enslaving recorded in the annals of history."[31] Marx also did much to whip up support for the Union among British workers. He was instrumental in organizing several pro-North workers' meetings and led the International Workingmen's Association to take a strong pro-North stand after its formation in 1864. Writing to Lincoln on behalf of the International in 1864, Marx declared: "From the commencement of the titanic American strife, the working-men of Europe felt instinctively that the star-spangled banner carried the destiny of their class, . . . and that for men of labor, with their hopes for the future, even their past conquests were at stake in that tremendous conflict on the other side of the Atlantic."[32]

Such utterances may have been inspired by polemical purposes more than by conviction, but it is nevertheless significant that European radicals were drawn to the Northern cause as a source of revolutionary propaganda. One reason for this can be found in the revolutionary's chiliastic worldview, which tends to see the final triumph of "good" over "evil" as an inevitable result of the law of history and progress. From this point of view, the defeat of slavery in America could be seen as part of an ineluctable movement toward the social millennium. Like the freeing of the Russian serfs and the resurrection of Italy, American emancipation was widely cited as proof that God (or History) was on the side of social progress.[33]

But those European radicals who saw the Civil War as a reflection of their own ideology greatly misconstrued the ideas and intentions of the men who actually fought that war. No doubt, the abolition of slavery was a progressive act. But though bourgeois liberals, socialists, and revolutionaries could all rejoice over this event, the really significant question was whether it was to be seen as a culmination or as a beginning of social progress. George Lichtheim has written: "The abolition of [American] slavery was the last great triumph of democratic liberalism and the termination of its heroic age. . . . But the abolition of slavery likewise signalized the depth of the gulf separating the most radical of liberals from the most moderate of socialists."[34]

The difference concerned their respective attitudes toward the private ownership of the means of production, toward wage labor, and toward capitalism in general. Liberals thought this was the best of all possible social and economic systems; socialists called for its destruction. Therein lies the obvious flaw in the notion that the Civil War and abolition were victories for the international proletariat. Socialists like Marx and Vésinier denounced both slavery and capitalism as exploitative systems. But the defeat of one form of exploitation in the South merely reinforced the other form in the North, which was the very embodiment of bourgeois democracy and laissez-faire capitalism. Many French socialists seem to have ignored this fact in their enthusiasm over emancipation. But America's postwar development—under the leadership of the same politicians who had headed the abolitionist crusade—would show that Northern capitalists had been the chief beneficiaries of the "Second American Revolution."[35]

There were a few observers on the French left who judged the capitalists and slaveholders by the same standard. One such radical was P.-J. Proudhon, who had never been a great admirer of the Americans. While he seemed to lean toward the Union at the time of the *Trent* crisis and during the early phases of the Mexican expedition, his deep-rooted distaste for the Yankees seems to have gotten the upper hand by mid-1862. Alluding frequently to the American war in his correspondence, he showed little indulgence for the slaveholders. But he leveled his harshest attacks at the North, whose stubborn struggle for political centralization and economic hegemony needlessly prolonged the bloodshed and condemned European workers to starvation. At the same time, Proudhon cried out against those European liberals and democrats who blindly supported the North's "anti-liberal" cause.[36]

Far from winning him over, Lincoln's emancipation policy seems to have driven Proudhon even further into the anti-Yankee camp. The news of the proclamation arrived while he was working on his federalist manifesto, *Du principe fédératif* (1863). Infuriated by the limited terms of Lincoln's decree and by the injustice of his colonization plan, Proudhon devoted part of his new book to a scathing critique of the North. Lincoln had doubly sinned in Proudhon's eyes: first, by attempting to impose the authority of the central government on the Southern states; secondly, by offering the Blacks a dismal choice between "deportation" and permanent legal inferiority. "And it is for this noble cause that they agitate the conscience of both hemispheres," he scoffed.[37] While he had no sympathy for slavery, Proudhon believed that the South had a constitutional right to separation, especially since the injustice of Lincoln's slavery policy deprived the Union of any claim to moral superiority. The Northern capitalists had equally violated the laws of human justice by creating a proletariat in their large industrial cities.[38] In the absence of any humanitarian motive, said Proudhon, "the blasphemous and hypocritical attack of the North against the South can only bring about the ruin of all the States and the destruction of the republic."[39] In October 1864, just three months before his death, he chided a Belgian friend for "admiring the so-called republicans of the United States as models of civic virtue and good government."[40]

Proudhon's view of the Civil War, like his opposition to the Polish insurrection and to Italian unification, ran against the current of French liberal and democratic opinion. Yet he was not entirely alone in attacking Lincoln from the left. His judgment was shared by the prominent liberal journalist Emile de Girardin, whose thinking was actually close to Proudhon's on a number of points.[41] Like Proudhon, Girardin was a passionate believer in individual liberty and an enemy of all centralized, authoritarian governments.[42] But unlike Proudhon, Girardin had been an enthusiastic admirer of the United States before the war: "I am an American at heart," he had declared in 1857.[43] Although his hatred of slavery had initially led him to oppose the secessionists, he had reservations about the North's right to retain the Southern states in the Union by force.[44] When he learned of the Emancipation Proclamation and of Lincoln's colonization plan, Girardin finally lost all patience with the North and bitterly attacked it in the columns of *La Presse,* the influential daily of which he was the founder and director.[45] The proclamation was too little and too late in his opinion, the colonization plan unjust and hypocritical. Since the North had no moral basis for opposing secession, Girardin now came out in favor of Southern independence. "The *voluntary separation* between the South and North followed naturally from the idea of liberty," he argued. "Once the South proposed it, the North had no right to refuse."[46] As for Lincoln: "His election was deplorable and his assumption of power was disastrous.... He has compromised and perverted everything. He has succeeded only in obscuring the question and turning against the North the sympathies which Europe had initially felt for it."[47] Although he would later change his mind about Lincoln, Girardin had attacked the president more violently than the most diehard conservative on this occasion.[48]

Near the end of the war, Lincoln and his countrymen were denounced by another prominent republican, Alphonse de Lamartine, the former leader of the Second Republic. Living and writing in seclusion under a borrowed roof, the aged poet took no active part in politics during these years. But he found the occasion to express his views on the Civil War in an essay on the American naturalist John James Audubon, published in 1865.[49] Judging by Lamartine's well-known republican and antislavery views, one would expect him to support the Union, which had openly adopted an abolitionist policy by the time this essay was written. Instead, he pronounced a thorough condemnation of the Yankees.

Although they had made emancipation the "noble banner of the present war," said Lamartine, the Northerners had no intention of conferring true liberty and equality upon the freed Blacks. Citing Lincoln's own declarations on the impossibility of social equality between the races, Lamartine declared abolition to be a mere pretext. What the North really sought, he said, was "the ruin of the South, whose Black capital, cotton culture, navy and prosperous commerce aroused the murderous jealousy of this people that is determined to reduce everything to its own level."[50] Lamartine further asserted, against all logic and factual evidence, that the slaves themselves "would rather endure the humiliations of legal servitude than the neglect of the so-called philanthropists of the North; and, ordeal for ordeal, they are right to prefer that of slavery, which gives them shelter, food and protection, to that of contempt and death in the states of the Union."[51]

This last declaration would seem more appropriate coming from a Confederate propagandist like George Fitzhugh than from a charter member of the Société pour l'abolition de l'esclavage and the author of an admiring book on the Haitian liberator Toussaint Louverture.[52] But in reality, Lamartine was neither proslavery nor pro-South: he was fundamentally anti-American. Denouncing the North's "hypocritical" emancipation policy was one means of expressing contempt for American civilization, which had become increasingly distasteful to him with the passing years. Like Proudhon, he attacked the North as the embodiment of this aggressive, materialistic, Anglo-Saxon culture whose emergence as a major power was alarming to many Europeans—regardless of their political opinions. Depicting the Yankees as a crude, arrogant, violent, intemperate, and licentious race, Lamartine declared that the "catastrophe" that had struck them was "a God-sent lesson to overly democratic peoples . . . that there is no future for those nations who believe only in the force of numbers and the brutality of conquest."[53]

In 1848 Lamartine had been a warm admirer of the United States, effusively declaring that "every Frenchman has for Americans the heart of Lafayette."[54] Now he judged that country as harshly as any reactionary. It is possible that the unhappy experience of the Second Republic had made him wary of popular democracy. But whatever faith he may have retained in democracy as a political ideal, it is clear that the United States had ceased to serve as a model of it in his eyes. The evolution of Lamartine's views reflects the general decline of the American image in French opinion during the 1850s. But unlike the majority of French liberals and democrats, Lamartine's ardor for America was not rekindled by the Civil War and emancipation.[55]

In attacking the North at this time, Lamartine, Proudhon, and Girardin were anomalies among French partisans of liberty. Most of the others, whatever initial reservations they may have had in some cases, had thrown their full weight behind the Union once Lincoln declared his emancipation policy. But the harsh critiques of this Yankee-bashing trio—based on a shared contempt for America's materialistic values, Anglo-Saxon culture, and increasingly dominant position on the world stage—foreshadowed the kind of visceral anti-Americanism that would become a tenet of the French left in the twentieth century.

CHAPTER 12

The Dénouement

Lincoln, the glorious, supreme representative of a holy cause, can pass into immortality without endangering his country, for the proud republican mold never fails to produce great characters for great circumstances.

—A. A. LEDRU-ROLLIN, April 1865

By the time of Robert E. Lee's surrender at Appomattox on April 9, 1865, the left's admiration for America had reached a new peak. Not since the first euphoric days of 1848 had there been such enthusiasm for the United States among French partisans of liberty. "The men of the North . . . have made more beautiful pages for history than all those of Greece, Rome, France, the Revolution and the Empire," wrote Henri Allain-Targé in April 1865.[1] His zeal is understandable, for in many ways the American Civil War had been an event without precedent in history: a vast republic had waged war for four years without succumbing to dictatorship or anarchy; a volunteer army of over one million men had been created, had triumphed, and was being quietly disbanded; and most important, a population of four million Black slaves had been delivered from their bondage.

But the left's rejoicing was soon darkened by tragedy. Only ten days after they had learned of Richmond's fall, the French were stunned by the news that Lincoln had been fatally shot at Ford's Theater by a diehard Confederate sympathizer. This event, reported in the Paris papers of April 26, 1865, touched off a spontaneous outpouring of sympathy for the United States. All day long, crowds of mourners gathered in front of the U.S. legation on the Rue de Chaillot, and American minister John Bigelow was besieged by individuals and delegations seeking to express their sympathies. Along with these popular demonstrations, messages of condolence arrived from the highest French government circles, including Napoleon III and the Corps législatif.[2]

For the left, the popular upsurge of emotion that followed Lincoln's assassination was a propaganda windfall, providing a rare forum for voicing democratic sentiments at a time when public meetings and demonstrations were prohibited and the press was strictly controlled. The martyred Lincoln became a symbol of liberty, equality, and fraternity—to eulogize him was one way of condemning the empire. Although expressions of condolence cut across party lines, an undeniable current of republicanism ran through the popular response to the U.S. president's death.

The left claimed Lincoln as a martyr to their own cause and an inspiration to those fighting for freedom in Europe. "Wherever there is a faithful friend of liberty, there is a mourner for Lincoln," wrote Edgar Quinet from Geneva. "But in this mourning, what hope for the world!"[3] From Guernsey, Victor Hugo proclaimed that "the thunderclap in Washington has shaken the earth." The American Union, he said, had "become the guide among nations . . . , pointing out to its sister nations the granite way to liberty and universal brotherhood."[4] Elisée Reclus, traveling in Sicily, learned of the fall of Richmond and the assassination at the same time. "My spirit is gripped, as if in a vise, by a mixture of stupor and profound joy," he wrote to his brother Elie. The tragedy had consecrated the American struggle and raised it to epic proportions, said Reclus: "The brave Lincoln could not have wished for a more glorious death. . . . The Union is reestablished, the American people are stronger than ever, slavery is abolished, and it is at the moment of these great events that Lincoln is struck down." Did not the friends of liberty in France, he asked, feel that "the history of the world now pivots around the United States?"[5]

Most of Reclus's fellow republicans would have answered that question with an emphatic yes. Allain-Targé eloquently expressed the mixture of grief and hope that Lincoln's martyrdom inspired among the men of the French left. "Tonight," he wrote on learning of the assassination, "I am as sad as if one of my own family had died. . . . I shall never forget my impression of this day." But the "martyr's blood was . . . shed to bear fruit"—and not only in America. The Union triumph was "the greatest victory in the world for the republicans of France." It had inspired and foreshadowed a sweeping democratization of French society:

The conservative interests, the principle of authority, privilege, caste, aristocratic monopolies,—all these things . . . that seemed as necessary to European society as slavery to the Southern aristocracy,—all this will be swept away by egalitarian democracy. [Conservatives] can retard and prolong their resistance, . . . but they must ultimately accept the consequences of the emancipation of the slaves in America, and of . . . the intellectual, moral and material emancipation of the people of Europe. . . . The bourgeoisie, which has established a society under its yoke of servile and insolent functionaries, . . . will share the fate of the men of the South. . . . [This bourgeoisie] will be swept away, and we will wind up here, as on the other side of the Atlantic, with the reign of equality, of right, of justice.[6]

One of the groups that reacted most demonstrably to Lincoln's death was the rising generation of republican *jeunesse* that would contribute so much to the opposition cause during the Second Empire's twilight years. Their political awakening had coincided with the period of the Civil War. Many of those who were just beginning to drink at the fountain of republicanism during these years were too young to remember the prewar decade, when American prestige had fallen so low. Their main impression of America had been formed during the heroic struggle to free the slaves. To them, Lincoln became a sort of folk hero, and the United States seemed the incarnation of the democratic ideal. L.-A. Prévost-Paradol noted shortly after the war, "for the young generations, admiration of the United States tends to supplant all others."[7]

An impressive demonstration of these sentiments occurred on April 28, when a group of three thousand students organized a march from the Latin Quarter to the American legation in the sixteenth arrondissement to express their sympathies. These young men (whose ranks included such future republican leaders as Georges Clemenceau) so alarmed imperial authorities with their raucous cries of "Vive l'Amérique! Vive la République!" that police blocked off the bridges over the Seine, dispersed the marchers, and made several arrests.[8] Only a handful actually made it to the American legation, but the declaration they read to Bigelow showed that the lesson of America's armed struggle for liberty was not lost on a young and militant generation of French republicans: "We mourn President Lincoln as our own countryman, for no country is inaccessible today, and we consider as ours any country where there are neither masters nor slaves, where all men are free or fight to become so. We are the countrymen of John Brown, of Abraham Lincoln and of M. Seward. We, the young, to whom the future belongs, must have the courage to learn how a people who has made itself free can keep its freedom."[9]

Many workers' delegations also expressed their sympathies to Bigelow. In Tarare workers in the muslin industry associated themselves "heart and soul with the addresses of the students and of the four [liberal] journals of Paris—addresses so conformable to the true sentiments of liberty, justice, and hope." [10] A group of 208 workers at Tours expressed their condolences in terms that were nothing short of revolutionary. It was hard to collect so many signatures, they explained, in a city "where liberty is limited by policemen and public functionaries, and where democracy's warmest partisans are among the common people." Apologizing for the smudges and fingerprints that soiled their declaration, these workers told Bigelow: "It is not you, a representative of a country where labor leads to the highest dignities of the nation, that will disdain our address because it carries the visible impress of hands devoted to work. These are hands that will break, in this country, all the bonds and fetters that are put on liberty, under the specious pretext of measuring and regulating its gait; these are the hands that will shake most cordially those of your citizens." [11]

The future Communard Félix Pyat similarly voiced the workers' admiration for Lincoln and their hostility toward the empire. Writing on behalf of the Commune révolutionnaire, a group of radical exiles that he headed in London, Pyat claimed to express the sentiments of all French workers and republicans: "As workers, white slaves, we are in solidarity with the blacks. Slaves of the ball-and-chain or of the daybook, we have the same cause, work; the same enemy, the master; the same friend, the . . . worker of Liberty, Abraham Lincoln. The President of abolition had to be a worker." French republicans, said Pyat, were compatriots of the Americans, who "guard over the government of Liberty in the New World as a trust and a model for the Old." [12]

Viewed from the perspective of the imperial authorities, these militant declarations by students and workers had to be worrisome. In the wake of Lincoln's death and the Union victory, it seemed that the image of the liberating American republic was being weaponized against the Bonapartist regime. Without intervening in French politics or embracing French radical ideas, as Michael Vorenberg has suggested, Lincoln actually helped topple the Second Empire. [13] Minister Bigelow seemed to foreshadow this in a May 1865 letter describing the martyred president's influence on French opinion:

The feeling in France . . . is very profound. Indeed I think Lincoln would gladly have sold his life to his assassin for the price his country will receive for it. The [imperial] government cannot resist the popular feeling and is obliged to join in the general reaction. The universal reflection in all circles now is that we have accomplished with our democratic government, results that could never have been accomplished with any other. The Republicans are taking advantage of this to keep the subject before the people as much as possible. The death of Lincoln, I think, is destined to work a radical change in the Constitution of France.[14]

The emperor's opponents soon launched a more organized campaign to honor the murdered president and celebrate the republican values he championed. On April 28 the historian Charles-Louis Chassin proposed in a letter to the *Phare de la Loire* that French democrats launch "a popular demonstration in honor of Abraham Lincoln, and in support of the principles that this great and honest man represented during his lifetime and to which his death has just given the supreme consecration." Since the laws of the empire would not permit French democrats to meet publicly to organize such a project, Chassin suggested that the liberal newspapers open a subscription to offer a gold medal to Lincoln's widow.[15] The *Phare*'s editor, Victor Mangin, enthusiastically supported the idea.

The Lincoln medal project immediately formed a rallying point for the democratic opponents of Napoleon III. There was no mistaking the political orientation of the committee chosen by Chassin and Mangin to execute this project. Most of them were illustrious "forty-eighters," including many political exiles whose hatred for "Napoléon le petit" was well known. Among them were Hugo, Quinet, Louis Blanc, Victor Schoelcher, Jules Michelet, Eugène Pelletan, Etienne Arago, Jules Barni, and Taxile Delord.[16] Imperial authorities at first attempted to discourage the project, seizing several subscription lists and confiscating some of the money that had been collected.[17] But the committee's many volunteer fundraisers continued their activities undaunted. One of them, the republican writer and feminist Juliette Adam, later recalled: "We were outraged by the assassination of a President. . . . We must honor our dear heroes, fallen or exiled for the good cause. I even took to the streets to collect money."[18] Remarking on the enthusiastic popular response to the project, Victor Chauffour wrote to Chassin: "You have succeeded in eliciting a civic act from men who had completely lost the habit."[19]

From the spring of 1865 until the closing of the subscription in December 1866, the *Phare de la Loire* and other democratic papers kept the example of Lincoln and American democracy before the public. The *Phare* regularly published lists of subscribers' names, along with readers' letters in support of the project. By the time the subscription was finally closed, some 44,554 French men and women had contributed.[20] Moreover, it was a truly popular subscription, for donations had been limited to ten centimes so that even the poorest could participate. Working-class contributors probably accounted for more than two-thirds of the total.[21] Along with their contributions, some workers expressed their sentiments in letters addressed to the *Phare* or to the Lincoln committee. Most of these documents are in the crude hand and style of those unaccustomed to expressing themselves in writing, but the sincerity of their sentiments is all the more credible for their mistakes in spelling and punctuation.[22]

The medal was struck in Switzerland by the French engraver Franky Magniada. On December 1, 1866, members of the committee presented it to the U.S. minister, who arranged for its transfer to Mrs. Lincoln.[23] To the very last, the committee had remembered the cause of the opposition in France while honoring the fallen American president. Even the medal's inscription contained an implicit denunciation of Napoleon III: "Dedicated by French democracy to Lincoln, twice-elected president of the United States; Lincoln the honest man, abolished slavery, re-established the Union, saved the Republic, without veiling the statue of liberty.[24] He was assassinated on April 14, 1865. Liberty. Equality. Fraternity."[25] In addition to citing the familiar revolutionary slogan banned by Napoleon III, this inscription was a condemnation of the once-elected *homme de décembre* who had violated his republican oath of office by staging a coup d'état and proclaiming himself emperor. An accompanying letter to Mrs. Lincoln underscored the distance separating the empire from the United States on the question of liberty: "If France had possessed the liberties enjoyed by the American Republic, we should have counted with us, not by thousands but by millions, the admirers of Lincoln and the partisans of the opinions to which he devoted his life and to which his death is consecrated."[26]

Placing the medal in Bigelow's hand, Pelletan asked the American minister to "tell Mrs. Lincoln that this little box contains the heart of France."[27] One month later the committee received a letter on the black-bordered mourning stationery of Mary Todd Lincoln. She thanked them for their "testimonial to the memory of my husband, given in honor of his services in the cause of liberty, by those who labor in the same great Cause in another land."[28] Mrs. Lincoln had laboriously copied the names of the twenty committee members at the bottom of her letter, although—apart from Hugo perhaps—she probably had not the vaguest idea who they were or what they really stood for.[29] It was beyond her power to know whether or not all these men were actually working for the "same great Cause" as her husband, and she probably remained unaware of the propaganda role that Lincoln's image had played in French politics.

Six months after the presentation of the Lincoln medal, French leftists seized the occasion to praise a more radical American hero—the abolitionist John Brown. The campaign was launched by the militant feminist and republican Augustine Girault Lesourd, who felt that the Lincoln medal subscription obscured the sacrifice that Brown, a true revolutionary hero, had made to the cause of liberty. Under the pseudonym that she used as a painter and author, Madame A. Gaël, she wrote to *La Coopération* to suggest that a similar medal be offered to Brown's widow. "This man was the initiator of the great movement and voluntarily gave his life for it," she noted. "Far less fortunate than Lincoln, he received nothing but insults and scorn for his devotion."[30] *La Coopération,* a workers' newspaper devoted to the cause of labor and democracy, enthusiastically embraced this idea. Other republican journals like the *Progrès de Lyon* and the *Phare de la Loire* also promoted the project; subscription lists circulated as far as England, Belgium, and Poland.[31] The warm and immediate response to this appeal shows that the French public had not yet lost interest in the Civil War themes of liberty and emancipation—nor had the left exhausted their usefulness.

The list of contributors was headed by Victor Hugo, that intransigent enemy of Napoleon III and lyrical promoter of the "universal republic." With his famous 1859 plea for Brown and his engraving of the martyred abolitionist, Hugo had done more than anyone to popularize the Brown legend in Europe.[32] When the *Coopération*'s editor invited him to take part in the project, Hugo responded enthusiastically. "A Lincoln medal calls for a John Brown medal," he wrote. "Let us pay this debt while waiting for America to pay hers. America owes John Brown a statue as tall as that of Washington. Washington founded the republic, John Brown promulgated liberty."[33] Elisée Reclus was also active in promoting this project and wrote a eulogistic biography of Brown for the *Coopération*.[34] Another radical publicist who promoted the project was C.-L. Chassin, who had earlier been the instigator of the Lincoln subscription. "In the history of the destruction of the last vestiges of the old servitudes and the definitive coming of the egalitarian republic," wrote Chassin, "two great names, Abraham Lincoln and John Brown, will remain united."[35] The abolitionist Schoelcher, who had served with Chassin and Hugo on the Lincoln committee, also responded enthusiastically to the new appeal.[36]

Like the Lincoln project, the Brown subscription sought to keep the themes of democracy and emancipation before the French public. Yet the tone of this project was more radical. Brown, even more so than Lincoln, was a figure with whom the most ardent revolutionaries could identify. Lincoln's greatness had been in his respect for the law and the Constitution; Brown's lay in his willingness to transcend the law in the pursuit of a higher justice. With the possible exception of Garibaldi (who himself contributed to the Brown medal), no other contemporary figure represented better than Brown the blend of high moral purpose and militant action to which the radicals aspired.[37]

The subscription lists, published regularly in the *Cooperation,* included the names of many well-known radicals: Blanc, Cluseret, Melvil-Bloncourt, Gustave Courbet, Charles Langlois, Raoul Rigault, Ange Guépin, André Léo, Elie Reclus, and Auguste Vacquerie.[38] As with the Lincoln project, these show a large number of collective donations from workshops, fraternal societies, and labor organizations.

The radical interpretation of Brown's career was articulated by the militant feminist and socialist André Léo in an article announcing the completion of the project in April 1869.[39] Recalling Madame Gaël's sentiments, Léo said it was unjust to praise Lincoln for finishing the work of emancipation without also praising Brown for "the more spontaneous, more generous and more devoted inspiration that began it." Both were men of "great and pure conscience," but Brown had acted on his conscience with "a higher and more inspired degree of energy." To Léo, his greatness lay precisely in the fact that he had taken up arms against injustice. When the law condoned such "monstrosities" as slavery, she wrote, there was "no other logic than the conscience, and any human being who has one is obliged to obey this supreme law."[40] To her, the lesson of Brown's example was the moral imperative of insurrection against unjust laws and authorities. Two years later—along with Vésinier, Reclus, Rigault, Cluseret, and numerous other admirers of Brown—Léo would act on this conviction by serving the revolutionary government of the Commune. Even in Paris, amid the blood and rubble of May 1871, John Brown's soul was marching on.

The Lincoln and Brown subscriptions show how the French left continued to exploit Civil War themes long after that struggle had ended. In the absence of a wider freedom of expression, these subscriptions were effective vehicles for opposition sentiments. They were also precursors of later campaigns—like the Jean-Baptiste Baudin and Victor Noir subscriptions—that would have important political repercussions during the Second Empire's last years.[41] But paying homage to Lincoln and Brown was only one of the many ways in which the American example was kept before the public during the postwar years. The image of the United States had emerged from the Civil War purified and redeemed in the eyes of the French left. If support for the Union had been a useful propaganda tool during the war, then celebrating the example of a triumphant and rehabilitated America would prove all the more effective during subsequent years, when the fortunes of the left were on the rise.

CHAPTER 13

A French Radical in the Union Army

My intention . . . in putting my sword at the service of the cause of the United
States, was to do from a democratic point of view what Lafayette had done in
a different sense. I think I may add, without an excess of vanity, that I had a
better knowledge of my profession than the little marquis.

—GUSTAVE CLUSERET, 1865

The great nineteenth-century painter Gustave Courbet is famous, among
other things, for *L'Origine du Monde,* the scandalously explicit nude
that now hangs in the Musée d'Orsay.[1] But he was also known for his
radical political views and his friendships with some of the leading leftists of
his day. Among them was P.-J. Proudhon, whom Courbet painted wearing a
worker's smock surrounded by his two children in the family's garden. Another
friend was Gustave Cluseret, to whom he gave painting lessons and who became
a competent watercolorist in his own right.[2] But when Courbet painted Cluseret's portrait, his subject wore neither a worker's smock nor artist's smock but a
dark blue military uniform with three medals on his breast and a single star on
his shoulder. This was the tunic he had worn as a volunteer in the Union army.
Cluseret's face is turned slightly to the left, but the penetrating gray eyes stare
straight ahead. His dark brown hair sits atop a high forehead. He sports a long,
pointy mustache, reminiscent of the emperor's, with whom, despite his sworn
enmity, he shared something else: a taste for intrigue and an unshakable belief
in his own destiny.[3]

If anyone can be said to embody the link between French radicalism and
American democracy at this time, Cluseret is the man. In 1862 he presented
himself in America as the military representative of the French left. After the
Civil War, he became one of the most ardent promoters of American-style democracy in France. In Cluseret's mind American ideals were so closely identified

with those of the far left that in 1871, as military chief of the Paris Commune, he would claim to be fighting for "the communal principle in France, which I saw working so well in America."[4]

Born in 1823, Cluseret came from a long line of army officers. He entered the French army as a lieutenant after graduating from the Saint-Cyr military academy in 1844. In 1848 he received the Legion of Honor when his Garde mobile battalion took eleven barricades during the June Days insurrections. Years later, reproached by fellow radicals for having aided the repression in 1848, Cluseret attributed this youthful exploit to political naïveté and military indoctrination. "Entirely devoted to my profession, I had never given any thought to politics," he explained.[5] That fault was soon remedied, for after 1848 he seems to have given little thought to anything but politics.

In 1850 he was temporarily put on the nonactive list for his involvement in socialist propaganda and his "advanced political opinions."[6] Reactivated with the rank of captain in 1853, Cluseret participated in the Algerian campaign the following year. In 1854 he distinguished himself in the Crimea, where he was wounded twice during the siege of Sebastopol.[7] From 1856 to 1858, Cluseret was nominally attached to the Arab Bureau in Algeria but seems to have spent most of his time managing a private farm, running an illegal commerce in wheat and livestock, living off base with his mistress, and dabbling in local political intrigues.[8] Cluseret's flagrant neglect of his duties and his habitual insubordination finally resulted in his forced resignation from the army in May 1858. Although he officially cited his Crimean wounds as the cause of his resignation, the report of his commanding officer tells another story: "Having abandoned his military duties in order to devote himself exclusively to commercial and colonial operations, M. Cluseret has put himself . . . in a bad situation which can only be rectified by his resignation."[9] After leaving the army, he went off to Italy to fight under Garibaldi in the campaign of the Two Sicilies. It was at the end of this operation that he decided to go to America, hoping "to contribute to the abolition of slavery and perfect myself in the art of war."[10]

Although high republican and humanitarian motives were ostensibly behind Cluseret's decision, there is little doubt that he also saw the Civil War as a stepping stone for his own personal success. No aspect of his career can be understood without taking into account the vanity, arrogance, and almost pathological ambition that lay at the bottom of his character. His contemporaries have left ample testimony to this effect. Karl Marx dismissed Cluseret as a "lousy, importunate, vain and over-ambitious babbler."[11] Edmond Lepelletier, a fellow Communard and later a historian of the Commune, voiced this judgment of Cluseret's character and career: "Jack-of-all-trades in the service of insurrectionary causes, fluttering cosmopolitan, he frequently changed uniforms and even nationality. It cannot be said that he also changed opinions, for he never had any opinions, not personal ones at any rate. Like a good *condottière,* he professed those opinions served by his sword. . . . His venturesome and agitated existence was a succession of struggles to succeed, rapid rises and headlong falls."[12]

Though these critics were right about Cluseret's ambition, the charge that he was merely a self-serving mercenary with no personal convictions seems a bit unfair since he consistently fought for causes linked with the progressive ideals of liberty, democracy, and equality.[13]

C luseret's entrance into the Union army was typical of the man. In September 1861 he contacted the American minister in Turin, George Marsh, and professed his desire to serve "the most beautiful cause in the world"—in exchange for a general's rank. Assured of this unofficially by Marsh, Cluseret left for Paris, where he sought to interest the leading French republicans in his self-appointed mission on behalf of liberty and democracy. After winning the support of such men as Henri Martin, Eugène Pelletan, Hippolyte Carnot, and Louis-Antoine Garnier-Pagès, Cluseret hurried off to London. There his mission received the blessings of Alexandre Ledru-Rollin, Alexander Herzen, and Karl Blind.[14] When he arrived in Washington, D.C., early in 1862, Cluseret presented himself to Massachusetts senator Charles Sumner, armed with impressive recommendations and touting himself as the quasi-official representative of French democracy. The republican party of France, he said, "sends its best wishes with me and implores me to continue the old traditions of French liberalism by taking up the sword of Lafayette."[15]

Sumner was, in fact, the perfect interlocutor for Cluseret. In addition to being one of the most powerful Republican senators and a prominent abolitionist, he was an unabashed Francophile. As a young man in the late 1830s, he had spent nearly a year in Paris, strolling the avenues, visiting the museums, and attending lectures at the Sorbonne. With the help of private tutors, he had become profi-

cient in the language and was an avid reader of the French press and French literature. In 1856, while recovering from his near-fatal caning by a proslavery congress-
man, Sumner returned to Paris and met a number of influential figures, including
Tocqueville and Lamartine. He visited the city again in 1858 and would make a
final pilgrimage in 1872, just two years before he died. Few Americans at this
time had a better knowledge of France and respect for its history and culture.[16]

When Cluseret appeared on his doorstep with his impressive letters of recommendation, Sumner was initially receptive to his offer of service and promised
to intercede for him. Contrary to the Frenchman's expectations, however, the
generalship he had counted on did not materialize. Instead, he was offered, and
reluctantly accepted, a commission as a colonel on the staff of General George
McClellan.[17] But McClellan did not take to him—"I did not like his appearance," as he later put it—and soon had him transferred to the command of General John C. Frémont in western Virginia.[18] At that point the indignant Cluseret
called upon Sumner to help get him the promised generalship; otherwise, he
hinted, the United States might lose his invaluable services and compromise the
good will of French republicans for the Union cause. "According to our military
usages," he haughtily informed Sumner, "it is impossible for me to serve other
than as a simple volunteer or as a general. Now, is it politic to lose the influence I
have on my former comrades-in-arms in France and Italy . . . who follow me with
their hopes? I should think not. Is it politic to rebuff so many sympathetic men
who, in sending me here, thought to affirm in the most effective way their hopes
and sympathies in favor of the American cause? I think not!"[19] Still unsatisfied, a
few months later he wrote, "I hope, Mr. Senator, that in circumstances so decisive
for my future and at the same time so interesting for our friends in Paris, you will
see fit to use your powerful intervention in my favor."[20] Cluseret returned to this
theme time and again in his correspondence with Sumner. To hear him tell it,
the cause of liberty and humanity itself depended on the success of his personal
ambitions.

For all Cluseret's arrogant bluster, there was some foundation to his claim to
represent French democracy. His letters of recommendation were genuine and
came from those Frenchmen whose good will was highly valued by Sumner as
well as Lincoln. For his part, the senator took Cluseret quite seriously, offering him his personal friendship and protection and using all his influence to
get him his general's commission. Elihu B. Washburne, future U.S. minister to

France, once overheard Sumner enthusiastically telling Lincoln about this "gallant Frenchman" sent by "our friends" in Europe to help fight for democracy.[21] Prodded by Sumner, the president finally did approve Cluseret's promotion to the rank of brigadier general after the Frenchman had distinguished himself against General Thomas "Stonewall" Jackson's forces at Cross Keys, Virginia, in June 1862.[22] Announcing this news on June 18, Sumner wrote to Cluseret: "You are, or soon will be, precisely what you desire. . . . I thank you and congratulate you with all my heart; you have done a good job which we can never forget."[23] The promotion was made official on October 14, 1862.[24]

Cluseret's advancement was also good news to those French republicans who took a special interest in his American military career and believed that his success there would have a positive effect on French opinion. In his correspondence with Sumner, Henri Martin rarely failed to put in a good word for Cluseret, and the senator kept Martin informed on Cluseret's progress. In July 1862, before learning of the generalship, Martin thanked Sumner for sending him American newspaper clippings

> reporting on the events in which our compatriot, Colonel Cluseret, played such an honorable role. . . . My friends—Carnot, Garnier-Pagès and others—will also be very satisfied to see that he is serving so worthily and usefully the good cause to which he has offered his sword: since we are interested here in our own *nationals* engaged in faraway struggles for liberty, it would have a good effect on opinion to see the services of this brave officer rewarded by the rank which he was promised at the time of his entrance into the American army, and which he has well earned since then. It would increase our public interest in the events of the war to see a French name figure among your generals.[25]

Addressing Cluseret as "our second Lafayette," Eugène Pelletan wrote in March 1863: "you have courageously won your general's epaulettes; you have a right to be proud." Stressing the importance of the officer's American activities to the democratic cause in France, Pelletan reminded him "that we have put more than one hope on your head; French democracy is with you. Continue to collect glory in America. It will be a treasure, I would almost say a ransom for us one day." He had sent several copies of his *Adresse au roi Coton* and asked Cluseret to give them to "Sumner, Seward and President Lincoln; you will not need a letter;

all of our political friends—Carnot, Simon, Favre, Henri Martin—sent advance word on your behalf as soon as you went to fight against slavery."[26]

Thus there seems to have been some substance to Cluseret's claim to represent French republicanism on the American battlefields. Judging by their own declarations, his "sponsors" apparently expected his military career to serve the cause of republican propaganda in France as well as that of abolitionism in America. It is possible, moreover, that they hoped their support would create a moral obligation on the part of the United States to aid the cause of European liberty after the war—hence Pelletan's curious use of the term "ransom" in relation to Cluseret's military service. Going beyond Cluseret's particular case, there is no doubt that many European republicans expected active assistance from the United States in exchange for their sympathies during the Civil War. While it accorded with their principles, their support for the Union was not entirely disinterested.

As for Cluseret, no one could ever accuse him of being disinterested. Having won his general's star, he immediately began quarrelling with his superior officers, accusing them of treachery and incompetence. Unfortunately for him, Frémont, with whom he got on well, suddenly left the army in July 1862, ceding his command to General Robert Milroy. In his frequent letters to Sumner, Cluseret complained of Milroy's corrupt profiteering and accused him of mistreating Southern civilians in the Shenandoah Valley.[27] Milroy, in turn, charged Cluseret with insubordination and had him arrested. In March 1863 the Frenchman resigned his commission rather than face charges.[28]

After leaving the army, Cluseret immersed himself in American journalism and politics. In 1864 he joined forces with Frémont and edited a short-lived newspaper, the *New Nation,* in support of his former commander's presidential campaign.[29] In that capacity Cluseret wrote dozens of editorials praising Frémont and bashing Lincoln as "the most unfit man in the nation for the presidency."[30] Following the general's withdrawal from the race in September 1864, Cluseret switched his support to Lincoln and, anticipating a Union victory, began calling for a radical approach to Reconstruction. Citing the example of the French Revolution, he wrote to Sumner, "Lee's head must fall, judiciously and in cold blood, in the name of law and morality."[31]

Cluseret's uncompromising view of Reconstruction coincided with a general radicalization of his political views at this time. In 1864 he joined the newly founded New York section of the International, having been converted to revolutionary socialism by the French exile Claude Pelletier.[32] He also came into contact with the Fenians, a New York–based group of Irish republicans who launched several ragtag "invasions" of Canada after the Civil War in a futile effort to promote Irish independence from England. Searching for new revolutionary causes to fight for, Cluseret offered his military services to the Fenians. Toward the end of 1866, he was off to Ireland, hoping to lead an insurrection against British rule. But the Fenian uprising fizzled, and Cluseret hastily fled the country under the threat of a death sentence, passed in absentia by a British court.[33]

Cluseret resurfaced in Paris in March 1867. Momentarily laying down his sword, he took up his journalist's pen and began attacking the regime of Napoleon III in the press. Arrested and briefly jailed by French authorities, he only escaped a long prison sentence by invoking the American citizenship he had gained on the battlefield.[34] He was finally deported as a threat to state security. By June 1869, he was back in New York, organizing for the International, propagandizing for Cuban revolutionaries, and sending incendiary articles to the French radical press.

Cluseret's brief Civil War career may not have lived up to the hopes of his French republican sponsors, but he himself managed to squeeze considerable mileage out of it. He did not win much glory on the battlefield—with less than a full year's service, he hardly had time for that. But he had gained the coveted title of "general," along with U.S. citizenship and the prestige of having fought against slavery. All of this burnished his reputation in France. Playing this role to the hilt, Cluseret tirelessly invoked the American example in his journalistic attacks on the Second Empire in the late 1860s. Having gone to the United States in 1862 as a representative of French republicanism, he returned to France to preach American-style democracy under the nose of Napoleon III. "I have raised the banner of our party and our country here," he wrote to Sumner from Paris in 1867, "and I shall preserve it here against all the world."[35] As we shall see, Cluseret would continue to pursue his political goals as a journalist, agitator, and finally the military chief of the Commune—a revolutionary insurrection that inspired only horror in the minds of most Americans.[36]

PART III

The Apotheosis of the American Image, 1865–1870

The United States, having astonished all Europe by triumphantly crushing out the most stupendous rebellion the world has ever known, and after one of the most gigantic wars in history, had bounded forward to a position of the first rank among the nations of the earth.

—ELIHU B. WASHBURNE, U.S. minister to France

During the years immediately following the Civil War, the United States enjoyed an unprecedented level of prestige abroad. This was especially true in France, where liberal and democratic ideas were steadily gaining momentum during the late 1860s. As the ardent republican Henri Allain-Targé remarked in January 1866, French opinion had been seized by "an incontestable infatuation with America." That infatuation was a boon for republican propagandists, who skillfully directed it toward their own ends. To an extent that would never have been possible before the war, the American example became a compelling argument in favor of a wide variety of goals pursued by the French left during the twilight years of the Second Empire.

CHAPTER 14

American Government and Politics
in the Eyes of the French Left

We must study the lessons provided by the American Republic, which is
increasingly becoming the authoritative teacher of free democracies.

—LÉON GAMBETTA, 1868

Our program is clear, we have proclaimed it a hundred times: we want
the peaceful and laborious democracy of the United States.

—ERNEST LAVIGNE, 1869

Major political developments were unfolding on both sides of the Atlantic during the years between the American Civil War and the Franco-Prussian War. In the United States the political scene was dominated by the question of Reconstruction. President Lincoln had hoped to readmit the defeated Southern states into the Union as rapidly as possible, without reprisals or excessive federal interference. Under his leadership, Reconstruction might have been a less painful experience, but Lincoln's death put the problem into the far less skillful hands of his vice president, Andrew Johnson. A Democrat, Johnson adopted Lincoln's lenient Reconstruction plan (with some modifications) and hastened to put it into effect during the summer and fall of 1865 while Congress was not in session. Freely granting pardons to former Confederate leaders, the new president allowed the Southern states to reenter the Union once they had elected new constitutional conventions, repealed the secession ordinances and officially abolished slavery. Each state could then organize a civil government and send its representatives to Congress. Apart from requiring the abolition of slavery, Johnson made no provision for the future social and civil status of the freedmen. All but two of the former Confederate states had been "reconstructed" on the basis of the Johnson plan by the time Congress convened in December 1865.[1]

Instead of accepting the fait accompli, however, the Radical Republican majority in Congress was indignant over the president's attempt to settle the question without consulting them. They repudiated the new Southern state governments, refused to seat their representatives, and set up a joint committee to work out a congressional plan for Reconstruction. Led by Thaddeus Stevens in the House and Charles Sumner in the Senate, the Radicals regarded the former Confederacy as a "conquered province" and insisted that the old planter aristocracy must be stripped of all power and influence before the Southern states could reenter the Union. They further demanded full political and civil rights for the Blacks—guaranteed by federal law and federal bayonets—amid talk of dividing the lands of confiscated plantations among the freedmen. The issue was thus joined between President Johnson and Congress.

The Radicals gained the upper hand after a sweeping victory in the congressional elections of November 1866. Armed with a two-thirds majority, which permitted them to override any presidential veto, they proceeded to put their own plan into effect. Under the Reconstruction Act of March 1867, ten Southern states were organized into five military districts and put under the command of governors appointed by Congress and supported by U.S. Army forces. New constitutional conventions were elected—this time with the participation of Black voters and delegates—and proceeded to draw up new state constitutions stripping former Confederate leaders of their political rights, enfranchising the freedmen, and guaranteeing their civil and political equality. Once new legislatures had been elected, they were required to ratify the Fourteenth and Fifteenth Amendments to the U.S. Constitution, which granted full citizenship and voting rights to the former slaves on a national scale. Only then could Congress officially readmit the former rebel states into the Union and seat their representatives. All the Southern states had been readmitted on this basis by 1870, and thus Reconstruction was theoretically completed, although it would be another seven years before the last federal troops withdrew from the old Confederacy.

But the Radicals were not satisfied with the triumph of their own Reconstruction plan. They also wanted to disgrace Johnson personally and weaken the institution of the presidency, making Congress the supreme power in the federal government. First they sought to reduce the president's control over his own cabinet by passing the 1867 Tenure of Office Act, which forbade the executive to remove his own appointees from office without the approval of the Senate.[2] When Johnson challenged this decree by firing Secretary of War Edwin N. Stanton, an ally of the Radicals, he was impeached by the House of Representatives for "high crimes and misdemeanors" and brought before the Senate for trial in March 1868. Despite the legal weakness of the case against Johnson, the Senate came within one vote of removing him from office. Thus disgraced, Johnson finished the remaining year of his term in a constitutional limbo, officially holding the title of president but effectively powerless before a Congress that governed unchallenged.

Shortly after Johnson's acquittal, the Republican Party nominated General Ulysses S. Grant, the Civil War hero, as its candidate in the November 1868 presidential election. Grant's easy victory seemingly put an end to the struggle between the executive and legislative branches, for he promised to cooperate closely with the Radicals and serve as a simple executor of the congressional will. Thus the American constitutional crisis, like the Reconstruction issue, appeared to be resolved by the end of the decade. In the eyes of its French admirers, American democracy seemed as triumphant in 1870 as it had been in 1865.

Meanwhile, another kind of political reconstruction was taking place in France. The late 1860s were difficult years for Napoleon III. His prestige damaged by foreign-policy failures, his energies sapped by age and illness, the emperor was no longer up to exercising absolute authority in the face of an increasingly powerful opposition. He therefore sought to shore up his regime and ensure the succession of his son, Louis-Napoleon, by granting a number of liberal reforms.[3]

In 1865 Napoleon III began to make overtures to the influential opposition deputy Emile Ollivier, hoping to forge an alliance between liberals and Bonapartists. Ollivier refused the emperor's offer of a ministerial post at that time but encouraged him to embark on a policy of liberalization. Their discussions led to the emperor's declaration of January 19, 1867, which granted the lower house of parliament, the Corps législatif, the right to question government ministers and promised to relax restraints on the press and public meetings. Contrary to the emperor's expectations, however, these half-measures had little positive effect on public opinion. Instead, they caused grumbling among conservative Bonapartists while failing to quiet critics on the left.[4]

Popular dissatisfaction with the regime was clearly registered by the May 1869 legislative elections, in which the opposition made significant gains. Despite the violence of the campaign in some areas, the results were not a mandate for revolution: the republican and radical candidates had made a clean sweep of the Parisian constituencies, but it was the more moderate center-left that had prevailed in the country as a whole. Sensing that the mood of the nation now favored his own prudent approach to reform, Ollivier engineered an alliance between liberals, Orleanists, and liberal Bonapartists in the new Corps législatif. In July 1869, 116 deputies signed his proposal calling for further liberalization and ministerial responsibility before the bicameral legislature.

In response to these demands, the emperor announced a series of significant constitutional modifications. The Corps législatif could now initiate laws and elect its own officers; the Senate was given the power to amend and veto bills; deputies could now be named as ministers; ministers were granted entrée into both houses and were declared "responsible." The transition from authoritarian to liberal empire was completed by a change of governing personnel. Old supporters like Eugène Rouher, Baron Haussmann, and Victor Duruy were ousted from office, and the emperor asked Ollivier to form a cabinet representing the left-center majority in the Corps législatif. A new constitution, embodying the various reforms announced by Napoleon III, was ratified by an overwhelming popular majority in the plebiscite of May 8, 1870. The Bonapartist regime seemed to have won a new lease on life.

Far from inaugurating an era of conciliation, however, the coming of the so-called Liberal Empire further polarized French politics, for if the reconstructed regime ultimately won the support of most liberals and moderates, it pushed the irreconcilable far left into a more determined opposition. As so often happens in politics, the siphoning off of moderate elements from the left tends to reinforce the radicalism and militancy of the rest.

Ironically, it was the emperor's own liberal concessions that permitted the irreconcilables to express their opposition with such virulence. Following the enactment of a new press law in March 1868, some 140 new journals appeared, most of them belonging to the opposition. Among the newcomers were a number of radical organs, including C.-L. Chassin's *Démocratie,* Charles Delescluze's

Réveil, Henri Rochefort's *Lanterne* and *Marseillaise,* Victor Hugo's *Rappel,* Eugène Pelletan's *Tribune,* Aimé Malespine's *Réforme,* and Henri Allain-Targé's *Revue politique.*[5] In the columns of these journals, the emperor's leftist opponents voiced their hostility to the regime with an unprecedented violence and audacity. The newly authorized public meetings also provided an important forum for the far left, including workers, socialists, and communists, whose views had earlier found but limited means of expression. The turbulent 1869 electoral campaign and the antiplebiscite meetings of 1870 provided further opportunities to attack the Second Empire. Never before had the enemies of Napoleon III enjoyed such freedom of expression—and never before had their voices rung out so loudly in opposition.

American Reconstruction as Viewed by the French Left

As they had done during the Civil War, the propagandists of the French left followed America's postwar development with great interest and often used its experience to support their own political ideology. They were fascinated by the events of Reconstruction, which, like the Civil War, they tended to see in the reflected light of their own revolutionary tradition. Their sympathies went instinctively to the Radical Republicans, who had led the abolitionist crusade and were now demanding full equality for the freedmen. It was the Radicals, it seemed, who were continuing the humanitarian and progressive movement that had begun with emancipation. In the eyes of many French observers, fiery Radical leaders like Representative Thaddeus Stevens resembled "the *Conventionnels* of '93" with their calls for the confiscation and redistribution of the great Southern estates. This parallel was enhanced by the fact that the more advanced Radicals like Stevens and Wendell Phillips themselves cited the French precedent in favor of confiscation.[6] In a sense, the French left was not wrong in seeing the Radicals as revolutionaries, for as C. Vann Woodward has observed, "history does not record a more drastic application of the democratic dogma" than the one they attempted during Reconstruction.[7]

As early as 1864, Sainte-Suzanne Melvil-Bloncourt analyzed the developing conflict between Northern partisans of "easy" Reconstruction and the advocates of the "conquered province" theory. Praising Charles Sumner as the "guiding spirit" of emancipation, he urged Congress to adopt his "policy of coercion" as the basis for its Reconstruction program.[8] The Radical Republicans were "the party of right and justice," said Melvil-Bloncourt, "therefore the future belongs to them."[9]

Georges Clemenceau, who had gone to America in 1865 to report on Reconstruction for the *Temps,* was another enthusiastic partisan of the Radicals. Unless their program was adopted, wrote Clemenceau in January 1867, there would be "no internal peace" for the rest of the century. "Anyone who hopes that the Sumners, the Stevenses, the Phillipses, the noblest and finest men of the nation, will stand silently by and see their country fall into moral ruin without making strong efforts to prevent it is hoping for this country's misfortune."[10]

Elisée Reclus declared that the Radicals' policy was that of "pure justice" and hoped that they would take advantage of their military victory to force a definitive solution of the race question on the basis of full equality.[11] Looking on the events of Reconstruction from his log cabin in Texas, Victor Considérant pronounced his wholehearted support for the Radicals' Reconstruction program. "Let them ruin and banish . . . the authors of the greatest, the most disastrous and the bloodiest crime which has ever been committed on earth," he wrote in 1867. "The slaveholding class, destroyed by the liberation of their slaves, must be finished off by the effective confiscation of their property for the benefit of the poor families of the North and South."[12] Another firsthand observer of Reconstruction, Edouard Portalis, similarly endorsed the policies of the Radicals, whom he called "the avant-garde of humanity in its march . . . towards that state of equality, liberty and union for which it was created. Our sons will be grateful to the Republicans of the United States for the blood which they have shed on behalf of human freedom, and for the intelligence which they have shown in their defense of free labor."[13]

If temperament and ideology drew the left's sympathies to the congressional Radicals, there was far less to recommend the president's case in their eyes. They had little understanding of the states' rights principles on which Johnson's policy was based, nor did they grasp the fact that the American system of checks and balances was being endangered by the congressional attack on the executive. Pierre Guiral, a modern biographer of the liberal journalist Prévost-Paradol, notes that he sided blindly against Johnson because he judged the president "from the point of view of a French partisan seeking above all a confirmation of his concept of French politics."[14]

That observation could apply equally well to the French left in general. Most of them viewed the struggle for control of Reconstruction strictly in the context of French politics, seeing it as proof that personal power was a constant threat to liberty. Johnson was portrayed as an analogue of Napoleon III: usurper, conspirator, aspiring dictator. Like the emperor, he was accused of trying to defy the people's representatives, violate the Constitution, and seize power for himself. Napoleon III actually reinforced this comparison by voicing his approval of Johnson's attempts to resist Congress.[15]

Allain-Targé was typical of those French republicans who linked the hated emperor with the disgraced president. Accustomed as they were to the trappings of despotism, he wrote, many Frenchmen might fail to see the gravity of Johnson's "crime"; indeed, partisans of the imperial regime were likely to "side with a chief executive who sought to abuse and threaten a parliament." While Johnson had not gone so far as to stage a coup d'état—unthinkable in republican America—he was nevertheless guilty of seeking a "personal government" and of trying to impose "his own will . . . , his own ideas, his own policy." This was an outrage in the eyes of the Americans, declared Allain-Targé, for it violated "the customs and practices of government of the people by the people." In an obvious swipe at the emperor, he charged Johnson with transgressing the spirit of the U.S. Constitution by assuming that "the President of a Republic is a sort of king, . . . whose mission is to think on behalf of and in the interest of the nation." In America, at least, such errors were soon rectified.[16]

Spurious as it was, the comparison between Johnson and Napoleon III was especially useful to the left at a time when the emperor was seeking to liberalize his image by casting himself as a sort of hereditary chief executive presiding over a constitutional regime. For the irreconcilables, it was important to show that even this mitigated role was dangerous where the people had no control over the executive. The Johnson example not only indicated the dangers of personal power—whatever its shape or form—but also showed that American-style republican institutions provided the only safeguard against such threats.

The American example seemed especially well suited to the left's arguments at this time, for the postwar years saw a drastic decline in the power and influence of the U.S. presidency. Johnson was virtually ignored during his last year in office, and his successor, Grant, would prove to be one of the weakest presidents in American history. It was not until the end of the century, in fact, that the presidency regained a preponderant role in the federal government.[17] This decline of executive power contributed significantly to the French left's enthusiasm for the American political model during the late 1860s. The presidency was one feature of the Constitution that had long caused misgivings among French republicans. In 1848, as we have seen in chapter 1, many of them had opposed the insertion of this "quasi-monarchical" institution into the Constitution of the Second Republic. Their hostility to a strong executive was reinforced in 1851 after Louis Bonaparte used the presidency as a stepping-stone to imperial restoration.

Thereafter, republicans had increasingly come to advocate parliamentary government, thus America's postwar political development seemed to confirm the constitutional views of the French left.[18] With Congress asserting its supremacy over the president, the United States seemed to be evolving toward their ideal of parliamentary democracy. Many French republicans, in fact, hoped to see the American presidency further weakened or even abolished in the wake of Johnson's impeachment.[19]

The dust had hardly settled after Johnson's Senate trial when the election of Grant provided the left with more polemical ammunition to use against Napoleon III. At a time when the extralegal origins of the Second Empire were being widely discussed (Eugène Ténot's famous exposé on the coup d'état had appeared shortly before Grant's election), this American military hero came to office through the peaceful working of the democratic process, promising to be a passive executor of the congressional will.[20] The contrast between his rise to power and that of Louis Bonaparte was not lost on the left. Rochefort, the radical editor of *La Lanterne,* hailed Grant's election in the lacerating style for which he was famous:

> The number of votes by which General Grant has been elected President proves that a coup d'état is not always necessary in order to win popular sympathy. Today General Grant is in the same situation that Louis Bonaparte found himself in on 10 December 1848. Both men were elected for four years, and both have sworn to protect the Republic. Thus, they could both use the same passport, except that under the article "special characteristics," one of them, I am not sure which, is described as an honest man. There is another important distinction: General Grant fought for the abolition of slavery, while today French generals only fight for the abolition of liberty.[21]

The same comparison was drawn by the future Communard historian Prosper Lissagaray. Responding to a progovernment journalist who had accused him of showing less respect for the emperor than the free American press did for their president, Lissagaray sarcastically noted that "Grant has never betrayed his oath of fidelity to the Republic, he has never staged a coup d'état, gunned down fifteen hundred bystanders in the streets, deported thousands of patriots, compromised his country in insane expeditions, exhausted the resources of the nation in order to enrich his favorites, damaged the reputation of the United States abroad, perverted universal suffrage, or mutilated its elected representatives."[22]

The republican lawyer Léon Gambetta, who would soon be catapulted to national prominence by his courtroom denunciation of the coup d'état, also portrayed Grant as an anti-Bonaparte.[23] Instead of attempting to seize absolute power by force, said Gambetta, the victorious general was content to remain "only the servant of Congress, the subaltern of civil power, the subordinate of the law." America's detractors had often predicted that the Civil War would lead to a military dictatorship, but events had proven the absurdity of such claims. "In this land of pure democracy, the whole nation is constantly involved in the management of its affairs," wrote Gambetta. "The militant vigilance of all the citizens of the republic poses an insurmountable barrier to any coup d'état. There is no place there for political usurpation." In Europe a military hero might become a Cromwell or a Bonaparte, he noted, but "in the radical democracy of America . . . he can only be a great citizen, a Washington or a Grant, obliged to respect the law. . . . There, democratic institutions condemn genius to virtue."[24]

Grant's first annual message to Congress on December 6, 1869, furnished the occasion for a fresh round of journalistic barbs hurled at Napoleon III. The temptation to contrast the two leaders was especially strong since the emperor had delivered his opening address to the French legislature a week earlier. Grant's written message had announced that peace and prosperity reigned throughout the United States; agricultural and industrial production surpassed all previous levels; the Treasury showed a fifty-million-dollar surplus, and the national debt was being rapidly repaid; Reconstruction was proceeding well; and the military budget was drastically reduced. In closing he had reiterated his pledge to execute the people's will, promising "a rigid adherence to the laws and their strict enforcement."[25] The emperor's address, delivered with much pomp and ceremony at the Louvre on November 29, announced the coming of constitutional government and promised to found the empire on liberty. But at the same time Napoleon III had declared his firm intention to "maintain order" in the face of the "subversive passions" stirred up by his adversaries on the left.[26]

Comparing these two addresses, republican journalists drew conclusions that were predictably unflattering for the emperor. Charles Delescluze's *Réveil*, for example, observed that Grant's message bore "no resemblance, in form or content, to the Imperial address of 29 November. . . . The President of the American Republic said nothing about hostile and subversive passions, nor did he see fit to threaten the use of force to maintain order; however, he did promise new reductions in the military budget. Lucky Americans!"[27]

The French left's view of postwar America bordered on the hagiographic. In their eyes the Union was continuing the progressive course it had embarked upon during the Civil War, and the soundness of its republican institutions received new demonstrations with each succeeding year. Writing in 1868, Gambetta cited America's postwar evolution as the irrefutable proof of democracy's excellence:

> Within the past few years, this Republic has given us the great example of a nation that . . . fearlessly sustains a gigantic struggle, that triumphs over its internal enemies without violating the law by any military or dictatorial necessity, that chases a foreign power from its borders with one bold gesture, that holds a conspiring president in check, and designates his successor in advance, patiently awaiting the constitutional end of his term before conferring the executive power upon a general whose greatest glory is his refusal to act like a military man.

The American experience, Gambetta concluded, had dissipated all doubts about the feasibility of democracy and compelled "the human race to follow the most salutary of examples."[28]

There is great irony in this French glorification of postwar America. No one familiar with the history of Reconstruction—and especially of Grant's corrupt administration—can suppress a smile upon reading these naïve panegyrics from across the sea. American historians have generally looked on the postwar decade as a "Tragic Era"—and so it was, despite the efforts of revisionists to find some bright spots in the period. The attempt to ensure equality and civil rights for Blacks ended in abject failure and neglect; the impeachment of Johnson was an inglorious and regrettable episode; and Grant, in the view of Samuel Eliot Morison, was "the most unfortunate chief magistrate in American history.... He was unfitted for the presidency by temperament, and less equipped for it than any predecessor or successor."[29]

Far from confirming the optimistic expectations of many French republicans, the Grant era would be besmirched by some of the worst political and financial scandals the United States has ever known. The stealing and squandering of the public wealth, the guilty collusions between government and private interests, and the speculative mania that characterized Gilded Age America far surpassed the malfeasance and cronyism of the Second Empire. Even the duc de Morny's manipulations and Baron Haussmann's financial irregularities were pale by comparison.[30] The United States was far from the summit of national greatness at the close of the Civil War decade: indeed, the country was on the threshold of what Vernon Parrington famously labeled the "Great Barbecue."[31]

It is true that the worst scandals of the Grant era occurred after the fall of the Second Empire, and these French observers cannot be blamed for failing to foresee the events of the next decade. But the left clearly misjudged the current and direction of America's postwar development. They did so because they did not really seek to understand it objectively, only to use it for domestic political purposes. Consciously or no, they puffed up the American image in order to prove that the republic was the best of all possible governments. They were especially anxious to stress this point at a time when many French citizens were being won over to the Liberal Empire. But as we shall see, the idealized image of this sweet land of liberty would begin to crumble as soon as the fall of the empire removed its usefulness as a propaganda weapon.

The U.S. Constitution vs. the Liberal Empire

The overarching goal of the irreconcilable left was the establishment of a democratic republic based on the principle of "popular sovereignty." That principle, implicit in the institution of universal suffrage, was held by the left to be inconsistent with any type of monarchy. Thus they opposed the hereditary personal government of Napoleon III, no matter what constitutional forms might adorn it. "If you are expecting our help in founding liberty with the Empire, you will never get it," Gambetta told Ollivier in a famous 1870 speech. "In our eyes, universal suffrage is not compatible with the form of government you recommend. You are only a bridge between the Republic of 1848 and the Republic of the future, and it is a bridge we intend to cross."[32]

As they worked to build that "Republic of the future," the irreconcilables looked constantly to the United States as a source of inspiration and propaganda. The more liberal the imperial regime became, it seems, the more its irreconcilable opponents were tempted to contrast it with a "true republic" like the United States. But it is not so clear that the U.S. Constitution actually represented the political principles of the men who were invoking it so freely against the Liberal Empire. It was natural enough for the left to contrast America's political freedom with the authoritarian regime of the 1850s. The Imperial Constitution of 1852 had attributed all effective power to Louis Bonaparte. The nonelected Senate had no legislative function; the Corps législatif served only as a rubber stamp for laws decreed by the executive; deputies could neither initiate laws, nor question ministers, nor even publish their debates; ministers were responsible only to the emperor and had free entrée in the chambers; the emperor was declared "responsible" only to the people, to whom he could always appeal in the form of plebiscites.[33] Founded on the principles of political repression and one-man rule, this constitution seemed to be diametrically opposed to the one the Americans had framed in 1787.

But the decade-long liberal evolution begun in 1860 transformed the empire into a political system that, in certain fundamental respects, resembled that of the United States. In his 1866 address, Napoleon III himself observed that the "constitutional forms" of the empire bore a "certain resemblance to those of the United States." Both systems were "wisely founded on a just balance between the different powers of the State," unlike English-style parliamentarianism, where "the chamber controls the ministers and the executive is without authority."[34] In the absence of basic liberties, this analogy seemed hollow, even absurd. But in a purely constitutional sense, the emperor had a point, and the subsequent extension of civil and political liberties would serve to reinforce the similarity to the U.S. system.

Republicans predictably mocked the emperor's 1866 observation. To them, it was obvious that the two constitutions were at antipodes. Allain-Targé, for example, asserted that the U.S. Constitution of 1787 and the Imperial Constitution of 1852 had only one thing in common: universal (male) suffrage. That single analogy, he argued, was in itself a condemnation of the whole imperial system, for "universal suffrage, democracy and equality do not go with centralization, heredity, bureaucracy, pomp, dynasty, permanent armies, a gagged press, restricted rights of assembly, speech, association, an irremovable and non-elective judiciary, a salaried clergy, prefects, etc."[35]

Allain-Targé continued to stress the contrast between the American and French political systems as the empire pursued its liberal evolution. Denouncing the "parliamentary fictions" of the liberals, he repeatedly called for American-style "government of the people by the people," which he depicted almost as a form of direct democracy: "Nothing must be done without the people, and they must put their confidence in no one."[36] Allain-Targé's remarks are typical of the way the French left used the U.S. Constitution to discredit the notion of a liberal empire. Yet it seems clear that he and many of his fellow republicans misunderstood some of the basic constitutional and political principles of the U.S. system.[37] In reality, the liberal regime that was inaugurated in 1870 bore more resemblance to the American system than the republicans realized—or cared to admit.

In seeking alternatives to the authoritarian empire, France had three basic constitutional models to choose from. First, there was the model of the Revolutionary Convention, where all power resided in a single elective assembly with no head of state and no upper chamber. Second, there was English-style parliamentary government, where the majority party within the legislative chamber controlled the cabinet and the monarchical head of state had little effective power. Third, there was representative government, based on a system of checks and balances between a legislative body and a strong, independent executive. The latter system had been tried in 1848 and had ended in the coup d'état of December 2, 1851. In reaction to that failure, most republicans now advocated some form of parliamentary government.[38]

Part of the reason that republicans were so hostile to the Constitution of 1870 was that it had revived old political ideas that had been discredited in 1848. Yet those ideas had roots in the republican tradition. Ollivier, the main author of the 1870 Constitution, came from an old republican family and had long been a leader of the republican opposition himself. His principal political idol was George Washington. His constitutional ideas were greatly influenced by the theories of Benjamin Constant and by the tradition of 1848. He disliked English-style parliamentarianism and believed instead in the principle of "mixed government." Based on a system of checks and balances between legislative and executive branches, Ollivier's 1870 document reproduced ideas that moderate republicans like Alexis de Tocqueville, Louis Cormenin, and Edouard Laboulaye had advocated in 1848.[39]

But if the Constitution of 1870 was linked to the tradition of 1848, so was the U.S. Constitution. Witness the profound influence the American example had on shaping the Constitution of 1848, particularly the institution of the presidency. It also had a certain influence on Ollivier's thinking: in 1870 he invoked the example of the independent American executive against those who were calling for more parliamentary power.[40] It could be reasonably argued, therefore, that the Constitution of 1870 belonged in the same political tradition as the Constitution of the United States and that many of those republicans who were attacking the Liberal Empire by citing the American example were themselves out of harmony with some of the basic principles of U.S. government.[41]

This is apparent in the way the American system was distorted or misconstrued by many French republicans in order to bring it more into line with their own ideas. In an 1870 pamphlet attacking the Liberal Empire, the Proudhonian Gustave Chaudey claimed that "the government of the United States of America is a parliamentary government *par excellence.*"[42] Gambetta likewise asserted that the American government was "entirely parliamentary."[43] Such assertions were intended to mark a contrast between the "parliamentary monarchy" of the empire and the "parliamentary democracy" of the American republic. But in fact, neither regime could be properly described as "parliamentary," for in both cases the representative body was counterbalanced by an independent executive who named his own cabinet and enjoyed broad prerogatives. The "parliamentary government" that Gambetta envisaged (and later helped establish) was quite a different thing from the American system he had praised while in opposition.[44]

The fact that the United States was a representative government with an independent executive and a bicameral legislature obviously bothered republicans who were criticizing these same features in the constitution of the empire.[45] There were, of course, significant differences between the Imperial Constitution of 1870 and the U.S. Constitution. Despite the broad liberties he had granted, the emperor still retained personal prerogatives that were far greater than those of a U.S. president. His power was perpetual and remained in his dynasty; he alone declared peace and war and made treaties; he could initiate laws; he appointed senators, prefects, and magistrates; and he could bypass the legislative chambers and appeal directly to the people through plebiscites. Yet, had the hereditary emperor been replaced by an elected president, the Constitution of 1870 could well have served as the basis of a representative republic, one that would have resembled the United States far more than the Third Republic, with its parliamentary bickering and unstable governments.

Indeed, there were those in the moderate republican camp who rallied to the Liberal Empire as at least a step in the right direction. Laboulaye, who was considered the greatest French expert on the U.S. Constitution at this time, defended the Constitution of 1870 against the advocates of "parliamentary usurpation." He justified both the independent executive and the plebiscitary principle as guarantees of "government by the people" as against an oligarchy of "deputies driven by their own petty ambitions and prejudices." Citing the U.S. Constitution as a model, he declared that France was now "heading in that direction."[46] The republican *jeunesse* booed Laboulaye out of his lecture hall at the Collège de France for saying such things, and opponents of the Liberal Empire accused him of betraying his longstanding belief in America's democratic principles.[47] Prévost-Paradol, who had often praised the American example during his years in opposition, made his peace with Napoleon III and was appointed ambassador to the United States in 1870. Other liberal admirers of the American republic, including Emile de Girardin, Charles de Montalembert, and Jean-Jules Clamageran, also embraced the Liberal Empire in 1870.[48] (Tocqueville, who died in 1859 and did not live to see the liberal reforms, had earlier reconciled himself to Louis Napoleon's presidency and even served as his foreign minister in 1849.)[49]

But if the Liberal Empire won the support of certain noted Americanophiles, it was the irreconcilable left that made the most use of the American example. It seems somewhat paradoxical that the republicans should be so anxious to invoke a model that, in many points, was inconsistent with their own constitutional ideas. But in citing the American example, they were not really searching for a constitutional model. Dazzled by America's enormous prestige after the Civil War, French republicans developed what Allain-Targé described as an "infatuation" with the United States.[50] For psychological reasons as well as propaganda purposes, they sought to bask in the reflected rays of American glory. In the eyes of many republicans, the triumphant republic symbolized the future success of their own cause—and in some cases the success of their personal ambitions as well. Writing to his father in September 1866, Gambetta said, "the future looks marvelously bright; my professional affairs and political hopes are all tinted in rose and gold, which doubles my energy and makes me cheerfully repeat each morning the war cry of the Americans: Go ahead!"[51] To Gambetta, as to many of his fellow republicans, the American image was associated with victory and success as well as republicanism. It was perhaps in this general and transcendent way, more than as a concrete constitutional model, that the American example had its greatest influence on the opponents of the empire.

The Basic Freedoms

The new laws on the press, public meetings, and the right of association marked an undeniable improvement over the repression of the authoritarian period. But considerable limits still remained on basic freedoms. The press law of March 9, 1868, abolished the preliminary authorization requirement for founding a newspaper and withdrew the right of imperial officials to warn, suspend, or suppress publications. But the government still retained significant controls over the press. It could forbid the sale of offending papers on the streets and in railway stations. Though arbitrary suspensions and suppressions of newspapers were no longer permitted, authorities could prosecute journalists and publishers for a long list of press-specific offenses. Those accused of such violations were tried before criminal courts without juries. Imperial authorities seemed determined to use these remaining powers to the fullest in order to compensate for the liberal concessions the law had granted. Within three months, some forty-one journalists were convicted of press offenses and three papers suppressed.[52]

The new law on public meetings, passed on March 25, 1868, also retained curbs on the rights of free speech and assembly. It allowed only those public meetings dealing with nonpolitical and nonreligious subjects to be organized without government authorization. Political meetings could be held by candidates to the Corps législatif only during the two weeks before an election. All public assemblies, moreover, had to be attended by a police officer, who could call speakers to order and arbitrarily disband the gathering whenever discussions touched on taboo subjects or passions rose too high. This proved to be an effective means of control, for policemen frequently interrupted the meetings and dissolved a great number of them.[53] Freedom of association was likewise circumscribed. The right to strike and form coalitions was given a limited scope by the law of May 1864, while the official tolerance granted to labor organizations in 1868 could be withdrawn at the whim of the government, as the proceedings against the International would later prove.

All this fell far short of the absolute freedoms guaranteed by the American Bill of Rights—and critics of the Liberal Empire never tired of pointing this out. Léon Journault, for example, mocked the emperor's liberal pretensions in an 1868 article on public meetings. Citing numerous cases of arbitrary intervention and dissolution of meetings by imperial police, he wrote: "So that is what the Empire calls liberty? Thank God there is another kind of liberty, one whose meaning cannot be misunderstood. . . . The echo of its voice comes to us . . . from across the Atlantic. . . . It is liberty that . . . dictated to Washington, Franklin and Jefferson this proud declaration: 'Congress shall make no law . . . abridging the freedom of speech, or of the press, or the right of the people to peaceably assemble.'" America's prodigious development and prosperity, argued Journault, were the fruits of "a full, absolute liberty without restrictions or limits; a liberty . . . that does not fear the masses and does not need the protection of a policeman. This is American liberty. . . . Does anyone dare to say that France is incapable of it?"[54]

The Civil War veteran Gustave Cluseret was one of those republican journalists who most often cited the American example to discredit the emperor's professed liberalism. When the ex–interior minister Victor de Persigny published a letter on the new press law in 1868, Cluseret sarcastically declared, "after seeing liberty applied in all its glory, force and grandeur by its founders in America, I was surprised to see it regulated by one of the men of December 2nd, a patriarch of the Imperial idea." Men like Persigny always talked of combining liberty with authority, wrote Cluseret, but they did not understand that liberty implied the "sovereignty of the individual, and consequently, the development of the individual in every sense. At least that is how we understand liberty in America."[55] Cluseret later contrasted America's absolute freedom of the press with imperial efforts to control newspapers through fines, stamp taxes, and intimidation. American leaders, he observed, "do not seek to frighten, stifle or repress the people. . . . Public opinion is their watchdog and their prime minister. . . . Thus the government seeks to facilitate the circulation and diffusion of ideas by all possible means." Napoleon III, meanwhile, "uses your [the public's] money to pay soldiers who hinder, repress and smother opinion. On which side do security, stability and prosperity lie? On the side of violence or on the side of liberty?"[56]

America's freedom of the press was similarly praised by Lissagaray, who observed that U.S. leaders—unlike imperial authorities—accorded their critics the same liberties as their admirers. "Nowhere does the press attack public men as furiously as in America," he wrote, but American statesmen were not "alarmed by these attacks, nor do they order their friends to avenge them, as the government of Napoleon III does, because their conscience tells them that such attacks are undeserved."[57]

Individual liberty, like freedom of the press, was another area where the constitutional protections enjoyed by Americans contrasted sharply with the limited rights of Frenchmen before the state. Under the Second Empire, citizens were deprived of many of the individual rights that Americans took for granted, such as habeas corpus, inviolability of domicile, and immunity against self-incrimination. The government's inquisitorial criminal code put the burden of proof on the accused; denied the rights to legal counsel and trial by jury in many cases; and curtailed freedom of opinion not only in the press and public meetings but also in the streets, shops, cafés, and restaurants, where police were liable to arrest anyone whose words or acts they judged dangerous to state security. The repressive law of *Sûreté générale*, passed after Orsini's 1858 assassination attempt against Napoleon III, granted the government almost unlimited powers of arbitrary arrest.[58] Citizens had no legal recourse against unjust acts on the part of authorities, for the famous Article 75 of the Constitution of 1799 (An VIII) gave public officials judicial immunity. Many of these limits on individual liberty predated the Second Empire, of course, but nonetheless belied the government's professions of liberalism and were vigorously denounced by the leftist opposition.[59]

The American example of individual liberty was frequently cited by critics of imperial repression. Edouard Portalis, for example, devoted a whole chapter of his 1869 book on the United States to the question of individual rights in France and America. In France, he observed, the individual had no defense against the state, while government officials were protected by Article 75. In America it was the other way around: the individual was surrounded by constitutional protections, while all officeholders were legally responsible before the courts for their conduct. In America the individual was sovereign and the government was his "servant." In France the individual was overwhelmed by the powers of the state. Citing numerous cases of arbitrary arrest, police brutality, dissolution of public meetings, and intimidation of voters by imperial authorities, Portalis charged that the "Liberal" Empire was more dependent than ever on violence and force. "But in America, where the people rule, [the government] is quite calm; it never clubs anyone, nor does it attack crowds or put voters in prison for seditious utterances."[60] Contrasting American police procedures and legal process with the arbitrary and inquisitorial methods of French authorities, he declared: "In the United States they punish the crime, but they respect the individual. . . . Individual liberty is surrounded by guarantees, and the dignity of a man is always respected. That is why this agglomeration of immigrants has become the greatest people in the world."[61] The Bill of Rights, said Portalis, "should be engraved . . . on the doors of the Palais Bourbon."[62]

In 1869 the contrast between American and French liberties received a striking and well-publicized illustration in a case involving a naturalized U.S. citizen, Cluseret. After fighting in the Civil War and winning U.S. citizenship, as we have seen, the former general had returned to France in 1867. There he had thrown himself into radical politics and journalism, attacking the imperial regime relentlessly in the republican press. Numerous warnings and a prison sentence had failed to silence his journalistic broadsides against the government. But his luck ran out in the spring of 1869, when he exposed a scandal in which several prominent Bonapartists were implicated. This affair concerned a bond swindle perpetrated by Cluseret's former Civil War commander, General J. C. Frémont, who had since become director of the shady Transcontinental, Memphis, El Paso, and Pacific Railroad. In May 1869 the Transcontinental began advertising its bonds in the French press and soon became one of the hottest items on the Paris Bourse. Cluseret, to whom Frémont had earlier confided his plan to dump worthless railroad bonds in France, now saw his chance to avenge an old personal grudge and to stir up some self-promoting publicity at the same time.[63] Proclaiming himself the defender of "the people's savings," he denounced Frémont's operation with the dogged persistence of a personal vendetta. When the fraudulent claims of the Transcontinental were exposed, the company's representatives hauled Cluseret into court on charges of defamation. But his accusations proved to be well founded, and the Transcontinental wound up completely discredited.[64]

Before these civil proceedings were terminated, however, Cluseret found himself in trouble with the government. Imperial authorities had long looked on him as a dangerous radical—French police spies had tracked him even in England and America—and now he had definitively made himself persona non grata by exposing a scandal involving several figures close to the government.[65] On June 5, 1869, a ministerial decree ordered Cluseret to leave the country immediately, citing the law of *Sûreté générale* and an 1849 statute authorizing the peremptory expulsion of foreign citizens deemed dangerous to state security. (Cluseret had lost his French citizenship by fighting in the American Civil War without the authorization of the emperor.)

This decree was delivered to Cluseret's home in the night by a band of police officers who threatened to smash the door down and haul him away by force. Cluseret first invoked his American citizenship. When that failed to satisfy the officers, he drew his pistol and told them, "I will fire my last bullet before I surrender and blow the brains out of the first man who violates my domicile."[66] After the policemen had prudently retreated, he got word to the American minister, Elihu B. Washburne, who took him under his protection. Although he was unable to get the decree withdrawn, Washburne arranged a compromise with the government that allowed Cluseret ten days to settle his affairs before leaving the country. The revolutionary adventurer thus had no choice but to pack his trunks once more and return to America. On June 19 he sailed for New York aboard the steamer *Péreire.*

But imperial authorities were mistaken if they thought that they had silenced Cluseret. In fact, the expulsion generated much more publicity for him and his radical political ideas than he ever could have done on his own, for his case was widely taken up and agitated by the republican press. Since Cluseret was an American citizen and a Civil War veteran, the opposition papers hammered home the contrast between individual rights in France and the United States.

Before leaving Paris, Cluseret published an indignant letter "To the President and People of the United States," relating the facts of his expulsion and denouncing "before the whole civilized world a law [*la loi de Sûreté générale*] that dates from the age of barbarism." He remarked: "The legislation that permits such an outrage against me today can be used tomorrow against any other American in France. . . . It is a shame for us and the civilization we represent to have endured such laws for so long. Our right, our duty, and our dignity require us to force those governments which rebel against civilization to conform to its laws."[67]

As soon as he reached the United States, Cluseret took his case up with his American political friends. With their help, he submitted a petition to Congress demanding that "the U.S. take such action as it shall judge proper, for securing to every American abroad, under any circumstances, a fair hearing and a trial of his case."[68] He also used his influence in New York journalistic circles to publicize his case in the American press.

While Cluseret was pursuing these activities across the Atlantic, his republican friends in France were also making political capital out of the incident. Here was a fresh opportunity to contrast the conduct of the American republic and that of the Second Empire in the field of individual liberty. The Cluseret affair brought the empire's whole system of repressive legislation under attack. Chassin ironically noted that Cluseret's expulsion was perfectly legal according to the arbitrary laws that existed in France, "but what a shameful legality for the people who proclaimed the RIGHTS OF MAN and declared itself the soldier of humanity from the tribune of the Convention."[69] Rochefort, editor of the satirical and ferociously anti-imperial *Lanterne*, observed that Cluseret had struck a blow for "individual rights" by brandishing a loaded pistol in the faces of the "ignoble agents" who sought to "invade his domicile. . . . What a fine lesson for those generals who politely allowed themselves to be arrested on the night of December 2nd!" Rochefort quipped. "With every passing day, it is becoming more obvious that France has only one thing to do: apply for American citizenship."[70]

Cluseret's case shows how the publicists of the left could turn a fairly minor incident involving a U.S. citizen into an "affair of state" that had few repercussions on the diplomatic level but provided the left with a symbolic confrontation between American liberty and imperial repression. Here again, the American example was helping deflate the liberal pretensions of the French government.

American Economy vs. Imperial Prodigality

The wastefulness and inefficiency of imperial finances was another favorite target for the opposition during these years. The empire was particularly vulnerable on this point, for the costs of the Mexican expedition and of Baron Haussmann's controversial transformation of Paris had helped push the floating national debt to 936 million francs by 1868. Faced with the expenses of army reorganization and the completion of Haussmann's project, the government had to resort to deficit spending and large-scale borrowing, which further increased the national debt. By 1869, the annual budget had swelled to 2.2 billion francs, and massive loans were necessary to keep the government solvent. The financial situation thus became an important political issue at this time—especially during the parliamentary election year of 1869—and the left effectively exploited it to discredit the Liberal Empire.

Critics not only accused Napoleon III's ministers of incompetence, mismanagement, and dishonesty but also denounced the inherent extravagance of the imperial regime, with its civil list, sinecures, luxury, and pomp. By contrast, republican governments were held to be cheap, efficient, and prosperous. Such claims were almost invariably backed up by allusions to the United States. The moment was, in fact, well chosen for illustrating America's economic resiliency and financial capacities. After a war whose military costs alone had topped 3 billion dollars, the American economy was prospering as never before. The national debt, a staggering 2.8 billion dollars at the end of the conflict—representing a 4,100-percent increase from 1860—was reduced during the postwar years at a rate that astonished French observers.[71]

The example of American prosperity was a mainstay of the left's economic case against the empire. Republican propagandists churned out endless streams of facts and figures contrasting the cheapness and efficiency of the U.S. government with the prodigality of the imperial regime. One 1869 pamphlet presented a fifteen-page statistical comparison between the two nations, showing, for example, that Napoleon III was paid 212 times more than the U.S. president; the emperor had twelve chateaux at his disposal, while the president had only one "modest wooden house"; the American education budget was nearly ten times higher than the empire's (214,451,700 francs vs. 21,950,821 francs); and that American workers earned far more than their French counterparts.[72] These differences were attributed mainly to the fact that "France is governed by one man, while the United States governs itself."[73] In publishing excerpts from this pamphlet, the *Tribune* remarked that it illustrated the advantages of "cheap government, which have been too often forgotten since the Empire has made us pay so dearly for its splendors and glories. . . . Only a democracy can be so economical and at the same time so magnificent."[74]

Opponents of the Liberal Empire took a particular delight in pointing out the enormous difference between the salaries of public officials in the United States and France. Noting that Grant had declined a salary raise and refused to give his son a government job, Delescluze's *Réveil* moralized: "economy and disinterestedness will remain the exclusive attribute of the Americans, while the most liberal and generous nepotism will continue to flourish and prosper in France, as in all monarchical countries."[75] Rochefort quipped in his *Lanterne* that the U.S. president's $25,000 annual salary was "just a shade less than the Emperor spends in one day."[76]

The postwar reduction of America's national debt provided further opportunities to embarrass an imperial government whose financial deficits were daily increasing. How was it, asked the future Communard Arthur Arnould, that the United States could reduce its debt while the empire tottered on the brink of insolvency? Simple: America had "No subsidized churches!—No state pensions to widows worth two million!—No generals with 350,000 francs a year!—No permanent army!—No civil list! That is how the United States manages to reduce its debt by one million francs a day!"[77]

Throughout the final years of the Second Empire, the American example was constantly used in this way to support the claim that a republic would be cheaper and more efficient than the imperial regime. This assertion had more to do with politics than economics, for assailing the state of French finances was above all a means of attacking Napoleon III. But for all their criticism of the empire, the republicans themselves were hardly paragons of fiscal rectitude. Within a short time after coming to power in 1870, they too were running up chronic deficits, and the financial scandals of the Third Republic would be easily as notorious as those of the Second Empire.[78] Nor, for that matter, did Grant's America long remain a model of frugal, efficient, and honest government. An orgy of speculation, corruption, and materialism erupted in the United States during the 1870s, a decade that also witnessed one of the worst economic depressions in the nation's history. Contrary to the oft-repeated claims of the anti-imperial propagandists, republicanism carried no guarantee of financial health or lofty public ethics on either side of the Atlantic. On this point, as on many others, the left's perception and exploitation of the American image were at odds with reality.

Decentralization

Before the coming of the Second Empire, most French republicans embraced the principle of the "one and indivisible state," which was part of the heritage of the French Revolution and traced its historical roots back to Colbert and Richelieu. In 1848 they had adamantly opposed any attempt to introduce decentralization or American-style federalism into the constitution of the Second Republic. At that time it was the conservatives who supported such measures in an effort to weaken the revolutionary influence of Paris. But the unitary principle had triumphed in 1848, and three years later Louis Napoleon was able to seize absolute power simply by laying hold of the capital city. His coup d'état showed the ease with which despotism, as well as revolution, could grasp power in a highly centralized state. The Constitution of 1852 pushed the principle of centralization even further, making it a cornerstone of the emperor's authoritarian regime. Thus the opposition parties were increasingly drawn to the principle of decentralization as a means of attacking the regime itself. The emperor's enemies on the left as well as the right could find a common ground on this theme.[79]

Proudhon's *Du principe fédératif,* published in 1863, had much to do with the left's rising interest in decentralization. The only way to reconcile the principles of liberty and authority, Proudhon argued, was to dismantle the centralized state and to put all political, industrial, and economic relations on a federal basis. The individual, not the state, would become the essential unit of social structure, and political authority would rise up from the local level, with the powers of the central government encompassing only those matters of general interest that could not be dealt with locally.[80] Despite certain resemblances between his system and that embodied in the U.S. Constitution, Proudhon seems to have been more influenced by the Swiss than the American example. This is partly because he felt Swiss conditions were more analogous to those of France and other European countries. But his lack of enthusiasm for the U.S. model was also due to his temperamental dislike of Anglo-Saxon civilization in general—and American civilization in particular. Moreover, at the time he was formulating his federal system during the American Civil War, he felt that the North was violating the federal principle by attempting to force the South to rejoin the Union.[81] Yet the American example was, in fact, quite relevant to the questions he had raised, and many of Proudhon's followers, like his close friend Chaudey, took a more positive view of American federalism.[82]

Another important call for decentralization was the Nancy Program of 1865. Hardly a revolutionary manifesto, it simply demanded increased administrative authority for municipalities and departments. It nonetheless generated a great deal of discussion and helped make the issue of decentralization a rallying point for various opposition parties. Instigated by a group of legitimists and Orleanists, the Nancy Program also received the endorsement of certain prominent republicans, including Pelletan, Jules Ferry, Louis-Antoine Garnier-Pagès, and Jules Simon.[83] In May 1870 the Ligue de la décentralisation was formed by a group of legitimists, Orleanists, and moderate republicans who encouraged the government to include decentralization among its liberal reforms.[84] The Ollivier government actually appointed a commission to study this question in 1870, but its work was cut short by the outbreak of the Franco-Prussian War.[85]

The American example was widely cited by republican partisans of decentralization. In his endorsement of the Nancy Program, for example, Ferry pointed to the United States as "the country that enjoys the most complete communal liberty."[86] Pelletan also invoked the American example in demanding the "liberation of the commune" (that is, the municipality) from "the devouring pantheism of the State."[87] Another republican anticentralist, Louis Joly, asserted that the only way to reconcile decentralization with democracy was an American-style federal system. The Nancy Program had erred in attempting to combine administrative decentralization with political centralization, said Joly, for administrative authority had to be accompanied by a corresponding political power both at the local and the national levels. The framers of the U.S. Constitution had solved this problem by attributing all matters of national interest to the central government and all matters of local interest to the governments of the individual states. The state governments, as well as the national government, had administrative and political authority in their respective spheres.[88] To those who argued that a federalized France would be weak and vulnerable, Joly cited the experience of the American Civil War as proof of the inherent strength and resiliency of a federation: "The last war gave dazzling proof that a regime like the American Union, highly centralized in everything that concerns general services, could bring the most tremendous struggles to a happy conclusion, a fact that had been subject to doubt until then."[89]

Léon Chotteau also argued that American-style federalism provided the best hope for establishing enduring political liberty in France. Responding to the 1869 *Manifeste de la Gauche,* which had made a timid call for municipal liberties, Chotteau criticized the republican deputies for their reluctance to attack the problem of centralization head on. "It is all very well for France to have one brain; but it would be far better if she had several, like the United States, where no city makes the law and each city leads its own life." Everyone complained of excessive centralization, said Chotteau, but the remedy that was most often proposed was merely "a less severe form of centralization." He insisted that France had to be "federalized in order to build freedom on its true base."[90]

Portalis for his part enthusiastically praised the American system of decentralized self-government in his 1869 study of the United States. Describing the local organization of American schools, churches, police organizations, militias, and municipal and state administrations, Portalis remarked that "such a system certainly discourages arbitrary imprisonments and coups d'état." He contrasted the efficiency and dynamism of America's local administrations with the cumbersome machinery of France's centralized bureaucracy—"this collection of official puppets"—and recommended that his countrymen "imitate the Americans" in this and other domains.[91]

But the left was not united on the issue of decentralization, despite its usefulness in attacking the imperial regime. The "one and indivisible Republic" remained the ideal of most Jacobin democrats as well as those socialists, such as Louis Blanc, who looked on the state as the guarantor of social equality. The republicans who had endorsed the Nancy Program were actually denounced as dupes of the reactionaries in some of the main republican papers.[92] The radical journalist J. Labbé, for example, branded the Nancy Program "a counterrevolutionary work" and declared, "We are against decentralization because we are for the revolution."[93]

There was one form of federalism that did have near-unanimous support among those on the French left at this time: the idea of binding the great European nations together to form a peaceful confederation, generally referred to as the "United States of Europe."[94] But as Léonce Ribert observed in 1868, there was a great difference between this sort of supranational federalism, which aimed at union, and the internal federalism that sought to "dissolve the great modern State in order to exalt the provinces." If the United States of Europe was ardently desired by all democrats, said Ribert, "the dismemberment of the great nations would be a terrible mistake." Unity was so vital to a nation's existence that even a federal republic like the United States had fought to preserve it against the secessionist threat during the Civil War, he observed.[95] Despite his belief in national unity, Ribert admitted that centralization had become excessive under the Second Empire, where "the State absorbs everything." But he felt that France would be "the last country in the world to be infected by the contagion of [federalist] ideas. Here, they would conflict not only with other ideas, but also with instincts; they would have to overcome an anti-federalist sentiment that our forefathers felt with an intense passion and still lives on in our souls."[96]

As we shall examine more closely in chapter 18, the anticentralists on the far left would have a brief heyday under the Paris Commune of 1871, some of whom claimed explicitly to be inspired by the American example. But ultimately, the Parisian revolt and its brutal repression discredited federalist ideas in the eyes of mainstream republicans: the men who went on to lead the Third Republic were almost unanimous in espousing the unitary state.

Military Reform

None of the issues debated during the final years of the Second Empire were to affect French destinies more than military reform. Napoleon III's attempts to beef up his armed forces through a wider use of the conscription contributed much to the unpopularity of his regime, while his failure to get an effective reform bill passed was largely responsible for the disaster that befell France in 1870.[97]

The stunning Prussian victory over Austria at Sadowa in July 1866 had first prompted Napoleon III to raise the question of military reform. In September of that year, he appointed a special commission to produce a plan for reorganizing the army. The commission's report, published in December, proposed to increase the armed forces from 400,000 to 800,000 men, to replace the old system of exemptions by the principle of universal military service, and to establish a new militia—the Garde nationale mobile—that could provide an additional 400,000 men in the event of war. Had it been adopted, such a plan would probably have put France on an even footing with Prussia in 1870. As it happened, however, the mere suggestion of extending conscription and increasing the armed forces met with howls of protest from nearly every segment of the public.

Faced with this resistance, Napoleon III and War Minister Adolphe Niel published a revised plan, which reduced the length of service by one year and required those who had procured exemptions (by drawing a "good number" in the lottery or by paying for a replacement) to serve in the reserves and the Garde mobile. But the new plan fared no better than its predecessor. Public debate over the project raged on for many months as opposition forces redoubled their propaganda against the proposed military reforms. In a way that was rare for the Second Empire, the public became directly involved in the debate at the grassroots level, denouncing the bill in the cafés and marketplaces, marching and demonstrating in defiance of imperial police, and flooding the Senate with petitions against the proposed law.

In the face of this determined opposition, the bill's sponsors further modified it so that the final version, adopted in January 1868, was completely emasculated. But popular hostility to military reform continued even after passage of the bill, and it remained an important issue in the elections of 1869. Feeling on this question was so intense that the plan was never effectively implemented, even in its watered-down version, for fear of touching off riots among the conscripts. When the Franco-Prussian War broke out in July 1870, the Garde mobile was only a list of names on paper.

The left's reaction to the military question seems paradoxical, for no other segment of political opinion outdid the republicans in their exaltation of French military glory. The legends of the triumphant Revolutionary armies, celebrated by poets like Béranger and Hugo, had long been a vital part of the republican ideology.[98] Up until 1848, in fact, the army itself had been considered a foyer of liberal and subversive ideas. But the use of the army against the people during the June Days and its subsequent role as a pillar of the Bonapartist regime had turned the left into staunch antimilitarists under the Second Empire.[99] As Gambetta's biographer later observed, the republicans of the 1860s opposed the army because it was "associated in their thoughts with the Imperial regime whose downfall they desired."[100]

If the left was united in opposing the kind of military organization the emperor advocated, what did they see as an alternative? What most republicans wanted, Jules Simon told the Corps législatif, was "an army that is not an army"— that is, a national militia instead of a permanent professional force.[101] The republicans were still laboring under the myth of Valmy and the levée en masse. In their eyes, standing armies were instruments of kings and despots; volunteer battalions, militias, and citizens' armies were the incarnation of democracy.[102] To those who were nurtured on this tradition, the onerous reforms proposed by Napoleon III seemed wholly unnecessary since the "nation-in-arms" could defend a country better than a regular army—especially if that nation was France!

While the idea of the nation-in-arms was not a recent addition to the republican ideology, it had been powerfully reinforced by the spectacle of the American Civil War. The creation of immense volunteer armies, the improvisation of new methods and tactics, and the ad hoc financing of the campaign with almost no preexisting military budget all helped convince republicans that volunteer battalions were the best guarantee of national security. The war, wrote Laboulaye in 1863, proved that "the best armies are citizens' armies. . . . A young and patriotic soldier is worth more than a mercenary grown old in his profession."[103] The rapid disbanding of Union forces after Appomattox, moreover, greatly impressed those who believed that permanent armies were a danger and an unnecessary burden in peacetime.[104] What greater proof was needed that a large military establishment was useless to a nation of democrats and patriots?

Echoed and amplified by the Civil War, the French Revolutionary tradition of the nation-in-arms provided a compelling argument against the proposed military buildup. In his 1866 study of U.S. military institutions, F.-P. Vigo-Roussillon cited these twin examples as a major source of public hostility to the permanent army: "It is asked whether it is useful and necessary to retain old soldiers and permanent regiments, when the history of the French Revolution, along with that of the American Civil War, proves that volunteer corps can provide good troops within a short time."[105]

No one was pushing that point more insistently than the partisans of the left. During the parliamentary debates over the Niel bill in December 1867, Jules Favre advised its sponsor to heed "the wise counsels given by North America, and after following their lessons in courage, . . . let him disband his army, and . . . seek not in permanent armies, but in the patriotism of his citizens, the means of defending the nation."[106] Gambetta, another leader of the republican opposition, likewise praised the disbanding of the Union armies and contrasted the American example with the militaristic intrigues of Napoleon III. "Trusting in their own energy to create a whole new army should adversity strike them again," he wrote, "[American soldiers] returned eagerly to their farms and workshops, unsoiled by militarism."[107]

Gambetta's ally Allain-Targé made effective use of the American example in an influential 1867 pamphlet attacking the government's proposed military reforms.[108] The way to meet the Prussian threat, he argued, was not a massive military buildup based on conscription, but rather a simplification of French foreign policy and a reorganization of the army along democratic lines. To avoid a confrontation with Prussia, France must abandon the old monarchical diplomacy based on force and rivalry and adopt a "democratic, pacifistic and reasonable policy" like that of the United States. It was not by military intervention, but rather "by the example of its greatness and prosperity . . . that the United States propagates its institutions and egalitarian customs," noted Allain-Targé.[109] He criticized the Niel project as being wasteful of men, money, and the productive capacities of the nation. By turning the country into a barracks, the French government was following the lead of Prussia rather than the more salutary example of the United States: "On the other side of the Atlantic, a new society, guaranteeing numerous rights . . . and unlimited freedom of action to the individual, reserving all its collective resources to produce . . . , advances more in twenty years than we do in a century;—meanwhile, the nations of Europe, struggling for preponderance, retard their civilization, their progress and the development of their well-being in pursuing the short-lived triumphs of this insane struggle." [110]

As an alternative to the conscript army of 800,000 recommended by the government, Allain-Targé outlined a plan for a "democratic" military organization. Along with a small regular force of full-time professionals, all eligible male citizens would be given rapid military training and assigned to units that would be activated only in case of war. Thus the nation's defense would depend on a large pool of trained civilians rather than a separate military caste. In arguing the feasibility of such a system, Allain-Targé turned again to the American example: "The twenty-one million citizens of the United States of the North furnished in four years, without permanent armies and practically without resorting to the draft [*sic*], *two million six hundred thousand* soldiers who waged six hundred twenty-five battles. . . . Is it necessary, then, for the men of a democracy to be professional soldiers in order to fight? . . . When a man knows how to carry a rifle, can he not pass immediately from civilian life into the camps?" [111]

Another critic of the emperor's army project was Emile de Girardin, the influential editor of *La Liberté,* who analyzed the military question in a long series of articles appearing in September 1866. In seeking to reorganize its army, said Girardin, France had two models to choose from: the Prussian system of obligatory military service with no exemptions, or the American system based on voluntary enrollment. But since obligatory service was incompatible with the democratic principle and the institution of universal suffrage, France had to choose "the American regime, with voluntary enrollment in case of war; and if that enrollment is insufficient, an appeal *en masse,* the nation-in-arms." In imitating the Americans, Girardin maintained, France had nothing to fear from Prussia or any other power: "Who would be insane enough to insult [France], brazen enough to attack her? . . . Isn't patriotism more invincible than militarism? . . . France under attack would be the revolution-in-arms!" [112] With such arguments as this, combining the American Civil War experience with their own idealized Revolutionary tradition, the French were lulled into believing that simple patriotism was a match for Otto von Bismarck's "blood and iron."

One of the most relentless critics of the government's proposed army reform was Cluseret, who boasted a firsthand knowledge of both the French and American military systems. No other publicist on the left was better qualified, by training, experience, and temperament, to lead the attack on this front. When the parliamentary debate over the Niel bill got under way in December 1867, Cluseret published a series of articles in the *Phare de la Loire,* mercilessly exposing the shortcomings of French army organization and declaring the inability of the proposed reforms to remedy the situation.[113] Over the next few years, he intensified his attack on the army in the radical press.[114] In June 1868 Cluseret's blistering criticisms of the army won him a two-month jail sentence for "inciting hatred and contempt for the government," but his opposition was in no way silenced by his stay at Sainte-Pélagie Prison. On the contrary, it was there that he met Eugène Varlin and other militants from the International, whose influence pushed him even further in the direction of revolutionary socialism. He also took advantage of his enforced leisure to write an influential book entitled *Armée et démocratie,* which contained a thorough condemnation of the emperor's reorganization plan and called for the creation of a truly democratic army.[115]

Cluseret naturally made wide use of the American example in his discussion of military matters. The Civil War experience, he said, had proven the superiority of democratic armies over permanent armies based on authoritarian principles. It had demonstrated "the force of republican institutions based on the common sense and devotion of the population."[116] The notion that political freedom was incompatible with effective military organization had been exploded by that war, argued Cluseret: "The success of America has definitely decided the question and proven that liberty has an answer for everything and cannot be found wanting."[117] The Americans—accustomed as they were to self-government, individual initiative, and pragmatism—had accomplished what no traditional military regime could do: "What European military organization would have been capable of arming, feeding, transporting and equipping so many troops, over such considerable distances, so quickly and so often? There is something there which in no way resembles the pigmy-like peoples of the past, but which reveals the giant people of the future, whose birth is shaking the foundations of the old world."[118]

Despite his great admiration for the Americans, Cluseret did not think France should slavishly imitate their system of military organization. The Civil War had caught the United States unprepared, and the early phases of the struggle had shown the shortcomings of an army made up of untrained volunteers.[119] In contrast to many of his fellow republicans, Cluseret had little faith in a spontaneous *levée en masse*. The nation's defenses had to be systematically organized—not as a permanent army, but as a democratic militia. Like Allain-Targé, he recommended a system of universal military training for all able-bodied male citizens. These trainees would be organized into militia units that could only be activated by the legislative assembly in the event of a national emergency.[120] The militia's training should be based on democratic principles, for the true military virtues were better instilled by habits of individual initiative and self-government than by the stultifying barracks life of the professional army.[121] The most important military quality was not the passive obedience of the French soldier but the "go ahead!" of the American: "In America, where there was not a single old soldier, the volunteers were more than a match for the soldiers of France.... Nothing can replace the enthusiasm, the initiative and the devotion of the man who acts with discernment according to his own judgment."[122]

From a tactical point of view as well, said Cluseret, the Americans had provided lessons that would revolutionize the practice of war. The rapidity of troop movements; the military use of railroads, telegraph, flag signals, and balloons; the system of reconnaissance by scouts; the widespread use of trenches; and the effectiveness of ironclad ships had all been demonstrated by the Civil War.[123] Thus French generals "must learn from the American generals the tactics that will govern all future operations."[124]

On the military questions, as in so many other areas, the American example played a central role in the left's attack on the imperial government and its policies. But subsequent events suggest that this example was neither well chosen nor well used in this case. In trying to adapt the Civil War experience to their propaganda purposes, opponents of the French army reforms often distorted or misconstrued the facts. It was widely claimed, for example, that conscription did not exist in America; in reality, both the Union and the Confederacy resorted to the draft many times during the war. Even more ill-founded was the frequent assertion that the North's army was composed entirely of volunteers, while the South had a regular army. It was often overlooked, moreover, that the Union did have a professional army led by highly trained career officers educated by the Military Academy at West Point. Although this army was too small to suppress the rebellion alone, it formed the nucleus around which the volunteer regiments were organized. From this cadre came the discipline, the know-how, and the administrative apparatus that were vital to the war effort. Thus it was erroneous and misleading to depict the war as a spontaneous *levée en masse*.

But the greatest flaw in these arguments was that they ignored the vast differences between American and European circumstances. As Vigo-Roussillon pointed out in his 1866 study of U.S. military strength, volunteer armies had succeeded in America only because they were pitted against the same kind of army. Had they been up against a large permanent army, the Americans would not have had time to organize and perfect themselves in the art of war. If the United States was surrounded by neighbors with permanent armies, it would be obliged to adopt the same system. Only the country's isolation permitted it to maintain such a small army. The situation was obviously different in Europe, where a reduction of permanent armies would only be feasible if it was done progressively and simultaneously by all nations.[125]

In hindsight, it is obvious that Vigo-Roussillon was right. With the Prussians arming themselves to the teeth across the Rhine, it would have been suicidal madness to reduce the size of the French army unilaterally as the Americans had done after the Civil War. As it turned out, it was also suicidal madness to refuse the badly needed military reforms put forth by the imperial administration. Looking back in later years, the radical feminist Juliette Adam, who had earlier launched the John Brown medal subscription, wrote that the memory of the republicans' opposition to the Niel project had become "a torture for those patriots who suffered the thousand deaths of that terrible year [1870–71]. The words which Jules Favre, [Victor] Magnin, [and] Jules Simon . . . pronounced at that time must have burned in their throats later on."[126]

"America" might well have figured among those throat-burning words. To the extent that it helped foster and sustain the left's opposition to military reform, the U.S. example arguably contributed to the disaster at Sedan.

CHAPTER 15

The Left Views American Society

Look at this nation, born yesterday, that clears the forests and populates the
deserts, whose founders were immigrants and whose presidents are workers, . . .
that uplifts women and ennobles labor, fights debauchery, suppresses poverty
and destroys ignorance. What made this nation?—Liberty."
—LÉON JOURNAULT, republican journalist, 1869

T
o most French republicans, even more so to socialists, political and social questions were interrelated, and their demands for social reform
were rarely devoid of political implications. Since the 1868 law on public meetings excluded politics from the agenda, the agitation of social questions
became especially useful as a vehicle for antigovernment propaganda: behind
the public discussions of education, labor, and women's rights was "politics and
nothing but politics," as the revolutionary Gustave Lefrançais observed.[1] It happened that the late 1860s marked a very active period for social movements in
France. It was during these years that the French labor movement got underway,
that French feminists launched the first organized campaign in favor of wom-
en's emancipation, and that the demands for universal free education and secularization (two issues that would preoccupy the leaders of the Third Republic)
emerged as major themes of the republican opposition. In all of these domains,
the American example added weight to the arguments of the left.[2]

The American Model of Republican Education

Education was an important issue in France throughout the nineteenth century,
and especially so during the Second Empire. This question took on a special importance after 1848, for the newly adopted institution of universal male suffrage
required a higher level of public enlightenment. This need became increasingly

apparent as the reforms of the Liberal Empire opened the nation's political life to a greater degree of popular participation. As government restraints on the press and public meetings were relaxed, Napoleon III's educational policy became one of the prime targets of the left opposition.[3]

It is ironic that the emperor's adversaries blamed him for the shortcomings of French education, for he himself was largely responsible for reviving the question of educational reform in the 1860s. During his first decade in power, Napoleon III had favored the extension of clerical education as part of his program for rallying Catholic supporters to his regime. But when he reversed his Catholic policy in 1859, he sought to reassert the government's control over education by curtailing the rights and privileges of clerical teachers and by expanding the state school system.[4] This effort was spearheaded by the historian Victor Duruy, a moderate republican who served as minister of education from 1863 to 1869. Although he was forced out of office before he could implement his whole program, Duruy nonetheless accomplished a great deal during his six years as minister. Under his administration, the number of state schools was greatly increased and their curriculum enlarged, primary education was made free for the majority of the students, and the system of state education for girls was improved, with the first girls *lycées* established in 1867.[5] Laudable as they were, Duruy's reforms fell short of the expectations of most republicans and radicals. Thus the left continued to criticize the government's educational program and to demand a fuller democratization of the school system.

On the question of education, as on many others, the left often turned to the American example for support. Since Alexis de Tocqueville's time, the American system of education had aroused the admiration and envy of French observers—whatever reservations they might have about other aspects of American life. Although it was generally agreed that the quality of European secondary and university education was superior, America's supremacy in the field of primary education went undisputed. Praise for American education was not limited to partisans of political liberty, but during the Second Empire, it was the liberals and republicans who showed the greatest interest in the U.S. school system and most insistently urged the government to emulate it. If the United States was the freest, most powerful, and most prosperous nation on earth, they argued, it was because the entire population was educated for democracy.[6] This longstanding French admiration for the American schools was reinforced by the Civil War, for it was widely claimed that the triumph of the Union had resulted from the North's superior system of education (just as the French defeat of 1870–71 would be attributed by many to the superiority of "the Prussian schoolmaster").[7]

French travelers during the early Reconstruction years were virtually unanimous in their praise of U.S. education. One of the most enthusiastic among them was the university professor Céléstin Hippeau, who had been sent by Duruy to make an official government report on the American system. Published in 1870, his study was a major contribution to the French debate over education—one that implicitly supported the arguments of the left. Hippeau attributed the excellence of the American school system mainly to the fact that it was based on the "democratic principles to which everything is subordinated in this, truly the freest country on earth."[8] The advantages of liberty were apparent not only in the classroom but also in the organization and administration of the schools, which reflected "the admirable power of private initiative in a country where the citizens ask nothing of their government."[9] In addition to instilling the democratic virtues, said Hippeau, the U.S. system constituted the most important source of social equality. The American primary school was "the first bond between the different classes of society," whereas French primary schools were "the point of departure for the inequality and separation of the classes."[10]

Unlike the American system, Hippeau observed, the overly centralized French government was incapable of successfully administering to the nation's educational needs. Pointing to the "miserable condition" of the *instituteurs* and the inadequacy of French school facilities, he called on the government to grant a greater measure of responsibility to the municipalities. French education would flourish if the local populations—like the Americans—could tax themselves, buy school buildings, hire teachers and administrators, and choose their own curriculum without state intervention. In education, as in other areas of administration, said Hippeau, "only such decentralization can enhance and develop all the resources that France possesses."[11] He became most critical of the French government when remarking upon "the enormous difference between the budgets that each of these nations devotes to popular education."[12] Before France could hope to match the Americans in the field of education, the government would have to transfer 400 million francs from "this war budget that never seems too big for an essentially military nation."[13] In his conclusion Hippeau energetically praised America's political liberties as well as its educational institutions: "Never has a greater example been given by a free and independent people; never has there been a more brilliant proof of the excellence of democratic institutions."[14] Although it was officially written for the imperial government, Hippeau's report was so enthusiastic about American democracy that it could almost be taken for a manifesto of the republican opposition. Indeed, his book received considerable attention from the republicans and was widely cited in support of their educational ideas.

If an official envoy of the French Empire could express such a high opinion of American education, it is not surprising that those travelers who openly sympathized with the left should do likewise. The feminist Olympe Audouard, for example, devoted much attention to the American educational system during her 1868–69 tour of the United States.[15] A moderate republican, Audouard praised the Americans' public schools as the mainstay of their democratic and egalitarian institutions. "In America," she wrote, "democratic sentiments are instilled in the hearts of its young citizens as soon as they enter school." This was not the case in France, where a distinction was made between those who could afford an education and those who could not.[16] French primary education, Audouard wrote, was "a torture for the young and a moral deformation of the human being." The *instituteurs* were almost always "morose and crotchety," for their existence was "one long struggle with poverty."[17] They instilled "passive obedience," while American teachers "respect the child as a citizen. . . . The young are shaped neither for obedience nor commandment. They are simply taught how to be free men."[18] As a feminist, Audouard particularly admired the fact that the U.S. educational system encouraged gender equality through the widespread use of women teachers, the institution of coeducation, and women's access to higher learning. Like Hippeau, she argued that France must "Americanize" its educational system in order to maintain a high rank among nations: "If we want progress, if we want to march with our century, we must copy America."[19]

Travelers of a more radical bent often went even further in touting American public education as a model for France. Edouard Portalis, who devoted a chapter of his 1869 book to this question, drew a comparison between the two countries that was highly critical of the imperial system. In France, where the central government controlled every aspect of education, schools turned out only "partisans and servants" of the state, whereas American schools produced "citizens," for the people themselves organized education on the local level. Like Audouard, he bewailed the class inequalities inherent in a French system that distinguished between those who could and those who could not pay for their education. In contrast, the American system instilled egalitarian sentiments by bringing children of all classes together and treating them alike. From kindergarten through high school, Portalis observed, the Americans provided students with millions of dollars' worth of free tuition, books, libraries, and facilities. In France "all knowledge has its price, all the ranks are to be bought." The political consequence of this was the continuation of "despotism," for the imperial regime was consistently supported at the polls by the ignorant and illiterate masses. Since Napoleon III could not be expected to abolish the "popular ignorance" that was the basis of his power, Portalis called on the French people to take matters into their own hands by organizing free and independent schools and educating their children for liberty, as the Americans did: "The day when all Frenchmen will go to school, they will have the government they will choose to give themselves, or better still, there will no longer be any government possible."[20]

Another radical traveler of these years was Léon Chotteau, who visited America in 1868 in order, he said, to study "the great Republic without the distorting lenses of the Empire."[21] Chotteau's trip produced a number of books on the United States, and he eventually emerged as one of the foremost "Americanists" of the Third Republic. He devoted much of his attention to the question of American education, using it, like Portalis and others, to advance the republican cause in France. If the American Revolution was followed by no counterrevolution, said Chotteau, it was because the Americans all "knew how to read and write." The French, on the other hand, had repeatedly fallen prey to despots because of popular ignorance. Chotteau praised the American school system as "an application of the federal principle in all its absoluteness." Organized on the local level by the citizens themselves, American schools taught self-government and independence. French schools instilled the principles of obedience, docility, and regimentation because they were controlled by a centralized hierarchy descending from the emperor himself—"the school-master of the nation."[22] By their pedagogical principles as well as by their organization, American schools were ideally adapted to the needs of a republican nation, said Chotteau, for they fostered the active development of the individual and encouraged students to express their opinions. As a result, these "young republicans" learned to speak, think, and act for themselves. Such teaching methods would be considered anathema in France, for the imperial authorities knew that "nothing is more dangerous than a population of orators."[23]

Among the greatest French admirers of the American educational system was the man who would later be responsible for implementing the republicans' educational program, Jules Ferry. In an 1870 lecture on public education, Ferry declared that the Americans had achieved "the realization, word for word, of the plan of our great Condorcet." Basing his arguments on Hippeau's report, Ferry pointed to the "humiliating" contrast between the educational systems of the American republic and the French Empire: "Over there, seven million children are taught free of charge, while in France, we count scarcely 500,000 children in the primary schools. . . . Free America spends 450 million [francs] every year on the public schools . . . [to give] the children of all classes an education which, in France, is received only by a small number of children of the bourgeoisie. (Applause.)"[24] France could not hope to equal "this noble Utopia" under its present government, argued Ferry, for an American-style school system required "liberty as its principal trait." It depended on "the local communities, on the ensemble of the citizens and their elected officials, and not on any [central] administration whatsoever." Another reason why imperial France could not create such a system, Ferry declared, was that it "confuses the glories of war with the glories of peace, and when you give 700 million francs to the war budget every year, it is not surprising that you find only 50 [million] for the people's education! It is sad to put these miserable figures next to the grandiose figures of young America!"[25]

Edouard Laboulaye, as we have seen, relentlessly cited the American example to promote the cause of liberty in France. His popular 1863 novel, *Paris en Amérique,* included a laudatory chapter on the school system that had made the Americans "the least ignorant people under the sun."[26] During the latter years of the Second Empire, Laboulaye played an active role in the campaign for educational reform, always pointing to the American system as the model to emulate. "While we are seeking to resolve this problem of a wise, peaceful, self-controlled, democracy," he declared in an 1869 lecture, "the Americans have already done so through their schools. That is how they have attained a perfect equality." Citing Presidents Lincoln, Johnson, and Grant as typical products of the American schools, Laboulaye observed that such careers would be impossible in France, where "the men who lack a primary education will never reach the highest ranks."[27]

The admiration expressed by such bourgeois republicans seems to have been shared by French workers. In his 1861 book on public education, for example, the typographer Henri Leneveux praised the American model of a broad-based practical instruction for the masses. By comparison, he found the French system "inferior in every way."[28] An 1869 public meeting, presided over by the radical Pierre Vésinier and attended largely by workers, pointed to the insufficiency of French primary education as major cause of social inequality. "It is especially this fact," said one speaker, "that perpetuates a class of workers and a class of capitalists, a distinction that does not exist in the United States, and is the greatest obstacle to a social solution."[29]

Beyond the question of the empire's school system, the decade of the 1860s witnessed numerous other signs of what Antoine Prost has called "the hunger for education" among the French people. It was at this time, for example, that public libraries first began to proliferate throughout the country.[30] This movement was supported mainly by private groups like the Société Franklin, founded in 1865 by Laboulaye and other liberal-minded citizens. As its name indicates, this group was directly inspired by the American example, espousing Benjamin Franklin's ideal of popular enlightenment.[31] Another product of this movement was Jean Macé's Ligue de l'enseignement, founded in 1866, which grew out of an earlier organization that promoted public libraries in Alsace. By 1870, the Ligue counted some 17,000 members throughout the country and was one of the most influential forces in favor of free, compulsory, and secular education.[32] Although he himself was a republican and anticlerical Freemason, Macé strove to keep his organization apolitical. Thus he purposely refrained from using the U.S. example as a propaganda weapon as some of the more partisan members of the republican opposition were doing. He nonetheless had a profound admiration for America's educational and political institutions.[33]

The example of American education continued to attract French attention after the fall of the Second Empire and the establishment of the Third Republic. The debate over education, in fact, intensified in the wake the Franco-Prussian War. Many republicans charged that the disaster at Sedan had resulted from the inferiority of the emperor's educational system. Catholics and conservatives, on the other hand, tended to blame both the defeat and the excesses of the Commune on the decline of religious and moral teaching in the schools. Whatever had gone wrong, it was generally felt that a reorganization of the French educational system was necessary to put things right again.[34] Education therefore became a paramount issue during the subsequent years as republicans struggled with conservatives and royalists for control of the new regime.

In this debate the republicans continued to use the American example against the right as they had previously done against the empire.[35] What they seemed to admire most about American public education were those aspects that reinforced democratic and egalitarian principles: gratuity, universality, the practical nature of the curriculum, secularism, access of the female population to all levels of learning, and the relatively high social and economic status of teachers. Many of these features were reflected in the sweeping educational reforms implemented under Jules Ferry in the 1880s. Yet in some ways the republicans' program differed from the American system they had so often cited as a model: the principles of centralization and anticlericalism that formed the basis of Ferry's program had no analogue in the ideology or practice of American educators. In attacking the educational system of Napoleon III, the republicans had loudly praised the local and autonomous organization of American schools, but this feature left no trace on Ferry's work.[36] In this respect the French school remained under the Third Republic what it had been under the Second Empire: an instrument of state power.

American Religion and French Anticlericalism

The French left had become increasingly anticlerical since 1848, when the Roman Catholic Church allied with Bonapartism to destroy the Second Republic. Anticlerical sentiments were intensified by the close relationship that existed between Napoleon III and the church during the first half of the Second Empire. In the minds of most republicans, anticlericalism and anti-Bonapartism went hand in hand. The anticlerical movement was also reinforced during these years by the spread of positivist philosophy, which had a special appeal for the younger generation of republicans.[37] Thus when the left began to revive its opposition movement during the 1860s, anticlericalism emerged as one of its major themes. The last two years of the empire constituted one of the high-water marks of French anticlericalism.[38] Demands for the separation of church and state and for the secularization of education found their way into virtually every political program that emanated from the left during these years.[39] These demands would continue to be a focal point—in fact, an obsession—of the republican movement for the rest of the century. As Léon Gambetta proclaimed in a famous 1877 speech: "Le cléricalisme, voilà l'ennemi!"[40]

Henry Blumenthal has noted that the anticlericalism of the republicans was "a typically French phenomenon" having no equivalent in the American experience.[41] Yet the American example did play a certain role in the heated French debates over the religious question. To be sure, that example was not ideally suited to the views of the anticlerical left: on the one hand, it supported the arguments in favor of separation and secularization of the schools, yet on the other, it clashed with the antireligious sentiments that most often underlay anticlericalism. For if the Americans had managed to keep religion out of politics, they remained a profoundly religious people. This fact was often cited against the anticlericals by those who claimed that religious faith was a necessary concomitant of liberty.[42]

Many positivists and freethinkers were put off by America's neo-Protestant religiosity, which they found no more compatible with the teachings of science than Catholicism. With their infinite variety of exotic sects, in fact, the Americans seemed to have outdone the Jesuits in demonstrating the absurdity, fetishism, and superstition that allegedly lay at the base of all religion. Auguste Comte, the father of positivism, had only contempt for American Protestantism, which he saw as a source of social disorder and individual demoralization.[43] Comte himself was politically conservative, but his scorn for American religiosity was shared by younger positivists and anticlericals in the republican camp.[44] Denouncing the "tyranny of the Bible," the freethinker Eugène Vacherot charged that the Americans had not understood "the true principles of religious liberty" since they refused to condone skepticism or atheism: "The purest and most perfect of philosophies will not do in America; one is not accepted there unless he belongs to a religious sect."[45] Proudhon, one of the most rabid of the anticlericals, likewise noted in 1860 that the American was "more Protestant, more Christian, more credulous than our forefathers of the eighteenth century; his liberty has only served to produce an infinity of sects, each more ridiculous than the last."[46]

But there were those among the anticlericals who found the American example to be a useful argument in favor of separating church and state. Speaking before the International Association for Progress in the Social Sciences in 1863, the freethinker Frederic Morin declared: "The conscience belongs only to man, and the government . . . has no right to intervene. Let us therefore carefully separate the temporal and the spiritual, following the example of the United States, where each religious communion exists freely and the government never thinks of interfering with them."[47]

Ulrich de Fonvielle, another anticlerical republican, enthusiastically praised the religious freedom he had observed in America while serving as a volunteer in the Union army. "Everyone thinks of religion what he pleases," he wrote from Washington in 1863. "Religious issues never envenom political questions."[48] Fonvielle's comrade-in-arms Gustave Cluseret, himself a confirmed atheist, likewise recommended that France establish "religious liberty as it exists in the United States." The American example proved the feasibility of separating church and state, he said, for religious institutions thrived there without government subsidies.[49]

Some anticlerical writers even sought to put the U.S. example more squarely in their camp by suggesting that Americans were themselves indifferent or hostile to religion. One 1869 article in the *Etats-Unis d'Europe* (the organ of the Ligue internationale de la paix et de la liberté) praised the United States for excluding religion from politics and public education. The writer further claimed that organized religion was declining in America, that George Washington had been a freethinker, and that "half the population remains outside of any religious community."[50] A similar assertion was made in 1866 by Henri Allain-Targé, who sought to reconcile his great admiration for the United States with his philosophical views. He charged that Tocqueville and Laboulaye had launched "a false and detestable theory" in suggesting that American democracy had been "the work of the Protestant religious spirit." On the contrary, he maintained, "the founders of the United States were all free thinkers, men of the Enlightenment, from Franklin to Jefferson."[51]

America's religious inclinations posed less of a problem for French Protestants, whose ranks included some of the leading republicans and liberals of this period.[52] Eugène Pelletan, Agénor de Gasparin, Laboulaye, Hippolyte Carnot, and Henri Martin all came from old Protestant families; Maurice Sand converted to Protestantism; while Charles Renouvier, Jules Simon, Jules Favre, and Edgar Quinet, though not converts themselves, felt that the Protestant religion was the one most conducive to political liberty.[53] Some of the most enthusiastic admirers of American institutions were to be found among this group, and not the least of America's attributes in their eyes was the fact that it embodied the Protestant faith and tradition. "America was the historic mission of Protestantism, its task, its glory, its creation," declared Pelletan.[54] To Protestant liberals and republicans, the U.S. example did not merely provide an argument in favor of separation, it also showed how political liberty could be founded on religion.

One of the main exponents of this view was Quinet, who traced the origins of American democracy back to the Reformation. The principles of individual liberty and self-government, he argued, followed naturally from the Protestant doctrine of free examination. Planted on the virgin soil of the New World, those principles had engendered the republican institutions of the United States. But political freedom could not flourish in countries where free examination had been forbidden by Catholicism, nor could it survive in the total absence of religious belief. In his view, the only hope for permanent liberty in France lay in the adoption of some form of neo-Protestant faith that would replace dogmatic Catholicism without destroying religion altogether.[55]

Quinet thought he had found such a faith in William Ellery Channing's Unitarianism, which combined elements of Protestant thought with Rousseauist deism and rationalism. This, he felt, was the religion "best reconcilable with our time, for it retains a shadow of Christian antiquity and thereby reassures the trembling mind of the peoples while joining hands with the boldest philosophy. Unitarianism is nothing other than the confession of faith of the Savoyard Vicar, which was for so long the soul of the French Revolution." The teachings of Channing and Ralph Waldo Emerson, said Quinet, were "practically identical" to the philosophy he and Jules Michelet had been expounding at the Collège de France.[56]

Channing's philosophy in fact had a great vogue in France during the Second Empire. Apart from Quinet, Channing had a strong influence on republican writers like Eugène Sue, Jean-Jules Clamageran, Eugene Despois, and Laboulaye (who translated his main works into French).[57] The militant feminist André Léo called Unitarianism the "twin brother of liberal French Protestantism."[58] George Sand read and greatly admired Channing (although she had reservations about the extreme individualism that underlay his philosophy).[59] Channing's admirers also included republican freethinkers like Gambetta and Allain-Targé, who had little indulgence for Catholicism or orthodox Protestantism.[60] Thus in the Yankee philosophy of Unitarianism, French liberal Protestants, rationalists, and freethinkers could find common ground.[61]

The influence of the American example was not only felt outside the Catholic

Church; liberal Catholics had long figured among the admirers of America's religious liberty. In the 1830s Tocqueville had observed that Catholicism was thriving in the United States, where it enjoyed complete freedom and independence from the state. He also noted that the Catholic clergy in America were among the firmest believers in democratic institutions.[62] Tocqueville's observations were encouraging to those who sought to reconcile Catholicism with political liberty in France. Henri Lacordaire, Lamennais, and Charles de Montalembert had all invoked the American example in 1848, when such a reconciliation seemed possible.[63] Even as the schism between the forces of liberalism and Catholicism widened during the ensuing years, the increasingly isolated liberal Catholics had continued to draw inspiration from the American experience.

Montalembert warmly praised America's religious liberty in his famous 1863 address, "A Free Church in a Free State."[64] He even planned to go to the United States in 1866 to study American religious and social institutions but was prevented from doing so by age and illness. Two other liberal Catholics, Guillaume de Chabrol and Emile Jonveaux, did visit the United States after the Civil War. Upon their return they published a number of articles on America in the liberal Catholic monthly *Correspondant,* stressing the benefits that Catholicism could derive from the separation of church and state.[65] These views were shared by other liberal Catholic publicists like Pierre Duval and Augustin Cochin.[66] The liberal Catholics thus joined Protestants and even anticlericals on this point.

These views were thoroughly condemned by the Vatican. The *Syllabus of Errors,* published in 1864, had flatly declared that religion was incompatible with any form of liberty. Five years later the church's commitment to absolutism was expressed even more clearly in the *Syllabus on Papal Infallibility.* Thus it is hardly surprising that the American example of religious and political liberty was anathema to French ultramontanes like Louis Veuillot, who violently attacked the liberal heresies in the columns of his *Univers.* In an 1867 article, Eugène Veuillot (Louis's brother) reproached the liberal Catholics for their "infatuation" with America, declaring categorically that the United States was "founded on a fundamental negation of the law of God."[67] Many of America's admirers would have protested against Veuillot's claim that the United States was "the land of apostasy," but he was not entirely wrong in seeing the American experience as an encouragement to the church's enemies. Ultimately, it was the anticlerical cause that had the most to gain by citing this example of a secular republican state.

A Workers' Republic: The Proletarian Image of American Society

To a modern reader, the idea of a "workers' republic" might call to mind the various communist regimes of the twentieth century. During the previous century, however, it was the United States that was most often associated with this idea. Many of those who were then seeking to improve the lot of Europe's proletariat cast an admiring gaze on America, where workingmen seemed to enjoy a higher degree of political power, social equality, and material well-being than anywhere else on earth.

As early as the 1830s, Tocqueville and Michel Chevalier had familiarized French readers with this image of the American worker. These two observers of Jacksonian America had described a society dominated by laboring masses whose democratic will could ride roughshod over the bankers and capitalists. American society, said Chevalier, was "Europe turned upside-down"—the workers were on top.[68] They observed that the American "Common Man" had attained an unprecedented level of material well-being along with his considerable political power. "While European societies are all more or less devoured by the sore of pauperism, to which even the cleverest of men has not yet been able to apply a healing balm, there are no poor people" in the United States, Chevalier noted. "Here, nothing is easier than to live by working, and to live well."[69] America thus appeared in the pages of Tocqueville and Chevalier as a sort of worker's paradise. Both writers had misgivings about the supremacy of the popular masses in the United States. But to those who were less timid in embracing egalitarian democracy, this republic of "farmers and mechanics" was often the object of enthusiastic admiration.[70]

The French view of the United States as a nation of workers was reinforced by the Civil War. The most serious flaw in that image had always been the existence of a class of "aristocratic" idlers in the South who exploited labor in the most blatant way. But secession had severed this slaveholding class from the Union, and the war had pitted the Northern champions of "free labor" against them. This served to purify and enhance the "workers' republic" image of the United States.

That image was actively promoted by Northern propaganda. Lincoln repeatedly claimed that the war was being waged by the "plain people" of the North in defense of popular government. Many of the Union's European sympathizers—

men like John Bright and Karl Marx in England, Pelletan and Laboulaye in France—also stressed the working-class character of the Northern population in order to discourage cotton-starved European textile workers from demanding intervention in the war. Marx declared in 1864 that "the workingmen" represented "the true political power of the North."[71] In his *Adresse au roi Coton*, Pelletan described American society as "an immense, heaving machine" dedicated to "the cult of work and liberty." Nurtured on labor and democracy, the American worker had become "a new man, the final word in man, the man master of himself, his own sovereign, his own policeman, his own priest, the absolute self, the Yankee."[72]

Through its diplomatic agents abroad, the U.S. government also touted the advantages enjoyed by American workers in hopes of attracting European immigrants to offset the North's labor shortage and fill the ranks of its armies.[73] This was one of the main objectives of the 1862 Homestead Act, which promised 160 acres of federal land to any U.S. citizen or properly registered immigrant who would occupy and work his claim for five years. In a State Department circular of February 8, 1862, Secretary of State Seward stressed the special advantages that the Homestead Act offered to European workers and urged that it be given the widest possible publicity abroad. In France the pro-Union press lauded the act as proof of the U.S. government's solicitude for the workers of the Old and New Worlds.[74] Two years later Congress passed the Act to Encourage Immigration in another effort to attract the European proletariat to American shores. Meanwhile, steamship companies and private agencies such as the American Emigrant Company, founded in 1864, also sent representatives abroad during these years to preach the benefits of the American way of life to the workers and peasants of Europe.[75]

These efforts to encourage immigration continued after the war and found a number of advocates in France.[76] The lure of America, said Emile de Girardin in 1868, was rapidly depopulating all the despotic countries of Europe, "for as long as those who love liberty will not find it in Europe . . . they will go seek it in America. . . . In ten years' time what great European state will be able to resist the effects of this emigration caused by its own despotism?"[77]

Napoleon III actually had little to worry about on that score, for these efforts had a very limited success in France. Although the number of French emigrants to the United States nearly doubled the year after the Civil War ended, the figures soon dropped back down to their previous low levels.[78] Though this campaign attracted only a modest number of French immigrants to U.S. shores, it nonetheless reinforced the image of America as a land of freedom and plenty, a haven for the oppressed workers of the Old World.

In the eyes of many French observers, the Union victory marked the definitive triumph of labor over exploitation in America. "The question is not at all . . . between the North and the South," wrote Victor Considérant in June 1865. "It is exclusively between Democracy and Aristocracy, both in the North and in the South; between the workers and the exploiters of labor, in the North as in the South; . . . between the masses who work and want to live comfortably from their own production, and the various cliques who want to live off the masses."[79] By victoriously defending the principles of free labor and democracy, argued Considérant, America had become "the social fatherland of the world's proletariat."[80] Thus the war seemed in his view more like a successful proletarian revolution than the sectional and constitutional struggle it really was.

The proletarian image of America owed much to the figure of Lincoln, the rail-splitter who had become president and freed the slaves. During the Civil War, the Union's French supporters had made much of Lincoln's working-class origins, as we have seen. Consecrated by victory and immortalized by martyrdom, his image remained an object of leftist adulation long after the war. Furthermore, Lincoln had been succeeded in office by two other working-class presidents, a fact that seemed to support even the most exaggerated claims about social equality and popular government in the United States.[81] More than any other single aspect of the American experience, perhaps, this succession of "proletarians" in the White House contributed to the idea of the country as a "workers' republic."

Allusions to Lincoln and his successors abounded in the leftist propaganda of the late 1860s. Writing in the *Courrier français* in 1866, for example, the Proudhonian journalist Pierre Denis recommended that his fellow French workers imitate "the people of America, where the government was yesterday in the hands of a woodcutter and is today in the hands of a tailor."[82] The 1869 program of the *Voix du peuple,* an organ of the radical workers' movement, called for the establishment of an "egalitarian" republic like the United States, where "everyone has the right to educate himself and live by his labor . . . , the right to vote laws and elect leaders . . . , the right to aspire to all offices of the government. May the woodcutter, like Lincoln, or the tailor, like Johnson, be called to represent their fellow citizens one day."[83]

During the years between Lee's surrender and the fall of the Second Empire, the image of the American "workers' republic" was widely exploited by the propagandists of the left. At a time when the French proletariat was growing increasingly restive under the empire, the exaggerated and idealized portrait of the American worker was a useful weapon in the hands of the opposition. Whether or not they believed in the accuracy of this image, it fit their polemical needs to show that only a republic could establish true social equality and economic well-being for its workers.

Edouard Portalis, one of the main propagators of this notion, portrayed the United States as the ideal egalitarian democracy. Whereas French society was infested by "an aristocracy of idlers" and a "multitude of parasites," America had "nothing but workers, all building, cultivating, constructing, thinking, inventing, perfecting."[84] Absolute social equality reigned among the Americans, he claimed: "There are no class distinctions among them, for the simple reason that they have had the good sense not to establish any."[85] In addition to social equality, American workers enjoyed high salaries that satisfied their material needs and opened the road of prosperity and happiness for all. "This continuous rise of salaries," wrote Portalis, "solves one of the greatest problems of modern civilization; it suppresses misery better than the solicitude of the State and the national workshops."[86] The Americans had thus avoided most of the social ills that plagued the industrial nations of Europe: class conflict, wage slavery, and the exploitation of labor by capital. If none of this existed in America, it was because "everyone there works and produces." Far from submitting to the "despotism of capital," labor actually had the upper hand there, Portalis asserted. All over the United States, workers were organizing unions and cooperative associations aimed at "abolishing wage labor, and success is crowning their efforts." They were "raising their expectations every day and forcing capital to retreat, like it or not." European labor was in a far weaker position, for there capital was defended by police, permanent armies, and state power, "whose crushing weight fatally brings the people to inertia and decadence, or to social revolution." Decadence and revolution did not threaten America, however, for "everyone there declares labor superior to capital. ... Wage labor will disappear in the United States just as slavery disappeared, but without a shock; no one will think of defending it, it will be struck from the social institutions by the tacit agreement of everyone's will."[87]

Eugène Pelletan, editor of the influential *Tribune,* frequently invoked the example of the American worker. "There is something greater than capital, and that is labor," he declared in an 1869 lecture. "Look across the ocean at the Americans, this people whose industriousness approaches heroism; over there a man does not quit working even if he has a fortune of a hundred million."[88] Writing in the *Tribune* in 1869, Pelletan again extolled the American's devotion to work. Under the empire, he wrote, France was wasting its energies in the pursuit of military glory, but "for the republican of Ohio, there is no greatness but labor, no glory but production.... Only the Yankee race has known how to do justice to Labor.... Work is something sacred in America; whether intellectual or material, it also glorifies the worker.... Whatever the name of the profession or the nature of the tool, they do not consider any work inferior in the great republican bee-hive.... [May] labor assume a place of honor in Europe as it has in America."[89]

The "workers' republic" image had another proponent in Eugène Chatard, who wrote on American affairs for Charles Delescluze's *Réveil*. "Over there, no one dies of hunger, no one even dreams of this life of humiliation," wrote Chatard in 1868. "Mechanics, carpenters, masons make four or five dollars a day. They are educated and enlightened gentlemen who bring up their families on the ideal of independence and the motto: Heaven helps those who help themselves."[90] The American workingman and bourgeois lived on terms of perfect equality, Chatard asserted: "There is far less difference between a worker and his boss in America than there is in Europe. They wear the same clothes and have the same manners because they have the same education.... This is the model which we propose to French workers."[91]

As useful as it may have been in promoting the republican idea in France, this utopian view of the American worker was far from reality. The Civil War was not a victory for labor, as was so often claimed, but instead a windfall for the capitalists, creating high demand and boosting industrial production and profits to unprecedented levels. The Radical Republicans, who had consolidated their political power during the war, were "the party of the industrial aristocracy ... and the rich factory owners of New England," as Georges Clemenceau rightly observed in 1867.[92] Workers, on the other hand, saw their standard of living devoured by soaring prices while their wages remained near prewar levels. The capitalists, moreover, had taken advantage of the military emergency to attack the unions, forming powerful employers' associations, blackballing union members, and hiring cheap immigrant and female labor to replace the men who had gone off to war. When Northern citizen-soldiers returned from the battlefields by the hundreds of thousands in 1865, they were faced with unemployment, sinking wages, and a soaring cost of living.[93]

Both in economic and political terms, those who had interpreted the Civil War as a victory of the workers over the exploiters were gravely mistaken. Equally mistaken were those who supposed that some ideological link existed between the triumphant Yankees and the forces of European socialism. It was probably Lincoln himself who best expressed the ideology that ultimately prevailed in the Civil War. To anyone who carefully studied his words, it should have been clear that the American ideals he articulated—despite their egalitarian overtones— were fundamentally incompatible with the ideals of the socialists. In his message to Congress on July 4, 1861, for example, the president described the war as a popular crusade for social justice: "This is essentially a People's contest. On the side of the union, it is a struggle for maintaining in the world, that form, and substance of government, whose leading object is, to elevate the condition of men—to lift artificial weights from all shoulders—to clear the paths of laudable pursuit for all—to afford all, an unfettered start, and a fair chance, in the race of life."[94]

Taken at face value, this talk of equality and popular government sounds rather radical. On closer inspection, however, it is obvious that Lincoln was not preaching equality as the socialists understood it, but rather the ideals of individualism, competition, and laissez-faire: "an unfettered start, and a fair chance, in the race of life" really means equality at the starting line and "the devil take the hindmost." This philosophy has more in common with the Social Darwinism of Herbert Spencer than with the socialist ideals of association, collectivism, and mutual aid.

Despite his working-class origins and his great respect for labor, Lincoln was as firm a believer in the capitalist system as any Yankee industrialist. His first annual message to Congress, in fact, contained a vigorous defense of capitalism. He was actually responding to the arguments of proslavery polemicists like George Fitzhugh, who borrowed socialist theories to attack the "free" society of the North.[95] But in refuting such arguments, Lincoln was also refuting the socialist critique of capitalism itself:

It is assumed [by critics of capitalism] that labor is available only in connection with capital; that nobody labors unless somebody else, owning capital, somehow by the use of it, induces him to labor. . . . [I]t is naturally concluded that all laborers are either hired laborers, or what we call slaves. And further it is assumed that whoever is once a hired laborer, is fixed in that condition for life. Now, there is no such relation between capital and labor, nor is there any such thing as a free man being fixed for life in the condition of a hired laborer. Both these assumptions are false, and all inferences from them are groundless.[96]

Having denied the charge that capitalism doomed the working class to perpetual wage slavery, Lincoln went on to celebrate the ideal of the self-made man and of the free-enterprise system that permitted and encouraged individual success:

Many independent men everywhere in these States, a few years back in their lives, were hired laborers. The prudent, penniless beginner in the world, labors for wages awhile, saves a surplus with which to buy tools or land for himself; then labors on his own account another while, and at length hires another new beginner to help him. That is the just, and generous, and prosperous system, which opens the way to all—gives hope to all, and consequent energy, and progress, and improvement of condition to all.[97]

This was the American dream: individual success through work, competition, and deferred gratification. Lincoln's America was indeed a "republic of workers"— workers scrambling for the top as he himself had done.

Lincoln's words help illustrate the divergence that often existed between American realities and the American image as perceived and used by many of those on the French left. The ideology expressed by Lincoln may have been in harmony with the thinking of most French liberals and bourgeois republicans, but it was totally inconsistent with the ideals of those socialists who were hailing the president as a symbol of proletarian ascendancy and applauding the Union victory as a step toward the revolutionary emancipation of the world's laboring masses. In this connection it is interesting to note that when the International congratulated Lincoln on his 1864 reelection and suggested that the Union had a role to play in liberating the world's workers from the tyranny of capital, he replied through his minister in London that the United States would abstain "everywhere from propagandism and unlawful intervention."[98] This was a restatement of traditional American policy, but by invoking it on this occasion, Lincoln obviously sought to dissociate the Union from any revolutionary cause abroad.

The Civil War nonetheless marked a turning point in the history of organized labor—and not just in America. In Europe the economic distress caused by the war contributed to the rising sense of working-class solidarity that gave birth to the International.[99] In a similar way the war had so severely undermined the economic position of the American worker as to make the growth of a national labor movement inevitable.[100] As early as 1862, pioneer labor leaders like William H. Sylvis began laying the groundwork for national organization. Shortly after the war came the founding of the National Labor Union (NLU). Claiming more than 800,000 members, it immediately began agitating for higher wages and a shorter working day.[101]

The 1860s also witnessed the parallel rise of the French labor movement, which had lain dormant during the first half of Napoleon III's reign. A slight revival of labor activity had begun after 1860, when the emperor relaxed some of the more authoritarian aspects of his regime in an effort to win support from liberals and workers. In 1862 he permitted a French workers' delegation to attend the London Exhibition, where they came into contact with English workers and were greatly impressed by the British trade unions. Thereafter, workers increasingly demanded the right to organize similar labor associations in France. Those demands were partially satisfied by the law of May 25, 1864, which gave them the right to form coalitions and to strike (subject to certain restrictions), and in 1868 the government agreed to tolerate trade unions. Armed with these new rights, French workers launched an active and militant labor movement, forming *chambres syndicales* in all the major cities and organizing a considerable number of strikes during the late sixties. The International, founded in 1864, also became an important center of French labor activism at this time. By the end of the decade, the labor question had become one of the main focal points of opposition to the Second Empire.[102]

Amid this ferment of labor activity on both sides of the Atlantic, French workers were often inspired and encouraged by the progress of their American counterparts.[103] French workers were especially impressed by the agitation for an eight-hour workday in the United States. Launched during the Civil War by

Boston mechanic Ira Steward, the eight-hour campaign soon developed into "a movement which ran with express speed from the Atlantic to the Pacific, from New England to California," as Marx enthusiastically noted in 1866.[104] The movement was further accelerated when the NLU adopted the eight-hour demand at its Philadelphia convention in 1866. Two years later this campaign bore fruit when Congress established the eight-hour workday for all employees of the federal government. Similar laws were subsequently adopted by a number of state legislatures.[105] This example of prolabor legislation was warmly applauded by French workers, whose average workday ranged between eleven and twelve hours at this time.[106]

Despite the utopian claims of many French propagandists, the position of the American worker was actually not so rosy. This was the message that American labor leaders delivered in the late 1860s when they forged their first direct contacts with European workingmen's movements. "Our cause is the same: it is a war between poor and rich," wrote NLU president Sylvis to the General Council of the International in 1869. "Labor is everywhere in an inferior position, capital is everywhere the same tyrant." Describing the plight of the American worker, Sylvis wrote: "The result of our last war has been to build up the most infamous moneyed aristocracy on the face of the earth. This money power is fast eating up the substance of the people. We have declared war on it and think we shall be victorious."[107]

Although the NLU never actually affiliated itself with the International, the two organizations maintained cordial ties. In September 1869 the NLU sent Andrew C. Cameron as a delegate to the International's Fourth Congress at Basel. According to the official report of the congress, the American's arrival in the meeting hall was "an extraordinary event," touching off a long and enthusiastic ovation. Cameron told the assembly that the U.S. political system was controlled by men "whose interests are opposed to our own, and who selfishly seek to perpetuate that opposition." The NLU thus refused to support either of the existing political parties, said Cameron, for it was useless "to hope for reforms from those who have created the evils of which we complain." He further deplored the effects of uncontrolled immigration, which was causing unemployment and depressing the wages of American laborers. He asked the International to cooperate in limiting European emigration to the United States and directing it away from overcrowded urban centers.[108] The firsthand testimony of men like Sylvis and Cameron must have surprised those Europeans who had thought of the Civil War as an egalitarian social crusade and a victory for the American workingman.

Another direct link between the American and European labor movements was provided by Gustave Cluseret, who had returned to the United States in June 1869 following his expulsion from France by imperial authorities. Shortly after his arrival in New York, Cluseret became involved in the labor movement there. In February 1870 he was named by both the International and the Parisian Chambre fédérale des sociétés ouvrières to represent them in the United States.[109] Throwing himself wholeheartedly into his new mission, Cluseret spent most of his time addressing workers' meetings, writing manifestoes, and organizing American sections for the International. "I am preaching the International as Peter the Hermit preached the great Crusade," he wrote to C.-L. Chassin in May 1870.[110] Cluseret's intimate contact with the U.S. labor movement, as well as his acquaintance with important journalists and politicians, put him in an exceptional position to observe American society on the threshold of the Gilded Age. His close-up view was transmitted to his colleagues on the French left through the numerous articles he sent to the leading republican journals back home.

Although he never lost his overall faith in the United States, Cluseret presented a far bleaker picture of the American worker than the one that prevailed in French republican propaganda. Like Sylvis and Cameron, he asserted that U.S. political leaders had no interest whatever in promoting the cause of labor. The Civil War, far from purifying American politics, had opened the floodgates of corruption, plunder, and avarice, with both parties rushing to the trough: "Today Democrats and Republicans have only one thing in view: to steal as much as possible from labor in one way or another. And to arrive more surely at their goal, they are perverting the institutions and violating the sincerity of universal suffrage." The American republic thus faced a critical moment in its existence, for the democratic principle, which the workers represented, was in danger of being destroyed by the capitalists and the politicians. "If the politicians prevail," Cluseret warned, "it will be all over for republican institutions."[111]

The social status of the American worker was also on the decline since the Civil War, declared Cluseret: "Although he is politically free, the working-man is socially the serf of the capitalist, whose demands and influence grow larger each day."[112] America was already beginning to feel "the fatal consequences of the relations that society has established between capital and labor. . . . Workers' meetings, . . . strikes, complaints and misery; in short, the whole traditional European parade of labor being oppressed by the capitalist, such is the spectacle which the big cities and manufacturing centers are beginning to present in America." [113] Formerly so powerful and highly respected, the American workingman now saw his position "threatened today in the New World just as in the Old. . . . The worker must reconquer step by step the whole society that the capitalist has stolen from him." [114]

The Yankee worker's fabled material well-being was likewise deteriorating. The prodigious growth of industrial production during the war had not benefited the workers, Cluseret noted, for prices had doubled or tripled during the 1860s while wages had remained stable. Thus the worker's standard of living was actually much lower than before the war. Moreover, the "constant flow of immigration" had increased competition in the labor market, creating unemployment and pushing down salaries. Nor did the western lands offer a panacea for the social problem, as many people claimed, for "the city worker will never transform himself into a laborer of the fields." [115] From the point of view of political influence, social standing, and material well-being, Cluseret claimed that the workingman was sinking into a position of inferiority in American society.

Despite the discouraging picture he had painted, Cluseret still felt that the United States offered the best chances for the ultimate triumph of labor. "Even with all its vices and pettiness," he wrote, "the great republic is still a hundred leagues ahead of European monarchy." [116] The existence of political freedoms and republican institutions made the organization of labor far easier in the United States than in Europe. Whereas French workers could not speak or meet freely without government harassment, noted Cluseret, the Americans enjoyed "the absolute liberty to say, write and do whatever they please. . . . In the United States, where the workers have all the political liberties, they can free themselves from dependence, from misery, without bloody struggles, and instead of the revolution that is elsewhere inevitable, they can perform a simple and peaceful reorganization." [117] This reorganization would be effected by the establishment of labor associations and cooperatives, through which workers could use their political power as voters and their economic power as producers and consumers to regain their rightful place in American society. Echoing an idea then current among U.S. labor leaders, Cluseret called for the formation of an independent "labor party, organized exclusively by workers and for workers . . . to give assault on the old privileges."[118] If the American workers could succeed in reorganizing society by democratic means, the cause of all workers would be advanced, for the interests of the proletariat were everywhere united.[119]

Cluseret's observations illustrate one of the main problems that the American example posed for those who believed in the necessity of social and economic reorganization. As it was most often used by the republican propagandists under the Second Empire, the American example encouraged an exclusive preoccupation with political institutions. It supported the belief that once a republic was established in France, social equality and material well-being for the masses would follow naturally, without recourse to revolution or socialistic measures. "Pauperism will disappear, and a satisfactory distribution of wealth will be established without violence or expropriation," wrote Eugène Chatard. "It cannot be said that this is an unrealizable Utopia, for this has already been achieved in the united States."[120] To Allain-Targé, the American experience proved that "political equality produces order and well-being for everyone." He hoped that France, like America, would establish a democracy based on "liberty, without which equality is a vain word; political liberty that mixes the ranks and unites men of all origins and all professions under the same flag, in a common cause; liberty whose doctrine has definitely vanquished the primitive socialist theory, that is, the communistic and dictatorial principle."[121]

It was not only bourgeois republicans who used the American example in this way to discredit the collectivist ideal. In 1870 the Parisian worker Denis Poulot declared that "to preach communism in France today . . . is not only inexpedient, it is an enormous blunder. In the United States of America, everyone realizes this. The Americans are made to understand everything, the French still have a long way to go."[122] Thus the American example was not only an effective weapon against the empire, it could also be turned against those on the far left who envisaged a different sort of "workers' republic."

It is not surprising, then, that some socialists and communists expressed reservations about the American model. The Proudhonian journalist A. Planquette, for instance, wrote that while Americans were "ahead of other peoples in their great political institutions," they were "unfortunately far behind from the point of view of economic institutions." Unless these institutions were perfected, he argued, the Americans risked "new secessions and perhaps bloodier struggles than the one they have just survived."[123] The future Communard Gustave Flourens observed that the American republic embodied the same bourgeois principles as the French Third Estate of 1789. The men of 1789, said Flourens, had stood for the power of the bourgeoisie, not of the people; they had understood nothing at all about the question of labor. "The United States of America, which was constituted under the influence of French ideas, is still at that stage," he wrote. "The Third Estate dominates." Rejecting all bourgeois republics, Flourens called for a "true republic . . . which is summarized in one word: Equality."[124]

Eugène Varlin, a militant leader of the International in France, likewise declared that "all the old political forms" were "powerless to satisfy the demands of the people." All existing governments—including the American republic—were based on the principles of "authority and subjugation of the masses," he wrote. "This authority can be more or less rigid, more or less arbitrary, but that does not change the basis of the economic relations, and the workers always remain at the mercy of the holders of capital." Varlin thus included the United States among the oppressive regimes of the past that the revolution would do away with. He held that the "privileges of success" were just as arbitrary as the "privileges of birth," and that it was unjust to put "the public wealth" at the disposal of either privileged class. He complained that "the spirit of individualism, developed to excess in most men," was a major obstacle to the organization of a revolutionary labor movement and to the establishment of true social equality.[125] In sum, Varlin's ideals of collectivism, solidarity, and class struggle conflicted with the very qualities that had made the United States attractive to many Europeans: individual liberty, the spirit of initiative, the opportunities for personal achievement and success, and the "self-made" ideal.

But if certain militants had misgivings about the American example, few dared to attack it outright at this time. This had not been the case before the Civil War, when the far left had vigorously denounced slavery, materialism, political corruption, and other flaws in the American model. But now—in the wake of the Union's glorious military victory, the emancipation of the slaves, and the apotheosis of the worker-president Abraham Lincoln—the American image had become almost sacrosanct. Like the Soviet Union during the first half of the twentieth century, in the eyes of the left, the United States represented "the future that worked." The idea of a triumphant "workers' republic" was so attractive—and so useful for propaganda purposes—that most of those on the French left continued to pay homage to it, even while pursuing goals that were often at odds with everything America really stood for.

French Feminism and the Image of the American Woman

The roots of French feminism go all the way back to the Great Revolution, and diverse voices in favor of women's rights could be heard throughout the nineteenth century. The movement to improve the condition of women was not strictly political, nor were all of its advocates to be found among the ranks of the left. But, in general, feminism advanced apace with the spread of democratic ideas. The emancipation of women had been an integral part of French socialist thought ever since the time of Fourier and Saint-Simon. Later socialist thinkers—with the notable exception of Proudhon—continued to link the cause of women with that of the oppressed masses.[126] But it was only during the latter half of the Second Empire that feminism developed into a distinct and coherent movement in France.

Certain influential republicans like Michelet, Victor Hugo, Jules Simon, and Ernest Legouvé began speaking out in favor of women during the 1860s, and the liberal reforms of 1868 opened the way for more organized agitation. In 1869 the republican journalist Léon Richer launched a feminist newspaper and subsequently founded the Association pour les droits des femmes. A more radical feminist group, the Société pour la revendication des droits des femmes, was formed by Noémie Reclus and André Léo in 1868.[127] The feminist movement was also advanced at this time by public meetings at which the question of women's rights was often debated.[128]

The French feminists of this period drew much inspiration and support from the example of the United States, whose women had long attracted the attention of European observers. In the 1830s Tocqueville had marveled at the freedom, independence, and self-reliance of the American woman. "Nowhere else does her position seem to be higher," he wrote, adding that the "singular prosperity and growing force of this people" owed much to "the superiority of its women."[129] Later travelers had rarely failed to comment (though not always approvingly) on the freedom enjoyed by American women.[130]

But the freedom these observers noted was a relative thing. It existed more in manners and social attitudes than in law. During the first half of the nineteenth century, in fact, the legal and political status of the American woman was little higher than that of her French sister. She could neither vote nor hold public office; if single, she was considered a legal minor (although she paid the same taxes as men); following the traditions of English common law, she was declared "civilly dead" upon her marriage, and her husband became the legal owner of her entire property and income; and she owed absolute obedience to her husband, who was permitted by law to administer corporal punishment to a recalcitrant spouse.[131] Certain legal reforms, mainly in the field of property rights, were adopted by several states starting in the 1840s; but in the United States, as in France, women remained second-class citizens throughout the period under consideration.[132]

Nonetheless, American women did enjoy certain advantages over their French counterparts. In the United States the institution of divorce allowed women to escape from the bondage of an unhappy marriage. For French women, there was no such escape from a cruel, drunken, or adulterous mate: divorce had been abolished in 1816 and would not be reestablished until 1884. With respect to social attitudes, the American girl had far greater freedom to move about, travel, study, and mingle with the opposite sex than the cloistered and chaperoned daughters of the French bourgeoisie. In public places American women were treated with a degree of deference and respect that often surprised European travelers. American girls generally exercised their own free will in choosing their husbands; love and emotional compatibility tended to be the main criteria for the choice of marital partners. In French bourgeois and aristocratic families, marriages were almost always prearranged on the basis of class, fortune, and dowry. Prospective brides rarely had any voice in the matter, and their romantic inclinations received little or no consideration.[133]

One of the greatest concrete advantages enjoyed by the American over the French woman during this period was in the field of education. American girls attended the same primary and secondary schools as boys, and the vast majority of schoolteachers were women. Starting in the 1830s, certain U.S. colleges and universities began to open their doors to women, and by the time of the Civil War, several hundred American women were practicing medicine and law. Nothing like this existed in France: the first state *lycées* for girls were established only after 1867 (and many of these were short lived); women formed a small minority of the secular teaching profession during this period; higher education and liberal professions remained closed to them until much later. Before the coming of the Third Republic, the education of French girls only lasted five or six years and was generally administered by nuns.[134]

American women also enjoyed certain political rights not shared by their

French sisters. Although they could not vote at this time, the republican rights of assembly, petition, free speech, and free press gave American women an opportunity to organize and agitate for reforms long before French women (or men, for that matter) could do likewise. In the United States women first exercised these rights on a significant scale as participants in the abolitionist movement, which became the seedbed of organized feminism. It was while fighting for the freedom of the slaves that the leading American feminists learned the skills of public speaking, organization, and political agitation that later served them in pursuing their own goals.

The Civil War, which marked the triumph of abolitionism, also gave a powerful impetus to the women's movement. The Republican Party's crusade to free Blacks from slavery and give them the vote provided the feminists with strong arguments in favor of their own liberation and enfranchisement. Furthermore, women's active contributions to the war effort—as volunteer service workers, nurses, and teachers to the freedmen—were cited by feminists as proof of their courage and patriotism. The necessities of wartime production had also brought great numbers of women into the workshop and the factory, which prompted the first attempts to organize working women and improve their condition. Out of the ferment of the post–Civil War years, an active women's movement grew up in the United States. Two national women's associations were formed in 1869 and immediately began agitating for the right to vote. Led by former abolitionists like Elizabeth Cady Stanton and Susan B. Anthony, this campaign soon bore fruit in the territories of Wyoming and Utah, where women were voting in local elections by 1870 (although five more decades would elapse before women throughout the country were fully enfranchised).[135]

In the light of all this activity in the United States, it is not surprising that French champions of women's rights should pay close attention to events across the Atlantic as their own movement was beginning to pick up momentum. Indeed, as has often been noted, the gains made by American women during this period greatly inspired the feminist cause throughout Europe.[136] "In the United States more than anywhere else, women have hastened their victory," wrote the radical feminist André Léo in 1869. "They make their demands with a rare vigor and resolution." Although they were still oppressed and exploited, said Léo, they had an immense advantage over their European sisters in their enjoyment of political liberty. America's freedom of press, speech, and assembly enabled them to organize equal-rights associations and agitate for reforms. "Success belongs to energy," she declared. "The women of the United States have powerfully advanced their work." Léo thus recommended the American example of organized agitation as a model for her fellow feminists in France.[137]

Madame A. Gaël, instigator of the John Brown medal subscription and a cofounder of the Société pour la revendication des droits des femmes, likewise declared in 1868 that "the North American women march towards progress more directly than we do; they are our experimenters." The United States, she said, was the vanguard of the "movement in favor of the intellectual and moral development of women taking place in the civilized societies of both hemispheres. The Americans are leading the way."[138]

French travelers of the postwar years, like their predecessors, often took a special interest in the condition of American women. On this subject, probably no French writer was more outspoken than the ardent feminist and republican Olympe Audouard. An attractive young woman, described by one writer as "beautiful, blonde and adventurous," Audouard had left her husband and embraced the literary life at age twenty-five.[139] In addition to writing stories, essays, and novels, she unleashed formidable polemical talents as a lecturer and author of virulent pamphlets proclaiming the intellectual and moral superiority of women.[140] After traveling widely in Turkey, the Middle East, and Russia, Audouard spent ten months in the United States in 1868–69, moving from the East Coast to the Far West, occasionally leaning out a train window to shoot at galloping herds of antelope.[141] (Evidently not averse to the use of firearms, she would later challenge *Figaro* editor Hippolyte de Villemessant to a duel; Villemessant wisely declined.)[142]

On her return from the United States, Audouard launched a vigorous campaign of public lectures intended to vaunt America's democratic system and the liberty enjoyed by its women. The sharp contrasts she drew with the French system earned her a police citation for publicly attacking the imperial government.[143] In fact, her main focus was not on political opposition to Napoleon III but on the social and legal liberation of French women. On that front she was a veritable revolutionary. And she tirelessly waved the American example as a battle flag, not only in her public lectures but also in two hefty travel books describing her experiences in the United States.[144]

Audouard was not an unconditional admirer of American society, but on the subject of women, her praise was unbounded.[145] "These men of the twentieth century," she wrote, "have understood that the human soul is of the same essence, whether its shell be masculine or feminine. They have understood and admitted that knowledge, science, erudition and intelligence . . . are the attribute of both sexes."[146] Thus the Americans had opened the gates of higher education to women, and their experience "triumphantly refutes all the objections made in France against the emancipation of women."[147] It was the unanimous opinion of the Americans, wrote Audouard, that "thanks to the legal emancipation accorded to their women, their intellectual level is at present higher than that of the men."[148] In addition to enjoying full educational equality, she asserted (with some exaggeration), American women found "all careers" open to them: "There are women doctors, women stockbrokers, women sea captains. One hundred thousand of them find honorable and lucrative careers in teaching. . . . In all the institutes and universities, one finds as many women as men among the professors."[149]

Audouard also felt that American women were better off in terms of manners and social conventions. In the coeducational state schools and in daily life, girls mixed freely and naturally with boys. They were informed about the ways of the world from an early age, and when the time came for marriage, they chose their own husbands. Unlike in France, noted Audouard, "marriages of money and speculation are unknown in America. These men, so hungry for gold, nevertheless marry according to their hearts; they marry a woman and not a fortune."[150] Adultery, a veritable epidemic in France, was "excessively rare" in the United States.[151] This was due not only to the possibility of divorce, Audouard felt, but also to "the fundamental honesty of the Yankee character. . . . Don Juans are very rare among them."[152] French men had a hypocritical double standard, regarding a husband's escapades with indulgence but severely punishing a wife's adultery. The Americans, on the other hand, had "one moral code, not two. Not wanting anyone to seduce his wife, the American does not seduce his neighbor's wife."[153] Unmarried girls were also protected against seduction by law and public opinion, which were severe toward seducers and compassionate toward their victims. In France seduction was not even considered a crime, and public opinion put all the blame on the fallen girl.[154] With their virtue thus protected, American women could travel alone without danger or embarrassment, for "the Yankee, better than any other people on earth, understands the respect due a woman."[155] Audouard concluded, "woman is queen in America, every man is ready to serve, aid and protect her."[156]

Although she greatly embellished the picture in order to heighten its polemical value, Audouard was not wrong in her basic claim that American women were far more emancipated than their European counterparts. This view was shared by every French traveler of this period, including those who had no special commitment to the feminist movement. University professor Célestin Hippeau was especially impressed by the achievements of American women during his 1868 visit. In Europe, he noted, the question of woman's intellectual emancipation was still at the speculative stage, but the practical experience of the Americans had already produced "admirable results" in this domain. It was largely because of their access to education, Hippeau felt, that women had gained "a much higher place in this society than in European nations."[157] No less laudatory was Léon Chotteau, who visited the United States in 1867–68. "If the Americans are a great people," he wrote, "they owe it to the American women, to their intelligence and their virtues."[158] The Lyon workers' delegation to the 1876 Philadelphia World's Fair observed: "The condition of women in America is superior to the condition of French women. . . . The laws and regulations are in their favor, and certainly one of the most remarkable facts is the deference and respect that the men manifest towards the women."[159] These workers were particularly impressed by the high intellectual and cultural level of American women, which they attributed to their superior educational opportunities.[160]

Though the American example provided a wealth of precedents and arguments for French feminism, it is not at all clear that it contributed to the women's movement in any substantive way. To a great extent, their different circumstances prevented French feminists from adopting the methods and strategies of the Americans. In the United States the vote formed the main focus of the feminist movement, whereas the French movement was more concerned with civil and social rights than with political ones. Only a small minority of French feminists were demanding the vote, while most of their male defenders opposed their immediate enfranchisement on the grounds that women were still too much under the influence of the Catholic Church and would vote as the priests dictated.[161] Thus, while they admired the gains of the American suffragists, most French supporters of the feminist cause regarded the vote as too distant a goal to base their movement on. They proceeded in a different way, relying on the gradual evolution of public opinion rather than on the open political agitation of the Americans.

Another difference between the American and French movements concerned their relationship to working women and to labor in general. The French movement was dominated by middle- and upper-class ladies, whose concerns with property rights, adultery, seduction, divorce, and higher education passed largely over the heads of working-class women. Female workers had no property to control, often lived in concubinage, and had no realistic chance of pursuing higher education or liberal professions under any circumstances. As it was generally presented in feminist propaganda, the image of the American woman was a bourgeois image and thus had little to do with the needs and concerns of French working women. Much was said about women teachers, doctors, and lawyers in the United States, but almost nothing about the female factory workers, washerwomen, seamstresses, shirt sewers, and cigar makers, who far outnumbered women in the liberal professions. If they thought about her at all, most French observers seem to have imagined the American factory girl in the idyllic setting of Lowell, Massachusetts, whose "model" textile mills were assumed by many to typify industrial conditions throughout the country.[162]

But American industrialism had changed drastically since the 1830s, when Chevalier had observed and enthusiastically described the Lowell mills in his *Lettres sur l'Amérique*.[163] By the time of the Civil War, which brought greater numbers of them into the industrial sector, women formed a significant—and particularly oppressed—segment of the American proletariat. This situation led to the first attempts to organize them, and a number of women's protective associations and trade unions were established in the major American cities during the postwar years. Working women won an important victory in 1868, when the biggest labor organization in the United States, the NLU, officially supported their right to work and demanded equal salaries for them.[164] Many of the postwar male labor leaders, moreover, were favorable toward women's suffrage and other questions raised by the feminists.

In this domain the American example might have provided a useful precedent for improving the miserable lot of French working women, whose condition had been so vividly described in Jules Simon's *L'Ouvrière* (1861). But the organization of working women in France was almost out of the question at this time. For one thing, the bourgeois feminists had little contact with this class and shared few common interests with them. For another, the male proletariat was generally opposed to the idea of gender equality and hostile to female competition: since women were paid only half as much as men, their presence in the labor force caused unemployment and drove salaries down. Apart from Eugène Varlin and a handful of others, French members of the International tended to share Proudhon's contemptuous view of feminists and openly protested against women's right to work in 1866. This attitude would characterize organized labor in France for the rest of the century.[165]

In the fields of politics and labor organization, the American example had little effect on the progress of French women. The same was not true of education, for this was one area where feminist demands fully coincided with the goals of the left opposition. The left, as we have seen, took a vital interest in the question of education. Their anticlerical sentiments made them especially anxious to reform the system of girls' education, which was still dominated by nuns at this time. The call for secular women teachers—for which the American practice was often cited as a precedent—was largely motivated by their desire to take female education out of clerical hands. Give women a secular education based on scientific principles and raise their intellectual level to that of the men, they argued, and you will destroy the ignorance and superstition through which the priests now control them. This view, shared by practically all the republicans, was summed up in Jules Ferry's famous 1870 remark, "Women must belong either to science or to the Church."[166] This phrase came at the end of a long passage praising the intellectual equality of men and women in the United States. The American experience, Ferry declared, "proved abundantly that as soon as women will have a right to an education as complete as that of men, their faculties will develop and we shall see that they are men's equals."[167]

Once they came to power after 1870, Ferry and his fellow republicans made educational reform one of their major concerns. Picking up the pieces of Victor Duruy's abortive efforts, they made some of their most impressive strides in the field of women's education. Women's teacher-training colleges (écoles normales) were established in every department in 1879, the first regular system of girls' secondary education was organized in 1880, the Sorbonne opened its lectures to women that same year, and the Paris law faculty admitted its first female student four years later.[168] As the old barriers were gradually removed, the educational and professional opportunities of French women began to approach those of the Americans by the end of the nineteenth century. American women remained far ahead in the field of civil and political rights, however. They had obtained the vote in a number of states by the end of the century, achieving full suffrage in 1920; French women did not vote until de Gaulle enfranchised them by executive decree in 1945.

French feminists continued to invoke the example of the American woman well into the twentieth century. Yet it was probably not in feminist propaganda that the U.S. example had its greatest influence in France. As Simon Jeune has observed, it was largely through literary works, novels, plays, and later the cinema that the French public became familiar with the image of the American woman.[169] The works of American authors like Louisa May Alcott, Henry James, and Mark Twain, with their portrayals of strong women, were widely translated and much remarked upon in France—not to mention the numerous French novels of this period, often pairing American females with French male characters.[170] These literary portrayals of American woman, Jeune suggests, played an important role both in shaping the expectations of French women and in modifying the attitudes of French society toward its own women.

CHAPTER 16

America's Emergence as a World Power, 1865–1870

Before our war we were to Europe but a huge mob of adventurers and shopkeepers. . . . But a democracy that could fight for an abstraction, whose members held life and goods cheap compared with that larger life we call country, was not merely unheard of but portentous. It was the nightmare of the Old World taking upon itself flesh and blood, turning out to be substance and not dream. . . . The young giant . . . had become the enfant terrible of the human household.

—JAMES RUSSELL LOWELL, 1869

T he United States emerged from the Civil War as a formidable world power—one that would have to be taken into account in any reckoning of international politics. There were indications, moreover, that its traditional aloofness from European affairs might be giving way to a more direct and aggressive role in the world. In June 1865 a permanent U.S. naval squadron plied European waters for the first time since the outbreak of the war, causing much speculation over a new departure in American foreign policy.[1] Secretary of State Seward's 1867 purchase of Alaska and his determined efforts to acquire territory in the Caribbean seemed to foreshadow a new splurge of expansionism. And America's growing hostility to the French presence in Mexico—like its truculent attitude toward England in the *Alabama* dispute—raised the threat of direct confrontations between the triumphant republic and its rivals in the Old World.[2] The "young giant" was clearly flexing its muscles. But whether America's emergence as a world power was, as James Russell Lowell suggested, a "nightmare" to Europeans depended very much on the political orientation of the observer.

In France this situation clearly alarmed the imperial government and the conservative classes in general. An official report on American military strength, ordered by the War Ministry in 1866, judged the United States to be "a maritime and continental power of the first order" and warned of the "dangers . . . to the peace and happiness of the world" that might result from the development of its military might.[3] A similar concern was expressed in the government's 1866 La Valette Circular, which noted that the United States and Russia were growing at a rate that threatened the security of Europe and called for increased unity among the Continental powers.[4] Michel Chevalier, an advisor to Napoleon III and a coauthor of the circular, had developed this theme three months earlier in the *Revue des deux mondes.* The Civil War, he observed, had "taught the United States the profession of arms, and they have given proof of great military qualities." Chevalier predicted that America would surpass Europe "in every domain" within the next three decades and that "armed struggles" between the Old and New Worlds were inevitable. "A divided and disunited Europe," he warned, would suffer "disastrous defeats in such a war as we must foresee."[5] (It is interesting to see men like Chevalier, who had earlier viewed American disunion as essential to European interests, now arguing for European unity to counterbalance the power of the reunited American republic.)

But if the growing strength of postwar America was alarming to many French observers, there was a strong tendency on the left to rejoice in its preeminence. The power of the United States was seen as a formidable weapon in the arsenal of European republicanism, a proof of the superiority of free nations, and, if need be, an active ally in the struggle against despotism. "We all know how well the democracy of the United States has refuted [its critics]," wrote Eugène Pelletan in 1868. "In less than a century, it has grown, by its powerful expansion, to the size of a whole continent and today it can say, without exaggeration, that it will henceforth make the world lean to its side!"[6] Democrats like Pelletan asked nothing better than for France to lean to the American side. To them, the power and prestige of the United States seemed to guarantee the triumph of their own cause.

The Showdown over Mexico

The dénouement of Napoleon III's ill-fated Mexican venture underscored the notion that U.S. power might serve as a weapon for French democracy. The Union victory had left France facing a reunited America whose military machine was in high gear and whose anger over the flouting of the Monroe Doctrine was daily increasing. Although President Johnson had officially declared America's neutrality in Mexico, there were numerous indications of a more belligerent attitude: General Philip Sheridan had 50,000 troops concentrated on the Mexican border, Northern newspapers were advertising for Civil War veterans to join the Juarist forces, and prominent generals like Grant were openly professing their desire to clear the French out at gunpoint. "The most alarming rumors are coming from America," declared the *Courrier français* in May 1865, shortly after General Lee's surrender at Appomattox. "A specter of war is hanging over the Atlantic."[7]

As soon as Seward had recovered from his wounds (he had been stabbed on April 13, 1865, as part of the Lincoln assassination plot), he stepped up his diplomatic demands for French withdrawal. In the fall of 1865, he sent General John M. Schofield to Paris to protest the continuing French presence in Mexico. In December he dispatched a firm message declaring that the failure to withdraw would put Franco-American relations in "imminent jeopardy." Finally, in February 1866 he fired off a virtual ultimatum demanding a fixed date for French evacuation.[8] Faced with the American threats, increasing pressures at home, and a troubled political situation in Europe, Napoleon III finally abandoned Maximilian to his fate. The last French troops left Mexico in March 1867. Captured by the Juarist forces, Maximilian was executed by a firing squad on June 19, 1867.[9]

Though open conflict with the United States was averted, the Mexican affair remained one of the major defeats of Louis Bonaparte's career, and his opponents on the left would continue to exploit it long after the last troops had returned. What made this issue especially attractive to the left was not simply that "Napoléon le petit" had suffered a humiliating setback, but the fact that he had been faced down and forced to withdraw by the great American republic. Paradoxically, this failure of French foreign policy was seen as a victory for French republicanism. "The Mexican retreat is complete and shamefully executed," wrote Henri Allain-Targé in January 1866. "[The emperor] lies, fooling no one, and in order to make people believe that he is not giving in to the United States, he goes down on his knees before them. . . . Never has such a humiliation been so calmly inflicted upon a despot by free men."[10] Referring to Seward's blunt notes demanding withdrawal, Allain-Targé remarked, "if this correspondence shames us as Frenchmen, does it not flatter us as Republicans?"[11]

The war scare over Mexico suggested the possibility that the United States might be drawn into a conflict that would topple the Second Empire and usher in a new republic. Though most French observers apprehended a war with the Americans, certain radicals actually welcomed this eventuality as a means of inciting revolution from without. As early as 1863 the revolutionary Auguste Blanqui had considered this possibility with relish. Napoleon III, he said, would "soon find himself at grips with the United States and I doubt that he will wriggle out of this war as he did in the Crimea and in Italy. If ever . . . a change can come to us from the outside, this is the only place to expect it." [12]

Certain other radicals actively attempted to encourage a Franco-American conflict in Mexico in the interests of European republicanism. In the early months of 1865, the republican exiles Alexandre Ledru-Rollin, Giuseppe Mazzini, and Karl Blind sent President Lincoln a confidential letter urging that he extend the struggle for liberty by launching an attack on imperial forces in Mexico "followed by an effective blow at headquarters in France and elsewhere." [13] In another letter to Lincoln, apparently written on the eve of the Union victory, Ledru-Rollin described the solidarity of interests between the American and European republicans and called on the United States to actively support revolutionary movements in the Old World. This, he suggested, was the recompense due to the European republicans for supporting the Union cause during the Civil War. France, Germany, and Italy were ripe for revolutions, said Ledru. "All they need, to win their liberty, is the assistance of a fraternal government . . . before which . . . the despotisms of Europe could not hold out six months. . . . Would it not be beautiful to see it one day inscribed in history that . . . President Lincoln, while establishing the unshakable foundations of democracy in the New World, contributed to the emancipation of democracy in the Old World?" [14]

If other republicans were not as bold as Ledru-Rollin in claiming their quid pro quo, many of them shared his hope that the United States would go on to attack the sources of European despotism after destroying slavery at home. Victor Considérant developed this theme in a series of letters addressed to Marshal François Bazaine, commander of the French forces in Mexico. Ever since the failure of his Réunion community in 1856, Considérant had been living in a secluded cabin near San Antonio, Texas. He had taken no direct part in the Civil War, although the Confederates offered him a commission in the rebel army upon learning that he was a former French army engineer. [15] From his vantage point near the Mexican border, however, he was an attentive observer of both the American war and the French expedition. In his letters to Bazaine, written shortly after the end of the Civil War, Considérant stressed the futility of the

Mexican venture and warned the marshal to withdraw immediately before the Americans chased him back to France. The Union was justly indignant over a foreign intervention that had sought "to destroy its power, to help divide it and to inoculate this Continent with the virus . . . of Monarchy."[16] Pointing to the buildup of Sheridan's forces in Texas, Considérant said it was only a question of time before the United States moved to enforce the Monroe Doctrine in Mexico. That doctrine was not, as most Europeans believed, an arrogant and selfish attempt to dominate the Western Hemisphere, he argued. It was rather a legitimate expression of America's "right and duty" to protect the principle of self-government from European usurpations. Considérant asserted that the United States had a "legitimate right of direct intervention in all the States of the Americas, from the Behring Strait to Cape Horn." He further urged the Americans to assert their "right . . . to intervene in the affairs of Europe itself."[17]

Not surprisingly, the Civil War veteran Gustave Cluseret was perhaps the most exuberant French champion of America's mission as international protector of democracy. During his long sojourn in the United States, Cluseret had closely followed the evolution of the Mexican venture, aided by confidential information from his former French army comrades serving in Mexico and by official documents furnished by his friend and protector Senator Sumner.[18] His study of this question resulted in a vigorous piece of pro-American propaganda entitled *Mexico and the Solidarity of Nations* (1866). This book argued that Bonaparte's Mexican expedition, like his pro-Southern Civil War policy, was an attempt to "attack the American giant, that living protest of right against might, or liberty against despotism."[19] Cluseret stated that the United States should respond to this aggression by "laying a heavy hand on the crown of Louis Napoleon. . . . What better ally could we have than a French Republic?"[20] He urged the Americans to pursue an aggressive foreign policy aimed at toppling all the monarchies of the Old World. "Life must be made as unendurable as possible to monarchical nations, and our people should be made the constant object of envy and jealousy."[21] Like Considérant, Cluseret believed that such a policy was the logical extension of the Monroe Doctrine, which embodied America's "divine mission" in the world. That doctrine was "destined to fix the battle-field upon which those two principles that have been opposed during so many centuries must come together . . . , freedom and absolutism." It was not only a question of American policy but also of "the future liberty of the world."[22] The Mexican affair, Cluseret declared, was only the precursor of "the irrepressible conflict between the new and old world, the past and the future, Europe and America."[23]

As a naturalized U.S. citizen, Cluseret might be suspected of expressing a purely American viewpoint here. But, in fact, many others on the French left seemed just as "American" as Cluseret during these years, identifying their cause so strongly with the United States that they actually rejoiced over the humiliations it inflicted on the French government. This attitude is all the more remarkable coming from a nation that nearly went to war in 1867—and did do so three years later—to avenge Prussian slights on their "national honor." Yet the American insults did not raise a flicker of patriotic protest from the chauvinistic French left. On the dubious reasoning that "the enemy of my enemy is my friend," American animosity toward Napoleon III was taken as a sign of active sympathy for French republicanism.

Shortly after Grant took office, for example, Léon Chotteau noted with satisfaction: "The incumbent President of the United States professes anything but friendship for the paternal government that is smothering us with its benevolence. . . . Never before has America detested the French government more thoroughly . . . and for good reason."[24] True enough. But like many of his fellow republicans, Chotteau mistakenly assumed that America's contempt for Napoleon III implied a commitment to liberate the French people from their servitude. Chotteau thus hoped that Grant's diplomatic representatives in Europe would "help the enslaved peoples to break their chains. They can do this . . . by establishing direct contacts with the masses."[25]

Charles Delescluze's *Réveil* likewise expressed the opinion that U.S. enmity for the French government was good for the cause of liberty.

> If the American people should one day intervene in European affairs, as everything indicates they will, the influence of American arms will certainly be employed to fight against the influence of French arms. Could the glorious American republic ever forget the moral support that France and England lent to the slaveholders during the Civil War? Meanwhile, as we wait for the inevitable explosion, this hostility has done us a real service. The evacuation of Mexico, solicited, if not imposed, by the cabinet at Washington, has brought some relief to the evils of this deplorable war. . . . [The U.S.] intervention, based on the eternal rules of justice, which are disagreeable to our government, could only have happy

results for our country. Whatever feelings she might have about the personal politics [of Napoleon III] . . . , will not America always be more favorable than hostile towards the peoples?[26]

The radical satirist Henri Rochefort, editor of *La Lanterne,* often gloated over the emperor's humiliation in Mexico and suggested that the United States was helping further the goals of the French left with its unbending defense of the Monroe Doctrine. Commenting on the retirement of American minister John Dix in 1869, for example, Rochefort reminded his readers that he was "the same person who informed Napoleon III that he had forty-eight hours to evacuate Mexico, where he had committed all sorts of atrocities for four years, or else the United States would yank out his ears. . . . And what the Left had not been able to achieve through four years of persuasion, General Dix obtained in five minutes with the threat of a well-deserved chastisement."[27]

Till the end of his reign, Napoleon III's opponents on the left would continue in this way to rub his face in the Mexican debacle and the humiliation inflicted by the American republic. Though the hoped-for U.S. intervention never materialized, the mere threat of it proved to be an effective weapon for the propagandists of the French left.[28]

The American Republic in a Revolutionary World

Having prevailed over the Southern slaveholders and the imperialists at its doorstep, the United States was repeatedly urged to cross the Atlantic and lead the fight for liberty abroad. Had it been so inclined, the late 1860s presented a number of occasions for such action: Italy, Crete, Spain, and Cuba were all rife with revolutionary turmoil during these years. With a powerful naval squadron patrolling the Mediterranean, the United States was in a favorable position for intervention. Thus many French republicans and radicals now expected to see the country swing its weight as vigorously in Europe as it had done in Mexico.

Among the most persistent advocates of American intervention in the Old World were the London-based band of French exiles led by Félix Pyat, known as the "Commune révolutionnaire." Along with his fellow exile Pierre Vésinier, Pyat issued frequent harangues calling for the assassination of Napoleon III and the overthrow of Europe's monarchies by any and all possible means. One of the means he envisaged was the direct assistance of the United States. As early as 1854, Pyat had appealed to America for money and guns to support an armed assault against the empire. He had also sent fellow exile Marc Caussidière on a fundraising tour of the United States, vainly hoping to fill the coffers of the French revolutionaries with American dollars as the Hungarian Lajos Kossuth had done a few years earlier.[29] After the Civil War, Pyat often cited the American republic as a model for European republicans and renewed his appeals for U.S. aid to the revolutionary movements of the Old World. When a revolt erupted in Spain in 1868, causing Queen Isabella to flee the country, Pyat drafted an address on behalf of the Commune révolutionnaire calling on "the great American Republic to use all of its moral and material influence to hasten the triumph of a social democratic and federal Republic in Spain."[30] In a separate address to the Spanish people, he declared: "Only the North American is truly free today. . . . The future is in the democratic republic. Your salvation is there!"[31] Several months later Pyat appealed to President Grant to intervene in Italy, where Garibaldi's red shirts were seeking to drive the Pope and his French protectors out of Rome. From there the United States could unleash revolutionary "pandemonium" throughout Europe. In his typically extravagant style, Pyat exhorted the American president:

> Lend a hand to Garibaldi as you did to Juarez! Rome will be free like Mexico! . . . Hero of the new world, you can become the hero of the old. Chosen leader of the American republic, you can become the chosen leader of the universal republic. Liberator of the African race, you can become the liberator of the human race. You can easily acquire a glory which will cross all the seas and tower over all the mountains. By unleashing Pandemonium, you can merit the admiration, and the gratitude of humanity. Washington proclaimed liberty for the United States. Monroe proclaimed it for the Americas. President Grant, proclaim it for the whole world. You can and must do it.[32]

Hopes of American intervention were also aroused by the 1866–69 revolt of the Greek Christians against their Turkish masters in Crete. Unlike the events in Spain and Italy, which left most Americans indifferent, the Cretan insurrection had touched off a wave of Philhellenism in the United States just as the Greek revolt of the 1820s had done half a century earlier. "The Cretans find much sympathy here," Georges Clemenceau reported from New York in January 1867. "Democrats and Republicans are vying in eloquence and, more to the point, in liberality."[33] Pro-Cretan rallies were held in a number of U.S. cities, and large sums of money were raised for the rebels. Encouraged by these signs, the insurgents appealed directly to the U.S. government for moral and material support. But Congress went no further than to pass a noncommittal declaration of sympathy. Public interest in the question rapidly waned after its initial burst of enthusiasm. By the summer of 1869, the Turks had finally suppressed the rebellion.[34]

The French left, which tended to support revolutionary movements everywhere, naturally sympathized with the Cretan insurgents as they had done with the Poles and the Italians. In 1867 Victor Hugo wrote a widely published address in favor of the Cretans, comparing their leader, General Ioannis Zimbrakakis, to Washington and John Brown as a soldier of liberty.[35] In January 1869 a representative of the Cretan provisional government, Constantin Vouloudaki, set out for the United States in a last-ditch effort to win American aid. Vouloudaki was encouraged in this endeavor by leading French republicans, who feted him during his passage through Paris.[36] At Vouloudaki's request, Hugo wrote an appeal to America on behalf of the Cretan cause, calling on the United States to assume a revolutionary international role:

> Europe refuses its role, America seizes it.
> An abdication is compensated for by a coming [avènement]. . . . Washington will hear the Cretan appeal and will come. Before long, the free American flag will be flying between Gibraltar and the Dardanelles. . . . This marks the arrival of the new world in the old world. We welcome this arrival. America is coming not only to the aid of Greece but also to the aid of Europe. . . . For America, it is the abandonment of local politics and the entry into glory.[37]

Cluseret likewise hoped that the Americans would use the Cretan insurrection to establish their influence in the Mediterranean and from there to republicanize Europe. "You would not believe," he wrote to Charles Sumner in the spring of 1868, "the influence of our country, which is growing daily here [in Europe]. The peoples hope and the governments tremble. Cost what it may, we must have a port in the Mediterranean and we shall have it in '69 through the

Eastern question [Crete] which is more and more attracting my attention."[38] In January 1869 he again wrote to the senator: "I urge you strongly to throw the full weight of your influence in favor of Greece. . . . The fruit is ripe and we are going to pick it."[39] Sometime later, seeing the chance for American intervention slipping away, Cluseret lamented, "this magnificent Eastern complication from which we should have emerged as the first people in the world, master of European destiny, without firing a shot, will all finish up to the satisfaction of Napoleon III."[40]

Just as the Cretan insurrection was flickering out, attention turned to Cuba, where a revolt against Spanish rule had broken out in October 1868. Americans had long taken a special, often predatory, interest in Cuba, whose proximity brought it under the protection of the United States according to the Monroe Doctrine. From the outset of the revolt, the American public showed a strong sympathy for the Cuban cause, with widespread demands for the government to recognize the belligerency or outright independence of the island. These sentiments were echoed in the House of Representatives, which unanimously adopted a pro-Cuban resolution proposed by the expansionist Nathaniel P. Banks in February 1869. A year later the House again declared its sympathy for the cause of Cuban independence and demanded to know why the government could not recognize the belligerency of the rebels. Although President Grant was personally inclined to take this step, he was dissuaded from doing so by Secretary of State Hamilton Fish, who doubted that the rebels could build a stable government and sought to avoid complications with the European powers. Thus in December 1869 and again in June 1870, Grant declared that it was impossible to recognize the belligerency of the Cubans or to aid them with anything but sympathy. Although the insurrection dragged on for ten years, the United States never wavered in its neutrality.[41]

The attitude of the French left toward America's Cuban policy at this time provides striking contrast with that of the 1850s. Before the Civil War, as we have seen, the Americans' enthusiasm for Cuban independence was generally associated with the expansionist designs of the slave power in the minds of French liberals and radicals. The participation of American volunteers in filibustering raids on Cuba had, in fact, contributed much to the left's disenchantment with the United States during that period.[42] But the destruction of slavery in the Civil War seems to have lifted the cloud of suspicion from American motives. "Now that the South is defeated on the battlefields and in public opinion," announced the *Revue du monde colonial* in 1865, "the future will show that Latin America has nothing to fear from the ambition of the men of the North."[43]

Thus, when the latest Cuban insurrection flared up, many French republicans and radicals now actively encouraged the United States to intervene on behalf of the insurgents, to assume the guardianship of an independent Cuba—or even to annex the island—all in the name of universal republican principles. C.-L. Chassin, for instance, hailed the passage of the Banks resolution as a sign that "the American people have decided to push the old world onto the republican road and to avenge, by the multiplication of free nations, the impotent insults of European emperors and kings. The revolutionary propaganda of the United States will soon make itself felt in the Eastern Hemisphere."[44] Reporting the passage of the second congressional resolution in favor of Cuba in 1870, the Civil War veteran Ulrich de Fonvielle declared American recognition to be a virtual fait accompli: "The majority of the citizens of the United States are burning to see the Spanish domination cease. . . . Thanks to the recognition of the Cuban Republic by the United States, we shall soon see the disappearance of the last vestige of slavery, that gangrene that European monarchy bequeathed to the New World."[45]

But the Americans continued to abstain from recognition or intervention, much to the chagrin of those who were counting on U.S. leadership of the worldwide republican cause.[46] Some of the loudest lamentations came from a familiar source, Cluseret, who had seen the Cuban insurrection as yet another opportunity for the United States to extend its dominion over the Western Hemisphere in the name of freedom. Disgusted with America's deepening isolationism, Cluseret tried to convince his friend Sumner to push in the Senate for the recognition and annexation of the island. "You will never make the European people understand the egoism of Washington," he wrote in January 1869. Now that the American republic was "alone able to dictate its will," he argued, "we ought to finish with Cuba and generally all the Antilles to which we are entitled geographically and morally by right of civilization."[47] Following his expulsion from France six months later, Cluseret actively promoted the Cuban cause in New York, where he edited a newsletter and organized rallies for the Cuban junta.[48]

In his semiofficial capacity as propagandist for the junta, Cluseret sent information on the insurrection to leading European republicans and revolutionaries. Hugo, in a total about-face from his prewar criticisms, answered him with a ringing declaration of faith in the United States: "I love America as my own country. The great Republic of Washington and John Brown is a glory to civilization. She must not hesitate to take her rightful place in the government of the world. From the social point of view, let her emancipate the workers; from the political point of view, let her deliver Cuba. Europe has her eyes fixed on America. What America does will be well done."[49]

So tenacious was this image of America as democracy's international gendarme that it seems to have been little affected by the U.S. government's repeated refusal to assume such a role. In his 1869 book on America, Edouard Portalis declared—contrary to all indications—that aid to foreign revolutions was an inflexible axiom of U.S. policy:

> The Americans are so well persuaded that a strong government is a plague, a permanent enemy of order, of property, of progress, that they encourage all the peoples who revolt and lend them a hand.... Their aversion to despotism is the same as it was during their earliest days. Just recently we have seen them support the Fenians in Ireland against the British aristocracy, the Cretans against the sultan, the Spanish liberals against the Bourbons, and the Cubans against the Spanish. The first European nation that will have the courage to free itself will find powerful allies in the Americans. Instead of permanent armies, it will have the alliance of the great American Republic to command respect for it.[50]

It mattered little, apparently, that the North had just upheld the principle of strong government in the Civil War, or that the United States had done nothing to aid the revolutions cited here. The myth was established and hung on doggedly.

As useful as it was for the left's propaganda purposes, the idea of America as ally and protector of European revolutions was pure fantasy. Apart from expressing varying degrees of sympathy, the United States did not aid the revolutionary movements of the 1860s in any way. Postwar America had other things to do besides leading international republican crusades. The Civil War had left behind an immense public debt and the internal problems of Reconstruction, all of which were to keep the country occupied for years. Since the days of Washington, moreover, U.S. foreign policy had been opposed to any kind of interference in the internal affairs of the Old World. If the Monroe Doctrine protected New

World republics from the monarchical encroachments of European powers, it also carried a corollary of nonintervention abroad. The Civil War, contrary to the assumptions of many Europeans, actually reinforced this isolationist tendency. Lincoln and Seward had fought tooth and nail to prevent European monarchies from recognizing what they consistently termed the "revolution" of the secessionists. In opposing the South's attempt at self-determination, they necessarily based their foreign policy on an antirevolutionary ideology.[51]

Seward's whole diplomatic effort was aimed at establishing the Union's status as a legitimate sovereign government fighting to suppress an illegal insurrection. Having succeeded in preventing European interference, he was little inclined to violate that principle by supporting revolts against European sovereigns. It was on these grounds that he had declined to aid Polish independence in 1863.[52] Neither Seward nor his immediate successors saw fit to reverse that policy after the Civil War. American diplomacy consistently renounced the role of active republican proselytism. As in 1848, the left's expectations of the United States far outstripped its desire or capacity to satisfy them.

The United States of Europe

The view of America as a natural ally of European republicanism was encouraged during these years by a movement known as the "United States of Europe." The authorship of this phrase is generally credited to Victor Hugo, who first used it in a speech before the 1849 Paris Peace Conference and thereafter did much to popularize the idea. Although the notion of a European confederation was hardly original with Hugo, he was largely responsible for grafting this idea onto the republican tradition after 1848. By the mid-1860s, the French left was almost unanimously in favor of the United States of Europe.[53]

One of the main sources of support for this idea was the Ligue internationale de la paix et de la liberté, founded in 1867 by the former Saint-Simonian Charles Lemonnier. Its original membership included such eminent figures as Hugo, Garibaldi, Louis Blanc, Jules Barni, Eugène Pelletan, Elisée Reclus, and Edgar Quinet.[54] Through its annual conventions, its newspaper, and the various books published under its auspices, the Ligue internationale preached the United States of Europe as the key to universal peace and brotherhood. A glance at its propaganda immediately reveals the influence of the United States: the success of the American federal system was constantly cited to prove the feasibility of a European republican confederation. "In order to better understand what the United States of Europe can become," wrote Lemonnier, "let us study the United States of America. . . . Let us transport to Europe the political constitution [of the United States]. . . . In place of the United States of America, put the principal nations of Europe . . . so that we would have the United States of Europe on this side of the Atlantic. . . . Who would not be moved by the power, the morality, the greatness of the results?"[55]

Despite the mantra-like references to it, the American union was actually a rather poor model for a European confederation. The common origin and history of the American states, their cultural and linguistic homogeneity, their limited sovereignty, and their integrated economy all created favorable conditions for a type of confederation that could never be duplicated in Europe. But so great was America's prestige during these years that it formed the main model and inspiration for the idea of European confederation.

In fact, the United States was more than a mere model to many partisans of the United States of Europe, who called for an active alliance between the future European federation and the American republic. The future Communard Vésinier, for instance, predicted in 1864 that these "two great confederations of free peoples" would "intervene" together in Asia and Africa "to emancipate the fellah, the coolie and the slave, to sow liberty everywhere and make it grow."[56] C.-L. Chassin, a cofounder of the Ligue internationale, repeatedly asserted that a confederation of European republics would find a natural ally and defender in "the United States of America, increasingly led by European faults to put their immense forces at the service of republican propaganda and to prepare the United States of Europe."[57] The American Republic, said Chassin, would protect the United States of Europe "in every corner of the world."[58]

Considérant also saw America as a model and ally for the United States of Europe. Interviewed in New York shortly before returning to France in 1869, Considérant declared that the Civil War and its aftermath had proven "the superiority of government by the people over that of one person or class." The American example had crushed Europe's "monarchical faith," making the formation of a federative European republic inevitable. "Once that is accomplished," he predicted, "Europe and America will unite to take over the government of the world and control its great interests."[59] Hugo seems to have imagined a sort of symbiotic relationship between America and a republicanized Europe. "Alongside the United States of America, we must have the United States of Europe," he wrote in 1870. "The two worlds must form one single Republic."[60] (This from the man who in 1840 had mocked America as a "soulless" republic and a "cold star" as he bewailed its rising influence in the world.)[61]

Like Hugo, many republicans seem to have assumed that the United States of America would naturally march hand in hand with the United States of Europe once that confederation came into being. But like the calls for American intervention in Crete, Cuba, and elsewhere, these scenarios attributed to the United States an activist international role that it was not yet prepared to assume. Many of these extravagant visions linking the United States of Europe with the United States of America also implied an American commitment to a far more radical brand of democracy than the Yankees themselves practiced at home. Socialist partisans of the United States of Europe might imagine, with the republican exile Amedée de Saint-Ferréol, that "the democracy of the old world will join its red flag to the star-spangled banner of the young United States of America," but the Americans' hostile reaction to the Commune would soon give the measure of their sympathy for French radicalism.[62]

American Expansionism in the Western Hemisphere

If America declined to interfere in the affairs of the Old World during these years, it seemed less timid in its own hemisphere. Held in check during the Civil War, the old expansionist urge began to reawaken afterward, enhanced by the belief that the United States was now the world's strongest military power.

The most ardent American expansionist of these years was Secretary of State Seward, who took advantage of the free hand given him in foreign affairs to launch a number of annexation projects during the Johnson administration. In 1866 he had begun negotiating with Denmark for the purchase of two Caribbean islands. He also recommended the annexation of the republic of Santo Domingo, whose president, Buenaventura Báez, had proposed that the island be taken under U.S. protection. While these negotiations were in progress, Seward seized upon Russia's sudden offer to sell Alaska to the United States. With his customary alacrity, the secretary railroaded a hastily drafted treaty through Congress in April 1867. A territory twice the size of Texas thus passed into American hands for $7,200,000. But the unpopularity of the Alaska purchase—derided by critics as "Seward's icebox" and "Seward's folly"—ultimately compromised his other expansionist projects. Congress began to show a growing reluctance to purchase and administer new territories at a time when the country faced a staggering war debt and grappled with the internal problems of Reconstruction. When Grant took office in 1869, he attempted to revive the Santo Domingo question and sent an emissary to the island to negotiate an annexation treaty. But the Senate finally rejected the agreement in 1870, thus ending the brief flurry of postwar expansionism.[63] Although the old urge for national aggrandizement was still alive, the economic and political circumstances of Reconstruction America were not yet ready to support the sort of imperialism that would erupt three decades later with the Spanish-American War of 1898.

Apart from the purchase of Alaska, these post–Civil War stirrings produced few concrete results, yet they aroused much interest and discussion in Europe. The French government was understandably alarmed at the prospect of unchecked U.S. expansion, a prospect that was especially disquieting since America's closest ally at this time seemed to be that other irrepressible giant, Russia. Already the two superpowers of the future seemed to be threatening Europe from both sides.[64] Concern over American expansion was also shared by certain liberals like Adolphe Thiers, Emile de Girardin, and L.-A. Prévost-Paradol, who bewailed France's shrinking influence in a world increasingly dominated by Anglo-Saxons.[65] Moving further to the left, however, one finds a great deal of enthusiasm for the idea of U.S. expansion. Many French republicans—like the Americans themselves—described the territorial aggrandizement of the United States in terms of "extending the area of freedom." It is not surprising that Americans should speak in these terms: like the justifications of the European colonialists, such a view provided a humanitarian rationale for what might otherwise appear to be (and most often was) naked self-interest. What is surprising is to hear America's "Manifest Destiny" ideology being spouted by prominent figures on the French left, traditionally a very chauvinistic breed.

Before the Civil War, as we have seen, most French republicans had opposed American expansionism because of its association with the slave power.[66] In 1851, for instance, Victor Schoelcher had written that, while the spread of free institutions was theoretically a good thing, European democrats would continue to denounce America's expansionist drives as long as the "stain of slavery" tarnished the U.S. Constitution.[67] But emancipation had removed this objection and thus freed the French left to use America's territorial growth—along with its military strength, prosperity, and political freedom—as a propaganda weapon to promote their own goals at home. During the postwar years, most French republicans had come to agree with Théodore Duret that "American expansion is indeed a magnificent spectacle, for it shows what can be achieved . . . by the union of democracy and liberty."[68]

So far did the left identify with America's democratic principles that they tended to interpret the extension of U.S. power and influence in the world—even when achieved at the expense of French national interests—as a victory for their own cause. In an 1869 attack on Napoleon III's foreign policy, Chassin fairly gloated over the fact that the United States was "ruining, in all of South America and even the Antilles, the few French influences and relations that have survived the irreparable faults of the Second Empire. Haiti, like Cuba, is gradually falling into the hands of the United States, and it is not difficult to foresee the day when the Old World will have no more colonies in the New."[69]

Writing in the *Démocratie* in 1870, Claude Sauvage expounded a sort of "domino theory," whereby most of the Western Hemisphere was destined to be absorbed by the United States. This ineluctable process was already well underway, said Sauvage, pointing to the "forthcoming" annexations of Santo Domingo, Haiti, and Cuba. Far from causing alarm, American expansion was seen as a victory for republican principles and a beneficial lesson for Europe: "The great American Republic never ceases to spread its direct action, because this action in no way resembles a conquest; the populations that are annexed to the United States, without losing their nationality, merely grow in liberty and prosperity. . . . Let us little Europeans, unitary and monarchist as we are, admire the all-powerful idea of the federal republic, and let us hasten to apply it to ourselves, if we do not wish our decadence to become irremediable."[70]

Ulrich de Fonvielle likewise seized upon the rumored American annexations to score a few easy propaganda points against the empire: "Whole populations are now seeking to be annexed to the Great Republic. [This is] the logical consequence of a sensible, honest, moderate and economical government, without a court or courtiers, without useless standing armies, without exorbitant budgets, without secret funds, pensions, subsidies, etc., etc. How many peoples have asked to be annexed to France since the creation of the Second Empire?"[71]

It is ironic that these French republicans imputed such high ethical motives and beneficial results to America's expansionist activities, for the same activities would have been loudly denounced had they come from Prussia, Austria, England—or even imperial France. Where the American republic was concerned, it seems, the hard rules of realpolitik had been suspended in the eyes of the French left.

The American Republic and the French Spirit of '92

The widespread tendency to exalt American power and glory illustrates the profound change that was taking place in the left's image of the United States during the postwar years. Ever since the French Revolution, the left had nurtured an extremely chauvinistic view of their country's "mission" to democratize the world and universalize the *droits de l'homme*.[72] The revolutionary messianism of the French left had reached a peak in 1848, when a chain reaction of European uprisings followed the February Revolution. For a brief moment, France did seem to be spreading the republican gospel to its Continental neighbors. As Hugo grandly proclaimed in March 1848, "Every nation should be happy and proud to resemble France!"[73]

But the coup d'état of 1851 had reduced the French left to such a state of impotence that their messianic self-image lost much of its credibility. Thus they were tempted to look elsewhere for their own (and the world's) political salvation. The American Civil War, coming at a time when reaction seemed firmly entrenched in France, revived their hopes and suggested that the "spirit of '92" was still burning in the New World. Morally cleansed and militarily triumphant, America emerged from the war with an enhanced democratic and egalitarian image, appearing as the new torchbearer of the Revolutionary tradition.

"The great humanitarian stance that the America of 1869 has taken over from the France of 1792," wrote Chassin, "proves to us that, despite the terrible fault we have committed in abandoning our own glorious republican tradition, our principles are becoming universal and will soon triumph."[74] In his 1869 book on military reform, Cluseret similarly declared, "By taking up the liberating mission abandoned by France, America has won her place in the sympathy of the peoples."[75] Hugo, in his appeal for Crete, exhorted the United States to seize the international role "abdicated" by France at the head of the revolutionary movement.[76] "America picked up in 1860 the revolutionary work momentarily abandoned by France," wrote the Proudhonian pamphleteer and future Communard Benjamin Gastineau at the end of the Civil War.[77]

Such comments suggest that postwar America was becoming a sort of surrogate for the messianic ideals of the French left. This reaction is all the more remarkable since the United States and France were, in Michel Crozier's phrase, "both sisters and rivals" in their claims to embody the universal values of liberty, democracy, and human rights.[78] For French leftists to concede the advantage to the Americans, even temporarily, represented an extraordinary shift in their thinking and their rhetoric. Yet even to some of the most diehard chauvinists, America seemed to be supplanting France as the world's chief disseminator of democratic ideals at this juncture.

One striking example is the high priest of French supremacy, Jules Michelet. As a historian, Michelet had made a career of glorifying France's preeminent place in the universe. At the same time, he had taken a condescending, often hostile view of the American parvenus. In 1831, for example, he wrote that the French people were "interested in the liberty of the whole world.... Every single thought of nations is revealed by France.... The youngest and most fecund nation in the world is not America, that serious child who will imitate for a long time to come. It is old France, rejuvenated by the spirit."[79]

But the experience of the Second Empire and the spectacle of the Civil War seem to have reversed these roles in Michelet's mind. Shortly after the Union victory, he jotted in his journal, "Is the Occident worn out, divided?—will America be her inheritor? ... Welcome, young child! You are the youngest and greatest, but are you yet capable?"[80]

Michelet's view of the United States became increasingly positive over the next few years. In 1867 he wrote that France should be proud of having aided the American Revolution, "when we have the joy of seeing this great America rising so high in its immensity,—the pride, the hope, the salvation of the world.... She opens and illuminates the future by her great examples, by the solidity of her government, in the face of a wavering Europe which cannot take a step without the earth crumbling beneath her feet."[81]

Three years later, his hopes for Europe further shaken by the outbreak of the disastrous Franco-Prussian War, Michelet again put his faith in the United States to regenerate the world: "America, daughter of Europe, is today her mother in democracy. [America] gives birth to her in liberty."[82] He could never have written those lines before the Civil War.

M ichelet's conversion to faith in the United States reflects the experience of the French left in general during these years. Having nurtured a certain image of France's revolutionary mission in the world, they were perplexed by its failure to live up to that image under the Second Empire. So they tended to project it onto the triumphant American republic. This way of thinking may have satisfied their psychological and ideological needs, but it did not generate much insight into the attitudes and motives of the Americans themselves. Often excessive and unrealistic in their claims for France, the left developed excessive and unrealistic expectations of America. This was all very well as long as these expectations remained in the realm of propaganda and rhetoric. But a big disappointment was in store in 1870, when something more substantial was needed to save the fledgling Third Republic from the Prussian invaders.

PART IV

L'Année Terrible and Beyond

O STAR of France!
The brightness of thy hope and strength and fame,
Like some proud ship that led the fleet so long,
Beseems to-day a wreck, driven by the gale—a mastless hulk;
And 'mid its teeming, madden'd, half-drown'd crowds,
Nor helm nor helmsman.
Dim, smitten star!
Orb not of France alone—pale symbol of my soul, its dearest hopes,
The struggle and the daring—rage divine for liberty,
Of aspirations toward the far ideal—enthusiast's dreams of
brotherhood,
Of terror to the tyrant and the priest. . . .
O star! O ship of France, beat back and baffled long!
Bear up O smitten orb! O ship continue on!
—WALT WHITMAN, "O Star of France, 1870–1871"

The Franco-Prussian War triggered the downfall of Napoleon III, the birth of the Third Republic, and, as a devastating aftershock, the bloody revolt of the Paris Commune. As the shattered country struggled to reassemble the pieces, the American example suddenly seemed to lose its relevance to the French left. There were many reasons for this: President Grant's undisguised preference for Prussia was seen as a betrayal of all the French; the leaders of the new regime found the American system at odds with the centralized parliamentary republic they envisioned; and the radical left saw the United States as a bastion of the kind of bourgeois republicanism that they rejected. In the wake of 1870–71, the left's former infatuation with the American model quickly faded.

CHAPTER 17

The Empire Strikes Out

No one on your side. All are agreed. This one,
Named Gladstone, says thanks to your executioners!
This other one, named Grant, mocks you. . . .
There is not one who doesn't spit in your face
As you hang on the cross.
Alas! What have you done to these nations?
You came to the side of those who wept, with these divine words:
Joy and Peace!—You shouted: Hope! Jubilation!
—VICTOR HUGO, "A la France."

On May 8, 1870, Napoleon III won a resounding victory when voters overwhelmingly supported the plebiscite on his liberal reforms.[1] As a result, despite the mounting republican opposition, the future of both the imperial regime and the Bonapartist dynasty seemed secure. The following month Prime Minister Emile Ollivier confidently declared that "at no other moment has peace in Europe appeared more assured."[2] Nineteen days later France declared war on Prussia.

The conflict had numerous underlying causes, but the main one was French concern over Prussia's rising power as Otto von Bismarck pursued the unification of the German states under the rule of Prussian king Wilhelm I. Bismarck calculated that a successful war against France would allow him to bring the remaining German states under his tent and make Prussia the supreme power in Europe. Like a master chess player, he used a dispute over the succession to the Spanish throne, and an insulting diplomatic telegram, to trick Napoleon III into committing a fatal error. The aging emperor fell for the gambit, and France declared war on July 19. In an upswell of patriotic fervor, crowds filled the streets of Paris with cries of "Vive la guerre!" and "A Berlin!" And thus the outmanned and ill-prepared French army set out to face Europe's most formidable military machine.

It is ironic that the event that finally brought down the Second Empire and ushered in the Third Republic also marked the end of the left's infatuation with America. Having held the United States in such exaggerated esteem during the preceding decade, French republicans were astounded to see the sentiments of the American people running strongly in favor of the Prussian invaders following the outbreak of hostilities. The main reason for this, as Gustave Cluseret noted, was that Americans could not forgive "Napoleon III's hatred for the great American Republic, which he tried to divide and ruin; all the services of Lafayette will not prevail against the resentment that is in every heart here."[3]

On the whole, Cluseret's observation was correct: the leaders of the American government and the vast majority of the population preferred Protestant Germany to the Roman Catholic empire that had encouraged their country's dismemberment and challenged them in Mexico. Judging imperial France to be the unprovoked aggressor in the affair, many Americans shared James Russell Lowell's sentiment: "Anything that knocks the nonsense out of Johnny Crapaud will be a blessing to the world."[4] This reaction was logical and foreseeable. But the fiercely patriotic French republicans, who only weeks earlier had gloated over America's hostility to the empire, could not easily accept the American preference for the Teutons who were invading their homeland and humiliating their armies.

To be sure, Americans were not unanimous in their support for Prussia. Among the nearly 5,000 Americans living in Paris at the outset of the war, many were dedicated Francophiles who sided with their host country. The Southern contingent, disproportionately large among these innocents abroad, remembered Napoleon III's preference for the Confederacy during the Civil War and tended to sympathize with the French. Some even gave more concrete support to the cause. Dr. Thomas Evans, the emperor's American dentist and confidant, set up a well-equipped field hospital, the American Ambulance, to treat wounded French soldiers brought back from the front. Up to 50 Americans and dual nationals died fighting as volunteers with the imperial forces. Back in the United States, there were currents of sympathy for France, not only in the South but also among Northern Democrats and Irish immigrants. But they represented a minority voice in a public opinion that largely sided with the Germans and was widely echoed in the U.S. press.[5]

Although he officially proclaimed American neutrality in the conflict, President Grant made no secret of his personal pro-German sympathies.[6] General Philip Sheridan, a famous Civil War hero, accompanied Prussian forces into the field as an observer.[7] The American minister in Berlin, George Bancroft, was an intimate friend of Bismarck's and an overt partisan of the German cause. Bancroft's counterpart in Paris, Elihu B. Washburne, though less biased in his attitude toward the belligerents, also blamed France as the sole aggressor and felt that the Prussian retaliation was justified.[8] Despite his efforts at evenhandedness, Washburne, a close personal friend of President Grant, inevitably aroused suspicions by agreeing to oversee German interests in France during the war. Although he undertook this responsibility with the permission of the French foreign ministry, Washburne's role as protector of German subjects and property won him the hostility of many patriotic Frenchmen, some of whom even suspected him of being a spy for Bismarck.[9]

The German chancellor hardly needed the help of a diplomatic spy in Paris. From the beginning of the conflict, his armies under Field Marshal Helmuth von Moltke outnumbered and outmaneuvered the French. On July 28 Napoleon III left Paris to take over the command of his embattled forces. Old and sick, suffering from bladder stones so painful that he could not even sit on a horse, he joined Marshal Patrice de MacMahon's army at Châlons, hoping that his presence would "magnetize the troops in the field."[10] Instead, his confused orders merely contributed to the fog of battle. On September 1 disaster struck the French: MacMahon's 100,000-man army was bottled up in the eastern town of Sedan. The marshal himself was gravely wounded and his troops decimated in the fighting. Napoleon III intentionally exposed himself to the enemy fire, hoping to fall honorably in battle. Failing to get himself killed, he ordered the white flag hoisted over the besieged citadel. On September 3 the Empress Eugénie, who had served as regent in Paris since the emperor's departure, received a brief dispatch from her husband: "The army is defeated and captured; I myself am a prisoner."[11] By that time, the Prussians were marching toward Paris.

Amid the spreading panic in the capital, the empress tried to rally her ministers and salvage the Bonapartist regime as crowds filled the streets and clamored for a republic. On the afternoon of Sunday, September 4, with angry hordes rattling the gates of the Tuileries Palace, Eugénie departed incognito in a horse-drawn cab. She arrived unannounced at the home of Dr. Evans, who exfiltrated her to Trouville and put her on a private yacht bound for England.[12] Her flight, paralleling that of Louis-Philippe twenty-two years earlier, marked the end of a reign. Later that afternoon the flamboyant Léon Gambetta climbed up on the sill of an open window of the Hôtel de Ville and, in his lilting southern accent, announced the birth of the Third Republic to the surrounding crowd. "Louis Napoleon Bonaparte and his dynasty have forever ceased to reign in France," he shouted.[13]

The September 4 proclamation touched off a momentary resurgence of sympathy between the "Sister Republics." Washburne was ecstatic over this sudden turn of events. "I am rejoiced beyond expression at the down fall of this miserable dynasty and the establishment of the Republic," he wrote to his brother back in Washington. "You never saw anything so quickly or handsomely done as this Revolution. It seems to me, even now, like a dream."[14] As in 1848, the United States was the first nation to recognize the new regime, an act marked by a cordial exchange of declarations between Washburne and the new foreign minister, Jules Favre.[15] A large crowd of French citizens gathered at the American legation to thank the U.S. minister.

Widely applauded in the republican press, the American recognition encouraged hopes of more active aid as France's provisional Government of National Defense continued the fight against the rapidly advancing enemy. Some in France even entertained fantastic dreams of seeing an American expeditionary force arrive to deliver them from the Teutonic grip.[16] This view, widely repeated in the French press, was judged a "strange hallucination" by Robert Sibbert, a Philadelphia physician living in Paris. "The example of Lafayette . . . is prominent before them," he wrote, "and they refuse to believe that assistance will not be sent."[17] Such hopes were, of course, groundless: no more in September 1870 than in December 1851 were Americans disposed to intervene militarily on behalf of a French Republic, however much they might sympathize with its principles. "Even if he existed," wrote the future Communard Armand Lévy, "an American Lafayette would be vainly awaited in France. . . . If we expect our salvation to come from anything but our own efforts, we will soon have to say bitterly: God is too high and the United States too far away."[18]

But if an armed U.S. intervention was obviously out of the question, there still seemed to be a possibility of American assistance on the diplomatic front. On September 12 Favre asked Washburne to use his good offices to obtain a swift and honorable peace from the Prussians. Upon querying Berlin, however, the State Department was informed that Bismarck had categorically rejected all outside interference. The U.S. government thereafter renounced any mediation efforts.[19] All realistic hope of American assistance had evaporated by the time of Grant's December 5 message to Congress, which ruled out U.S. participation in a peace mission unless requested by both parties.[20]

The failure of American mediation was a great disappointment for the French, who now found themselves almost completely isolated on the diplomatic front as they pursued an increasingly desperate military campaign. On January 26, 1871, with Paris besieged and battered by German artillery shells, the French government, led by Adolphe Thiers, finally surrendered and negotiated an armistice with Bismarck.

Any faith that French republicans may have retained in American friendship was shattered by Grant's message of February 7, 1871, which warmly congratulated the victors on the constitution of the new German Empire under the leadership of the Prussian king. The president enthusiastically declared: "The union of the states of Germany into a form of government similar in many respects to that of the American union, is an event which cannot fail to touch deeply the sympathies of the people of the United States. . . . The adoption in Europe of the American system of union, under the control and direction of a free people, educated to self-restraint, cannot fail to extend popular institutions and to enlarge the peaceful influences of American ideas."[21]

The French were stunned by Grant's message, which was published in French newspapers shortly before the German armies were to make their triumphal march through Paris, as stipulated by the armistice.[22] Hugo poured his outrage into the verses of his *L'Année terrible*.[23] Like the execution of John Brown twelve years earlier, Grant's "atrocity" had shaken Hugo's faith in the United States:

> It is because of him that a grieving history will one day say:
> —France aided America, and drew
> Its sword, and gave everything to deliver her.
> And, people, America stabbed France!— . . .

[Grant] displays before the universe, on a shameful chariot,
America kissing the heel of Caesar.[24]

Hugo's indignation was shared by Frenchmen of all political colors, but resentment was especially strong among republicans, who had held this Civil War
hero in such high esteem only a few months earlier. So tenacious was their bitterness that when Grant died in 1885, he was widely criticized in the French press
as an enemy of France and a traitor to the republican cause.[25]

CHAPTER 18

Paris in Arms!

When the crowd, now silent,
Will roar like the Ocean,
And be prepared to die,
The Commune will rise again.
We shall return in countless masses,
We shall arrive by every road, avenging specters,
We shall come holding hands.
—LOUISE MICHEL, May 1871

It is a riot of madmen and idiots mixed with bandits.
—GEORGE SAND, 1871

The Prussians were not the only enemies the new republican regime had to contend with. Almost immediately after September 4, 1870, various radical elements in Paris launched a furious propaganda campaign against the more moderate leaders of the Government of National Defense. Preaching a combination of revolutionary and patriotic ideals, the far left intensified its agitation as the siege wore on and French military hopes waned. By the time the armistice was signed, the government faced an insurrectionary threat more formidable than the Prussian battalions. It did not help the Parisians' mood that the National Assembly elections in early February produced a monarchist majority, largely on the strength of the rural vote, or that the formal peace treaty, signed on February 19, 1871, imposed harsh terms on France: the loss of Alsace and part of Lorraine and a staggering five-billion-franc indemnity to Germany.[1]

Enraged by the surrender and humiliated by the Germans' triumphal march through the capital on March 1, rebellious units of the Garde nationale refused to disarm as stipulated by the armistice. On March 18 Thiers sent a regular army force to the largely working-class district of Montmartre to seize the cannons that had been amassed there. The Garde nationale troops, backed by an angry mob, refused to give them up. The tide turned against the regulars when one of their regiments turned their rifle butts in the air and joined the rebellion.

Georges Clemenceau, then mayor of the eighteenth arrondissement that included Montmartre, later described the scene he witnessed that day: "Suddenly a terrific noise broke out, and the mob which filled the courtyard burst into the street in the grip of some kind of frenzy. Among them were chasseurs, soldiers of the line, National Guards, women and children. All were shrieking like wild beasts without realizing what they were doing. I observed then that pathological phenomenon which might be called blood-lust."[2]

Amid the melee, two army generals were seized and executed, their bodies abused by the mob and, according to some reports, urinated on by several women in the crowd.[3] As word of the insurrection spread, barricades sprang up throughout Paris, prompting Thiers and his government to abandon the capital and retreat to Versailles. It was the beginning of the bizarre seventy-day episode known as the Paris Commune, during which the city was ruled by a ragtag band of citizens and besieged by the Versailles troops, all under the watchful eye of Prussian forces, which remained on the outskirts of the city.

Many causes had contributed to the Parisian revolt: the sense of being betrayed by the government's capitulation, the long months of misery and privation during the German siege, the frustrated socialist and democratic aspirations of the Parisian workers, the desire for local self-government, hostility toward the conservative rural populations, and the revolutionary fervor of the neo-Jacobins and Blanquists prominent among the Communards. Though the rhetoric of the Commune was often tinged with Proudhonist and other socialist doctrines, it is impossible to ascribe any single ideology to this movement; the motives, ideals, and backgrounds of those who participated in it varied greatly.[4] Yet it is safe to say that it was a movement of the left, fiercely dedicated to the principles of republicanism and patriotism.[5]

It is interesting to note how many of its supporters had counted among the admirers of the American republic during the preceding decade. Under the Second Empire, as we have seen, Communards like Cluseret, Reclus, Vésinier, Pyat, Lissagaray, Rochefort, Vermorel, Lullier, and others had often used the American example to promote democratic ideas. After the insurrection of March 18, a number of Communard papers explicitly identified their cause with that of the American republic. The Commune's *Journal Officiel,* for example, declared on March 31: "The people have come of age, as in the United States, and they intend to govern themselves. . . . A new age has begun, the age of the worker, *novus ordo soeculorum,* as the Americans say. For a new age, a new flag, . . . the red flag!"[6] The republican press baron Edouard Portalis, who sympathized with the Commune but did not join it, explicitly linked the Parisian insurrection to the North's fight for "free labor" during the American Civil War. The predecessors of the Communards, he declared, were "Lincoln, Henry Ward Beecher, Grant and all those great spirits who demanded the emancipation of labor, of which the freeing of the Negroes was only a consequence." The true cause of the Union, said Portalis, had been that of "proletarians struggling against the encroachments of parasitism. . . . In fact, the Civil War was only one more episode in the old struggle between equality and liberty on one hand, and on the other, the egoism of those *ambitious* and *over-fed* men who want to *monopolize wealth and exploit labor.*"[7] Portalis's astounding conclusion: "the fight that is now raging under the walls of Paris is only the sequel and continuation of that war."[8] Lincoln would have turned over in his grave at the suggestion that he shared a common cause with the "secessionists" of the Commune. But that conclusion did not seem so illogical to those on the French left who had interpreted the Civil War in terms of their own ideology.[9]

Such allusions to the American example were largely rhetorical. But in at least one area, the U.S. model had a particular relevance to the Commune. In seeking to wrest the city of Paris from the control of a conservative national government, the Communards were reacting in part to twenty years of oppressive imperial centralization. But they were also giving a positive expression to federalist ideas popularized by Proudhon and others during the 1860s.[10] Indeed, as Roger L. Williams has observed, the overarching idea of the Commune was federalism—the replacement of "the nation-state with a federal state" comprising "small self-governing groups or units."[11] While it would be a mistake to exaggerate the American influence, a number of Communards explicitly cited the United States as a model of the sort of communal federalism they sought to establish in France.

In the opinion of Gustave Cluseret, who served as the Commune's war minister *(Délégué à la guerre),* the American example was paramount:

> The Central Committee and the International always followed the practical road of the communal revolution. For them, as for me, the revolution of 18 March never did and never will mean anything but the Municipal Council invested with full powers to control all the interests of the commune without exception, and attached to the central power by a simple federal bond, as in America. After eighty years of experience, the American system is obviously practicable, for not only has it survived, it has also succeeded in assuring the liberty and prosperity of a great people. The secret of her prosperity is to be found in the liberty and economy promoted by the independence of the communes. What is good for America is good for France.[12]

According to Cluseret, the Commune was directly—indeed, almost exclusively—inspired by the American example. Others voiced the same view. Charles Lullier, who served briefly as the Commune's military chief, declared that he had fought for the sort of "municipal liberty" that had existed "in the United States since its founding." Defending himself before a military court after the fall of the Commune, Lullier told his inquisitors: "My political ideas are those that predominate on the other side of the Atlantic; my principles are those that reign over the free land of the United States. Nothing more, but nothing less. I have drawn my convictions from this source; this civilization has furnished my models and guides. . . . These principles, to which I have devoted my whole life, were endangered by the Assembly of Bordeaux. I drew my sword in order to save them."[13]

Pierre Vésinier, who had earlier eulogized John Brown, declared in April 1871 that "the communes of France in general, and that of Paris in particular, must become revolutionary, democratic and social federations. . . . Paris will be the Washington of France."[14] Pierre Denis, a Proudhonian socialist on the staff of Jules Vallès's *Cri du peuple,* suggested that Paris and Versailles could come to terms with each other by agreeing to form "a peaceful federation [like] the United States."[15]

This idea probably received its fullest expression from Emile de Girardin, who sympathized with many of the grievances of the Communards, though he did not participate in their movement. On May 5, 1871, Girardin founded a newspaper, *L'Union française,* in which he promoted the idea of saving France by copying the U.S. federal system. His plan called for the division of France into fifteen states, each with its own senate and chamber of deputies. The proposal won some support, but the Commune finally suppressed his paper. (Girardin then went to Versailles, made his peace with Thiers, and began attacking the Commune in the press.)[16]

The Commune focused national attention on the issues of decentralization and federalism, but the movement ultimately tended to discredit these ideas in the eyes of most republicans. Denouncing the Communards before the National Assembly at Versailles in May 1871, Ernest Picard told his colleagues: "They call themselves federalists. Well, gentlemen, you may entertain whatever opinions you like on federalism and the Girondists; but he who professes such opinions under the present circumstances, in the face of a foreign enemy who occupies France, is a destroyer of national unity, and deserves not the least bit of sympathy or indulgence from any school or party."[17]

This view was shared by most of Picard's fellow republicans in the wake of 1870–71. Following the brutal repression of the Commune, the influence of the Proudhonian and socialist decentralists virtually disappeared from the republican ideology. Once again, as in 1848, it was the monarchists who called for decentralization, while the republican leaders—men like Gambetta, Ferry, and Thiers—emerged as champions of the one and indivisible state. This is one of the reasons why the American model had less relevance to French republicanism after 1871.

The Communards were mistaken if they imagined that some affinity existed between the Stars and Stripes and their red flag, which American minister Washburne cursed in May 1871 as "that hated emblem of assassination and pillage, anarchy and disorder."[18] Washburne's sentiments were shared by the vast majority of his property-minded countrymen, and the American press denounced the Communards in the most violent terms. Nor was America's opprobrium limited to the insurgents themselves. As they had done after June 1848 and again after the 1851 coup d'état, many Americans contemptuously pronounced the whole French people incapable of self-government and suited only for some form of authoritarian discipline.[19]

And yet, as Philip M. Katz has shown, there were pockets of American sympathy and support for the Commune.[20] In addition to Cluseret, a number of Americans and dual-nationals actually fought alongside the Parisian insurgents. Analogies to the Civil War were frequent in the U.S. press, and many Southerners identified the Communards' attempted secession with their own Lost Cause.[21] (Thiers also made this analogy, vowing that "any attempted secession . . . will be energetically repressed in France as it has been in America.")[22] Some American labor activists, including the former abolitionist Wendell Phillips, defended the Commune as a heroic workers' movement. In one of the most surprising reactions, General Benjamin "Beast" Butler, the infamous first commander of New Orleans under Union occupation, stated that the Communards were "fighting for the right of local government . . . [that] embodies all republican institutions. . . . I might have said that the Commune had the example of our fathers as a precedent."[23]

By and large, though, American opinion was openly hostile to the Communards. Words like "cannibals," "bandits," and "assassins" were commonly used to describe them. To be sure, there were numerous excesses. Among them the summary executions of the two generals seized at Montmartre on March 18, the demolition of Thiers's mansion on the Place St. Georges, and the toppling of the Vendôme column, with its bronze statue of Napoleon, denounced as a symbol of "barbarity" and "militarism."[24] But the Commune was not a murderous re-enactment of *La Terreur* of 1793. Several foreign visitors marveled at what one Englishman called "the extreme tranquility of the streets."[25] A California businessman who stayed in Paris for the entire duration of the Commune reported that he "saw and heard of *no single act of pillage or murder.*"[26]

The real bloodbath took place when the Versailles troops finally entered Paris on May 21 and slaughtered thousands of Parisians—most estimates range between 17,000 and 20,000—during the so-called *Semaine sanglante* (bloody week, May 21–28).[27] It was at that point, not only out of desperation and vengeance but also to slow the advance of the enemy, that certain Communard leaders ordered the torching of the Tuileries, the Hôtel de Ville, the Palais de Justice, and several other government buildings.

The Commune's most notorious act was the May 25 execution at La Roquette Prison of Archbishop of Paris Georges Darboy and three other clerics, who had earlier been taken hostage in the hopes of exchanging them for the revolutionary

August Blanqui and other Communard prisoners. The next day fifty other hostages were set upon and killed by an angry mob. In all, an estimated one hundred hostages were killed in the final days of the Bloody Week.[28] These appalling acts of violence had come only at the end of the Commune's ten-week insurgency, but they would largely define the movement in the popular imagination. As Cluseret lamented in his memoirs, the main thing that would mark the Commune in the eyes of history was the fact that it had assassinated the archbishop.[29]

In fact, Cluseret had earlier tried to aid Washburne in his attempt to secure Darboy's release. On April 23 the U.S. minister went to see Cluseret at the Ministry of War, assuming (incorrectly) that he was the "directing man in affairs here."[30] Though he had opposed the archbishop's arrest and sympathized with his plight, Cluseret told Washburne that the matter was not within his jurisdiction. Darboy, he explained, was not being held for a crime but as a hostage and that "under the circumstances it would be useless to take any steps" to release him. Cluseret did, however, agree to accompany Washburne to the Police Prefecture to meet with the Commune's chief of police, Raoul Rigault, and request an authorization to visit the archbishop.[31] Permission granted, the American minister headed over to Mazas Prison, where Darboy was brought to meet him in an empty cell.

Washburne was shocked by the archbishop's haggard appearance and long, unkempt beard. "He seemed to appreciate his critical situation and to be prepared for the worst," the minister reported to Secretary of State Hamilton Fish, adding: "He had no word of bitterness or reproach for his persecutors, but, on the other hand, remarked that the world judged them to be worse than they really were. He was patiently awaiting the logic of events and praying that Providence might find a solution to these terrible troubles without the further shedding of human blood."[32]

Washburne returned two days later with a pile of newspapers and a bottle of Madeira for the beleaguered prelate. But his efforts to negotiate Darboy's release in exchange for Blanqui met with a cold refusal from the government in Versailles.[33] Thiers, for his part, was reportedly furious over the American's attempt to meddle in the hostage affair, calling his actions "very peculiar behavior" (conduite très singulière).[34]

Nor did Washburne's moves on Darboy's behalf ingratiate him with the anticlerical Communards. On the contrary, his humanitarian efforts compounded their suspicions of complicity with Thiers and Bismarck. The American minister was bitterly attacked in the clubs and press—one radical orator even proposed that he be hanged—and national guardsmen attempted to requisition his apartment at one point.[35] These rumors multiplied after the fall of Paris and found their way into a number of Communard memoirs.[36] As a result, many radicals subsequently came to believe that the United States had contributed morally and materially to the defeat of the Parisian revolution.

In fact, Washburne had tried to act as a neutral and evenhanded diplomat. But the execution of the hostages, along with the destruction and bloodshed of the final week, led him to condemn the Commune's "career of murder, assassination, pillage, robbery, blasphemy and terror."[37] At the same time, he recoiled at the excesses of the Versailles forces. "There has been nothing but a general butchery since Wednesday last," he wrote on May 29, "men, women and children, innocent and guilty alike. The rage of the soldiers and the people knows no bounds."[38] His overall conclusion, shared by many Americans, was that the "frightful excesses of the Commune have brought reproach upon the sacred name of the Republic, and the good name of Republicanism everywhere suffers."[39]

CHAPTER 19

The Aftermath

The political question is settled; the Republic exists and nothing will undo it;
the social question remains. It is simpler and more terrible.
—VICTOR HUGO, *Choses vues*

The Commune marked a definitive breach between the far left and the
partisans of bourgeois republicanism in France. Formerly united in
their struggle against the Second Empire, these two currents of the
French democratic tradition flowed in very different directions after 1871. As
Theodore Zeldin points out, the bourgeois republicans became more conservative and the socialists more extremist.[1]

This divergence is well illustrated by the case of Gustave Cluseret. The outbreak of the Franco-Prussian War found Cluseret in New York, where he had
been living since his expulsion from France one year earlier.[2] Shortly after the
commencement of hostilities, he packed his bags once again and sailed for Europe, hoping to wield his sword against the Prussians as he had earlier done
against the Southern slaveholders. Turned away at the French border by imperial
authorities, he only succeeded in entering Paris on September 5, following the
proclamation of the republic. But when the Government of National Defense
also refused his military services, Cluseret began to attack them in the press as
charlatans and traitors.[3]

The Civil War veteran then made his way to Lyons, joining forces with local
radicals agitating for a revolt against the central government and the creation of
a revolutionary commune. When their attempted insurrection failed on September 28, 1870, Cluseret moved on to Marseilles, where antigovernment forces also
were planning to proclaim their own independent commune. He agreed to take
command of the local Garde nationale and led a march on city hall on October
30. But government troops soon gained control, and Cluseret spent the next five

months in hiding. He returned to Paris a few days after the March 18 uprising and, on April 3, was named the Commune's war minister.[4]

Cluseret's short-lived tenure as a military commander ended badly. Faced with the disorganization of the Garde nationale, the incompetence of its officers, and the lack of any autonomy from the Commune's faction-ridden political authorities, he was unable to mount an effective defense force. On April 30, following the apparent fall of strategic Fort d'Issy to government troops, Cluseret was arrested, jailed, and charged with treason.[5] His trial was underway at the Hôtel de Ville on May 21 when word arrived that the Versailles army had entered the city. The Commune Council acquitted Cluseret in a hasty vote, after which most of its members scattered to the barricades. Judging discretion the better part of valor, Cluseret sought refuge with a priest whom he had previously permitted to hear the confession of the imprisoned Archbishop Darboy. The former war minister spent the next five months posing as a seminary student and finally fled the country in October 1871 disguised as a Belgian priest. While waiting for his train at the Gare du Nord, he was approached by a group of French soldiers who, taking him for a true clergyman, asked for a blessing. Cluseret, socialist and anticlerical though he was, obliged them with a few mumbled words and a sign of the cross. His escape came none too soon: on August 30, 1872, a Versailles military court condemned him to death in absentia.[6]

Cluseret's progression from republican "Lafayette" in America to proto-Bolshevik in Paris illustrates the chasm that opened up between radicals like himself and the bourgeois republicans with whom he had made a common cause against Napoleon III. Looking back after the fall of the Commune, Cluseret wrote:

It is no secret that I have spent much of my life as a conspirator. Among my accomplices were Pelletan, Carnot, Henri Martin. . . . Their journals, the *Siècle,* the *Tribune,* the *Phare de la Loire,* were my own. Today they look on me as their enemy, I look on them with regret. This is because our goals were not the same. They conspired only in order to replace those in power and continue the same work. My goal went much further. Since the first stage of their journey was the same as mine, we started out together. But when they arrived at the resting place, they stopped. I kept going.[7]

Both Cluseret and his republican allies had exalted U.S. democracy before 1871. But the American example, for all its ideological elasticity, could not bridge the gulf that separated the far left from the bourgeois republicans in the wake of the Commune. To many of Cluseret's fellow radicals, America now appeared to belong in the enemy camp. To a great extent, this feeling was due to their hostility toward all bourgeois republics after the repression of the Commune. But America's own social and political development during the 1870s also did much to destroy the idealized democratic image that had emerged from the Civil War. After witnessing the events of that decade—the political corruption of Grant's administrations, the failure of Reconstruction, the financial panic of 1873, the mounting violence of industrial clashes—the far left could hardly continue to view the United States as the vanguard of human progress. Formerly persuaded that political liberty would eliminate class conflict and social inequality in America, Cluseret came to feel that "the same causes are producing the same effects on both sides of the Atlantic."[8] He now predicted that "the ruin of the United States" would come from the "persecution of labor by capital, which is already well underway."[9]

Elisée Reclus, another Communard who had expressed great faith in the American republic at the end of the Civil War, similarly turned away in disgust.[10] Commenting on the bloody smashing of the 1877 railroad strike by the U.S. Army, Reclus bitterly denounced the "bourgeois capitalists" who controlled the American government. "Their inspiration is the repression of the Paris Commune," he wrote. "The heroes they propose to imitate are Thiers and his lap-dog [Marshal Patrice] MacMahon ordering the massacres!"[11] Fifteen years later, in his geographical study of the United States, Reclus offered scathing criticisms of American racism, capitalism, and imperialism.[12] For him, the American image seems to have come full circle since he had first gazed in horror on the New Orleans slave market in 1856. Although the Civil War and the emancipation of the slaves had momentarily rekindled his faith in American democracy, that faith was shattered again within a few years.

The reactions of men like Cluseret and Reclus reflect America's declining prestige in the eyes of the far left during the years after 1871. Never again would European radicals look on the United States with such hope and expectation as they did during the 1860s. No subsequent American event would fire their imagination as the Civil War had done. No American leader after Lincoln would ever appear to them to embody the democratic aspirations of the world's laboring masses. With the passage of time, the European left would tend more and more to look on the United States as an enemy of progress. In the twentieth century, as Sir Denis Brogan has noted, the left came to see America "less as the holder of the lamp of liberty than as the last stronghold of the old, bad, order, refusing to go forward herself and busily bolstering up the decaying capitalist system by bribes and threats all over the world."[13]

A s for the bourgeois republicans, they also grew increasingly cool toward the United States after the fall of the Second Empire. "The paradox of the 1870s," writes Philippe Roger, "was that political circumstances that should have favored a rediscovery of the American political model led instead to its nearly universal refusal by the very people in France who had been its most ardent defenders: the new government's republican instigators."[14]

One reason for this sudden disaffection was America's reaction to the Franco-Prussian War. In the minds of many French republicans, the United States seemed to have abandoned its "Sister Republic" in 1871, just as it had done in after the coup d'état in 1851. Edgar Quinet, a longtime admirer of the United States, angrily noted in 1872 that republican America had joined with monarchical Europe in "throwing stones at France. This is hardly surprising, considering the way they accepted and applauded all the infamies of the Empire! Not a single honest and loyal word has come to us from Europe or America."[15] Republican leader Jules Favre came to believe that the Americans had assisted Prussian espionage activities during the war.[16] The experience of the "Terrible Year" even seems to have dampened Henri Allain-Targé's ardent pro-Americanism. Shortly after the fall of the Commune, he coauthored a report that accused the Americans of seeking to take advantage of France's misfortunes in order to

> wrest away our national wealth and industrial glory, which they hope to see disappear along with our political and military preponderance.... America is soliciting the emigration of our discouraged workers. Her tireless agents prowl ceaselessly about the prison camps at Versailles and in our faubourgs.... They tell our shattered [working-class] population that the present situation is definitive; that France is forever lost to democracy. They take away our families one by one. They persuade them that work, progress, wealth and all the old French civilization will be transported to the New World.[17]

To a great extent, the stark turnaround of former pro-American cheerleaders like Allain-Targé reflected a major shift in French circumstances. The fall of the Second Empire had greatly reduced the propaganda value of the American example. The republicans no longer faced the problem of toppling the Bonapartist regime, but rather that of giving concrete and durable institutions to their new republic. Their main adversaries were now the legitimists and Orleanists who, with a view to a royalist restoration, were seeking to frame a constitution that would lend itself to a monarchical system of government. America's basic constitutional principles—decentralization, checks and balances, bicameralism, and an independent executive—were actually closer to the ideas of the monarchists than of those of the French republicans. As Louis Blanc wrote to his American friend Moncure Conway in 1872, most republicans had by then come to look on the institution of the presidency as "a mere stepping-stone to ascend the throne." Those who still favored a presidency and a bicameral legislature, said Blanc, did so largely because "they are under the impression that that institution works well in the United States. To correct such an error is to do good service to the cause of republican institutions."[18]

The monarchist ideas triumphed in the Constitution of 1875, which established a bicameral legislature and a strong presidency. But when the republicans won undisputed control of the regime in 1877, they largely refashioned it in their own image, rendering the presidency innocuous and establishing a system of "government by deputies" that would last until the debacle of 1940.[19] The parliamentary republic they founded was actually much closer to the English than to the American political system.[20] Thus, by the time they gained ascendancy in the government, most republicans had shed their previous infatuation with America and proceeded to take a very different road. Flatly contradicting his earlier praise for the U.S. model, Léon Gambetta declared in 1876, "there is no way to compare America with France."[21]

Edouard Laboulaye, having grown increasingly conservative in old age, was one of the few French republicans to remain a partisan of American political doctrines. In 1880 he complained that the leaders of the Third Republic had "forgotten all the principles of liberty in favor of the authoritarian traditions of despotism, and the French Republic is moving further and further away from American ideas."[22] Laboulaye showed his own devotion to those ideas in 1875 by launching a subscription to finance the building of a monumental statue to celebrate the centennial of American independence. Created by French sculptor

Frédéric Bartholdi, the 151-foot-tall Statue of Liberty—officially named Liberty Enlightening the World—was erected on an island in New York harbor in 1886.[23]

Before shipping the statue to the United States, Bartholdi assembled it at his worksite near the Parc Monceau in 1884 and allowed the public to view it. Among the visitors was eighty-two-year-old Victor Hugo, in what turned out to be his last outing. Judging the colossus "très beau," he contemplated it silently for a long moment, hands in his pockets, then spontaneously remarked, "The great, turbulent ocean watches over the union of two great pacified lands." Bartholdi's entourage wrote down the words and asked permission to engrave them on the pedestal. Hugo died of pneumonia six months later, believing his citation would be enshrined on a bronze plaque at the feet of Lady Liberty. Instead, the chosen text was a passage from the now-famous poem by Emma Lazarus, "The New Collosus" ("Give me your tired, your poor, your huddled masses . . .").[24]

In a way, it was fitting that Hugo's paean to the transatlantic bond was not used, for the "traditional Franco-American friendship" that the statue embodied was marked by a certain coolness in the early years of the Third Republic. On the diplomatic front, although no serious conflicts arose between the two governments, relations were characterized by a sort of mutual indifference. Moreover, since American manners and society provided easy targets for criticism during the Gilded Age, it is not surprising that many French writers and travelers judged the United States with great severity during the 1870s.

Typical of this group was the liberal journalist and economist Gustave de Molinari. Sent to cover the 1876 Philadelphia World's Fair for the *Journal des débats,* he blasted the Yankee politicians who had "unleashed the Civil War, ruined the South by confiscation and plunder, raised the budget of the Union to fantastic levels, wasted the public wealth, and introduced theft and embezzlement into the highest levels of government."[25] Molinari's harsh view, shared by many of his contemporaries, forms a striking contrast to the idealized image of America that French republicans had been brandishing against Napoleon III a few years earlier.[26]

One French republican who had closely observed the United States for nearly half a century was the journalist Frédéric Gaillardet. Coauthor with Alexandre Dumas of a wildly successful play in 1832, Gaillardet sailed for New Orleans five years later, intending to follow in the footsteps of Alexis de Tocqueville and Michel Chevalier by writing a book about American democracy.[27] In 1839 he purchased the New York–based *Courrier des Etats-Unis* and filled its columns with effusive praise of the American example. Following his return to France, where he ran unsuccessfully for a seat in the Chamber of Deputies in 1848, Gaillardet continued writing for various journals and working on his still-unfinished book about America. Published posthumously in 1883, a year after Gaillardet's death, the book turned out to be a top-to-bottom refutation of Tocqueville that set the tone for all the anti-American diatribes that followed. Its title: *L'Aristocratie en Amérique.*[28] Gaillardet's personal disappointment in America was emblematic of a large-scale rejection of the U.S. model by French republicans in the decades following the *Année terrible.*

History, it seems, was repeating itself. As it had happened after 1848, a moment of exaggerated enthusiasm for the United States was followed by a period of severe criticism as unrealistic expectations gave way to inevitable disappointments. Like a disenchanted lover, the French left woke up to the realization that the American republic neither deserved nor reciprocated their former infatuation. To compound their disillusionment, it was the conservatives who used the American example against them in the early decades of the Third Republic.[29] The stage was thus set for the anti-Americanism that would typify the French left—and not only the left—through much of the twentieth century.

Conclusion

During the years between the 1848 February Revolution and the founding of the Third Republic, the French left's view of America fluctuated between extremes of naïve adulation and severe criticism. If their enthusiasm for the United States could be plotted on a graph, it would resemble a sine wave, with peaks at 1848 and 1865, a trough in the middle, and another downward turn after 1870. How do we account for these shifts in opinion?

To a great extent, the left's view of America was affected by the political situation in France. Certain scholars have suggested that domestic politics was actually the major factor in shaping French attitudes toward the United States. René Rémond has written: "The French think of themselves, or their own regime, when they think of the United States: they think in terms of the use they can make of the American example, either to recommend or condemn it. . . . The American experience is like a mirror that reflects the image, only slightly distorted, of French opinion."[1] Durand Echeverria has observed, "The American mirage . . . as seen by the French reveals the countenance of France far more than that of America."[2] Changes in French attitudes toward the United States, Echeverria argues, had little to do with the actual evolution of American politics and society: they can be traced mainly to the shifting political situation in France. As a general rule of thumb, he suggests that French opinion tended to be pro-American whenever the nation was governed by a regime judged less liberal than that of the United States; but whenever a regime was established that offered political liberties roughly equivalent to those of the United States, an anti-American reaction set in.

Echeverria's "rule" seems inadequate to fully account for the evolution of opinion during the period under consideration. Propaganda needs certainly had much to do with shaping the left's view of the United States, but that view was not a mere reflection of the French political situation. It was during the 1850s, for example, that the propaganda needs of the left were greatest, for the defeated and scattered partisans of republicanism then had nothing but rhetoric to level at Napoleon III. Yet instead of extolling American democracy, most of them took skeptical, often hostile views of American politics and society at this time.

Nor can the French political situation alone account for the left's extraordinary infatuation with America during the late 1860s. The Second Empire underwent a considerable liberalization during these years, and the Constitution of 1870 established a regime that bore a certain resemblance to the U.S. political system. According to Echeverria's rule of thumb, this liberalization should have reduced the usefulness of the American example as a propaganda weapon. But we have seen that just the opposite occurred: the more liberal the empire became, the more its adversaries on the left vaunted the American example. Thus the state of French politics can only partially explain the left's changing view of the United States. The whole picture cannot be understood without also taking into account the situation of American politics and society. Both factors were at work, even if one or the other might dominate at a given moment.

The brief burst of pro-Americanism that followed the Revolution of 1848 was largely the product of French circumstances. Following their sudden rise to power, republicans hailed the United States as their "official model" and "Sister Republic." But the initial enthusiasms soon gave way to more critical views as the American model was subjected to closer scrutiny. Many of those on the left felt that the U.S. constitutional doctrines of federalism, bicameralism, and an independent presidency were out of harmony with their own circumstances and traditions. Democrats and socialists on the far left, moreover, saw the American ideals of individualism, self-help, competition, and laissez-faire as obstacles to the social and economic reforms they envisaged. On the whole, the American example proved more useful to the moderates and conservatives in 1848, and this tended to make it suspect in the eyes of the left. After the coup d'état, the defeated French republicans of all stripes were disappointed by America's failure to actively defend the Second Republic and by the contempt that many Americans expressed for the French people in the wake of the events of 1848–51.

During the following decade, the left's increasingly hostile attitude toward the United States was mainly due to American factors: rapacious expansionism, the aggravation of the slavery controversy, the mounting violence of sectional passions, the mediocrity of U.S. political leadership under Franklin Pierce and James Buchanan, and the general vulgarity and materialism of American society as depicted by the exiles and travelers of the 1850s. By the end of this decade, the American image had reached an all-time low in the eyes of the French left.

It was an American event, the Civil War, that reversed this negative view and rekindled the left's enthusiasm for the United States. During that struggle, America had cleansed itself of the moral blot of slavery, demonstrated the strength and resiliency of its republican institutions, and emerged as a first-rate military and economic power. Abraham Lincoln's death consecrated the Union's emancipating crusade, and the martyred worker-president became a hero to partisans of democracy the world over. The events of the late 1860s—the beginnings of Radical Reconstruction, the enfranchisement of the freedmen, the impeachment of Andrew Johnson, and the election of Ulysses Grant—all seemed to confirm the idea that the United States was continuing to follow the progressive political and social evolution begun during the Civil War.

The years between the Civil War and the fall of the Second Empire represent the high-water mark of American prestige in the eyes of the French left: at no other time in the nineteenth century did they manifest such a powerful and sustained enthusiasm for the United States. It happened, furthermore, that the political fortunes of the left had begun to rise during the Civil War years, and the influence of democratic ideas in France increased steadily throughout the 1860s. As the emboldened left intensified their attack on the imperial regime, they found one of their most useful propaganda weapons in the image of the triumphant American republic and thus cited its example in favor of a wide variety of political and social goals. Encouraged by Napoleon III's forced withdrawal from Mexico under the threat of American intervention, many of his adversaries on the left hoped to see the United States assume an active role as a defender of republicanism throughout the world. It appears, then, that the left's extraordinary enthusiasm for America during these years resulted from the fact that their propaganda needs corresponded with U.S. events at this juncture, just as the amplitudes of two colliding waves are mutually reinforced at the point of intersection. The opposite had occurred during the 1850s, when the French and American "waves" were out of phase.

A combination of French and American factors was likewise responsible for the falling off of the left's sympathy for the United States during the 1870s. Embittered by America's pro-German stance in 1870, French republicans began to take an increasingly critical view of their "Sister Republic" during the ensuing years. They found ample grounds for criticism in the political corruption, financial scandals, and general sordidness that characterized Gilded Age America. With the fall of the Second Empire and the founding of the Third Republic, moreover, the American example had outlived its usefulness as a propaganda tool. Thus U.S. political doctrines exerted little influence on the thinking of French republicans after 1870, and the centralized parliamentary regime they founded was very different from the American republic they had lauded while in opposition. As for the radical and socialist far left, the bloody suppression of the Commune had made them increasingly hostile to all bourgeois regimes—including that of the United States. Far from living up to the egalitarian and democratic image that had emerged from the Civil War, America ultimately came to epitomize the worst aspects of the capitalist order in the eyes of the far left.

Despite the important role that the American example played in the French democratic propaganda of the 1860s, the left's view of the United States does not seem to have been a very perceptive one. Objective and dispassionate analysts like Alexis de Tocqueville were rare during these years of political turbulence, and allusions to America were seldom devoid of polemical content. The Civil War and the emancipation of the slaves had made America a symbol of triumphant democracy. Rejoicing over the victory of "their" principles in the United States, those on the French left tirelessly invoked that symbol for their own purposes at home. Yet the American example seems to have had surprisingly little positive effect on their thinking. What they praised most about the United States were those things that confirmed their own ideological views or suited their particular propaganda purposes. Used in this selective way, the American example could be adapted to the needs of widely differing and even conflicting ideologies. Thus Orleanists, liberals, republicans, socialists, and revolutionaries could all find support for their particular creeds in the example of the United States. But it is doubtful that many French observers actually changed their own political thinking on the basis of the American experience. Across the ideological spectrum, as Sophie Body-Gendrot has noted, French judgments of the United States were often based on "myths and a profound incomprehension of American democracy" more than on political realities.[3]

In many ways, in fact, the ideas and traditions of the French left were at odds with the American experience. In the United States democratic and egalitarian principles had had no ancien régime to fight against; in France those principles had to struggle with attitudes and institutions inherited from a feudal past. This fact gave the French democratic movement a revolutionary character that was foreign to the American political tradition. We have seen, furthermore, that U.S. constitutional principles clashed with some of the fundamental ideas and prejudices of the French republican tradition, while America's social ideals of individualism, competition, and laissez-faire caused misgivings on the radical and socialist left.

Historical and cultural differences between the two countries also dulled the left's perception of America. As partisans of liberty, they had certain political ideals in common with the Americans. But as Frenchmen—products of an ancient Latin and Roman Catholic civilization—they often had difficulty in comprehending this young Anglo-Saxon Protestant society whose temperament and values were so different from their own. To a great extent, too, the left's ability to understand the United States on its own terms was hindered by the chauvinistic worldview that so many of them shared with Jules Michelet: even as they applauded the triumph of democracy in America, most of those on the left harbored the belief that French principles and genius were somehow at the bottom of it all. With their view thus clouded by their own preconceptions and ideological beliefs, few Frenchmen really grasped the nature of American democracy or learned any enduring political lessons from the example of the United States. Despite the countless allusions to it throughout these years, it was more as a general inspiration and a propaganda tool than as a positive model that American democracy influenced the thinking of the French left. The French case, finally, illustrates a larger phenomenon: the subjective ways by which internal factions in one country have viewed foreign powers throughout history.

NOTES

ABBREVIATIONS

AN	Archives Nationales, Pierrefitte-sur-Seine
BHVP	Bibliothèque Historique de la Ville de Paris. Hôtel Lamoignon, Paris
BN	Bibliothèque Nationale de France, Paris
DBMOF	Jean Maitron, ed., *Dictionnaire biographique du mouvement ouvrier français* (Paris: Editions ouvrières, 1964–77)
PGR	Procureur général's report
RDM	*Revue des deux mondes*
RMC	*Revue du monde colonial, asiatique et américain*
SHD	Service historique de la Défense, Chateau de Vincennes, Paris
SP	Charles Sumner Papers, bMS Am 1.4, Houghton Library, Harvard University, Cambridge, Mass.

PREFACE

1. Throughout this study, the word "radical" is used in the English sense to denote people of progressive political views; it does not refer to France's Parti radical, created in 1901, or to the "radical" label that was used by French republicans under the July Monarchy.

2. Wherever possible, I have tried to avoid using the gender-specific term "Frenchmen" since a number of women were present and active in the French left, as we shall see. In some contexts, the term is unavoidable, as it describes the reality that, in France, the worlds of politics, economics, and journalism were largely dominated by males during the period under study.

3. Skard, *American Studies in Europe,* 1:131.

CHAPTER 1

1. See Hayat, *1848,* chap. 1; and Price, *1848 in France,* 11–51.

2. Tocqueville, *Ecrits et discours politiques,* 2:750–751.

3. Featherstonhaugh and Mason, "Le Départ de Louis-Philippe," 202–205. During his long exile before coming to power, Louis-Philippe, then known as the duc d'Orléans, traveled in the United States from 1796 to 1800 and met with such political leaders as George Washington, Alexander Hamilton, and John Jay. In 1839, nine years after he had ascended the throne as Louis-Philippe King of the French, he confided to his prime minister, François Guizot, that his travels in the United States had had a large influence on his political views. See Bishop, "Louis Philippe in America." See also Louis-Philippe, *Journal de mon voyage d'Amérique.*

4. Price, *1848 in France,* 28; Girard, *La IIe République,* chap. 6.

5. George Sand to Charles Poncy, Mar. 9, 1848, in Sand, *Correspondance,* 3:9–10.

6. Girard, *La IIe République,* 24.

7. Rush quoted in McCullough, *Greater Journey,* 184.

8. McCullough, *Greater Journey,* 185.

9. For the effects of the February Revolution on Franco-American relations, see Rémond, *Etats-Unis devant l'opinion française,* 2:831–858; Curtis, *French Assembly of 1848;* Blumenthal, *Reappraisal of Franco-American Relations,* 8–20; Chinard, "Comment l'Amérique reconnut la République de 48"; and Pincetl, "Relations de la France et des Etats-Unis."

10. Curtis, "American Opinion of the French Nineteenth-Century Revolutions," 254–262.

11. White, *American Opinion of France,* 213.

12. Lamartine quoted in Rémond, *Etats-Unis devant l'opinion française,* 2:834.

13. An economist and former member of the Saint-Simonian "church" at Ménilmontant, Chevalier (1806–79) had visited the United States in 1833–35 and published his two-volume *Lettres sur l'Amérique du Nord* in 1837. Along with Tocqueville, he was one of the main sources of French information on America, but he cast a more conservative and critical eye on the United States.

14. See Gray, *Interpreting American Democracy in France.*

15. Curtis, *French Assembly of 1848,* 329–330; Rémond, *Etats-Unis devant l'opinion française,* 2:850–851.

16. Tchernoff, *Parti républicain,* 123–125; Soltau, *French Political Thought,* xxvi.

17. See, for example, Blanc, *L'Organisation du travail,* 153–154; Michelet, *Le Peuple,* 265–273; Leroux, *De l'égalité,* 263; Ledru-Rollin, *De la décadence de l'Angleterre;* Blanqui, *Critique sociale,* 2:73; and Proudhon, *Correspondance,* 14:77–79.

18. Victor Hugo, "Les deux côtés de l'Atlantique," in Hugo, *Œuvres complètes. Poésie,* 72–73. Hugo's critique of America's mercantile culture was shared by his fellow poet Charles Baudelaire (1821–67), who fought on the barricades in 1848 and briefly wrote for a revolutionary newspaper, but lost faith in democracy after the 1851 coup d'état. In his 1856 introduction to a volume of Edgar Allen Poe's tales, Baudelaire called American society "a vast prison" and scathingly described the United States as "a gigantic and infantile country, naturally jealous of the old continent. Proud of its material development, [which is] abnormal and almost monstrous, this newcomer in history has a naïve faith and the omnipotence of industry. Time and money have such an enormous value over there! Material activity [is] exaggerated to the proportions of a national mania." Baudelaire, introduction to Poe, *Histoires extraordinaires,* viii–x. On Baudelaire's political action in 1848, see Cogniot, *La Lyre d'Airain,* 92–93.

19. Frédéric Mitterrand, *Napoléon III et Victor Hugo,* 51–53.

20. Hugo quoted in Jeanneney, *Victor Hugo et la République*, 29–30.

21. Jeanneney, *Victor Hugo et la République*, 29–30.

22. Rémond, *Etats-Unis devant l'opinion française*, 852–853. In this context, it is interesting to note that Baudelaire denounced Franklin as "the inventor of the morality of the counting house, the hero of a century devoted to materialism" and bewailed the fact that "Americanism has practically become a fashionable passion." Baudelaire, introduction to Poe, *Nouvelles histoires extraordinaires*, x.

23. Tocqueville quoted in Curtis, *French Assembly of 1848*, 231. See also Montalembert's invocation of the American example of laissez-faire in his famous speech against nationalization of the railroads in *Discours*, 3:31–32. See also M. Chevalier, "La question des travailleurs," 1062.

24. Hugo, *Choses vues, 1847–1848*, 337.

25. See Echeverria, "L'Amérique devant l'opinion française," 62. For an interesting discussion of federalism as a reactionary doctrine in France and a democratic one in America, see Palmer, *Age of the Democratic Revolution*, ii, 27.

26. Galante Garonne, *Philippe Buonarroti*, 30, 126; Rémond, *Etats-Unis devant l'opinion française*, 2:669–671.

27. Tocqueville, *Souvenirs*, 182.

28. Tocqueville, *Souvenirs*, 185.

29. Tocqueville, *Souvenirs*, 187.

30. Duvergier de Hauranne quoted in Curtis, *French Assembly of 1848*, 249–250.

31. *Représentant du peuple*, May 8, 1848. See also *Père Duchêne*, June 22, 1848; *Révolution démocratique et sociale*, Nov. 8, 1848; and Ledru-Rollin, *Voix du proscrit*, Feb. 16, 1851, 233–237.

32. Blanc, letter of Oct. 7, 1848, in *Almanach républicain* (1849): 180.

33. Tocqueville, *Souvenirs*, 189.

34. Lamartine, *La Présidence*, 52–54. It did not take long for Lamartine to regret those words. Appalled by Bonaparte's rising popularity during the run-up to the presidential election, he declared, "France is lost! After the original [Napoléon I], the pale copy. . . . And it will be worse!" Quoted in Mitterrand, *Napoléon III et Victor Hugo*, 58.

35. Tocqueville, *Souvenirs*, 186.

36. Robert Badinter, "Modèles américains des institutions, vus par les constituants français," in Fauré and Bishop, *L'Amérique des Français*, 22.

37. Quoted in McCullough, *Greater Journey*, 202.

38. Harriet Howard (1823–65), endowed with an enormous fortune by one of her many lovers, met Louis Napoleon at a London reception in 1846, became his mistress, and put her millions at his disposal. She accompanied him to France in 1848 and continued her relationship with him until 1853, when he married the Spanish countess Eugénie de Montijo in order to produce a legitimate heir. See Alain Decaux, *L'Empire, l'amour et l'argent*, 28–59. Tocqueville described Miss Howard as Louis Napoleon's "mistress . . . or to speak more correctly his favorite, since he always had several mistresses at the same time." Tocqueville, *Souvenirs*, 260.

39. Hugo had actually supported Louis Napoleon's election as president in 1848, hoping that "given the impossibility of becoming great like Napoleon, he would perhaps seek to be great like Washington." Hugo, *Choses Vues, 1849–1869*, 111.

40. Thompson, *Louis Napoleon and the Second Empire*, 116–124.

41. On Hugo's Guernsey life, see Mitterrand, *Napoléon III et Victor Hugo*, chap. 11, 12, and passim.

42. Mitterrand, *Napoléon III et Victor Hugo*, 264.

43. Thompson, *Louis Napoleon and the Second Empire*, 124; Cobban, *History of Modern France*, 160.

44. Blanc, *Histoire de la Révolution de 1848*, 124. See also Vacherot, *La Démocratie*, 362.

45. Williams, *America Confronts a Revolutionary World*, 98.

46. Blumenthal, *France and the United States*, 54–55.

47. Curtis, "American Opinion of the French Nineteenth-Century Revolutions," 256–258. American abolitionists, however, did applaud the French antislavery decree. See, for example, Horace Greeley's *New York Tribune*, Apr. 5, 12, 1848; Harriet Beecher Stowe, *Sunny Memories of Foreign Lands*, 2:409–410; and resolution of June 26, 1848, "congratulating [the French government] on the passage of the Decree for the emancipation of the Slaves in all the French Colonies and dependencies," American and Foreign Anti-Slavery Society Minutes, f. 5, Amistad Research Center, Tulane University, New Orleans.

48. White, *American Opinion of France*, 123–124.

49. White, *American Opinion of France*, 123–124.

50. On his distaste for American society, see, for example, Louis Napoleon to his mother, Apr. 24, May 8, 1837, quoted in Dansette, *Louis-Napoléon à la conquête du pouvoir*, 131. He praised American dynamism in an 1860 conversation with U.S. minister Charles J. Faulkner: "[Napoleon III] said that during his brief visit to the United States, he had been most deeply impressed with the energy, activity, and vitality which pervaded every class of society . . . , so much so that when he returned to his country, it seemed to him that all Europe was asleep." Quoted in Case and Spencer, *United States and France*, 19.

51. Blumenthal, *Reappraisal of Franco-American Relations*, 21–22.

52. Blumenthal, *France and the United States*, 63.

53. Arthur J. May, "L'Amérique et les revolutions du milieu du siècle dernier," in Fejto, *Le printemps des peuples*, 2:408; Blumenthal, *France and the United States*, 61–62; White, *American Opinion of France*, 131–132.

54. J. W. De Forest to A. W. De Forest, Dec. 28, 1851, De Forest Papers, Bieneke Library, Yale University, New Haven, Conn. For some other American travelers' opinions on France's unfitness for republicanism, see Mrs. J. W. Hincks, letters from Paris, Mar. 7, Apr. 25, and July 21, 1848, Hincks Family Papers, MSS 147, vol. 1, folder 11, Howard Tilton Memorial Library, Tulane University, New Orleans; Mrs. Avenel, letter from Paris, July 30, 1848, Avenel Family Papers, MSS 86, folder 1, ibid.; and Jarves, *Parisian Sights*, 200, 203–204.

55. Buchanan quoted in Calman, *Ledru-Rollin après 1848*, 117.

56. Blumenthal, *Reappraisal of Franco-American Relations*, 22.

57. Webster quoted in White, *American Opinion of France*, 130.

58. Ribeyrolles, *L'Homme*, Oct. 15, 1854.

59. Proudhon to Joseph Mazzini, Mar. 1852, in Proudhon, *Correspondance*, 4:263.

60. Sanders, "Au peuple de France," *L'Homme*, Oct. 18, 1854. On Sanders's relations with the French republicans, see chapter 2 below.

61. Tocqueville to Sedgwick, Dec. 4, 1852, in Hawkins, *Newly Discovered French Letters*, 189. Theodore Sedgwick III (1811–59) had met Tocqueville in Paris and aided his research on America democracy; they remained lifelong friends. Hugh Brogan, *Alexis de Tocqueville*, 255–256.

CHAPTER 2

1. Copans, "French Opinion of American Democracy," 70–71. By contrast, it is interesting to note that radical Communarde Louise Michel later applauded the U.S. intervention in favor of Cuban independence during the Spanish-American War in 1898: "I must salute . . . the generous people of the United States who, to aid the deliverance of this heroic island, wage the war of liberty." Michel, dedication to *La Commune.*

2. See, for example, Du Pasquier de Dommartin, *Les Etats-Unis et le Mexique;* Félix de Cour-mont, *Des Etats-Unis, de la guerre du Mexique, et de l'Ile de Cube* [sic]; and A. de Moges, *De l'in-fluence prochaine des Etats-Unis sur la politique de l'Europe.*

3. Tocqueville to Theodore Sedgwick, Dec. 4, 1852, in Hawkins, *Newly Discovered French Let-ters,* 188.

4. Schoelcher, "L'Insurrection de Cuba et les Etats-Unis," 463–464.

5. Curti, "Young America," 34–55.

6. Eyal, *Young America Movement.*

7. On Sanders's diplomatic career, see Curti, "Young America"; and Curti, "George N. Sanders."

8. Buchanan quoted in Curti, "Young America," 48.

9. Herzen quoted by Peter Dreyer, *The Nation,* July 31, 1976, 37.

10. Curti, "Young America," 48–52. A controversial figure known for his business failures as well as his political extremism, Sanders (1812–73) later served as a Confederate agent in Canada during the Civil War and was suspected of involvement in the assassination of Abraham Lincoln. Andrew Johnson issued a $25,000 reward for his arrest. Sanders escaped capture and fled to Europe. The charges were finally dropped but the suspicions about his involvement remain to this day. See Squires, "Controversial Career of George Nicholas Sanders," 10, 130, and passim.

11. On Soulé (1801–70), see Chancerel, *L'Homme du grand fleuve;* Green and Kirkwood, "Re-framing the Antebellum Democratic Mainstream"; Ettinger, *Mission to Spain of Pierre Soulé;* Tinker, *Ecrits de langue française en Louisiane,* 434–451.

12. Ettinger, *Mission to Spain of Pierre Soulé,* 497.

13. This charge was made in Congress by Representative L. D. Evans of Texas. See Calman, *Ledru-Rollin après 1848,* 118–119.

14. Blumenthal, *Reappraisal of Franco-American Relations,* 27.

15. Ettinger, *Mission to Spain of Pierre Soulé,* 497.

16. Ettinger, *Mission to Spain of Pierre Soulé,* 492.

17. Tinker, *Ecrits de langue française en Louisiane,* 446.

18. Blumenthal, *Reappraisal of Franco-American Relations,* 29.

19. Hugo to Sanders, Oct. 31, 1854, Autograph File, Houghton Library, Harvard University, Cambridge, Mass. On Sanders's close relationship with Ledru-Rollin, see Calman, *Ledru-Rollin après 1848,* 106–109.

20. See *Almanach de l'exil* (1855), 207; and *L'Homme,* Nov. 7, 15, 1854.

21. Quoted in Calman, *Ledru-Rollin après 1848,* 109–112. For similar reactions to Sanders's re-jection, see Curti, "Young America," 52–53.

22. See Filler, *Crusade against Slavery,* 193; and Garrison, introduction to *Joseph Mazzini,* xi–xvi.

23. Ledru-Rollin to Sanders, Aug. 1, 1854, in Calman, *Ledru-Rollin après 1848,* 115.

24. Ribeyrolles, *L'Homme,* Jan. 3, 1855.

25. Michelet, *La Femme,* 211.

26. Quinet to Francisco Bilbao, July 8, 1856, in Quinet *Lettres d'exil,* 1:282–284.

27. Vacherot, *La Démocratie,* 33–34, 362. See also Charles Delescluze, *Voix du proscrit,* Jan. 1, 1851, 143.

CHAPTER 3

1. Laboulaye, *Discours populaires,* 268–69.

2. Santineau, *Schœlcher,* 12.

3. Schoelcher, "Loi du 18 septembre 1850," 174–204.

4. Basterot, *De Québec à Lima,* 152.

5. See Curtis, *French Assembly of 1848,* 15; *Représentant du peuple,* Apr. 29, 1848.

6. Ribeyrolles, *Voix du proscrit,* Jan. 1, 1851, 135–137 (emphasis in original).

7. Hugo, *Choses vues, 1849–1869,* 277.

8. Lucas, *Littérature anti-esclavagiste,* 65–92; Gray, *Interpreting American Democracy in France,* 56–57.

9. George Sand quoted in Sideman and Friedman, *Europe Looks at the Civil War,* 132–133.

10. Michelet, *L'Amour,* xviii–xix.

11. Lucas, *Littérature anti-esclavagiste,* 159–171.

12. Geffroy, *Clemenceau,* 181.

13. Lucas, *Littérature anti-esclavagiste,* 212.

14. Jones, *Blue and Gray Diplomacy,* 15.

15. Koht, *American Spirit in Europe,* 123.

16. Wilson, *Patriotic Gore,* 6–8.

17. Laboulaye, introduction to Channing, *Œuvres.*

18. See chapter 15 below.

19. Schoelcher, "L'Esclavage aux Etats-Unis," 792–793.

20. Tocqueville, in *Letters on American Slavery,* 8.

21. Victor Hugo to Maria Weston Chapman, July 6, 1851, in *Letters on American Slavery,* 7.

22. Melvil-Bloncourt, *Homme ou singe,* 10. See also Ribeyrolles, *L'Homme,* Feb. 22, 1854.

CHAPTER 4

1. Bunle, *Etudes démographiques,* 22, 52; L. Chevalier, "L'Emigration française," 142.

2. Copans, "French Opinion of American Democracy," 26.

3. Monaghan, *French Travelers in the United States,* ix.

4. Jeune, *De F. T. Graindorge à A. O. Barnabooth,* 16–19.

5. On the anti-American books of conservative British travelers like Thomas Hamilton, Basil Hall, and Captain Marryat, see Crook, *American Democracy in English Politics,* esp. 113–136, and passim.

6. Jouve, *Voyage en Amérique*, 1:217. For other hostile books by conservative French travelers of this period, see Marmier, *Les Ames en peine;* Marmier, *Lettres sur l'Amérique;* Domenech, *Journal d'un missionnaire;* Bellegarrigue, *Femmes d'Amérique;* and Alembert, *Flânerie parisienne.*

7. Jeune, *Graindorge,* 16.

8. "Transatlantic Tourists," 545.

9. See esp. Assollant, *Scènes de la vie des Etats-Unis;* Eyma, *Excentricités américaines;* Eyma, *Les femmes du nouveau monde;* Eyma, *Le Trône d'argent;* and Comettant, *Trois ans aux Etats-Unis.*

10. French consular reports listed as many as thirty-eight political exiles living in the United States during this period. Bertrand, "Exil et transportation," 13.

11. The French exile community in New York formed a "Société de la Montagne," which organized meetings and demonstrations and published a short-lived newspaper, *Le Républicain.* See Weill, *Histoire du parti républicain en France,* 292. Saint-Ferréol names a number of French exiles who settled in Louisiana, New York, Texas, Kansas, and elsewhere in the United States. See Saint-Ferréol, *Les Proscrits français en Belgique,* 2:17, 32, 36, 129. A number of Ledru-Rollin's allies also emigrated to the United States from England. See Calman, *Ledru-Rollin après 1848,* 108–109.

12. Saint-Ferréol, *Les Proscrits français en Belgique,* 2:5.

13. Michelet, *Le Peuple,* 266.

14. Michelet, *Le Peuple,* 24.

15. Notes dated June 26, 1860, Papiers Michelet, A.3915, ff. 181, 184, BHVP.

16. Charles Delescluze, *Révolution démocratique et sociale,* Dec. 26, 1848. Cabet's Icarian colony is discussed later in this chapter.

17. Charles Delescluze, *Voix du proscrit,* Feb. 19, 1851, 240–242.

18. *L'Homme,* Sept. 27, 1854 (ellipses in the original).

19. *L'Homme,* Sept. 27, 1854. Despite his repeated criticisms of emigration, Ribeyrolles finally became so discouraged by his long exile that he left for Brazil, where he died in poverty in 1860. See *DBMOF,* 3:309.

20. Proudhon to Charles Edmond, Jan. 10, 24, 1852, in Proudhon, *Correspondance,* 4:188, 198.

21. Saint-Ferréol, *Les Proscrits français en Belgique,* 2:131.

22. Savardan, *Naufrage au Texas,* 325. Some exiles did make it in America. The anarchist Claude Pelletier, for example, went into business in New York manufacturing artificial flowers and wound up a millionaire. See *DBMOF,* 3:192.

23. Rude, *Voyage en Icarie,* 53, 229. On the criticism of American society by *quarante-huitard* refugees, see Arthur J. May, "L'Amérique et les révolutions du siècle dernier," in Fejto, *Le printemps des peuples,* 2:432.

24. On Reclus's life and ideas, see Clark and Martin, *Anarchy, Geography, Modernity;* and Vincent, *Elisée Reclus.*

25. Elisée Reclus, "Fragment d'un voyage à la Nouvelle-Orléans," 190. The New Orleans slave market also made a vivid impression on Frédéric Olinet, who witnessed this "heartbreaking" spectacle on his way to join the Icarians at Nauvoo. Olinet, *Socialisme,* 73–77. The same sight is said to have turned the young Abraham Lincoln into an antislavery man during an 1831 visit to New Orleans.

26. Elisée Reclus to Elie Reclus, n.d. [1855], in Elisée Reclus, *Correspondance,* 1:96.

27. Elisée Reclus, *Correspondance,* 1:96–97.

28. Elisée Reclus, *Correspondance,* 1:105; Vincent, *Elisée Reclus,* 104.

29. Elisée Reclus, *Correspondance,* 1:93.

30. Elisée Reclus, *Correspondance,* 1:90. This is apparently a word-play on *vomito-negro,* a Spanish term for yellow fever, the dreaded disease that ravaged the population of New Orleans with repeated epidemics until its connection with mosquitoes was discovered in 1905.

31. Elisée Reclus, *Correspondance,* 1:92–93. Reclus's negative impressions of America were not limited to his experiences in the slave state of Louisiana: while employed at the Fortier plantation, he made a brief trip to Chicago, where the horrors of the stock yards and industrialized slaughterhouses helped turn him into a lifelong vegetarian: Vincent, *Elisée Reclus,* 90–91.

32. Elisée Reclus, "Fragment d'un voyage," 190–191. Regarding yellow fever, Reclus himself was infected with this often-fatal disease in the autumn of 1853 but recovered after a short convalescence. Vincent, *Elisée Reclus,* 88.

33. Elisée Reclus, "Le Mississipi," 632.

34. Elisée Reclus, 'Fragment d'un voyage," 190–191.

35. Proudhon to Charles Edmond, Nov. 27, 1857, in Proudhon, *Correspondance,* 7:306; Tajan-Rogé's revelations about American society prompted Proudhon to remark: "The Yankees do not yet understand this humanitarian element called ART: in this domain, they are below the level of their neighbors the Eskimos, just as they are beneath the standards of civilized commerce with their eternal bankruptcies. Why doesn't somebody have the idea of visiting them with a hundred warships and a hundred thousand men?"

36. Tajan-Rogé, *Les Beaux-arts aux Etats-Unis,* viii, 11–12, and passim. On Tajan-Rogé's radical political activities, see *DBMOF,* 3:427.

37. Cabet, *Voyage en Icarie,* 535, 540.

38. D. Carrel to Cabet, Nov. 18, 1849, Papiers Cabet, MSS 1052, f. 65, BHVP.

39. Roiné to Cabet, Dec. 10, 1848, Papiers Cabet, f. 286, BHVP.

40. On the enormous influence of Cabet's book and his ill-fated American adventure, see Sutton, introduction to Cabet, *Travels in Icaria.* See also Prudhommeaux, *Icarie et son fondateur Etienne Cabet;* and Cabet, *Colonie Icarienne aux Etats-Unis.*

41. Tocqueville, *Souvenirs,* 180.

42. Quoted in Beecher, *Victor Considérant,* 298. Beecher's book offers a thorough account of Considérant's American colonization experiment in chapters 13–15.

43. Considérant, *Au Texas,* 34, 83.

44. Considérant, *Au Texas,* 159–160 (emphasis in original).

45. Considérant, *Au Texas,* 173.

46. Savardan, *Naufrage au Texas;* Considérant, *Du Texas;* Considérant, *European Colonization in Texas;* Maurice Dommanget, *Victor Considérant,* 46–48.

47. Dommanget, *Victor Considérant,* 48; Beecher, *Victor Considérant.*

48. See, for example, the journal of the Icarians Crétinon and Lacour, edited by Fernand Rude, *Voyage en Icarie.* See also Olinet, *Socialisme;* and Savardan, *Naufrage au Texas,* esp. 319–325.

49. See *Atelier,* Feb. 15, 1848; Blanqui, *Critique sociale,* 1:198–199; and Marx and Engels, *Communist Manifesto,* 116–117.

50. Considérant, *European Colonization in Texas,* 11.

CHAPTER 5

1. Tocqueville to Sedgwick, Sept. 19, 1855, in Hawkins, *Newly Discovered French Letters,* 208–209.

2. Tocqueville to Sedgwick, Aug 29, 1856, in Hawkins, *Newly Discovered French Letters,* 220. See also Tocqueville to Jared Sparks, July 15, 1857, in Hawkins, "Unpublished Letters of Alexis de Tocqueville," 207–208.

3. Tocqueville to Sumner, Mar. 28, 1858, in Hawkins, "Unpublished Letters of Alexis de Tocqueville," 216.

4. Montégut, "Une conversion américaine," *RDM* 15 (May 1, 1858): 197.

5. Michelet, *La Femme,* 211.

6. In all, Brown's band killed four people and wounded five; ten of his men were killed and five escaped. See Reynolds, *John Brown.*

7. On French newspaper reaction to the Brown affair, see Copans, "French Opinion of American Democracy," 83.

8. Hugo, "John Brown," in *Œuvres politiques complètes,* 551–552.

9. Hugo, *Choses Vues, 1849–1869,* 347 (Dec. 28, 1859).

10. Hugo to M. Heurtelou, Mar. 31, 1860, in Hugo, *Œuvres politiques complètes,* 557.

11. Hugo's engraving of Brown is reproduced in Honor, *L'Amérique vue par l'Europe,* 306. Michelet bought a copy of Hugo's engraving in Paris. See Michelet, *Journal,* 3:15. Edgar Quinet, upon receiving a bust of John Brown as a gift in 1871, wrote: "I see the modern Spartacus. This bust speaks of the future. When I look at it, I think I see, already, the liberation not only of the blacks but also of the whites." Quinet to M. X***, July 2, 1871, in Quinet, *Lettres d'exil,* 4:275.

12. One scholar has identified twenty-seven references to Brown in Hugo's work. See Dupont, *L'Amérique dans l'œuvre de Victor Hugo,* 23–28. For some other French works on Brown, see Pontécoulant, *John Brown à M. Victor Hugo* (Paris, 1860); Lucienes, *Le Gibet de John Brown;* Fernand, *John Brown;* Chevalier and Pharaon, *Drame esclavagiste;* and Vésinier, *Le Martyr de la liberté.* The left's use of the Brown legend during the late 1860s is discussed below in chapter 11.

13. See Gavronsky, *French Liberal Opposition,* 52–54; and Karsky, "L'Influence de Abraham Lincoln," 17–19.

14. Gavronsky, *French Liberal Opposition,* 54–57; Karsky, "L'Influence de Abraham Lincoln," 39.

15. Proudhon, *Qu'est-ce que la propriété?,* 73. Citing Tocqueville's and Chevalier's works on America, Proudhon wrote, "we have the proof today that even with the most perfect democracy it is possible not to be free."

16. See Curtis, *French Assembly of 1848,* 245.

17. Proudhon seems to have followed the evolution of the American slavery question with interest. His notebooks indicate that he had read Laboulaye's translation of Channing's works on slavery and society. See, for example, Proudhon's "Carnets," Dec. 1, 1857, Proudhon MSS, N. a.fr. 14275, vol. 11, f. 501, BN.

18. Louis Blanc (among others) had also made this point, saying that only the availability of land in America had obviated the social problems inherent in the principle of free competition. Blanc, *L'Organisation du travail,* 153–154. See also Vacherot, *La Démocratie,* 33–34.

19. Proudhon to Dulieu, Dec. 30, 1860, in Proudhon, *Correspondance,* 10:271–277.

CHAPTER 6

1. A large number of works have been devoted to various aspects of Franco-American relations during the Civil War. Among the most useful are Case and Spencer, *United States and France;* Case, *French Opinion on the United States and Mexico;* Jones, *Blue and Gray Diplomacy;* Doyle, *Cause of all Nations;* Sainlaude, *Le Gouvernement impériale et la guerre de sécession;* West, *Contemporary French Opinion on the Civil War;* Jordan and Pratt, *Europe and the American Civil War,* chaps. 9–10; Owsley, *King Cotton Diplomacy;* Blumenthal, *Reappraisal of Franco-American Relations,* chap. 5; and Gavronsky, *French Liberal Opposition.*

2. Martin to Sumner, Jan. 27, 1863, SP, vol. 137, f. 47.

3. Laboulaye, *Discours populaires,* 274–275.

4. Wellesley and Sencourt, *Conversations with Napoleon III,* 192.

5. Quoted in Case and Spencer, *United States and France,* 301. Apparently, the emperor's pro-South sympathies were not one sided. As Jeffrey Zvengrowski has shown, Confederate president Jefferson Davis was a longtime Francophile who saw Bonapartist France as a model for the Confederate States. See Zvengrowski, *Jefferson Davis, Napoleonic France, and the Nature of Confederate Ideology.*

6. Aumale to Sumner, Aug. 30, 1861, SP, vol. 136, f. 68.

7. Comte de Paris to François Buloz, July 29, 1862, in Sideman and Friedman, *Europe Looks at the Civil War,* 157. Another French nobleman, Prince Camille de Polignac (1832–1913), served as a volunteer major general on the Confederate side. See Gavronsky, *French Liberal Opposition,* 79.

8. West, *Contemporary French Opinion on the American Civil War,* 14–15; Case and Spencer, *United States and France,* 40.

9. Gasparin, *Uprising of a Great People,* 8–9.

10. Gasparin, *Uprising of a Great People,* vi.

11. Gasparin, *L'Amérique devant l'Europe,* 541.

12. Elisée Reclus, "De l'esclavage aux Etats-Unis. I"; Reclus, "De l'esclavage aux Etats-Unis II."

13. Elisée Reclus, "De l'esclavage aux Etats-Unis, II," 154.

14. Mercadier to Beluze, May 1861, in Beluze, *Lettres Icariennes,* 2:140.

15. Beluze, *Lettres Icariennes,* 2:157.

16. Proudhon to Félix Delhasse, Aug. 8, 1861, in Proudhon, *Correspondance,* 11:162.

17. Napoléon-Jérôme Bonaparte (1822–91), or Prince Jérôme-Napoléon, a first cousin of Napoleon III and a close friend of George Sand's, was a member of the National Assembly under the Second Republic and a senator under the Second Empire.

18. M. Sand, "Six Mille lieues à toute vapeur. II," 635–686; M. Sand, "Six Mille lieues. III," 903–947. George Sand had personally sent the articles to her friend François Buloz, founder and editor of the *RDM.* See G. Sand to Prince Jérôme-Napoléon, Jan. 7, 1862, in Sand, *Correspondance,* 4:306.

19. M. Sand, "Six Mille lieues. II," 676.

20. M. Sand, "Six Mille lieues. II," 684–686.

21. M. Sand, "Six Mille lieues. III," 912–913.

22. See, for example, her letter to Georges Rochet, Sept. 1842, in Sand, *Correspondance,* 5:776. Sand writes that "excessive liberty" in America produced "the most complete and regrettable in-

difference" among the population; American society was a "machine" driven by "personal interest, cupidity and the love of material pleasures ... no one thinks, believes, or loves there."

23. G. Sand to Barbès, Jan. 8, 1862, in Sand, *Correspondance,* 4:308.

24. West Virginia, which separated from Virginia in 1861 over the secession issue, was not formally admitted into the Union until June 20, 1863.

25. Franklin, *Emancipation Proclamation,* 15–19.

26. Lincoln to Greeley, Aug. 22, 1862, in Lincoln, *Collected Works,* 5:388–389. Lincoln's exchange of letters with Greeley was widely cited in the French semi-official press as proof that the North was not concerned with freeing the slaves: see Gavronsky, *French Liberal Opposition,* 184.

27. Letter of Sept. 15, 1861, in Blanc, *Lettres,* 1:183–192.

28. Blanqui to Lacambre, Feb. 1, 1862, in Dommanget, *Blanqui,* 35.

29. Blanqui to Lacambre, Feb. 14, 1862, in Dommanget, *Blanqui,* 35.

30. Elisée Reclus, "Les livres sur la crise américaine," 509.

CHAPTER 7

1. For detailed accounts of the *Trent* affair, see Case and Spencer, *United States and France,* chap. 6; Jones, *Blue and Gray Diplomacy,* 83–113; and Ferris, Trent *Affair.*

2. Case and Spencer, *United States and France,* 192.

3. Case and Spencer, *United States and France,* 192–193.

4. Case and Spencer, *United States and France,* 223–230; Jordan and Pratt, *Europe and the Civil War,* 206.

5. Once liberated, Mason and Slidell took up their respective posts in London and Paris, where they argued, cajoled, and intrigued in favor of British and French recognition of the Confederacy— in the end to no avail.

6. Gavronsky, *French Liberal Opposition,* 101–105; Case and Spencer, *United States and France,* 200.

7. Case and Spencer, *United States and France,* 198–199.

8. Prévost-Paradol, *Journal des débats,* Dec. 7, 1861. For other French reactions along these lines, see Gavronsky, *French Liberal Opposition,* 106; Gasparin, *Une parole de paix;* Assollant, *Cannoniers à vos pièces!;* and Elisée Reclus, "Le coton et la crise Américaine," 177. A number of the procureurs généraux (in Besançon, Lyons, and Nancy) reported that the *Trent* incident had aroused widespread anti-English sentiments, causing public opinion to favor French neutrality. See Case, *French Opinion on the United States and Mexico,* 248, 252, 254.

9. Letter of Dec. 2, 1861, in Blanc, *Lettres,* 1:276–277.

10. Letter of Dec. 8, 1862, in Blanc, *Lettres,* 1:283.

11. Blanc, *Lettres,* 1:298.

12. Proudhon to Chaudey, Dec. 30, 1861, in Proudhon, *Correspondance,* 11:312–314. See also Proudhon to Gouvernet, Dec. 19, 1861, ibid., 297–298.

13. Proudhon to Gouvernet, Jan. 2, 1862, in Proudhon, *Correspondance,* 11:316.

14. Blanqui to Lacambre, Feb. 14, 1862, in Dommanget, *Blanqui.* 35.

15. Letter of Mar. 23, 1862, SP, vol. 136, f. 89 (emphasis in original).

CHAPTER 8

1. On the Mexican expedition, see Martin, *Maximilian in Mexico;* Castelot, *Maximilien et Charlotte;* Blumenthal, *France and the United States,* 106–116; Bemis, *Diplomatic History of the United States,* 388–394; and Case, *French Opinion on the United States and Mexico,* chaps. 8–10.

2. Duruy, *Notes et souvenirs,* 2:115.

3. Jones, *Blue and Gray Diplomacy,* 285.

4. Napoleon III to Forey, July 3, 1862, in Case, *French Opinion on the United States and Mexico,* 327.

5. Napoleon III to comte August-Charles Flahault de la Billarderie, Oct. 9, 1861, in Bemis, *Diplomatic History of the United States,* 388.

6. Stève Sainlaude, "France's Great Design and the Confederacy," in Doyle, *American Civil Wars,* 107–124.

7. Chevalier, *La France, le Mexique,* 31.

8. Case and Spencer, *United States and France,* 545.

9. Seward quoted in White, *American Opinion of France,* 152.

10. Quoted in H. Blumenthal, *France and the United States,* 109.

11. Quinet, *L'Expédition du Mexique,* 15–18, 29 (emphasis in original).

12. Quinet, *L'Expédition du Mexique,* 29.

13. Michelet to Dumesnil, July 2, 1863, Lettres de Michelet à Alfred Dumesnil, Papiers Michelet, vol. 4, f. 273, BHVP. Michelet was referring to the Polish uprising against the Russian Empire that erupted in January 1863. It was definitively crushed by the Russians the following year, leaving some 25,000 insurgents dead. Napoleon III voiced sympathy for the Poles but never seriously considered military intervention on their behalf.

14. Vésinier, *Le Martyr de la liberté,* 285–290.

15. Proudhon to Defontaine, Apr. 12, 1862, in Proudhon, *Correspondance,* 12:53. See also Proudhon to M. X***, June 22, 1862, ibid., 12:132.

16. Speech of Feb. 6, 1863, in Favre, *Discours parlementaires,* 3:220–221. See also Picard, *Discours parlementaires,* 1:279.

17. Speech of May 13, 1864, in Favre, *Discours parlementaires,* 2:444–449.

18. Case and Spencer, *United States and France,* 563–564.

CHAPTER 9

1. Fohlen, *L'Industrie textile,* 285.

2. W. de Fonvielle, "Considérations sur le commerce de l'Union américaine," 6.

3. PGR, Colmar, Jan. 9, 1862, in Case, *French Opinion on the United States and Mexico,* 251.

4. *Rapports des membres de la section française,* 4:359, 5:20. On the crisis in French export industries, see Case and Spencer, *United States and France,* 162–64; Blumenthal, *Reappraisal of Franco-American Relations,* 155–56; and David H. Pinkney, "France and the Civil War," in Hyman, *Heard Round the World,* 120–28.

5. PGR, Lyons, Apr. 4, May 4, 1861, in Case, *French Opinion on the United States and Mexico,* 12.

6. Agriculture Ministry to Prefect of the Rhône, May 12, 1862, F¹² 4476 D, AN.

7. Official statistics cited in Gavronsky, *French Liberal Opposition,* 119.

8. *Rapports des délégués lyonnais,* 144–145.

9. On the economic aspects of the cotton crisis, see Beckert, "Emancipation and Empire," 1405–1438; Beckert, *Empire of Cotton,* esp. chap. 9; Fohlen, *L'Industrie textile,* 253–369; Dunham, *Anglo-French Treaty of Commerce,* 195–214; and Cordier, *La Crise cotonnière dans la Seine-Inférieure.* See also the diverse reports on the "Situation industrielle" contained in F¹² 4476 D and E, AN.

10. Fohlen, *L'Industrie textile,* 304.

11. Blumenthal, *Reappraisal of Franco-American Relations,* 156.

12. See chapter 10.

13. *Le Temps,* Dec. 26, 1862

14. Fohlen, *L'Industrie textile,* 265.

15. Fohlen, *L'Industrie textile,* 265–267.

16. Hector Pessard, *Le Temps,* Dec. 26, 1862.

17. Noël to Michelet, Jan. 23, 1863, Papiers Michelet, A.4817, vol. 20, f. 35, BHVP. See also Noël to Michelet, Dec. 30, 1862, ibid., f. 32. For other firsthand accounts of working-class suffering in Rouen, see the letters of Dr. E. C. Hellis in Chaline, *Deux Bourgeois en leur temps,* 177, 179–80.

18. E. Noël, *Opinion nationale,* Feb. 20, 1863.

19. *Nouvelliste de Rouen,* Apr. 3, 1863; Noël to Dumesnil, Feb. 21, Mar. 14, 1863, Correspondance Alfred Dumesnil–Eugène Noël, vol. 8, ff. 355, 366, BHVP.

20. PGR, Paris, June 15, 1862, in Case, *French Opinion on the United States and Mexico,* 81.

21. On the 1863 elections, see Tchernoff, *Parti républicain,* 402–408.

22. Quoted in Fohlen, *L'Industrie textile,* 275.

23. Fohlen, *L'Industrie textile,* 276.

24. Fohlen, *L'Industrie textile,* 268–271.

25. On the various relief efforts, see Fohlen, *L'Industrie textile,* 264–71. See also "Souscriptions pour les ouvriers de la Seine-Inférieure," F1¹⁰ III Seine-Inférieure, vol. 17, ff. 350–375, AN. See also dossiers 10 MP 1413 and 1 MP 3237, Archives Départementales de la Seine-Maritime, Rouen.

26. See Owsley, *King Cotton Diplomacy,* chap. 11; and Case and Spencer, *United States and France,* chap. 9.

27. Case and Spencer, *United States and France,* 359–363.

28. Case and Spencer, *United States and France,* 386–396.

29. Case and Spencer, *United States and France,* 397.

30. Fohlen, *L'Industrie textile,* 267.

31. Quoted in Sideman and Friedman, *Europe Looks at the Civil War,* 211.

CHAPTER 10

1. Blumenthal, *France and the United States,* 84.

2. Jordan and Pratt, *Europe and the Civil War,* 230.

3. Bernstein, *Essays in Political and Intellectual History,* 128.

4. Harrison, "British Labour and the Confederacy"; Harrison, "British Labour and American Slavery."

5. Harrison, *Before the Socialists,* 56.

6. Ellison, *Support for Secession,* 195–96. The findings of Harrison and Ellison have been corroborated by Norman Longmate, *Hungry Mills,* chap. 19.

7. Jones, epilogue to Ellison, *Support for Secession,* 200. Jones's list of propagandists for this myth could be extended to include the London exile Louis Blanc, whose letters to the *Temps* helped propagate the views of Cobden and Bright in France, where partisans of the Union were just as anxious as their English brethren to believe that the workers were voluntarily enduring their misery in the interest of antislavery and democracy. See, for example, letter of April 5, 1863, in Blanc, *Lettres,* 1:116.

8. Forcade, *RDM* 43 (Feb. 1, 1863), 745. This passage has been cited by the following writers: Krebs, "Lincoln et la France," 38; Sears, "Neglected Critic of Our Civil War," 541; Karsky, "L'Influence de Abraham Lincoln," 123; Sideman and Friedman, *Europe Looks at the Civil War,* 212–213; Lemaître, *La Guerre de Seession en photos,* 39; and Chinard, *L'Amerique de Abraham Lincoln,* 26–27.

9. Bernstein, *Essays in Political and Intellectual History,* 121–33.

10. On the *Times's* editorial line during the war, see Hamilton, "The London Times and the American Civil War."

11. Bernstein, *Essays in Political and Intellectual History,* 128.

12. Bernstein, *Essays in Political and Intellectual History,* 129.

13. Bernstein, *Essays in Political and Intellectual History,* 129.

14. Antonetti, *Histoire contemporaine politique et sociale,* 276.

15. Bernstein, *Essays in Political and Intellectual History,* 133.

16. Diverse reports contained in F^{12} 4651, F^{12} 4476 D and E, and F^{1C} III, AN.

17. On the effects of the cotton crisis in this region, see Pierrard, *La Vie ouvrière à Lille,* 464–467.

18. Préfet du Nord, Feb. 27, 1862, F^{1C} III Nord 15, f. 308, AN.

19. Préfet du Nord, Mar. 12, 1862, F^{1C} III Nord 15, f. 316, AN.

20. Préfet du Nord, Mar. 3, 1862, F^{1C} III Nord 15, f. 376, AN.

21. Procureur général, Douai, July 6, 1864, BB^{30} 377, AN.

22. Préfet du Haut-Rhin, May 16, 1862, F^{12} 4651, f. 354, AN.

23. Préfet du Haut-Rhin, July 19, 1862, F^{1C} III Haut-Rhin 14, AN.

24. Préfet du Haut-Rhin, Apr. 4, 1863, F^{12} 4651, f. 635, AN.

25. PGR, Rouen, Apr. 12, 1862, BB^{30} 387, AN.

26. Préfet de l'Aisne, Jan. 4, 1862 (copy), F^{1C} III Nord 15, AN.

27. Préfet de la Haute-Vienne, May 29, 1864, F^{12} 4651, f. 586, AN.

28. *Rapports des délégués lyonnais,* 144–145.

29. *Délégations ouvrières à l'Exposition universelle de Londres,* 58.

30. Harrison, *Before the Socialists,* 53.

31. "Aux travailleurs," *Opinion nationale,* Jan. 26, 1863.

32. See their appeals in *Opinion nationale,* Jan. 20, 24, 30, 1863. See also Coutant's letter on the workers' subscription in *Le Temps,* Jan. 8, 1863.

33. Lynn M. Case, "A Voice Crying in the Wilderness," in Osgood, *Napoleon III and the Second Empire,* 119.

34. S. Bernstein, *Essays in Political and Intellectual History,* 132. There is some evidence that an effort in 1862 to elicit a statement in support of Lincoln failed to arouse much enthusiasm among Parisian workers and was finally abandoned. See Henri Martin to Cluseret, Apr. 27, 1862, SP, vol. 134, f. 106.

35. Proudhon, *De la capacité politique,* 197 (emphasis in original).

36. Proudhon to Chaudey, Sept. 1, 1862, Proudhon, *Correspondance,* 14:237.

37. Proudhon to X***, Aug. 9, 1863, in Proudhon, *Correspondance,* 14:277.

38. Proudhon to Jottrand, Oct. 23, 1864, in Proudhon, *Correspondance,* 14:78. Proudhon also delivered a lengthy attack against the Yankees in *Du principe fédératif,* chap. 13 and passim.

39. Leneveux, *La Propagande de l'instruction,* 160. *L'Atelier,* published between 1840 and 1850, was an influential workingmen's newspaper espousing Christian socialist principles.

40. Corbon, *Le Secret du peuple de Paris,* 232.

41. Anon., "La Fête de Courcelles," Y^c 7182, f. 415, BN. On the significance of such songs as expressions of working-class attitudes, see Pierrard, *Les Chansons en patois de Lille.*

42. PGR, Douai, July 1, 1865, BB^{30} 377, AN.

43. Louis Longret, "L'Espoir de vivre heureux," Y^c 7182, f. 550, BN.

44. PGR, Rouen, Jan. 9, 1862, BB^{30} 387, AN.

45. PGR, Colmar, July 4, 1861, BB^{30} 376, AN.

46. See Eugène Noël's 1863 description of mothers in Rouen registering their daughters as prostitutes in chapter 9.

47. PGR, Colmar, Oct. 9, 1861, BB^{30} 376, AN.

48. PGR, Colmar, July 14, 1862, BB^{30} 376, AN.

49. Prefet du Haut-Rhin, July 19, 1862, F^{1C} III Haut-Rhin 14, AN.

50. PGR, Colmar, Jan. 24, 1863, BB^{30} 376, AN.

51. *L'Industriel Alsacien,* Oct. 26, 1862.

52. *L'Industriel Alsacien,* Feb. 16, 1862.

53. *L'Industriel Alsacien,* Nov. 9, 1862.

54. *Journal du Haut-Rhin,* esp. Nov. 16, 23, 1862, and Feb. 1, 1863.

55. PGR, Colmar, Jan. 24, 1863, BB^{30} 376, AN.

56. G. Imbert-Koechlin, *Industrial Alsacien,* Feb. 2, 1862 (emphasis added). In 1862 Imbert-Koechlin was instrumental in setting up a French company to promote cotton production in Algeria as an alternative to American cotton.

57. See Pierrard, *La Vie ouvriere à Lille,* 464.

58. Préfet du Nord, Oct. 7, 1861, F^{1C} III Nord 15, f 163, AN.

59. PGR, Douai, July 3, 1863, BB^{30} 377, AN.

60. Avocat général, Douai, Oct. 2, 1863, BB^{30} 377, AN.

61. *Chambre consultative des Arts et Manufactures,* Cambrai, Dec. 30, 1861, F^{12} 4476 D, AN.

62. *Mémorial de Lille et du Nord de la France,* Jan. 15, 1863.

63. *Echo du Nord,* Jan. 15, 1863. The *Journal populaire* was not authorized as a political newspaper and thus had no official editorial policy on the American war. Yet occasional allusions to the struggle in the "faits divers" column seemed favorable to the South. One such item reported the capture of the Union steamer *Chesapeake* by Confederate agents, which the journal admiringly described as "bold and energetic men, capable of launching into all sorts of adventures and skill-

ful enough to succeed at the most dangerous missions." *Journal populaire,* Feb. 16, 1864. Another praised "the courage of the ladies of Charleston." Ibid., Feb. 29, 1864. Yet another reproduced a long article from the *Richmond Examiner* denouncing a Yankee plot to assassinate Jefferson Davis and burn down the Confederate capital. Ibid., Mar. 8, 1864. In that same issue an article on the economic crisis noted that "the mere hope of seeing the American conflict come to an end, and thus reopen this important market, can encourage our manufacturers to continue giving jobs to a large number of their workers." Ibid., Mar. 8, 1864.

64. PGR, Rouen, July 10, 1862, BB^{30} 387, AN.

65. On Monseigneur Bonnechose's relief activities during the cotton crisis, see Cordier, *La Crise cotonnière dans la Seine-Inférieure,* 96; and Besson, *Vie du Cardinal Bonnechose,* 1:423–24. See also the vivid description of working-class suffering in Bonnechose, *Lettre de sa Grandeur Monseigneur l'Archeveque de Rouen,* 375: "Should we be surprised to see our countryside traversed day and night by suffering hordes who go from farm to farm asking for bread and shelter, to see our railroad stations besieged by poor children, appealing to the pity of travelers, or to see the ravages of hunger and cold on the gaunt and hollow faces of the miserable beings who wander around our cities? But what the public cannot perceive . . . is the despair, the wretchedness, the anxieties of the families retained in their sad hovels by infirmed relatives, by young infants, or by the shame of begging. All of that is happening before our eyes, and before the eyes of God, and it fills the soul with an immense bitterness."

66. Bonnechose quoted in Senior, *Conversations with Distinguished Persons,* 2:213.

67. M. Loyest, président de la Chambre consultative des Arts et Manufactures de Cholet, July 8, 1862, F^{12} 4476 D, AN (emphasis in original).

68. PGR, Nancy, Apr. 12, 1863, BB^{30} 381, AN.

69. Chambre consultative de Poitiers, "Rapport sur le mouvement industriel et commercial du Département de la Vienne, pendant le premier Semestre de l'année 1864," n.d., F^{12} 4476 D, AN.

70. Longret, "L'Espoir de vivre heureux."

CHAPTER 11

1. Lincoln, "Preliminary Emancipation Proclamation," in Franklin, *Emancipation Proclamation,* 46–49.

2. Lincoln, "Preliminary Emancipation Proclamation," 46–49.

3. Message of Dec. 1, 1862, in Lincoln, *Collected Works,* 5:527–537.

4. Lincoln, "Emancipation Proclamation," in Franklin, *Emancipation Proclamation,* 91–93.

5. *Siècle,* Oct. 12, 1862; *Phare de la Loire,* Oct. 8, 1862. On the initial French response to the proclamation, see West, *Contemporary French Opinion on the American Civil War,* 85–86; Case and Spencer, *United States and France,* 328–332; and Gavronsky, *French Liberal Opposition,* 184–188.

6. Letter of Feb. 3, 1863, in Blanc, *Lettres,* 2:412–413.

7. Elisée Reclus, "Les livres sur la crise américaine," 512.

8. Michael Vorenberg, "Liberté, Egalité, and Lincoln," in Carwardine and Sexton, *Global Lincoln,* 99–100. Though he never visited the United States, Dumas did have an indirect link

to America through his notorious 1867–68 affair with the actress Adah Isaacs Mencken, a New Orleans–born creole who took Europe by storm with her acting, singing, and especially her nude performances on horseback. Thirty-three years her elder, Dumas was much mocked in the press for his conspicuous liaison. See Troyat, *Alexandre Dumas*, 498–501.

9. In his message of December 8, 1863, Lincoln announced that 100,000 former slaves were in Union military service. Lincoln, *Collected Works*, 7:49.

10. Pelletan, *Adresse au roi Coton*, 1–3. Pelletan, like Agénor de Gasparin a cofounder of the Union des Eglises évangéliques de France, voiced a positive view of the United States, shared by many French Protestants, based on American traditions of religious liberty and freedom of conscience. French Protestants also had a strong attachment to the abolitionist cause. See, for example, *American Slavery, Address of French Protestant Pastors*.

11. Pelletan, *Adresse au roi Coton*, 10.

12. Pelletan, *Adresse au roi Coton*, 36–38.

13. Pelletan to Cluseret, Mar. 29, 1863, SP, vol. 137, f. 77.

14. On the reception of Laboulaye's book in France, see Jeune, *Graindorge*, 60–61; and Gavronsky, *French Liberal Opposition*, 199. The BN catalogue lists twenty-one editions of *Paris en Amérique* between 1863 and 1887. On Laboulaye's career as a champion of American democracy, see Gray, *Interpreting American Democracy in France*.

15. Elisée Reclus, "Les Noirs américains depuis la guerre. I," 364–394; Reclus, "Les Noirs américains. . . . II," 691–722.

16. Elisée Reclus, "Les Noirs. . . . II," 722.

17. Elisée Reclus, "Histoire de la guerre civile aux Etats-Unis," 556.

18. Elisée Reclus, "Histoire de la guerre civile aux Etats-Unis," 624.

19. Melvil-Bloncourt, "Homme ou singe," 143–147.

20. Melvil-Bloncourt, "Chronique de l'Amérique du Nord," *RMC* 9 (Aug. 1863): 205–206.

21. Melvil-Bloncourt, "Chronique de l'Amérique du Nord," *RMC* 11 (June 1864): 464.

22. Melvil-Bloncourt, "Chronique de l'Amérique du Nord," *RMC* 14 (Feb. 1865): 257. Melvil-Bloncourt (1823–80) had a brief but interesting political career. He was elected to the National Assembly as a deputy of Guadeloupe in April 1871 but renounced his seat and cast his lot with the Commune. Appointed director of infantry and artillery battalions by Gustave Cluseret, Melvil-Bloncourt served in the War Ministry until the insurrection was crushed, then calmly took up his seat in the National Assembly. His role in the Commune was discovered in 1874, at which point he fled to Geneva and narrowly escaped a death sentence, pronounced in absentia.

23. Pyat, *Au peuple des Etats-Unis*.

24. Vésinier, *Le Martyr de la liberté*, 6 (emphasis in original).

25. Vésinier, *Le Martyr de la liberté*, 191–193.

26. Vésinier, *Le Martyr de la liberté*, 303.

27. Vésinier, *Le Martyr de la liberté*, 362–363.

28. Vésinier, *Le Martyr de la liberté*, 272.

29. Vésinier, *Le Martyr de la liberté*, 363–364.

30. V. I. Lenin, "Letter to American Workers," quoted in editor's introduction to Marx and Engels, *Civil War in the United States*, xxiv.

31. Marx and Engels, *Civil War in the United States,* 24, 48, 81, and passim. Marx's influence on the French left was limited during the period under discussion, though he had lived in Paris briefly (1842–45, 1848–49), was an astute observer of French politics and social movements, and kept in close touch with Parisian members of the International: Noël, *Dictionnaire de la Commune,* 253–254.

32. Karl Marx, "To Abraham Lincoln," in Marx and Engels, *Civil War in the United States,* 279–280.

33. Brogan, *Price of Revolution,* 76.

34. Lichtheim, *Short History of Socialism,* 25–26.

35. The classic statement of this argument is that of Beard and Beard, *Rise of American Civilization,* esp. chap. 18. See also Novack, *America's Revolutionary Heritage,* 260–261.

36. See Proudhon, *Correspondance,* 12:79–80, 132, 14:237–38.

37. Proudhon, *Du principe fédératif,* 132.

38. Proudhon, *Du principe fédératif,* 72–74, 300–311. On this point, Proudhon shared the analysis of proslavery theorists like George Fitzhugh, who argued that the North's "pauperism" was more inhumane than the South's chattel slavery. See Wilson, *Patriotic Gore,* 341–364; McKitrick, *Slavery Defended,* 34–50.

39. Proudhon, *Du principe fédératif,* 307. Proudhon repeated the same charges in his posthumously published *De la capacité politique des classes ouvrières,* 197–98.

40. Proudhon to Lucien Jottrand, Oct. 23, 1864, in Proudhon, *Correspondance,* 14:78–79. See also ibid., 50, 64, 277.

41. Emile de Girardin (1802–81) founded *La Presse* in 1836, served multiple terms as a deputy, and was a leading voice of the liberal opposition during the Second Empire.

42. Proudhon himself noted the similarities between their ideas in a letter to Girardin on February 29, 1863. Proudhon, *Correspondance,* 12:322. See also Zeldin, *Emile Ollivier,* 93.

43. Girardin, *La Liberté,* 314.

44. For his hatred of slavery, see Girardin to the American Anti-Slavery Society, 1855, in *Letters on American Slavery,* 8–9.

45. *La Presse,* Dec. 19, 20, 22, 25, 29, 1862. This was later reprinted in Girardin, *Paix et liberté,* 59–77.

46. Girardin, *Paix et liberté,* 60 (emphasis in original).

47. Girardin, *Paix et liberté,* 71.

48. Girardin, *La Presse,* Apr. 27, 1865.

49. Lamartine, *Cours familier de littérature,* 81–114.

50. Lamartine, *Cours familier de littérature,* 91.

51. Lamartine, *Cours familier de littérature,* 92.

52. Lamartine, *Toussaint Louverture.*

53. Lamartine, *Cours familier de littérature,* 85.

54. Quoted in Curtis, *French Assembly of 1848,* 80.

55. Lamartine's anti-Union stand further discredited him in the eyes of the far left, which had been hostile to him ever since 1848. When Lamartine died in 1870, the Russian anarchist Mikhail Bakunin sarcastically noted, "M. de Lamartine is dead, after having launched a last eloquent plea in

favor of the slaveholding planters and against the republicans of the North, liberators of the black race, in the United States of America." M. Bakunin, *La Marseillaise,* Mar. 2, 1870.

CHAPTER 12

1. Henri Allain-Targé to his mother, Apr. 1865, in Allain-Targé, *République sous l'Empire,* 23. A close friend of Léon Gambetta, Allain-Targé (1832–1902) was active in the republican opposition during the final years of the Second Empire and later served in the government of the Third Republic.

2. Many of these messages are contained in the U.S. government–published *Assassination of Abraham Lincoln.*

3. Quinet to V. Mangin, May 14, 1865, in Quinet, *Lettres d'exil,* 3:11.

4. Hugo quoted in Sideman and Friedman, *Europe Looks at the Civil War,* 307.

5. Elisée Reclus, *Correspondance,* 1:244–246.

6. Allain-Targé to his mother, Apr. 1865, in Allain-Targé, *République sous l'Empire,* 22–25. See also Louis Blanc's letter to Charles Francis Adams expressing sympathy on behalf of all the London exiles: Blanc to Adams, Apr. 27, 1865, quoted in Gastineau, *Génies de la liberté,* 244.

7. Prévost-Paradol, *Courrier du dimanche,* Sept. 24, 1865.

8. *Phare de la Loire,* 2 May 1865; Tchernoff, *Parti républicain,* 358; Chinard, *l'Amérique de Abraham Lincoln,* 27–28; Lissagaray, *Histoire de la Commune,* 26.

9. Quoted by Chinard, *L'Amérique de Abraham Lincoln,* 28. See also Declaration on Lincoln's death signed by forty-three members of "la Jeunesse Israélite," Papiers Chassin, C.P. 5647, vol. 9, f. 82, BHVP.

10. Quoted by Bernstein, *Essays in Political and Intellectual History,* 131.

11. Bernstein, *Essays in Political and Intellectual History,* 131–132.

12. Pyat, *Au peuple des Etats-Unis,* n.p. Pyat's incendiary writings from London "gave the Imperial police nightmares." Noël, *Dictionnaire de la Commune,* 314–315. Pyat (1810–89) returned to France from his long exile after the fall of the empire in September 1870 and played a leading role in the uprising of the Commune.

13. Michael Vorenberg, "Liberté, Egalité, and Lincoln," in Carwardine and Sexton, *Global Lincoln,* 95. Vorenberg goes even further, speculating that Lincoln, in death, may have "helped to set in motion the events leading to the Paris Commune." Ibid., 102.

14. Bigelow to William Cullen Bryant, May 16, 1862, quoted in Vorenberg, "Liberté, Egalité, and Lincoln," 95.

15. Chassin, *Phare de la Loire,* Apr. 28, 1865.

16. The correspondence of the committee and other documents relating to the Lincoln medal project are preserved in Papiers Chassin, C.P. 5647, vol. 9, ff. 24–182, BHVP.

17. *Courrier français,* June 10, 1865.

18. Adam, *Mes Sentiments et Nos Idées,* 22–23.

19. Chauffour to Chassin, July 16, 1865, Papiers Chassin, vol. 9, f. 39, BHVP.

20. *Phare de la Loire,* Dec. 3, 1866.

21. On the subscription forms preserved in the Chassin papers, about 70 percent of those listing their professions are workers and artisans.

22. See Papiers Chassin, C.P. 5647, vol. 9, BHVP.

23. *Phare de la Loire,* Dec. 3, 1866.

24. This reference to a statue is metaphorical. The actual Statue of Liberty by Frédéric Bartholdi was only completed in 1884. See chapter 19 below.

25. A photographic reproduction of the medal appears in Honor, *L'Amérique vue par l'Europe* 321.

26. Papiers Chassin, vol. 9, f. 177.

27. Pelletan quoted in Chinard, *L'Amérique de Abraham Lincoln,* 29.

28. Mrs. Lincoln to committee, Jan. 3, 1867, Papiers Chassin, vol. 9, f. 182.

29. Hugo was actually well known in the United States at this time, thanks to *Les Misérables,* which appeared in translation there in 1862. With a few exceptions, it was critically acclaimed in both the North and the South, despite the author's abolitionist convictions. Hugo's book was especially popular among the soldiers of Lee's Army of Northern Virginia, who read it in pamphlet form in the trenches. Mispronouncing its title, they gave themselves the nickname "Lee's Miserables." See Louis P. Masur, "In Camp, Reading 'Les Miserables,'" *Opinionator* (blog), *New York Times,* Feb. 9, 2013, https://opinionator.blogs.nytimes.com/2013/02/09/in-camp-reading-les-miserables/, accessed June 23, 2019. See also Power, *Lee's Miserables.*

30. Madame A. Gaël, *Coopération,* June 30, 1867. Lesourd later explained her motivation in a letter to a friend: "At the time of the subscription to give a medal to Mme. Lincoln, while I fully supported that homage to the widow of a man so just and so great, I thought with sadness that another widow, whose sacrifice was voluntary, whose misfortune was greater, and whose devotion was total, the widow of John Brown, was forgotten. As always, the initiator [of emancipation] was overshadowed by the one who completed his work and garnered all the glory of success." Quoted in *Les États-Unis d'Europe,* Mar. 22, 1868.

31. *Coopération,* July 14, Aug. 25, 1867.

32. See chapter 5 above.

33. Hugo to Paul Blanc, July 3, 1867, in *Coopération,* July 14, 1867.

34. Elisée Reclus, *Coopération,* July 14, 1867.

35. Chassin, *Coopération,* July 14, 1867. Chassin and several other members of the Lincoln committee were invited to serve on the Brown committee by the editor of the *Coopération.* See Papiers Chassin, vol. 9, f. 324.

36. See Schoelcher's letter in *Coopération,* July 28, 1867.

37. For Garibaldi's contribution, see *Coopération,* Aug. 25, 1867.

38. See lists in *Coopération,* July 14, 28, Aug. 25, Sept. 8, 22, Oct. 22, 1867.

39. André Léo was the pseudonym of novelist Victoire Léodile Bera (1824–1900), socialist, anarchist, member of the International, and later an active supporter of the Commune.

40. André Léo, *Démocratie,* Apr. 11, 1869. Léo reported that 10,000 people had contributed to the subscription and that the medal had been struck gratis by the Belgian engraver J. Würden.

41. Jean-Baptiste Baudin (1811–51), a republican deputy, was killed on the barricades opposing Louis Napoleon's coup d'état. Victor Noir (1848–70), an opposition journalist, was shot dead by

Prince Pierre Napoleon, a cousin of Napoleon III. Another political subscription was sponsored by the *Siècle* in 1867–68 to erect a statue to Voltaire in Paris. As a vehicle for the widespread anticlerical sentiments of the left, this project received over 200,000 subscriptions—four times more than the Lincoln and Brown subscriptions combined. On the Voltaire subscription, see Guiral, *Vie quotidienne en France,* 236–237.

CHAPTER 13

1. A reproduction and history of this painting appears on the website of the Musée d'Orsay, https:// www.musee-orsay.fr/en/collections/works-in-focus/search/commentaire/commentaire_id/the -origin-of-the-world-3122.html. Courbet (1819–1877), a prolific self-taught painter, scandalized contemporaries with his challenges to the academism and romanticism of his day. A supporter of the Paris Commune in 1971, he encouraged the toppling of the Vendôme column and was later ordered to pay for its reconstruction. He died the day before the first installment was due. Noël, *Dictionnaire de la Commune,* 103–104.

2. Jack-of-all-trades that he was, Cluseret also proved to be a competent art critic, though his comments usually carried a political message. In a short-lived art review that he cofounded with Jules Vallès in 1868, he praised his friend Courbet as "the premier painter of our times." Cluseret, "Le Salon II," *L'Art,* May 1, 1868.

3. Victor Hugo, who met Cluseret after returning to Paris in September 1870, described him as "a rather tall man, with a full, round face, bold and shadowy eyes, military mustache and bearing, a respectful manner." Hugo, *Choses vues, 1870–1885,* 182 (June 5, 1871).

4. Cluseret, *Mémoires,* 2:112.

5. Cluseret, *Tribune,* Feb. 11, 1869.

6. E. Falières to Gen. Renson, May 3, 1872, Dossier Cluseret, Classement Officier 11793/N, SHD.

7. "Etats de service," Dossier Cluseret, SHD.

8. Merle to War Ministry, Nov. 9, 1857, Jan. 9, Feb. 23, 1858, Dossier Cluseret, SHD. Cluseret also raised eyebrows by living off-barracks with a local woman, his only known liaison with a member of the opposite sex. See Braka, *L'honneur perdu du général Cluseret,* 35.

9. Report, May 28, 1858, Dossier Cluseret, SHD.

10. Cluseret, *Mémoires,* 3:17–18.

11. Marx quoted in Katz, *Appomattox to Montmartre,* 6.

12. Lepelletier, *Histoire de la Commune,* 3:94. Lepelletier did not always have such a cynical opinion of Cluseret; see his laudatory article on him in the *Réforme,* June 22, 1869.

13. Katz, *Appomattox to Montmartre,* 6.

14. Cluseret to Sumner, n.d. [Feb. 1862?], SP, vol. 137.

15. Cluseret to Sumner, n.d. [Feb. 1862?], SP, vol. 137. Cluseret brought with him, as his aide-de-camp, the French republican Ulrich de Fonvielle, who had served with him in Italy and would later figure as a principal witness against Prince Pierre Napoleon in the sensational Victor Noir affair in 1870. See Fonvielle's letter from Washington in *Revue du monde colonial* 6 (Mar. 1862): 211.

16. McCullough, *Greater Journey*, 6–7, 59, 225–233, 334, and passim.

17. Cluseret to Sumner, Feb. 27, 1862, SP, vol. 136, f. 80.

18. McClellan, *McClellan's Own Story*, 143.

19. Cluseret to Sumner, Feb. 27, 1862, SP, vol. 136, f. 80.

20. Cluseret to Sumner, [May or June 1862?], SP, vol. 136, f. 119.

21. Washburne, *Recollections*, 2:107.

22. In his detailed account of this battle, Cluseret claims he defied Frémont's order to retreat and achieved an unexpected victory by outmaneuvering Jackson's forces. Cluseret, *Mémoires*, 2:163–167.

23. Sumner to Cluseret, June 18, 1862, quoted in Cluseret, *Mémoires*, 3:19.

24. Braka, *L'honneur perdu du général Cluseret*, 39.

25. Martin to Sumner, July 20, 1862, SP, vol. 137, f. 9. See also Martin to Sumner, Mar. 23, 1861, ibid. vol. 136, f. 89.

26. Pelletan to Cluseret, Mar. 29, 1863, SP, vol. 137. Cluseret cites other letters in the same vein from Carnot and Martin in his *Mémoires*, 3:22–26.

27. Cluseret to Sumner, n.d. [Jan. 1863?], SP, vol. 137, f. 43. See also Cluseret, *Mémoires*, 3:22–25; and Henri Martin, article on Cluseret's resignation, *Siècle*, Apr. 6–7, 1863.

28. Katz, *Appomattox to Montmartre*, 8.

29. Katz, *Appomattox to Montmartre*, 9–10.

30. Quoted in Phalen, *Democratic Soldier*, 30.

31. Cluseret to Sumner, Apr. 27, 1865, quoted in Katz, *Appomattox to Montmartre*, 11.

32. *DBMOF*, 3:192. Pelletier (1816–80) served as a socialist deputy from 1848 until 1851. Expelled after the coup d'état, he emigrated to New York, where he made a fortune manufacturing artificial flowers.

33. Cluseret, "My Connection with Fenianism," 37–42. See also Cluseret, *Mémoires*, 2:136, 3:118.

34. Katz, *Appomattox to Montmartre*, 6.

35. Cluseret to Sumner, Sept. 6, 1867, SP, vol. 143.

36. Cluseret's Civil War background would have much to do with his selection as military chief of the Commune in 1871. See *Journal Officiel* (Paris Commune), Apr. 6, 1871.

CHAPTER 14

1. Foner, *Reconstruction;* Stampp, *Era of Reconstruction*, chaps. 2–5; Morison, *Oxford History of the American People,* vol. 2, chap. 14.

2. Congress repealed this act in 1887.

3. Louis-Napoléon Bonaparte (1856–79), the prince impérial, lived in exile with his parents in England following the French defeat in the Franco-Prussian War. He later joined the English army and was killed in a skirmish with Zulu warriors in southern Africa.

4. Zeldin, *Emile Olivier*, 86–104.

5. Bellanger et al., *Histoire générale de la presse française*, 2:345–355; Collins, *The Government and the Newspaper Press in France*, chap. 12.

6. See, for example, Hofstadter, *American Political Tradition*, 155–156.

7. Woodward, *Reunion and Reaction*, 15.

8. Melvil-Bloncourt, Chronique de l'Amérique du nord," *RMC* 11 (May 1864): 467–468.

9. Melvil-Bloncourt, Chronique de l'Amérique du nord," *RMC* 11 (Apr. 1864), 951. For Melvil-Bloncourt's critique of Johnson's reconstruction policy, see ibid., 15 (June 1865): 403–417. In April 1865 he had launched a national subscription in favor of the American freedmen. See ibid. (Apr. 1865): 5–7.

10. Clemenceau, *American Reconstruction*, 84.

11. Elisée Reclus, "Histoire des états américains," 766–767. See also the minority resolution presented to the 1867 Paris Anti-Slavery Conference by Reclus, Melvil-Bloncourt, Chassin, Cluseret, and others, calling on the Radicals to establish complete racial equality throughout the United States. *Special Report of the Anti-Slavery Conference*, 14.

12. Considérant, *Mexique*, 187–188.

13. Portalis, *Etats-Unis*, 196. Portalis (1845–1918), a radical journalist, had gone to the United States in 1867–68 to study its republican institutions. This book, published upon his return to France, was an influential piece of anti-imperial propaganda that used the American example to attack the regime of Napoleon III.

14. Guiral, *Prévost-Paradol*, 451.

15. Michael Vorenberg, "Liberte, Egalité, and Lincoln," in Carwardine and Sexton, *Global Lincoln*, 103.

16. Allain-Targé, "Le message du président Johnson," 206–209. See also Chotteau, *Les Américains d'aujourd'hui;* and Chatard, *Le Réveil*, July 9, Aug. 15, 1868.

17. Rossiter, *American Presidency*, 96.

18. Zeldin, *Emile Ollivier*, 67.

19. On the weakening of the U.S. presidency, see Grousset, Castagnary, and Sarcey, *Le Bilan de l'année 1868*, 67; Grousset, *Le Rêve d'un irréconciliable*, 9; Chotteau, *Démocratie*, Mar. 20, 1870; Chassin, *Democratie*, June 6, 1869; and Vaïsse, *La république universelle*, 12. It is worthy of note that Louis Blanc, who had opposed the American constitutional model in 1848, approvingly cited the relative weakness of the U.S. presidency in an 1875 speech criticizing the "excessive powers" attributed to the president of the Third Republic. See Blanc, *Histoire de la Constitution du 25 février 1875*, 281–282.

20. Ténot, *Paris en decembre 1851*.

21. Rochefort, *La Lanterne*. Nov. 7, 1868.

22. Lissagaray, *Réforme*, Oct. 31, 1869.

23. As a young lawyer in 1868, Gambetta denounced the emperor's coup d'état in his defense of Charles Delescluze, who was charged with opening a subscription to erect a statue of Jean-Baptiste Baudin, the republican deputy killed on the barricades resisting the coup on December 3, 1851. Delescluze was sentenced to six months in prison and ordered to pay a 2,000-franc fine, but Gambetta's eloquent plea cemented his position as a rising hope of the republican opposition. See Barral, *Léon Gambetta*, 17–21.

24. Gambetta, "Le général Grant," 33–35. Grant and Gambetta later met in Paris at a dinner party arranged by the American portraitist George Healy in 1876. See McCullough, *Greater Journey*, 336.

25. Richardson, *Compilation of Messages and Papers of the Presidents*, 8:27–42.

26. Delord, *Histoire illustrée du Second Empire*, 5:440–443.

27. Favre, *Réveil*, Dec. 9, 1869. For other comments on Grant's message, see Gambon, *Marseil-*

laise, Dec. 24, 1869; and Laborde, *Réforme,* Dec. 9, 23, 1869. For other positive allusions to Grant by French republicans, see Trébois, *Tribune,* June 14, 1868; Vapereau, ibid., July 28, 1868; Légault, ibid., Oct. 18, 1868; Cluseret, ibid., Mar 14, 1869; Chatard, *Réveil,* Sept. 17, 1868; Chotteau, *Le Travail,* Nov. 21, 1869; Chotteau, *Les Véritables Républicains;* Ladet, "La campagne présidentielle," 131–33; Clemenceau, *American Reconstruction,* 199–200, 286; and Portalis, *Etats-Unis,* 191–195.

28. Gambetta, "Le général Grant," 35.

29. Morison, *Oxford History of the American People,* 3:29, 33.

30. Charles de Morny (1811–65) was the illegitimate son of Hortense de Beauharnais and thus the half-brother of Napoleon III. One of the chief instigators of the coup d'état, he made a fortune on stock and real-estate speculations during the Second Empire.

31. Parrington, *Beginnings of Critical Realism in America,* 23–26.

32. Gambetta quoted by Pradalié, *Le Second Empire,* 47.

33. Godechot, *Les Constitutions de la France depuis 1789,* 279–300.

34. Napoleon III, *Discours prononcé par Sa Majesté Napoléon III à l'ouverture des chambres.*

35. Allain-Targé to his father, Jan. 1866, in Allain-Targé, *République sous l'Empire,* 41–42. See also Allain-Targé's comparison between the French and American Constitutions in *Courrier du dimanche,* Feb. 11, 1866.

36. Allain-Targé, "Le Message du président Johnson," 207–208.

37. For a good example of the way the American political tradition could be twisted to fit the French republican ideology, see Allain-Targé, *République sous l'Empire,* 39–40. Denying the influence of Anglo-Saxon and Protestant traditions on the evolution of American democracy, Allain-Targé claimed that the American political system was almost entirely the work of Jefferson whom he described as a "democrat, socialist" and a son of the French Enlightenment.

38. Zeldin, *Emile Ollivier,* 67–68.

39. Zeldin, *Emile Ollivier,* 141–145. Louis Marie de Lahaye de Cormenin (1788–1868) was a deputy under the Second Republic and a member, along with Tocqueville, of the commission that drafted the 1848 Constitution. He protested the coup d'état but was later reconciled to the imperial regime.

40. Darimon, *Histoire d'un parti,* 280.

41. With its bicameral legislature, the Constitution of 1870 was even closer to the American system than that of 1848.

42. Chaudey, *L'Empire parlementaire,* 61.

43. Gambetta, speech of Apr. 5, 1870, in Gambetta, *Discours et plaidoyers politiques,* 1:205.

44. On the difference between the representative system of the United States and the parliamentary government of the Third Republic, see Bainville, *La Troisième République,* 11.

45. For his arguments against American-style bicameralism, see Gambetta, *Discours et plaidoyers politiques,* 1:212. On the republicans' hostility to the idea of an upper chamber, see also Bainville, *La Troisième République,* 46.

46. Laboulaye quoted in *Démocratie,* June 12, 1870. Several years later, during the debates over the constitutional laws of 1875, Laboulaye cited the American example of a strong, independent presidency against republicans like Blanc and Gambetta who sought to make the assembly supreme. See Deslandres, *L'avènement de la troisième république,* 395–396.

47. See Chassin, *Démocratie*, June 12, 1870.

48. Zeldin, *Emile Ollivier*, 120.

49. Tocqueville, a reluctant republican who would have preferred a liberal constitutional monarchy, accepted Louis Napoleon's 1848 election as a fait accompli and cultivated a good working relationship with him during his four months of service in the prince president's cabinet from June to October 1949. Tocqueville considered him an "extraordinary man . . . not because of his genius but because of the circumstances that had pushed his mediocrity so high." *Souvenirs*, 229–231. Had Tocqueville lived longer, it is not unlikely that he would have supported the Liberal Empire.

50. Allain-Targé to his father, Jan. 13, 1868, in Allain-Targé, *République sous l'Empire*, 38.

51. Gambetta to his father, Sept. 3, 1866, in Gambetta, *Gambetta par Gambetta*, 255.

52. Collins, *The Government and the Newspaper Press*, 148–151.

53. See the daily accounts of the public meetings appearing in the *Tribune populaire* starting in 1868.

54. Journault, *Tribune*, Oct. 17, 1869.

55. Cluseret, *Courrier français*, Jan. 21, 1868. Victor de Persigny (1808–72), fervent supporter of Louis Napoleon and one of the architects of the 1851 coup d'etat, served as a senator and interior minister under the Second Empire.

56. Cluseret, *Marseillaise*, Mar. 1, 1870.

57. Lissagaray, *Réforme*, Oct. 31, 1869. For similar references to America's freedom of press, speech, assembly and association, see Hugo, *Rappel*, May 4, 1868; Ferry quoted in *Réveil*, May 20, June 1, 1869; *Tribune populaire*, Oct. 17, 1869; and *Etats-Unis d'Europe*, Jan. 19, 1869.

58. Felice Orsini (1819–58), an Italian revolutionary, led a bombing attack on the emperor's cortège on January 14, 1858. Napoleon III and the empress survived, but 8 people died and 150 were injured. Orsini and two accomplices were captured and executed. See Thompson, *Louis Napoleon and the Second Empire*, 177–180.

59. Green, *Comparative View of French and British Civilization*, 106–109.

60. Portalis, *Etats-Unis*, 101–113.

61. Portalis, *Etats-Unis*, 168.

62. Portalis, *Etats-Unis*, 63.

63. Though Frémont was the only U.S. commander Cluseret got along with, the two had quarreled over control of *The New Nation* newspaper, which was launched to support Frémont's abortive 1864 presidential candidacy. See Florence Braka, *L'honneur perdu du général Cluseret*, 54.

64. For Cluseret's main articles on the Transcontinental scandal, see *Réforme*, May 16, 1868; *Démocratie*, June 6, 1869; and *Phare de la Loire*, Sept. 20, 1869. For Frémont's riposte, see Frémont, *Exposé de la situation*, 16–18. See also Washburne, *Recollections*, 1:11–12. Ironically, Frémont had been a great hero of the French left during the Civil War because of his advanced views on emancipation, and Cluseret had supported his presidential candidacy in 1864.

65. "General Cluseret's Dossier," *London Daily Telegraph*, Apr. 24, 1871.

66. Cluseret, *Démocratie*, June 20, 1869.

67. Cluseret, "A Son Excellence le président des Etats-Unis et au peuple américain," *Démocratie*, June 20, 1869.

68. Cluseret, "To the Honorable Senate and House of Representatives of the United States," *Démocratie*, May 24, 1870.

69. Chassin, *Démocratie,* June 13, 1869. See also Mangin, *Phare de La Loire,* June 19, 1869.

70. Rochefort, *Lanterne,* June 19, 1869. See also Légault, *Tribune,* June 13, 1869; Godchaux, ibid., Sept. 5, 1869; and Lepelletier, *Réforme,* June 22, 1869.

71. The U.S. national debt had increased by 4,100 percent during the Civil War. See Noll, "Repudiation."

72. The figures on educational spending may be exaggerated. The total given for France seems accurate, but it is difficult to estimate the total amount of money spent on American education at this time. Since the federal government had no direct role in education, there was no single education budget. Money for schools came from individual state governments, local municipalities, and private philanthropy, making it almost impossible to arrive at an accurate figure for the total amount spent on American education.

73. [Gardanne], *La France et les Etats-Unis comparés,* passim. See also L. Bouffard, *L'Empire français et la République des Etats-Unis* (Paris, 1869).

74. Légault, *Tribune,* July 18, 1869.

75. Favre, *Réveil,* May 25, 1869.

76. Rochefort, *Lanterne,* Dec. 12, 1868.

77. Arnould, *Rappel,* May 4, 1869. The widows' pensions refers to the 20,000-franc annual stipends granted to the already well-endowed widows of two prominent Bonapartists, Senator R.-T. Troplong and Count Alexander Walewski, natural son of Napoleon I and cousin of Napoleon III.

78. Zeldin, *France,* 1:583–584, 635.

79. Tudesq, "La décentralisation et la droite en France," 64. During the latter part of his reign, Napoleon III himself became aware of the drawbacks of excessive centralization, both as a political liability and as a source of administrative inefficiency, and sought means of reducing it. See Zeldin, *France,* 1:537–538.

80. Proudhon, *Du principe fédératif.*

81. See chapter 10 above.

82. See Chaudey, *L'Empire parlementaire,* 25, 28, 61. See also Chaudey, speech at the 1867 Congress of the Ligue internationale de la paix et de la liberté, cited in Delord, *Histoire illustrée du Second Empire,* 5:188; and Chaudey to Lefort, Nov. 28, 1868, cited in Tchernoff, *Parti républicain,* 525.

83. For the text of the Nancy Program, see *Courrier du dimanche,* Aug. 13, 1865.

84. *Ligue de la décentralisation. Séance du 27 mai 1870.*

85. See Zeldin, *Emile Ollivier,* 123.

86. Ferry, *Discours et opinions,* 1:560.

87. Pelletan, *Tribune,* Feb. 11, 1869. See also Pelletan's call for decentralization in *Annales de l'Association internationale pour le progrès des sciences sociales,* 329.

88. Joly, *La Fédération,* 47–48. Joly bases much of his argument on Tocqueville's analysis of American federalism.

89. Joly, *La Fédération,* 63. See also Légault, *Tribune,* Aug. 29, 1869; and Daniel Levy, *Réforme,* June 30, 1869.

90. Chotteau, *Travail,* Nov. 12, 1869. In 1871 Chotteau drafted a project for a federal constitution based roughly on the American model: France would be divided into twenty-four states, each

having an independent bicameral legislature; the central government would also have a bicameral legislature but no president. Chotteau, *On demande une constitution.*

91. Portalis, *Etats-Unis,* 15–24.

92. Zeldin, *France,* 1:537.

93. Labbé, *Le Manifeste de Nancy,* 29, 32.

94. See chapter 16 below.

95. Here we see how arguments based on the Civil War could cut both ways: some invoked it on behalf of unitarism, others on behalf of decentralization and federalism. In reality, the triumph of Union over secession—and the unprecedented growth of federal power during reconstruction— would tend to support the centralist position.

96. Ribert, "Le Fédéralisme," 82–85.

97. Wright, "Public Opinion and Conscription in France," 26–45; Case, *French Opinion on the United States and Mexico,* 234–237.

98. Lestocquoy, *Histoire du patriotisme en France,* 122–23.

99. Zeldin, *France,* 1:508, 518–19; Thompson, *Louis Napoleon and the Second Empire,* 229.

100. Deschanel, *Gambetta,* 50.

101. Simon, *La Politique radicale,* 224.

102. Lestocquoy, *Histoire du patriotisme en France,* 123.

103. Laboulaye, *Paris en Amérique,* 315–16.

104. Within seven months after Lee's surrender, the Union army was reduced from over 1,000,000 men to 183,000. By the end of 1866, it numbered a mere 25,000 officers and men, a figure that remained constant for the next thirty years. See Morison, *Oxford History of the American People,* 2:499.

105. Vigo-Roussillon, *Puissance militaire,* 380.

106. Speech of Dec. 23, 1867, in Favre, *Discours parlementaires,* 3:321.

107. Gambetta, "Le général Grant," 34. Gambetta later found himself in a position to apply some of the lessons of the American Civil War when, after famously escaping the besieged capital in a balloon, he became minister of war at Tours in 1870. There, along with Charles de Freycinet, he mustered an auxiliary corps of 578,900 men, modeled directly on the volunteer regiments of the Union army. See Freycinet, *La Guerre en province pendant le siège de Paris,* 52–54. For other allusions to the disbanding of the Union armies after the Civil War, see Elisée Reclus, "Histoire des états américains," 758–759; Rochefort, *Lanterne,* Aug. 14, 1869; Audouard, *A travers l'Amérique. Le Far West,* 134–138; Elie Reclus, *Démocratie,* Feb. 21, 1869; Laugel, *Les Etats-Unis pendant la guerre,* 233–237; and Pascal, *A travers l'Atlantique et dans le Nouveau Monde,* 271–272.

108. Allain-Targé, *Le Projet de réorganisation de l'armée.* On this pamphlet's influence among republicans, see Adam, *Mes Sentiments et Nos Idées,* 190.

109. Allain-Targé, *Projet de réorganisation de l'armée,* 12.

110. Allain-Targé, *Projet de réorganisation de l'armée,* 22–23.

111. Allain-Targé, *Projet de réorganisation de l'armée,* 28 (emphasis in original). Allain-Targé compares the patriotic citizens' armies of the North to those of the French Revolution in "L'Obéissance passive," 159. He contrasts France's huge military budget with America's minimal expenditures in *Les Déficits,* 31–31.

112. Girardin, *Le Succès,* 365–380 passim.

113. See Cluseret, *Phare de la Loire,* Dec. 24, 26, 28, 1867, Jan. 8, 17, 24, Feb. 5, 1868.

114. See *Tribune,* June 14, 1866, June 28, 1868, Feb. 14, Mar. 3, 25, Apr. 8, 15, 18, 1869; *Démocratie,* Mar. 7, Apr. 11, May 2, 1869; *Marseillaise,* Mar. 20, 1870; and *Courrier français,* Jan. 4, 5, 8, 20, 1868.

115. Cluseret, *Armée et démocratie.* On this book's influence, see Mocqueris, *Tribune,* Feb. 28, 1869; and Frambourg, *Un Philanthrope et démocrate nantais,* 340.

116. Cluseret, *Armée et démocratie,* 25.

117. Cluseret, *Armée et démocratie,* 28.

118. Cluseret, *Armée et démocratie,* 23.

119. Cluseret, *Armée et démocratie,* 15–19.

120. Cluseret, *Armée et démocratie,* 66.

121. Cluseret, *Armée et démocratie,* 20.

122. Cluseret, *Armée et démocratie,* 65–66. See also ibid., 110–111.

123. Cluseret, *Armée et démocratie,* 132–142.

124. When Cluseret became war delegate of the Commune in 1871, he attempted to apply some of his Civil War lessons in defending Paris against the Versailles army. See Cluseret, *Mémoires,* 1:166, 112. Louis Rossel (1848–71), the young polytechnician who served under Cluseret and later replaced him as the Commune's war delegate, shared his respect for the military lessons of the American Civil War. Rossel wrote: "The Civil War was an industrial, progressive, and humanitarian war. . . . Applied to this terrible science, we see all the exuberance of a people seriously active, young, intelligent, and incapable of fear. . . . If we want to do something new, that is where we must take the elements and shrink them down to our size." Rossel, *Abrégé de l'art de la guerre,* xvi–xix. Captured after the fall of the Commune, Rossel was executed on October 7, 1871.

125. Vigo-Roussillon, *Puissance militaire,* 392–393.

126. Adam, *Mes Sentiments et Nos Idées,* 191.

CHAPTER 15

1. Lefrançais, *Etude sur le mouvement communaliste,* 42. Lefrançais (1826–91) was a socialist and anarchist who took part in the Paris Commune alongside his friend and ally Elisée Reclus.

2. A meaningful development of the themes treated in this chapter will occasionally require a look at French views of American society before and after the period under discussion, but the main focus is on the use made of the American example during the latter years of the Second Empire.

3. Anderson, *Education in France,* 129–130.

4. Prost, *Histoire de l'enseignement en France,* 179–183.

5. On Duruy's work, see Prost, *Histoire de l'enseignement en France,* 182–184; Anderson, *Education in France,* chap. 7; Duruy, *Notes et souvenirs;* and Duruy, *Administration de l'Instruction publique.*

6. See Copans, "French Opinion of American Democracy," 196–202.

7. See, for example, C. Plomb, *Démocratie,* Feb. 6, 1870; Laveleye, "L'Enseignement populaire dans les écoles américaines," 277–278, 300; Jules Barni, *L'Instruction républicaine,* 9; and Chotteau, *Tribune,* Oct. 11, 1868.

8. Céléstin Hippeau, *L'Instruction publique aux Etats-Unis,* iii.

9. Hippeau, *L'Instruction publique aux Etats-Unis*, 340.

10. Hippeau, *L'Instruction publique aux Etats-Unis*, 34.

11. Hippeau, *L'Instruction publique aux Etats-Unis*, 11–12.

12. Hippeau, *L'Instruction publique aux Etats-Unis*, 10.

13. Hippeau, *L'Instruction publique aux Etats-Unis*, 134.

14. Hippeau, *L'Instruction publique aux Etats-Unis*, 341.

15. Audouard's views on American women are discussed later in this chapter.

16. Audouard, *A travers l'Amérique. North America*, 44–45.

17. Audouard, *A travers l'Amérique. North America*, 49–52.

18. Audouard, *A travers l'Amérique. North America*, 54–55.

19. Audouard, *A travers l'Amérique. North America*, 53–54.

20. Portalis, *Etats-Unis*, 199–224 passim.

21. Chotteau, preface to *L'Instruction en Amérique*. This book is an enlarged and revised version of articles that appeared in the *Tribune*, the *Cloche*, and other radical papers in the late 1860s.

22. Chotteau, *Tribune*, Oct. 11, 1868.

23. Chotteau, *Tribune*, Jan. 3, 1869. See also *Tribune*, Oct. 18, Nov. 1, 1868.

24. Ferry, *De l'égalité d'éducation*, 17–24 passim.

25. Ferry, *De l'égalité d'éducation*, 17–24. The contrast between the American and French budgets, in fact, provided republicans with one of their most useful arguments in favor of expanding education and reducing the permanent army. See, for example, Carnot, parliamentary speech of Apr. 7, 1865, in Simon, *L'Instruction populaire en France*, 152–153; Simon, *L'Ecole*, 104–108; Audouard, *A travers l'Amérique. North America*, 42; Chotteau, *Tribune*, Oct. 11, 1868; Portalis, *Etats-Unis*, 224; and [Gardanne], *La France et les Etats-Unis comparés*, 13–15.

26. Laboulaye, *Paris en Amérique*, chap. 27.

27. Laboulaye, *Discours populaires*, 282–283.

28. Leneveux, *La Propagande de l'instruction*, 164, 183. Leneveu (1817–93), a socialist with ties to Proudhon and Blanqui, edited the workers' newspaper *L'Atelier*, was active in the syndicalist movement, and promoted workers' education.

29. *Réforme*, Dec. 25, 1869. For similar references to the U.S. example at public meetings, see *Marseillaise*, Apr. 23, 1870; and *Tribune*, Sept. 6, 1869. For positive views of American public education by a French workers' delegation to the United States, see *Exposition universelle de Philadelphie 1876*, 120–126.

30. Prost, *Histoire de l'enseignement en France*, 183. See also Tchernoff, *Parti républicain*, 317–319.

31. See Laboulaye, "La jeunesse de Franklin," in *Discours populaires*, 161–181; and "Horace Mann," ibid., 206–225. Both of these lectures were given under the auspices of the Société Franklin.

32. Prost, *Histoire de l'enseignement en France*, 183–184.

33. Macé, *La Ligue de l'enseignement*, 215, 228–229, 343, and passim. Yet another manifestation of this "hunger for education" was the *Entretiens de la rue de la Paix*, a series of public lectures organized by the future Communard Prosper Lissagaray and Albert Leroy. An important forum for republican ideas, these lectures were intended to rival the official teaching of the state universities by providing free and independent higher education. Here, too, the influence of the American example was felt, not only in the republican orientation of many of the speakers but also in the use of public lectures as a source of popular culture and education.

34. Prost, *Histoire de l'enseignement en France,* 184–185.

35. See Laveleye, *L'Instruction du peuple,* 335–463; Barni, *Ce que doit être la république,* 13–15; Barni, *L'Instruction républicaine,* 9–10; Lamarle, *De la nécessité de l'instruction,* 8, 31, 33–34; Guer, *La Liberté et l'éducation;* and Thévenin, *L'Instruction primaire,* 4–14.

36. See Ferry's praise of America's decentralized school system in his comments on the Nancy Program in *Discours et opinions,* 1:560.

37. Tchernoff, *Parti républicain,* 300–303.

38. Guiral, *Vie quotidienne en France,* 236.

39. Tchernoff, *Parti républicain,* 553.

40. Gambetta, *Discours devant la Chambre des députés,* May 4, 1877.

41. Blumenthal, *France and the United States,* 137.

42. See, for example, Joly, *La Fédération,* 68; and Le Play, *Réforme sociale,* 1:136–146.

43. Hawkins, *Auguste Comte and the United States,* 10–12.

44. See Georges Clemenceau's mocking description of the camp meetings he had observed in America during the late 1860s in *La Mêlée sociale,* 185.

45. Vacherot, *La Démocratie,* 34–35. The American "prejudice" against atheism and free thought was often noted. See, for example, Léo, "La Colonie américaine," 1076; Cluseret, *Mémoires,* 2:197; and Savardan, *Naufrage au Texas,* 99.

46. Proudhon to Dulieu, Dec. 30, 1860, in Proudhon, *Correspondance,* 10:274.

47. *Annales de l'Association internationale pour le progrès des sciences sociales,* 206.

48. U. de Fonvielle, "Correspondance des Etats-Unis," 212–213.

49. Cluseret, *Démocratie,* May 9, 1869. For other favorable comments in the radical press concerning the separation of church and state in the United States, see Burat, *Voix du peuple,* July 10, 1869; and F.-X. de Trébois, *Tribune,* July 18, 1869. On secular education in America, see Journault, *Tribune,* Oct. 31, 1869; Plomb, *Démocratie,* Feb. 6, 1870; and Laveleye, *L'Instruction du peuple,* 290–292.

50. *Etats-Unis d'Europe,* Jan. 19, 1868. This unsigned article was possibly written by C.-L. Chassin, a freethinker and enthusiastic admirer of the United States who was one of the editors of this paper.

51. Allain-Targé to his father, Jan. 13, 1866, in Allain-Targé, *République sous l'Empire,* 39. This was to be the theme of a public lecture Allain-Targé planned to give.

52. It is not meant to imply here that an absolute barrier existed between anticlericalism and Protestantism. There were many Protestants among the anticlericals, and Protestant thought had a certain influence of the anticlerical movement. See Zeldin, *France,* 1:628.

53. Tchernoff, *Parti républicain,* 307.

54. Pelletan, *Profession de foi,* 353. See also Pelletan, *Adresse au roi Coton,* 1–4; Gasparin, *L'Amérique devant l'Europe,* 495–496; Fisch, *Les Etats-Unis en 1861,* 6; and Laboulaye, *Paris en Amérique,* chaps. 17, 19, and 21.

55. Quinet, *Le Christianisme et la Révolution française,* 179–199; Quinet, *L'Enseignement du peuple,* 41–44.

56. Quinet to Eugène Sue, Dec. 27, 1856, in Sue, *Lettres sur la question religieuse.* Elsewhere, Quinet called Emerson "the most idealistic writer of our times . . . a man who heads into the future

by the same path as us." Quinet, *Christianisme et la Révolution,* 195–196. Michelet, however, did not share his friend's admiration either for American Protestantism or for Channing's philosophy. Recalling the history of the American Revolution, he wrote in 1867: "The sons of the Puritans, in spite of everything people think, were in no way republicans. Their great book, the Psalms, is the book of a King. . . . These people of Biblical spirit were very submissive." It was not Protestantism, but French Enlightenment philosophy that gave Americans their notions of liberty, observed Michelet. *Histoire de la France au 18e siècle,* 229–233. In notes made on June 26, 1860, Michelet wrote that the Americans' "Biblical superstition and the pale neutralism of Channing show a great poverty of spirit." Papiers Michelet, A. 3915, f. 181, BHVP.

57. On Channing's influence among French republicans, see Tchernoff, *Parti républicain,* 307; Weill, *Histoire du parti républicain en France,* 348; Soltau, *French Political Thought,* 115; and Copans, "French Opinion of American Democracy," 130–133. Proudhon read Laboulaye's translation of Channing's works. See Proudhon's "Carnets," Dec. 1, 1857, Proudhon MSS, N.A.fr. 14275, vol. 11, f. 501, BN.

58. Léo, "La Colonie américaine," 1078.

59. Writing to her son Maurice during his 1861 tour of the United States, Sand described Channing's *Œuvres sociales* (in Laboulaye's 1854 translation) as "a very beautiful book that, for me, embodies all the heart and intelligence of America. . . . [I find] in him an extraordinary enthusiasm and charity, an eloquence. . . . [But] if Channing's ideal is beautiful and grand, if it is achievable—as I believe—it will not be through the doctrine of individualism. That is something I refuse with all my conscience, all my heart and all my faith." George Sand to Maurice Sand, Sept. 1, 1861, in Sand, *Correspondance,* 5:283–287.

60. See Allain-Targé, *République sous l'Empire,* 38; and Deschanel, *Gambetta,* 146. See also Lullier, *Mes cachots,* 259, 416.

61. It is interesting to note here that Ernest Renan, whose rationalist viewpoint resembles Channing's in many respects, found this American philosopher too cold, superficial, and pragmatic for his liking. See Renan, "Channing et le mouvement unitaire aux Etats-Unis," 1085–1107.

62. Tocqueville, *Démocratie en Amérique,* 1:301–303.

63. Rémond, *Etats-Unis devant l'opinion française,* 2:837, 846, 851.

64. Soltau, *French Political Thought,* 192.

65. Similar observations were made by other travelers. See Duvergier de Hauranne, *Huit mois en Amérique,* 2:131; Audouard, *A travers l'Amérique. North America,* 190–193; and Portalis, *Etats-Unis,* 8–13. For an interesting letter by a republican priest describing the advantages of American religious liberty and separation for the church, see *Réforme,* Oct. 18, 1869.

66. Meng, "A Century of American Catholicism as Seen through French Eyes," 39–49.

67. E. Veuillot, "Etudes sur les Etats-Unis," 75–101.

68. M. Chevalier, *Lettres sur l'Amérique du nord,* 1:284–85. See also Tocqueville, *Démocratie en Amérique,* 1:251–52, 183.

69. M. Chevalier, *Lettres,* 1:144–45. See also Tocqueville, *Démocratie en Amérique,* 1:181, 363, 2:42.

70. In subsequent years many socialist writers approvingly cited Tocqueville's and Chevalier's descriptions of the American workingman. See Blanc, "De la démocratie en Amérique," 114–116;

Pierre Leroux, "Les Etats-Unis," in Leroux and Renaud, *Encyclopédie nouvelle*, 5:96–97; Considé-rant, *Au Texas*, 165–71; Morhard, *Travail, liberté, propriété pour tous*, 29–31; and Guépin, "Situation et avenir des Etats-Unis," 122–123. For another socialist appreciation of the American spirit of work, see Pecqueur, *Des améliorations matérielles*, x–xi, 113–114.

71. Marx and Engels, *Civil War in the United States*, 280.

72. Pelletan, *Adresse au roi Coton*, 3, 8–9.

73. Curti and Blair, "Immigrant and the American Image," 204.

74. See Léon Plée, *Siècle*, Mar. 30, 1863; Mangin, *Phare de la Loire*, Oct. 25, 1862; and *Journal de Rouen*, Apr. 6–7, 1863.

75. Erickson, *American Industry and the European Immigrant*, 11–12. The American Emigrant Company had agents in Marseilles and Le Havre.

76. See P. Vinçard, *Démocratie*, Jan. 17, 1869; *Tribune*, Jan. 2, 1870; Audouard, *A travers l'Amé-rique. Le Far West*, 108–112; and Audouard, *A travers l'Amérique. North America*, vi. In 1869 a Bel-gian section of the International wrote to the organization's General Council that "socialist ideas can only advance with great difficulty in our old Europe" and advised "mass emigration to America." Association Internationale des Travailleurs, *Compte-rendu du IVe congrès international*, 49.

77. Girardin, *La Voix dans le désert*, 90–91.

78. The figures on French emigration to the United States from 1865 to 1870 are as follows: 3,583 (1865); 6,885 (1866); 5,237 (1867); 1,989 (1868); 3,879 (1869); and 4,009 (1870). Bunle, *Etudes démographiques*, 52.

79. Considérant, *Mexique*, 135.

80. Considérant, *Mexique*, 194.

81. Lincoln, who had worked at a number of odd jobs before going into law and politics, was most often referred to by French publicists as a "bûcheron" (lumberjack). His successor, Andrew Johnson, had actually been an illiterate tailor up to the age of twenty. Johnson's successor, Ulysses Grant, was in fact a career soldier and a graduate of West Point, but he was widely referred to as a "tanneur" because he had worked in his father's leather-goods store in Galena, Illinois, for a time.

82. P. Denis, *Courrier français*, Nov. 4, 1866.

83. *Voix du peuple*, 1869 prospectus. For other allusions to Lincoln, Johnson, and Grant as working-class heroes, see Girault, *Tribune*, Dec. 19, 1869; Vésinier, *Le Martyr de la liberté*, 303; Beluze, *Lettres Icariennes*, 2:113; Pyat, *Rappel*, Nov. 20, 1869; Chatard, *Réveil*, Aug. 6, 1868; Pelletan, *Le Travail au XIXe siècle*, 32; and Laboulaye, *Discours populaires*, 178.

84. Portalis, *Etats-Unis*, 26–27.

85. Portalis, *Etats-Unis*, 35.

86. Portalis, *Etats-Unis*, 38.

87. Portalis, *Etats-Unis*, 38–40.

88. Pelletan, *La Femme au XIXe siècle*, 24.

89. Pelletan, *Tribune*, Feb. 7, 1869. See also Pelletan, *Le Travail au XIXe siècle*, 32.

90. Chatard, *Réveil*, Oct. 22, 1868.

91. Chatard, *Réveil*, Aug. 6, 1868.

92. Clemenceau, *American Reconstruction*, 97.

93. Foner, *History of the Labor Movement in the United States*, 1:339–340.

94. Lincoln, *Collected Works*, 4:438.

95. See McKitrick, *Slavery Defended*.

96. Lincoln, *Collected Works*, 5:51–52.

97. Lincoln, *Collected Works*, 5:52–53.

98. Charles Francis Adams to A. M. Cremer, Jan. 31, 1865, quoted in Marx and Engels, *Civil War in the United States*, 282.

99. Bernstein, *Essays in Political and Intellectual History*, 136.

100. Carlton, *History and Problems of Organized Labor*, 65; Foner, *History of the Labor Movement in the United States*, 1:339–340.

101. Foner, *History of the Labor Movement in the United States*, 1:344–346, 370–388.

102. Dolléans, *L'Histoire du mouvement ouvrier*, 1:267–316; Zeldin, *France*, 1:205–206.

103. See for example, A. Verdure, *Tribune*, Oct. 24, 1869. See also *Tribune*, Aug. 30, 1868; *Réveil*, June 9, 1869; *Travail*, Nov. 21, 1869; *Démocratie*, Mar. 27, 1870; and *Marseillaise*, June 6, 1870.

104. Marx, *Capital*, 309. It was largely on the strength of the American example that the 1866 Congress of the International at Basel adopted an eight-hour demand.

105. On the eight-hour movement, see Foner, *History of the Labor Movement in the United States*, 1:363–369; and Lewis, *History of American Political Thought*, 254–58.

106. On the American eight-hour law, see Martin Nadaud to Charles Delescluze, Jan. 7, 1870, in Nadaud, *Discours de Martin Nadaud à l'Assemblée législative*, 310–11. See also P. Vinçard, *Démocratie*, Nov. 15, 1868; and E. Chatard, *Réveil*, Aug. 6, 1868.

107. W. H. Sylvis to J. G. Eccarius, May 26, 1869, in Association Internationale des Travailleurs, *Compte-rendu du IVe congrès international*, 23.

108. Association Internationale des Travailleurs, *Compte-rendu du IVe congrès international*, 150–152.

109. Togno, *Démocratie*, Mar. 6, 1870.

110. Cluseret, *Démocratie*, May 29, 1870.

111. Cluseret, *Démocratie*, Apr. 3, 1870.

112. Cluseret, *Marseillaise*, Apr. 2, 1870.

113. Cluseret, *Démocratie*, Mar. 27, 1870.

114. Cluseret, *Démocratie*, July 10, 1870.

115. Cluseret, *Démocratie*, Mar. 27, 1870.

116. Cluseret, *Démocratie*, Apr. 3, 1870.

117. Cluseret, *Démocratie*, Feb. 27, 1870.

118. Cluseret, *Démocratie*, July 10, 1870.

119. Cluseret, *Démocratie*, Mar. 27, 1870. Cluseret's observations on the declining position of the American worker were subsequently confirmed by the French labor delegation that attended the Philadelphia World's Fair in 1876. See *Exposition universelle de Philadelphie 1876*, 83–84, 88–89, 126–127, 143–144, and passim. For another French worker's view of postwar America, see P. A. Seauret, "Souvenirs d'un ouvrier français," 61–74, 169–193. Written by a Frenchman who had emigrated in 1876, this article presents a scathing critique of American society from a socialist worker's point of view. Although it deals with a later period than the present study, it is an important document for anyone interested in tracing the subsequent evolution of the American image in France.

120. Chatard, *Réveil,* Oct. 22, 1868.

121. Allain-Targé, *Les Déficits,* 26–27.

122. Poulot, *Question sociale,* 336.

123. A. Planquette, *Courrier français,* Sept. 2, 1866.

124. G. Flourens, *Marseillaise,* Mar. 5, 1870.

125. E. Varlin, *Marseillaise,* Mar. 11, 1870.

126. See Proudhon, *La Pornocratie.*

127. Noémie Reclus (1828–1905) was the wife of Elie Reclus and sister-in-law of Elisée Reclus. Like her friend André Léo, Reclus was a militant feminist, socialist, and an active supporter of the Commune.

128. Thomas, *Les Pétroleuses,* chap. 1; Zeldin, *France,* 1:345–348; Guiral, *Vie quotidienne en France,* 78–82.

129. Tocqueville, *Démocratie en Amérique,* 2:206, 222. Tocqueville's observations on American women were cited by later French feminists. See, for example, Richer, *Le Livre des femmes,* 66. Tocqueville's views were also refuted by critics of French feminism. See, for example, Baudrillart, "L'Agitation pour l'émancipation des femmes en Angleterre et aux Etats-Unis," 661; and Carlier, *Le Mariage aux Etats-Unis.*

130. See M. Chevalier, *Lettres,* chap. 13; Eyma, *Les Femmes du nouveau monde;* Savardan, *Naufrage au Texas,* 324–325; Bellegarrigue, *Femmes d'Amérique;* Etourneau, *Les Mormons,* 275; and Considérant, *Au Texas,* 151.

131. French women who were married under the "régime dotal" actually had it better in this respect: their real estate and the principal of their dowry could not be alienated by their husbands.

132. Debbie Woodroofe, "The Suffrage Movement," in Novack, *America's Revolutionary Heritage,* 365–366; Barbara M. Solomon, "The Seneca Falls Declaration," in Boorstin, *American Primer,* 376–378.

133. On French attitudes toward marriage during this period, see Zeldin, *France,* 1:285–303. On the French view of the independent, self-reliant American woman, see Zeldin, *Histoire des passions françaises,* 147–148.

134. Prost, *Histoire de l'enseignement en France,* 261.

135. Woodroofe, "Suffrage Movement," 366–368, 372–373.

136. See Koht, *American Spirit in Europe,* 44–55; and Silberschmidt, *The United States and Europe,* 36. For reciprocity's sake, mention should be made here of George Sand, whose personal quest for sexual equality had a strong influence on the American feminists. The American journalist Moncure Conway noted in his memoirs, "all the aspiring and discontented women known to me in America—poets, orators, reformers—were the offspring of George Sand." Conway, *Autobiography,* 2:262.

137. Léo, *La Femme et les moeurs,* 159–162. Léo's praise of the American feminists did not prevent her from making some severe judgments concerning the manners and pretensions of the affluent American women she observed in Paris. See Léo, "La Colonie américaine," 1065–1080.

138. Gaël, *La Femme médecin,* 21, 62. See also Niboyet, *Le Vrai Livre des femmes,* 80, 168, 169; Cheminat, *Quelques observations sur l'Américaine;* Monod, *La Mission des femmes en temps de guerre,* chap. 5; Daubié, *L'Émancipation de la femme,* 101, 122; Legouvé, *Histoire morale des femmes,* 183, 236, 380; Richer, *Le Livre des femmes,* 1, 80, 164; Richer, *La Femme libre,* 206–220, 285–290; Pelletan, *La*

Femme au XIXe siècle, 22; Assollant, *Le Droit des femmes,* 49, 172–176, 297; Michelet, *La Femme,* 422–423, 451.

139. Jeune, *Graindorge,* 106.

140. See, for example, Audouard, *Guerre aux hommes;* and Audouard, *Le Luxe des femmes.*

141. Jeune, *Graindorge,* 106–107.

142. Ernot, "Olympe Audouard dans l'univers de la presse."

143. *Le Gaulois,* Mar. 31, 1869, cited in Jeune, *Graindorge.*

144. Audouard, *A travers l'Amérique. Le Far West;* Audouard, *A travers l'Amérique. North America.*

145. Space limits do not permit a detailed look at the numerous allusions to the United States by French partisans of women's rights. Audouard touches on the main themes, however, and her commentary may be considered as representative.

146. Audouard, *A travers l'Amérique. North America,* 54.

147. Audouard, *A travers l'Amérique. North America,* 335.

148. Audouard, *A travers l'Amérique. North America,* 335.

149. Audouard, *A travers l'Amérique. North America,* 337.

150. Audouard, *A travers l'Amérique. North America,* 348.

151. Adultery was a personal sore point for Audouard, who left her husband, a Marseilles notary, because of his alleged philandering. See Gabrielle Houbre, *Le Livre des courtisanes,* 53.

152. Audouard, *A travers l'Amérique. North America,* 358.

153. Audouard, *A travers l'Amérique. North America,* 366.

154. Audouard, *A travers l'Amérique. North America,* 368.

155. Audouard, *A travers l'Amérique. Le Far West,* 231.

156. Audouard, *A travers l'Amérique. North America,* 366–367. Simon Jeune suggests that Audouard's rosy impression of women's position in the United States reflected the fact that her own physical attractiveness and foreign exoticism made her the object of special attentions from the American men she met. See Jeune, *Graindorge,* 107.

157. Hippeau, *L'Instruction publique aux Etats-Unis,* 79–81.

158. Chotteau, *L'Instruction en Amérique,* 55.

159. *Rapports de la délégation ouvrière lyonnaise,* 136.

160. *Rapports de la délégation ouvrière lyonnaise,* 125–126, For other travelers' observations on the condition of American women during this period, see Simonin, *Le Grand ouest des Etats-Unis,* chap. 19; and Duvergier de Hauranne, *Huit mois en Amérique,* 1:112, 433, 2:210, 217–219.

161. Richer, *La Femme libre,* 238–239; Zeldin, *France,* 1:346–348.

162. See, for example, Mercier, "Le Travail des femmes," 339.

163. M. Chevalier, *Lettres,* chap. 13. Judging by the frequent references to it, Chevalier's description of Lowell seems to have constituted the French public's main source of information on the condition of American working women.

164. Foner, *History of the Labor Movement in the United States,* 1:341–344, 382–388.

165. Thomas, *Les Pétroleuses,* 37; Zeldin, *France,* 1:345–346. One of the very few French organizations devoted to women's labor at this time was L'Ouvrière, société coopérative pour le travail des femmes; the statutes of this organization appeared in the *Voix du peuple,* Apr. 24, 1869.

166. Ferry, *De l'égalité d'éducation,* 29.

167. Ferry, *De l'égalité d'éducation*, 26–27.

168. Prost, *Histoire de l'enseignement en France*, 263–265; Zeldin, *France*, 1:344. The first woman to attend Paris's Ecole de Médecine was actually an American, Mary Putnam (1842–1906; daughter of U.S. publisher George Putnam), who began her studies in 1868 and graduated with honors in July 1871. She was an intimate friend of the progressive Reclus family and lodged with them in Paris. See McCullough, *Greater Journey*, 288–289; and Vincent, *Elisée Reclus*, 230.

169. Jeune, *Graindorge*, 467–469.

170. Jeune, *Graindorge*, 124–125. Simone de Beauvoir cited Louisa May Alcott's *Little Women* as the book in which she "recognized my own face and my destiny." Quoted ibid., 467.

CHAPTER 16

1. Field, *America and the Mediterranean World*, 313–316.

2. During and after the Civil War, Washington aggressively pursued claims against Britain for the damages inflicted on U.S. shipping by the British-built CSS *Alabama*. In 1872 an arbitration tribunal awarded the United States $15,500,000 in gold. Moore, *History and Digest of the International Arbitrations to Which the United States Has Been a Party*, 1:653.

3. Vigo-Roussillon, *Puissance militaire*, vi, 373, 380, 439.

4. Case, *French Opinion on the United States and Mexico*, 233.

5. M. Chevalier, *La Guerre et la crise européenne*, 784–785. In 1867 the imperial minister of state, Eugène Rouher, similarly invoked the threat of American power as an argument for European unity. See Thompson, *Louis Napoleon and the Second Empire*, 273–274. See also Girardin, *Le Succès*, xxiv.

6. Pelletan, *Tribune*, Nov. 8, 1868.

7. A. L. Duquesne, *Courrier français*, May 27, 1865.

8. Bemis, *Diplomatic History of the United States*, 393–94; Case, *French Opinion on the United States and Mexico*, 402–403.

9. Castelot, *Maximilien et Charlotte*, 595–598.

10. Allain-Targé to his father, Jan. 1866, in Allain-Targé, *République sous l'Empire*, 42–43.

11. Allain-Targé to his father, Jan. 7, 1866, in Allain-Targé, *République sous l'Empire*, 45.

12. Blanqui to Lacambre, Aug. 18, 1863, in Dommanget, *Blanqui*, 40.

13. Calman, *Ledru-Rollin après 1848*, 204.

14. Ledru-Rollin as quoted in Calman, *Ledru-Rollin après 1848*, 206. It is not known whether this letter was actually sent. On May 25, 1865, Mazzini addressed a similar plea to the American abolitionist Moncure Conway, urging the United States to accept its international "mission" for freedom by attacking the French in Mexico and sending money and arms to French and Italian republicans. Conway, *Autobiography*, 2:61–63.

15. Dommanget, *Victor Considérant*, 48.

16. Considérant, *Mexique*, 82–84.

17. Considérant, *Mexique*, 168–171.

18. Landy, "French Adventurer," 321.

19. Cluseret, *Mexico and the Solidarity of Nations*, 105.

20. Cluseret, *Mexico and the Solidarity of Nations*, 106.

21. Cluseret, *Mexico and the Solidarity of Nations,* 109.

22. Cluseret, *Mexico and the Solidarity of Nations,* 104, 106.

23. Cluseret, *Mexico and the Solidarity of Nations,* 109.

24. Chotteau, *Travail,* Nov. 21, 1869.

25. Chotteau, *Travail,* Nov. 21, 1869.

26. Favre, *Réveil,* May 9, 1869. See also Favre, ibid., Aug. 1, 1869; and H. Tolain, *Courrier français,* Jan. 18, 1868.

27. Rochefort, *Lanterne,* June 5, 1869. See also *Lanterne,* Aug. 1, Nov. 28, Dec. 12, 1868, May 15, July 17, 1869.

28. See F. Kohn, *Démocratie,* Aug. 1, 1868; U. de Fonvielle, *Marseillaise,* Dec. 25, 1869; J. Ferry, *Temps,* July 26, 1868; Portalis, *Etats-Unis,* 215; Saint-Ferréol, *Les Proscrits français en Belgique,* 2:160–161; Perdiguier, *Comment constituer la République,* 63; Pelletan, *Les Uns et les Autres,* xvi; and Lissagaray, *Histoire de la Commune,* 25, 30.

29. Tchernoff, *Parti républicain,* 135, 139.

30. Pyat quoted in *La Cigale* (Brussels), Nov. 1, 1868.

31. *La Cigale* (Brussels), Oct. 11, 1868.

32. Pyat, "Adresse française au président Grant," in *Démocratie,* Mar. 28, 1869. This address was transmitted to Grant by the American minister in London. A firm believer in nonintervention in Europe, the president was surely unreceptive to such appeals. But it is interesting to note that Wendell Phillips, the most radical of the American reformers, had expressed exactly the same idea as Pyat, calling for U.S. aid to Garibaldi as a retaliation for the French expedition in Mexico. See Hofstadter, *American Political Tradition,* 153.

33. Clemenceau, *American Reconstruction,* 82.

34. May, "Crete and the United States," 286–293; Field, *America and the Mediterranean World,* 317–323.

35. Hugo, *Œuvres politiques complètes,* 578–579.

36. Michelet, *Journal,* 4:91; *Démocratie,* Jan. 21, 1869.

37. Hugo, "Appel à l'Amérique," in *Œuvres politiques complètes,* 589.

38. Cluseret to Sumner as quoted in Landy, "French Adventurer," 317.

39. Cluseret to Sumner, Jan. 13, 1869, in Landy, "French Adventurer," 328–29.

40. Cluseret to Sumner, n.d., in Landy, "French Adventurer," 329.

41. Bemis, *Diplomatic History of the United States,* 434–436; Williams, *America Confronts a Revolutionary World,* 128–129.

42. See chapter 2 above.

43. Lamarque, "La Doctrine Monroe," 391.

44. Chassin, *Démocratie,* Mar. 21, 1869.

45. U. de Fonvielle, *Marseillaise,* Feb. 8, 1870. For similar comments, see Fonvielle, ibid., Jan. 4, 1870; J. Labbé, ibid., Feb. 15, 1870; Arthur de Fonvielle [brother of Ulrich and Wilfrid], ibid., Mar. 8, 1870; F.-X. de Trébois, *Tribune,* Apr. 4, 1869; and Elie Reclus, *Démocratie,* Mar. 21, 1869.

46. For expressions of disappointment at America's failure to aid Cuba, see Elisée Reclus, "L'Insurrection de Cuba," 271; A. Togno, *Démocratie,* Dec. 26, 1869; E. Lefèvre, ibid., May 29, 1870; and E. Gellion-Danglar, ibid., Mar. 6, 1870.

47. Cluseret to Sumner, Jan. 13, 1869, quoted in Landy, "French Adventurer," 328.

48. Cluseret, *Mémoires*, 3:149. In a letter to the *Démocratie* dated May 29, 1870, Cluseret reported on a banquet he had organized at Delmonico's, attended by Horace Greeley, Charles A. Dana, and various representatives of the Cuban junta.

49. Hugo to Cluseret, Apr. 22, 1870, quoted in Cluseret, *Mémoires*, 3:147–148. This letter was also published in *Rappel*, May 21, 1870, and *Démocratie*, May 22, 1870.

50. Portalis, *Etats-Unis*, 112. Two years later Portalis quoted this same passage in the Commune's *Journal Officiel* (April 5, 1871), suggesting that American sympathies were in favor of the Communards.

51. Williams, *America Confronts a Revolutionary World*, 116–117.

52. Blumenthal, *France and the United States*, 103.

53. Voyenne, *Histoire de l'idée européenne*, 127; Dumont-Wilden, *L'Evolution de l'esprit européen*, 159.

54. The Ligue internationale also had a number of American members, including Charles Sumner. See J. Lefèvre, *Tribune*, Oct. 11, 1869.

55. Lemonnier, *Les Etats-Unis d'Europe*, 127–129. See also *Annales du congrès de Genève*, 272–273, 262–263. On the history of the Ligue internationale, see Delord, *Histoire illustrée du Second Empire*, 5:107–125; Tchernoff, *Parti républicain*, 467–470.

56. Vésinier, *Le Martyr de la liberté*, 168–169.

57. Chassin, *Démocratie*, Feb. 21, 1869. See also Chassin, *Démocratie*, June 20, 1869.

58. Chassin, *Démocratie*, May 22, 1870.

59. Considérant, "Union républicaine de l'Europe et de l'Amérique," *Démocratie*, Sept. 19, 1869, reprinted from *New York Weekly Sun*, Aug. 25, 1869.

60. Hugo to Colonel Berton, Feb. 27, 1870, in *Marseillaise*, Mar. 14, 1870. See also A. Desmoulins, *Réforme*, June 6, 1869; Charles Delescluze, *Réveil*, July 16, 1868.

61. See chapter 1 above.

62. Saint-Ferréol, *Les Proscrits français en Belgique*, 2:169. For the U.S. response to the Paris Commune, see chapter 18 below.

63. Smith, "Expansion after the Civil War"; Bemis, *Diplomatic History of the United States*, 396–404.

64. Blumenthal, *France and the United States*, 131–134.

65. See Thiers, "Adresse aux électeurs," *Réveil*, May 18, 1869; Girardin, *Condamné du 6 mars*, 305, 373; and Prévost-Paradol, *La France nouvelle*, 397–418.

66. See chapter 2 above.

67. Schoelcher, "L'Insurrection de Cuba et les Etats-Unis," 453–454.

68. Duret, *Tribune*, June 24, 1869. Théodore Duret (1838–1927), journalist and art critic, was a leading defender of the Impressionists and a friend of Edouard Manet, who painted his portrait in 1868.

69. Chassin, *Démocratie*, May 9, 1869.

70. C. Sauvage, *Démocratie*, Feb. 6, 1870.

71. U. de Fonville, *Marseillaise*, Jan. 5, 1870. For similar comments, see Elie Reclus, *Démocratie*, Mar. 21, 1869; Elie Reclus, "Traité de commerce entre la Chine et les Etats-Unis," 231–235; Légault, *Tribune*, Sept. 27, 1868, Apr. 1, 1869; H.-E. Chevalier, ibid., Sept. 13, 1868; Pelletan, ibid., Nov. 8, 1868; and Allain-Targé, *Projet de réorganisation de l'armée*, 12.

72. Soltau, *French Political Thought*, 98.

73. Quoted in Jeanneney, *Victor Hugo et la République*, 29–30. See chapter 1 above.

74. Chassin, *Démocratie*, Mar. 21, 1869.

75. Cluseret, *Armée et démocratie*, 225.

76. Hugo, *Œuvres politiques complètes*, 589.

77. Gastineau, *Histoire de la souscription populaire à la médaille Lincoln*, 6.

78. M. Crozier, "Remarques sur l'antiaméricanisme des Français," in Fauré and Bishop, *L'Amérique des Français*, 191.

79. Michelet, *Introduction à l'histoire universelle*, 73.

80. Michelet, *Journal*, 3:311 (Aug. 1865).

81. Michelet, *Histoire de la France au 18e siècle*, 250.

82. Michelet, *Journal*, 4:225 (Nov. 28, 1870).

CHAPTER 17

1. The official results were 7,350,000 for and 1,538,000 against. Plessis, *De la fête impériale au mur des fédérés*, 220.

2. Ollivier quoted in Cornut-Gentille, *Le 4 septembre 1870*, 21.

3. G. Cluseret, letter from New York, July 16, 1870, in *Démocratie*, Aug. 7, 1870.

4. J. R. Lowell to Charles Eliot Norton, Aug. 28, 1870, quoted in White, *American Opinion of France*, 178. On American reaction to the Franco-Prussian War, see ibid., chap. 6; Blumenthal, *Reappraisal of Franco-American Relations*, chap. 7; Curtis, "American Opinion of the French Nineteenth-Century Revolutions," 263–269; and Jeune, *Graindorge*, 97–98.

5. Katz, *Appomattox to Montmartre*, 26–33. Of the 5,000 or so American residents living in Paris at the war's outbreak, Katz estimates that only about 175 remained in December 1870.

6. See Stanton, *Grant and the French*.

7. In fact, Sheridan had first asked to accompany the French army but had been denied permission to do so by the emperor. The American's presence in the enemy camp was nonetheless seen by many Frenchmen as a sign of pro-German sentiment. See, for instance, Michelet, *La France devant l'Europe* 117.

8. Washburne, *Recollections*, 1:33–34. Washburne, in fact, acted honorably, even heroically. Alone among diplomatic representatives of a neutral country, he insisted on remaining in Paris throughout the ensuing siege of the capital, braving the privations and enemy artillery bombardments in order to look after the interests of American citizens and German nationals and to inform his government about the dire situation in the city. See McCullough, *Greater Journey*, 267–279.

9. Washburne to Bismarck, Jan. 19, 1871, in Washburne, *Franco-German War*, 132; Washburne to Fish, 5 Feb. 1871, ibid., 142.

10. Cornut-Gentille, *Le 4 septembre 1870*, 32.

11. Cornut-Gentille, *Le 4 septembre 1870*, 20.

12. Cornut-Gentille, *Le 4 septembre 1870*, 123–128; McCullough, *Greater Journey*, 260–263.

13. McCullough, *Greater Journey*, 259–260.

14. E. B. Washburne to William Washburn [*sic*], Sept. 7, 1870, in Washburne, *Elihu Washburne*, 45.

15. Washburne, *Franco-German War,* 65–66.

16. See, for example, *Journal des débats,* Sept. 15, 1870; and *Annuaire encyclopédique* (1869–71), 1538.

17. Sibbet, *Siege of Paris,* 134, quoted in Katz, *Appomattox to Montmartre,* 33.

18. A. Lévy, *Patriote,* Sept. 12, 1870. See also *Patriote,* Sept. 17, 1870. Lévy (1827–91) was a republican lawyer and journalist, a passionate supporter of the Polish and Italian causes, and a partisan of the Commune.

19. Washburne to Fish, Sept. 13, 1870, in Washburne, *Franco-German War,* 69; Washburne to Fish, Oct. 9, 1870, ibid., 79–80; Hoffman, *Camp, Court and Siege,* 166–169; H. Blumenthal, *Reappraisal of Franco-American Relations,* 197–200.

20. Stanton, *Grant and the French,* 14.

21. Grant quoted in Stanton, *Grant and the French,* 14.

22. Stanton, *Grant and the French,* 9–10.

23. On September 5, 1870, the day after the Third Republic was proclaimed, Hugo had returned to Paris and ended his twenty-two-year exile. He remained there under the Prussian bombardments, exhorting his compatriots to continue their resistance and personally financing the manufacture of two cannons. Elected to the National Assembly on February 8, 1871, he delivered a blistering condemnation of the "infamous peace" and shortly afterward resigned his parliamentary seat. His views on the Commune were ambivalent—"It's a good thing badly done"—but in subsequent years he worked tirelessly for national reconciliation and amnesty. When he died in 1885, the national funeral procession that accompanied his body to the Panthéon was the largest in the history of France. See Jeanneney, *Victor Hugo et la République,* 45–49; Noël, *Dictionnaire de la Commune,* 203–204; and Bressant, *Les Funérailles de Victor Hugo.*

24. Hugo, *Œuvres complètes,* 11:67–68. See also Hugo, *Choses vues, 1870–1885,* 113 (Nov. 25, 1870).

25. Stanton, *Grant and the French,* 9–10.

CHAPTER 18

1. Williams, *French Revolution of 1870–1871,* 116–119.

2. Clemenceau quoted in Williams, *French Revolution of 1870–1871,* 113. Clemenceau, as we have seen, had reported on Reconstruction in the United States. As prime minister he would go on to lead the French delegation at the Versailles treaty negotiations that imposed harsh terms on Germany following World War I. When President Woodrow Wilson asked if he had ever been to Germany, Clemenceau famously replied, "No, but the Germans [have] been to France twice in my lifetime."

3. McCullough, *Greater Journey,* 307.

4. Zeldin, *France,* 1:738–40.

5. Tombs, *Paris Commune,* 116–120. In French the term "commune" simply refers to a municipality, having no political connotation and no relation to communism or other revolutionary ideology. The Paris Commune, referring to the 1871 revolt of Parisians against the central government, was of course a political and revolutionary movement.

6. *Journal Officiel* (Paris Commune), Mar. 31, 1871. See also ibid., Apr. 1, 5, 1871; *Cri du peuple,* Apr. 2, 1871; and *Prolétaire,* May 15, 1871.

7. Portalis, *Journal Officiel* (Paris Commune), Apr. 5, 1871 (emphasis in original).

8. Portalis, *Journal Officiel* (Paris Commune), Apr. 5, 1871.

9. Portalis was hardly alone in making this analogy. Among Americans, particularly Southerners, comparisons between the Civil War and the Commune were common, as will be discussed below.

10. Concerning the influence of Proudhon's ideas on the Commune, see, for example, Rougerie, *Paris libre,* 46–47.

11. Williams, *America Confronts a Revolutionary World,* 152.

12. Cluseret, *Mémoires,* 1:39. See also ibid., 2:3, 14, 112. Hugo, who disapproved of the excesses of the Paris Commune but supported some of its aims, similarly called for a federation of communes as the basic building blocks for a federal Europe. Hugo, *Choses vues, 1870–1885,* 302 (Dec. 29, 1872).

13. Lullier, *Mes cachots,* 126, 385. A graduate of the French naval academy, Lullier (1838–91) had tried unsuccessfully to offer his services to the U.S. Navy in 1862. He visited the United States in 1871, returning just before the outbreak of the Commune.

14. Vésinier, *Paris-libre,* Apr. 12, 1871. See also Considérant, *La Paix en 24 heures,* 1; and Stupuy, *Fédéralisme,* 2, 4–5, 7.

15. P. Denis, *Cri du peuple,* Apr. 8, 1871. Denis (1828–1900), who played an important role in drafting the Commune's federalist manifesto of April 19, was a great admirer of the United States. See Denis article, recommending that French democrats follow the American example, in *Courrier français,* Nov. 4, 1866.

16. Girardin, *L'Union française.* On Girardin's activities during the Commune, see Bellanger et al., *Histoire générale de la presse française,* 2:375–376.

17. Speech of May 9, 1871, in Picard, *Discours parlementairesm,* 3:124.

18. Washburne to Hamilton Fish, May 22, 1871, in Washburne, *Franco-German War,* 203.

19. Bernstein, "The American Press Views the Commune," in *Essays in Political and Intellectual History,* 169–82; White, *American Opinion of France,* 208–209.

20. Katz, *Appomattox to Montmartre,* 44–46.

21. Katz, *Appomattox to Montmartre,* chap. 5.

22. Thiers quoted in Tombs, *Paris Commune,* 2. Interestingly, one historian of the Commune compares Thiers with Lincoln, Cavour, and Bismarck, all "champions of the strong nation-state." Williams, *French Revolution of 1870–1871,* 152.

23. Butler quoted in Katz, *Appomattox to Montmartre,* 94.

24. Tombs, *Paris Commune,* 9.

25. Tombs, *Paris Commune,* 4.

26. Frank M. Pixley quoted in Katz, *Appomattox to Montmartre,* 53 (emphasis in original).

27. Williams, *French Revolution of 1870–1871,* 151. Jacques Rougerie puts the death toll as high as 30,000. See *Paris libre,* 257. On the "Bloody Week," see, for example, ibid., chap. 6; Tombs, *Paris Commune,* 177–186; Williams, *French Revolution of 1870–1871,* 145–152; and Noël, *Dictionaire de la Commune,* 337–339. For a dramatic eyewitness account of this event by the American minister, see Washburne, *Elihu Washburne,* 185–203.

28. Rougerie, *Paris libre,* 257.

29. Cluseret, *Mémoires,* 2:211.

30. Washburne to Hamilton Fish, Apr. 23, 1871, in *New York Times,* May 13, 1871.

31. Raoul Rigault (1846–71) was a journalist, Blanquist revolutionary, and passionate anticlerical who personally ordered the arrest of Archbishop Darboy and the execution of numerous political enemies. On the morning of April 24, 1871, he was captured and executed by Versailles troops. Washburne described him as "one of the most hideous figures in all history. . . . Bold, energetic and cynical, he was consumed by the most deadly hatred of society and the most intense thirst for blood." Washburne, *Elihu Washburne,* 173. Interestingly, Rigault had been an active supporter of the John Brown medal subscription in 1867.

32. Washburne to Fish, Apr. 23, 1871, in *New York Times* May 13, 1871.

33. McCullough, *Greater Journey,* 318.

34. Edwards, *Paris Commune,* 213, cited in Washburne, *Elihu Washburne,* 189. Washburne apparently had limited respect for Thiers, whom he judged "bright and smart—tough as a pine knot," but "impatient under criticism. . . . When a man is struck with such blindness it is but little use in talking to him." Washburne diary, Mar. 31, 1871, quoted in Washburne, *Elihu Washburne,* 169.

35. Washburne to Fish, June, 1871, in Washburne, *Franco-German War,* 212–13; Washburne to Fish, Mar. 23, 1871, ibid., 162–65. On Parisian hostility to Americans at this time, see also Hoffman, *Camp, Court and Siege,* 249, 272; and Boyland, *Six Months under the Red Cross,* 109.

36. See, for example, Cluseret, *Mémoires,* 2:115, 125–126; Malon, *La Troisième défaite du prolétariat français,* 454–56, 515; Lefrançais, *Etude sur le mouvement communaliste,* 346–47; and Vuillaume, *Mes cahiers rouges au temps de la Commune,* 296–97.

37. Washburne, *Elihu Washburne,* 202 (diary, May 28, 1871).

38. Washburne, *Elihu Washburne,* 203 (diary, May 29, 1871).

39. Washburne to Fish, June 2, 1871, quoted in Katz, *Appomattox to Montmartre,* 49.

CHAPTER 19

1. Zeldin, *France,* 1:744–745.

2. See chapter 14 above.

3. See Cluseret, *Marseillaise,* Sept. 7, 1870; and Cluseret, *Lettre du général Cluseret à Gambetta.* Victor Hugo, himself freshly returned from exile, recounted that Cluseret came to him on September 7, saying: "This government . . . betrays [France]. It will give up Paris. You, Victor Hugo, appoint me as a general. Your signature will suffice. I will raise a an army of fifty thousand men and I will repel the Prussians." Hugo, *Choses vues, 1870–1885,* 182 (June 5, 1871).

4. Cluseret, *Mémoires,* 2:137–139; Katz, *Appomattox to Montmartre,* 12–15.

5. In reality, the fort was abandoned by the Parisians, then reoccupied under Cluseret's command. It finally fell on May 8 after a violent combat and severe casualties among the Communards. See Noël, *Dictionnaire de la Commune,* 216–217.

6. Cluseret, *Mémoires,* 2:172, 192–193; Braka, *L'honneur perdu du général Cluseret,* 172–176; Katz, *Appomattox to Montmartre,* 15–20; Noël, *Dictionnaire de la Commune,* 78.

7. Cluseret, *Mémoires*, 2:266–67. In fact, Cluseret's political evolution "kept going" in surprising directions after his return to France following amnesty in 1880. Elected to the Chamber of Deputies in 1888, this former internationalist revolutionary broke with the socialists and moved progressively to the right, becoming a nationalist, xenophobe, anti-Semite, defender of the army, and rabid anti-Dreyfusard. See Braka, *L'honneur perdu du général Cluseret*, 219–275.

8. Cluseret, *Mémoires*, 1:10n (dated 1887).

9. Cluseret, *Mémoires*, 2:242.

10. Reclus's career as a Communard was brief though consequential. After enrolling as a simple soldier in the Garde nationale, he was captured during a disorganized sortie on April 5, 1871, and spent six months in prison awaiting trial. On November 15 a military tribunal convicted Reclus of "bearing arms in the insurrectional movement" and ordered him deported to the penal colony of New Caledonia. Thanks to petitions signed by nearly one hundred eminent scientists, including Charles Darwin, the sentence was commuted to ten years' banishment. During his exile in Switzerland, Reclus was active in anarchist and communist circles and continued his prodigious output as a writer, publishing dozens of books and articles on geography, politics, and society. His nineteen-volume *Nouvelle géographie universelle* is still recognized as a classic in its field. He died in Ixelles, Belgium, in 1905 and was buried next to his brother Elie, who had served as director of the Bibliothèque nationale during the Commune. See Vincent, *Elisée Reclus*, 241–255 and passim.

11. Elisée Reclus, *La Grève d'Amérique*, 15.

12. Elisée Reclus, *Nouvelle géographie universelle, Les Etats Unis*, 99–106 and passim.

13. Brogan, *Price of Revolution*, 231.

14. Roger, *American Enemy*, 98.

15. Quinet to Alphonse Chadal, May 2, 1872, in Quinet, *Lettres d'exil*, 4:342. See also J. Michelet, *La France devant l'Europe*, 117. Such complaints reflected a typical reaction in defeated nations to blame their misfortune on some betrayal from within or "stab in the back" by foreign powers. This phenomenon is astutely analyzed by Wolfgang Schivelbusch in his study of the American South after the Civil War, France after the Franco-Prussian War, and Germany after World War I. See Schivelbusch, *Culture of Defeat*.

16. See Favre's deposition in *Enquête parlementaire sur l'insurrection du 18 mars*, 2:50–51.

17. Allain-Targé et al., *Note adressée à nos collègues MM. les membres du conseil municipal de Paris*, 10, 18–19. Allain-Targé's claim seems exaggerated. The average annual number of French emigrants to the United States was actually far lower during the decade 1871–80 (5,800) than during the pre–Civil War decade 1851–60 (7,600). See Wilcox, *International Migrations*, 206.

18. Blanc to Conway, Oct. 7, 1872, in Conway, *Autobiography*, 2:264. At Blanc's suggestion, Conway wrote a pamphlet entitled *Republican Superstitions as illustrated in the Political History of America*. Blanc then used some of his arguments to oppose the inclusion of a presidency and a senate in the French constitutional debates. See Conway, *Autobiography*, 2:267; and Blanc, *Histoire de la Constitution du 25 février 1875*, 116.

19. Zeldin, *France*, vol. 1, chap. 19.

20. Sibert, *La Constitution de la France du 4 septembre 1870*, 107–108; Bainville, *La Troisième République*, 11.

21. Gambetta, *Journal Officiel*, Dec. 29, 1876, quoted in Roger, *American Enemy*, 100–101.

22. Laboulaye to Mary L. Booth, July 11, 1880, quoted in Simon Jeune, *Graindorge*, 100. Another diehard Americanophile, Edouard Portalis, likewise accused Gambetta and the Opportunists of abandoning the American principles they had extolled under the Second Empire. See Portalis, *Deux républiques.*

23. On the history of the statue, see Berenson, *Statue of Liberty;* and Trachtenberg, *Statue of Liberty.*

24. *Temps,* Nov. 29, 1884; Hugo, *Choses vues, 1870–1885,* 448 (Nov. 30, 1884); Belot and Bermond, *Bartholdi,* 434.

25. Molinari, *Lettres sur les Etats-Unis et le Canada,* 360. The Belgian-born Molinari (1819–1912), an ardent champion of free trade and free-market economics, was editor of the liberal *Journal des débats* from 1871 to 1876.

26. In the same vein, see Jannet, *Les Etats-Unis contemporains.*

27. The play was entitled *La tour de Nesle: drame en 5 actes.* Gaillardet, who claimed sole authorship, went to court and even fought an inconclusive duel with Dumas to establish his exclusive right to the royalties.

28. Roger, *American Enemy,* 101–120.

29. Nicholas Wahl, "La démocratie américaine vue par des lunettes françaises," in Fauré and Bishop, *L'Amérique des Français,* 99.

CONCLUSION

1. Rémond, *Etats-Unis devant l'opinion française,* 2:862–863.

2. Echeverria, "L'Amérique devant l'opinion française," 51–62.

3. Sophie Body-Gendrot, "Mirages et myopies des Français à propos du système politique américain," in Fauré and Bishop, *L'Amérique des Français,* 85.

BIBLIOGRAPHY

MANUSCRIPT SOURCES

Amistad Research Center. Tulane University, New Orleans, La.
   American and Foreign Anti-Slavery Society Minutes, 1848–59
   American Missionary Association Archives, French Correspondence, 1867–74
Archives Départementales de la Seine-Maritime, Rouen
Archives du Ministère de la Guerre. Chateau de Vincennes, Paris
   Classement officiers: Dossier Cluseret
Archives Nationales, Pierrefitte-sur-Seine
   Dossier Cluseret
   Procureur général reports
Bibliothèque Historique de la Ville de Paris. Hôtel Lamoignon, Paris
   Correspondance Alfred Dumesnil–Eugène Noël
   Papiers Cabet
   Papiers Chassin
   Papiers Michelet
   Révolution de 1848 MSS
Bibliothèque Nationale de France, Paris
   Blanqui MSS
   Proudhon MSS
Bieneke Library. Yale University, New Haven, Conn.
   John W. De Forest Papers
Houghton Library. Harvard University, Cambridge, Mass.
   Charles Sumner Papers
   Miscellaneous French letters
Howard Tilton Memorial Library. Tulane University, New Orleans, La.
   Avenel Family Papers
   Hincks Family Papers
Louisiana State University Libraries, Baton Rouge, La.
   Pierre Soulé Papers, 1850–1901

PRIMARY PRINTED SOURCES

Newspapers and Journals

L'Almanach de l'exil (1855)

Almanach Icarien, astronomique, scientifique, pratique, industriel, statistique, politique et social. (1845–48)

Almanach républicain (1849–50)

L'Art (1868)

L'Atelier (1840–50)

Coopération (1866–68)

Courrier français (1864–68)

L'Evènement (1848–51)

Les Etats-Unis d'Europe (1867–70)

L'Homme (1853–55)

Journal Officiel de la République française (1871–76)

Journal Officiel de la République française [Paris Commune edition] (1871)

Lanterne (1868–69)

Liberté de penser (1847–52)

Marseillaise (1868–70)

Mémorial de Lille et du Nord de la France (1862–65)

L'Opinion nationale (1861–65)

Patrie en danger (1870–71)

Phare de la Loire (1861–71)

Presse (1862–65)

Proscrit (1850)

Rappel (1869–71)

Réforme (1869–70)

Représentant du peuple (1848)

Réveil (1868–71)

Révolution démocratique et sociale (1848–49)

Revue des Deux Mondes (1848–71)

Revue du monde colonial, asiatique et américain (1861–65)

Revue politique (1868–69)

Siècle (1861–71)

Temps (1861–71)

Travail, ed. Léon Say and Léon Walras (1866–67)

Travail, ed. P. Douvet (1869)

Tribune (1868–70)

Tribune populaire (1869–70)

Voix du peuple (1869)

Books and Articles

Adam, Juliette Lambert. *Mes Sentiments et Nos Idées avant 1870.* Paris: A. Lemerre, 1905.

Alembert, Alfred d'. *Flânerie parisienne aux Etats-Unis.* Paris: Librairie théâtrale, 1856.

Allain-Targé, François-Henri-René. "De la responsabilité ministérielle aux Etats-Unis." *Revue politique* 3 (February 13, 1869): 147–150.

———. *Les Déficits, 1852–1868.* Paris: Le Chevalier, 1868.

———. "Le Message du président Johnson." *Revue politique* 1 (August 15, 1868): 206–209.

———. "L'Obéissance passive." *Revue politique* 2 (November 14, 1868): 158–159.

———. *Le Projet de réorganisation de l'armée.* Paris: E. Dentu, 1866.

———. *La République sous l'Empire: Lettres 1864–1870.* Edited by Suzanne de la Porte. Paris: Grasset, 1939.

Allain-Targé, François-Henri-René, et al. *Note adressée à nos collègues MM. les membres du conseil municipal de Paris.* Paris, [1871].

American Slavery, Address of French Protestant Pastors. Paris, 1863.

Annales de l'Association internationale pour le progrès des sciences sociales. 2e session, Congrès de Gand. Paris: Guillaumin et Cie., 1863.

The Assassination of Abraham Lincoln, President of the United States of America, and the Attempted Assassination of William H. Seward, Secretary of State, and Frederick W. Seward, Assistant Secretary, on the Evening of the 14th of April, 1865. Washington, D.C.: Government Printing Office, 1866.

Association Internationale des Travailleurs. *Compte-rendu du IVe congrès international tenu à Bâle en septembre 1869.* Brussels: Editeur scientifique, 1869.

Assollant, Alfred. *Cannoniers à vos pièces!* Paris: E. Dentu, 1861.

———. *Le Droit des femmes.* Paris: A. Anger, 1868.

———. *Scènes de la vie des Etats-Unis. Acacia. Les Butterfly. Une Fantaisie américaine.* Paris: Hachette, 1859.

Audouard, Olympe. *A travers l'Amérique. Le Far West.* Paris: E. Dentu, 1869.

———. *A travers l'Amérique. North America, constitution, moeurs, usages, lois, institutions, sectes religieuses.* Paris: E. Dentu, 1871.

———. *Guerre aux hommes.* Paris: E. Dentu, 1866.

———. *Le Luxe des femmes, réponse d'une femme à M. le Procureur général Dupin.* Paris: E. Dentu, 1865.

Barni, Jules. *Ce que doit être la république.* Amiens: A. Caron, 1871.

———. *L'Instruction républicaine.* Paris: A. Le Chevalier, 1872.

Basterot, Florimond Jacques, comte de. *De Québec à Lima, journal d'un voyage dans les deux Amériques en 1838 et en 1839.* Paris: Hachette, 1860.

Baudelaire, Charles. Introduction to *Histoires extraordinaires,* by Edgar Allen Poe. Translated by Charles Baudelaire. Paris: Michel Lévy Frères, 1856.

———. Introduction to *Nouvelles histoires extraordinaires,* by Edgar Allen Poe. Translated by Charles Baudelaire. 1859. Reprint, Paris: A. Quantin, 1884.

Baudrillart, Henri. "L'Agitation pour l'émancipation des femmes en Angleterre et aux Etats-Unis." *Revue des Deux Mondes* 101 (October 1, 1872): 661.

Bellegarrigue, A. *Les femmes d'Amérique.* Paris: Blanchard, 1853.

Beluze, J.-P. *Lettres Icariennes.* 2 vols. Paris: Chez l'auteur, 1859–62.

Besson, M. *Vie du Cardinal Bonnechose.* Paris: Retaux-Bray, 1887.

Bigelow, John. *Retrospections of an Active Life.* New York: Baker & Taylor, 1909.

Blanc, Louis. "De la démocratie en Amérique." *Revue républicaine* 5 (1835): 129–163.

———. *Discours politiques, 1847–1881.* Paris: Germer-Baillière, 1882.

———. *Histoire de la Constitution du 25 février 1875.* Paris: G. Charpentier, 1882.

———. *Histoire de la Révolution de 1848.* Paris: Lacroix, Verboeckhoven, 1870.

———. *Lettres sur l'Angleterre.* 2 vols. Paris: A. Lacroix, Verboeckhove, 1865–66.

———. *L'Organisation du travail.* 5th ed. Paris: Société de l'industrie fraternelle, 1847.

Blanqui, Louis-Auguste. *Critique sociale.* 2 vols. Paris: F. Alcan, 1885.

Bonnechose, Marie-Gaston. *Lettre de sa Grandeur Monseigneur l'Archeveque de Rouen au clergé et aux fidèles de son diocèse, en faveur des ouvriers sans travail.* Rouen, 1862.

Boyland, George Halstead. *Six Months under the Red Cross, with the French Army.* Cincinnati: Robert Clarke, 1873.

Cabet, Etienne. *Colonie Icarienne aux Etats-Unis d'Amérique. Sa constitution, ses lois, sa situation matérielle et morale, après le premier semestre 1855.* Paris, 1856.

———. *Voyage de M. Cabet.* New York: F. Malteste, 1849.

———. *Voyage en Icarie.* 1840. Reprint, Paris: J. Mallet, 1842.

Carlier, Auguste. *Le Mariage aux Etats-Unis.* Paris: Hachette, 1860.

Chaline, Jean-Pierre. *Deux bourgeois en leur temps.* Rouen: Impr. Lecerf, 1977.

Channing, W. E. *Œuvres de W. E. Channing. De l'esclavage précédé d'une étude sur l'esclavage aux Etats-Unis par Edouard Laboulaye.* Translated by Edouard Laboulaye. Paris: Lacroix-Comon, 1855.

———. *Œuvres sociales de W. E. Channing, traduites de l'anglais, précédées d'un essai sur la vie et les doctrines de Channing et d'une introduction par M. Edouard Laboulaye.* Paris: Lacroix-Comon, 1854.

Chaudey, Gustave. *L'Empire parlementaire, est-il possible?* Paris: Le Chevalier, 1870.

Cheminat, Eugénie. *Quelques observations sur l'Américaine des Etats-Unis.* Paris: E. Dentu, 1873.

Chevalier, Henri-Emile, and L. Pharaon. *Un Drame esclavagiste.* Paris: Charlieu et Huillery, 1864.

Chevalier, Michel. *La France, le Mexique et les Etats confédérés.* Paris: E. Dentu, 1863.

———. *La Guerre et la crise européenne.* Paris: Garnier, 1866.

———. "La Guerre et la crise européenne." *Revue des Deux Mondes* 43 (June 1, 1866): 784–785.

———. *Lettres sur l'Amérique du Nord.* 2 vols. Paris: C. Gosselin, 1836.

———. "La question des travailleurs." *Revue des Deux Mondes* 21 (March 15, 1848): 1057–1986.

Chotteau, Léon. *Les Américains d'aujourd'hui. Le président Andrew Johnson.* Paris: G. Retaux, 1868.

———. *L'Instruction en Amérique.* Paris: Rodière, 1873.

———. *On demande une constitution.* Paris: Heymann, 1871.

———. *Les Véritables Républicains. Biographies de Ulysses S. Grant, président, et de Schuyler Colfax, vice-président de la République des Etats-Unis.* Paris: Degorce-Cadot, 1869.

Clemenceau, Georges. *American Reconstruction, 1865–1870, and the Impeachment of President Johnson.* Edited by Fernand Baldensperger. Translated by Margaret MacVeagh. New York: Dial, 1928.

———. *La Mêlée sociale.* Paris: G. Charpentier et E. Fasquelle, 1895.

Cluseret, Gustave Paul. *Armée et démocratie.* Paris: A. Lacroix, Verboeckhoven, 1869.

———. "Behind the Scenes at the Commune." *Fraser's Magazine* 6 (1872): 782–801.

———. *Lettre du général Cluseret à Gambetta.* Paris: Impr. de Berthelemy, 1871.

———. *Mémoires du général Cluseret.* 3 vols. Paris: J. Lévy, 1887–88.

———. *Mexico and the Solidarity of Nations.* New York: Blackwell, 1866.

———. "My Connection with Fenianism." *Fraser's Magazine* 6 (1872): 37–42.

———. "The Paris Commune of 1871." *Fraser's Magazine* 7 (1873): 360–84.

Comettant, Oscar. *Trois ans aux Etats-Unis.* Paris: Pagnerre, 1858.

Considérant, Victor. *Au Texas.* Paris: Librairie Phalanstérienne, 1854.

———. *Du Texas, premier rapport à mes amis.* Paris: Librairie Sociétaire, 1857.

———. *European Colonization in Texas: An Address to the American People.* New York: Baker, Godwin, 1855.

———. *La France imposant la paix à l'Europe, lettre aux membres du gouvernement provisoire de la République.* Paris: Le Chevalier, 1870.

———. *Mexique. Quatre lettres au maréchal Bazaine.* Brussels: C. Muquardt, 1868.

———. *La Paix en 24 heures, dictée par Paris à Versailles. Adresse aux Parisiens.* Paris: Gouzren et Ledreux, 1871.

Conway, Moncure Daniel. *Autobiography, Memories and Experiences.* 2 vols. Boston: Houghton-Mifflin, 1904.

———. *Republican Superstitions, as illustrated in the Political History of America.* London: H. S. King, 1872.

Corbon, Anthime. *Le Secret du peuple de Paris.* Paris: Pagnerre, 1863.

Cordier, Alphonse. *La Crise cotonnière dans la Seine-Inférieure, ses causes et ses effets.* Rouen: Impr. de C.-F. Lapierre, 1864.

Courmont, Félix de. *Des Etats-Unis, de la guerre du Mexique, et de l'Ile de Cube* [sic]. Paris: Moquet, 1847.

Daubié, Julie-Victoire. *L'Émancipation de la femme.* Paris: E. Thorin, 1871.

Darimon, Alfred. *Histoire d'un parti. Le Tiers parti sous l'Empire.* Paris: E. Dentu, 1887.

Délégations ouvrières à l'Exposition universelle de Londres en 1862. Paris: M. Chabaud, 1864.

Domenech, Abbé. *Journal d'un missionnaire au Texas et au Mexique.* Paris: Gaume Frères, 1857.

Du Pasquier de Dommartin, H. *Les Etats-Unis et le Mexique.* Paris: Guillaumin, 1852.

Duruy, Victor. *Administration de l'Instruction publique, 1863–1869.* Paris: J. Delalain, 1870.

———. *Notes et souvenirs.* 2 vols. Paris: Hachette, 1901.

Duvergier de Hauranne, Ernest. "Les Etats-Unis en 1867: Un an de guerre politique." *Revue des Deux Mondes* 42 (November 15, 1867): 475–515.

———. "Le Président Johnson et le Congrès américain." *Revue des Deux Mondes* 46 (December 15, 1866): 785–828.

———. *Huit mois en Amérique: Lettres et notes de voyage, 1864–1865.* 2 vols. Paris: A. Lacroix, Verboeckhoven, 1866.

Enquête parlementaire sur l'insurrection du 18 mars. 3 vols. Paris: Cerf, 1872.

Etourneau, M. *Les Mormons.* Paris: Bestel, 1856.

Exposition universelle de Philadelphie 1876. Rapports de la délégation ouvrière lyonnaise. Lyons: Impr. Jevain, 1877.

Eyma, Xavier. *Excentricités américaines.* Paris: Michel Lévy Frères, 1859.

———. *Les femmes du nouveau monde.* Paris: D. Giraud, 1853.

———. *Le Trône d'argent.* Paris: Michel Lévy, 1860.

Favre, Jules. *Discours parlementaires.* 4 vols. Paris: Plon, 1881.

Fernand, Jacques. *John Brown, mort pour l'affranchissement des noirs.* Paris: C. Vanier, 1861.

Ferry, Jules. *De l'égalité d'éducation.* Paris: Société pour l'instruction élémentaire, 1870.

———. *Discours et opinions.* Edited by Paul Robiquet. 7 vols. Paris: A. Colin, 1893–98.

———. *Conférence populaire faite à la Salle Molière le 10 avril 1870.* Paris: Au Siège de la Société, 1870.

Fisch, Georges. *Les Etats-Unis en 1861.* Paris: Dentu, 1862.

Fonvielle, Ulrich de. "Correspondance des Etats-Unis." *Revue du monde colonial* 6 (1862): 212–214.

———. *Scènes de la vie militaire aux Etats-Unis.* N.p., [1866?].

Fonvielle, Wilfrid de. "Considérations sur le commerce de l'Union américaine." *Revue du monde colonial* 6 (January 1, 1862): 6.

Freycinet, Charles de. *La Guerre en province pendant le siège de Paris, 1870–1871.* Paris: M. Lévy Frères, 1871.

Gaël, A. [Augustine Guirault]. *La Femme médecin, sa raison d'être au point de vue du droit, de la morale et de l'humanité.* Paris: E. Dentu, 1868.

Gaillardet, Frédéric. *De l'aristocratie en Amérique.* Paris: E. Dentu, 1883.

Gambetta, Léon. *Discours et plaidoyers politiques.* 11 vols. Paris: Ed. Joseph Reinach, 1880–85.

———. *Gambetta par Gambetta: Lettres intimes et souvenirs de famille.* Edited by P. B. Gheusi. Paris: Paul Ollendorff, 1909.

———. "Le général Grant." *Revue politique* 1 (June 13, 1868): 33–35.

[Gardanne, comte de]. *La France et les Etats-Unis comparés.* Paris: Le Chevalier, 1869.

Garrison, William Lloyd. Introduction to *Joseph Mazzini, His Life, Writings and Political Principles.* New York: Hurd and Houghton, 1872.

Gasparin, Agénor, comte de. *L'Amérique devant l'Europe: Principes et intérêts.* 1862. Reprint, Paris: C. Lévy, 1879.

———. *The Uprising of a Great People.* Translated by Mary L. Booth. New York: Charles Scribner, 1862.

———. *Une parole de paix sur le différend entre l'Angleterre et les États-Unis.* Paris: Michel Lévy Frères, 1861.

Gastineau, Benjamin. *Les Génies de la liberté, avec des lettres de George Sand, Victor Hugo et Louis Blanc.* Paris: A. Lacroix, Verboeckhoven, 1865.

———. *Histoire de la souscription populaire à la médaille Lincoln, la médaille de la liberté.* Paris: A. Lacroix, Verboeckhoven, [1865].

Girardin, Emile de. *Le Condamné du 6 mars. Questions de l'année 1867.* Paris: Michel Lévy Frères, 1868.

———. *Force ou richesse. Questions de l'année 1864.* Paris: Plon, 1864.

———. *La Liberté.* Paris: Librairie nouvelle, 1857.

———. *Paix et liberté. Questions de l'année 1863.* Paris: Plon, 1864.

———. *Pouvoir et impuissance. Questions de l'année 1865.* Paris: Michel Lévy Frères, 1867.

———. *Le Succès. Questions de l'année 1866.* Paris: Michel Lévy Frères, 1867.

———. *L'Union française. Extinction de la guerre civile par l'adoption de la constitution américaine.* Paris: Impr. Serrière, 1871.

———. *La Voix dans le désert. Questions de l'année 1868.* Paris: Plon, 1869.

Grousset, Paschal. *Le Rêve d'un irréconciliable.* Paris: Madre, 1869.

Grousset, Paschal, A. Ranc Castagnary, and Francisque Sarcey. *Le Bilan de l'année 1868, politique, littéraire, dramatique, artistique et scientifique.* Paris: A. Le Chevalier, 1869.

Guépin, Dr. Ange. "Situation et avenir des Etats-Unis." *Almanach Icarien* (1848): 118–128.

Guer, Guerlin de. *La Liberté et l'éducation. L'Instruction primaire aux Etats-Unis.* Paris: Berger Levrault, 1880.

Henry, Fortuné. *Chants de ma prison.* Toulouse: M. Gimet, 1862.

Hippeau, Célestin. "L'Education des femmes et des affranchis en Amérique." *Revue des Deux Mondes* 93 (September 15, 1869): 450–476.

———. *L'Instruction publique aux Etats-Unis. Ecoles publiques, collèges, universités, écoles spéciales. Rapport adressé au ministre de l'instruction publique.* Paris: Didier, 1870.

Hoffman, Wickham. *Camp, Court and Siege: A Narrative of Personal Adventure and Observation during Two Wars: 1861–1865; 1870–1871.* New York: Harper & Brothers, 1877.

Hugo, Victor. *Choses vues, 1847–1848.* Edited by Hubert Juin. Paris: Gallimard, 1972.

———. *Choses vues, 1849–1869.* Edited by Hubert Juin. Paris: Gallimard, 1972.

———. *Choses vues, 1870–1885.* Edited by Hubert Juin. Paris: Gallimard, 1972.

———. *John Brown.* Paris: Dusacq, 1861.

———. *Œuvres complètes. Poésie.* Vol. 12. Paris: Albin Michel, 1935.

———. *Œuvres de Victor Hugo.* [Vol. 11], *Les Châtiments, l'Année terrible.* Paris: Flammarion, 1913.

———. *Œuvres politiques complètes. Œuvres diverses.* Edited by Francis Bouvet. Paris: J. J. Pauvert, 1964.

Jannet, Claudio. *Les Etats-Unis contemporains, ou les mœurs, les institutions et les idées depuis la guerre de sécession.* Paris: E. Plon, 1876.

Jarves, James Jackson. *Parisian Sights and French Principles, Seen through American Spectacles.* New York: Harper & Brothers, 1852.

Joly, Louis. *La Fédération, seule forme de la décentralisation dans les démocraties. Réponse au projet de Nancy.* Paris: Garnier Frères, 1866.

Jouve, E. *Voyage en Amérique.* Lyons: Impr. de Vve Mougin-Rusand, 1853–55.

Labbé, J. *Le Manifeste de Nancy et la démocratie.* Paris: E. Dentu, 1865.

Laboulaye, Edouard. *Discours populaires.* Paris: Charpentier, 1869.

———. *Les Etats-Unis et la France.* Paris: E. Dentu, 1862.

———. *Paris en Amérique.* 1863. Reprint, Paris: Charpentier, 1870.

———. *Souscription pour l'érection d'un monument commémoratif du centième anniversaire de l'indépendance des États-Unis: Union franco-américaine, signé E. Laboulaye.* Paris, 1875.

Ladet, Ulysse. "La campagne présidentielle." *Revue politique* 1 (July 18, 1868): 131–133.

Lamarle, Amédée. *De la nécessité de l'instruction dans une république.* Amiens: A. Caron, 1872.

Lamartine, Alphonse de. *Cours familier de littérature.* Vol. 20. Paris: Par l'auteur, 1865.

———. *La Présidence. Discours prononcé à l'Assemblée nationale par M. de Lamartine.* Paris: Michel Lévy Frères, 1848.

———. *Toussaint Louverture: poème dramatique.* Brussels: Vve. Wouters, 1850.

———. *Trois mois au pouvoir.* Paris: Michel Lévy Frères, 1848.

Laugel, Auguste. *Les Etats-Unis pendant la guerre, 1861–1865.* Paris: G. Ballière, 1866.

Laveleye, Emile de. "L'Enseignement populaire dans les écoles américaines." *Revue des Deux Mondes* 40 (November 15, 1865): 273–300.

———. *L'Instruction du peuple.* Paris: Hachette, 1872.

Ledru-Rollin, Alexandre-Auguste. *De la décadence de l'Angleterre.* Paris: Escudier Frères, 1850.

———. *Discours politiques et écrits divers.* Paris: G. Ballière, 1879.

Lefrançais, Gustave. *Etude sur le mouvement communaliste à Paris en 1871* Neuchâtel: Impr. de G. Guillaume Fils, 1871.

———. *Souvenirs d'un révolutionnaire.* Edited by Jan Černy. 1902. Reprint, Paris: Editions de la Tête de Feuilles, 1972.

Legouvé, Ernest. *Histoire morale des femmes.* 1849. Reprint, Paris: Didier, 1869.

Lamarque, J. de. "La Doctrine Monroe." *Revue du monde colonial* 15 (June 1865): 391.

Lemonnier, Charles. *Les Etats-Unis d'Europe.* Paris: Librairie de la Bibliothèque démocratique, 1872.

Leneveux, Henri. *La Propagande de l'instruction.* Paris: Impr. de Dubuisson, 1861.

Léo, André [Léonide Béra Champseix]. "La Colonie américaine." *Paris-Guide, par les principaux écrivains et artistes de la France* 2 (1867): 1065–1080.

———. *La Femme et les moeurs. Liberté ou monarchie.* Paris: Le Droit des Femmes, 1869.

Lepelletier, Edmond. *Histoire de la Commune de Paris.* 3 vols. Paris: Mercure de France, 1911–13.

Le Play, Frédéric. *La Réforme sociale en France.* 3 vols. Paris: Dentu, 1867.

Leroux, Pierre. *De l'égalité.* Paris: Impr. De P. Leroux, 1848.

Leroux, Pierre, and J. Reynaud, eds. *Encyclopédie nouvelle.* 8 vols. Paris: Ch. Gosselin, 1836–41.

Letters on American Slavery from Victor Hugo, de Tocqueville, Emile de Girardin, Carnot, Passy, Mazzini, Humboldt, de Lafayette &c. Boston: American Anti-Slavery Society, 1860.

Ligue de la décentralisation. Séance du 27 mai 1870. Paris: Impr. de Dubuisson, 1870.

Ligue internationale de la paix et de la liberté. *Résolutions votées par les vingt-et-un premiers congrès. Receuil officiel.* Geneva, 1888.

———. *Annales du Congrès de Genève.* Geneva, 1868.

Lincoln, Abraham. *The Collected Works of Abraham Lincoln.* Edited by Roy P. Basler, Marion Dolores Pratt and Lloyd A. Dunlap. 9 vols. New Brunswick, N.J.: Rutgers University Press, 1953–55.

Lissagaray, Prosper-Olivier. *Histoire de la Commune de 1871.* 1876. Reprint, Paris: Maspero, 1967.

Louis-Philippe (Louis-Philippe-Joseph d'Orléans). *Journal de mon voyage d'Amérique.* Paris: Flammarion, 1976.

Lowell, James Russell. "On a Certain Condescension in Foreigners." *Atlantic Monthly* 23 (1869): 82–94.

Luciennes, Victor. *Le Gibet de John Brown.* Paris: Castel, 1861.

Lullier, Charles-Ernest. *Mes cachots.* Paris: Chez l'auteur, 1881.

Macé, Jean. *La Ligue de l'enseignement à Beblenheim, 1862–1870.* Paris: G. Charpentier, 1890.

Malon, Benoît. *La Troisième défaite du prolétariat français.* Neuchâtel: G. Guillaume fils, 1871.

Marmier, Xavier. *Les Ames en peine, contes d'un voyageur.* Paris: A. Bertrand, 1851.

———. *Lettres sur l'Amérique.* Paris: A. Bertrand, 1851.

Marx, Karl. *Capital.* Translated by Eden Paul and Cedar Paul. 1867. Reprint, New York: Dutton, 1974.

Marx, Karl, and Frederick Engels. *The Civil War in the United States.* Newark, N.J.: International Publishers, 1961.

———. *The Communist Manifesto.* 1848. Reprint, London: Penguin, 1973.

McKitrick, Eric L., ed. *Slavery Defended: The Views of the Old South.* New York: Prentice Hall, 1963.

Melvil-Bloncourt, Sainte-Suzanne, vicomte de. *Au dernier défenseur de l'esclavage, réponse à M. Poussielgue.* Paris: Impr. de H. Carion, [1861].

———. "Des projets des Américains sur la presqu'île de Samana." *Revue politique* 1 (July 25, 1868): 154–157.

———. "Homme ou singe, ou la question de l'esclavage aux Etats-Unis." *Revue du monde colonial* 5 (August 1861): 143–147.

———. *Souscription en faveur des affranchis des Etats-Unis d'Amérique.* Paris: Impr. De Walder, 1865.

Mercier, Achille. "Le Travail des femmes." *Revue politique* (September 27, 1868): 339.

Michel, Louise. *La Commune.* 1898. Reprint, Paris: Editions Stock, 1978.

Michelet, Jules. *L'Amour.* Paris: Hachette, 1858.

———. *La Femme.* 1859. Reprint, Paris: G. Charpentier, 1889.

———. *La France devant l'Europe.* Florence: Le Monnier, 1871.

———. *Histoire de la France au 18e siècle.* Vol. 17, *Louis XV et Louis XVI.* Paris: Chamerot et Lauwereyns, 1867.

———. *Introduction à l'histoire universelle.* Paris: Hachette, 1831.

———. *Journal.* Edited by Paul Viallaneix and Claude Digeon. 4 vols. Paris: Gallimard, 1959–76.

———. *Le Peuple.* 1846. Reprint, Paris: Calmann Lévy, 1877.

Moges, Alfred de. *De l'influence prochaine des Etats-Unis sur la politique de l'Europe.* Paris: Impr. de Wiesener, 1856.

Molinari, Gustave de. *Lettres sur les Etats-Unis et le Canada.* Paris: Hachette, 1876.

Monod, Mme. William. *La Mission des femmes en temps de guerre.* Paris: Nouvelle Bibliothèque des Familles, 1870.

Montalembert, Charles-René Forbes, comte de. *Discours de M. le comte de Montalembert.* 3 vols. Paris: Jacques Lecoffre, 1860.

———. *La Victoire du Nord aux Etats-Unis.* Paris: E. Dentu, 1865.

Morhard, G. *Travail, liberté, propriété pour tous: Appel d'un Américain aux riches et aux prolétaires d'Europe.* Paris: Les Principaux Libraires, 1846.

Nadaud, Martin. *Discours de Martin Nadaud à l'Assemblée législative (1849–1851). Questions ouvrières en Angleterre et en France.* Paris: C. Dumont, 1884.

Napoleon III. *Discours prononcé par Sa Majesté Napoléon III à l'ouverture des chambres, le 22 janvier 1866.* Paris: Impr. de G. Jousset, Clet, 1867.

———. *Papiers et correspondance de la Famille Impériale.* Paris: Imprimerie Nationale, 1871.

Niboyet, Eugénie. *Le Vrai Livre des femmes.* Paris: E. Dentu, 1863.

Olinet, Frédéric. *Socialisme. Voyage d'un Autunois en Icarie, à la suite de Cabet.* Autun: Impr. de Dejussieu, 1898.

Pascal, César. *A travers l'Atlantique et dans le Nouveau Monde.* Paris: Grassart, 1870.

———. *Meeting en faveur des esclaves émancipés dans les Etats-Unis d'Amérique.* Paris: Grassart, 1866.

Pecqueur, Constantin. *Des améliorations matérielles dans leurs rapports avec la liberté.* Paris: C. Gosselin, 1840.

Pelletan, Eugène. *Adresse au roi Coton.* Paris: Pagnerre, 1863.

———. *La Femme au XIXe siècle.* Paris: Pagnerre, 1869.

———. *Profession de foi du dix-neuvième siècle.* Paris: Pagnerre, 1852.

———. *Le Travail au XIXe siècle.* Paris: Pagnerre, 1869.

———. *Les Uns et les Autres.* Paris: Pagnerre, 1873.

Pelletier, Claude. *Les Soirées socialistes de New-York.* New York, 1873.

Perdiguier, Agricol. *Comment constituer la république.* Paris: L'Auteur, 1871.

———. *Despotisme et liberté.* Paris: E. Dentu, 1864.

Picard, Ernest. *Discours parlementaires.* 4 vols. Paris: E. Plon, 1882–90.

Pierre Bonaparte et le crime à Auteuil. Paris, 1870.

Pontécoulant, Alfred de. *John Brown à M. Victor Hugo.* Paris: Libr. Théâtrale, 1860.

Portalis, Albert-Edouard. *Deux républiques.* Paris: G. Charpentier, 1880.

———. *Les Etats-Unis, le self-government et le césarisme.* Paris: A. Le Chevalier, 1869.

Poulot, Denis. *Question sociale. Le Sublime, ou le travailleur comme il est en 1870 et ce qu'il peut être.* Paris: A. Lacroix, Verboeckhoven, 1872.

Prévost-Paradol, Lucien-Anatole. *La France nouvelle.* Paris: Michel Lévy Frères, 1868.

Projet de décentralisation. Nancy: Vagner, Imprimeur-Librairie-Editeur, 1865.

Proudhon, Pierre-Joseph. *Correspondance.* 14 vols. Paris: A. Lacroix, 1875.

———. *De la capacité politique des classes ouvrières.* Paris: E. Dentu, 1865.

———. *De la Justice dans la Révolution et dans l'Église, nouveaux principes de philosophie pratique adressés à S. E. Mgr Mathieu.* Paris: Garnier frères, 1858.

———. *Du principe fédératif et de la nécessité de reconstituer le parti de la Révolution.* Paris: E. Dentu, 1863.

———. *La Pornocratie ou les Femmes dans les temps modernes.* Paris: A. Lacroix, 1875.

———. *Qu'est-ce que la propriété? ou Recherches sur le principe du droit et du gouvernement. Premier mémoire*. 1840. Reprint, Paris: Garnier-Flammarion, 1966.

Pyat, Félix. *Au peuple des Etats-Unis*. N.p., [1865].

———. *La Présidence*. Paris: Impr. de Schneider, 1848.

Quinet, Edgar. *Le Christianisme et la Révolution française*. Vol. 3, of *Œuvres complètes d'Edgar Quinet*. Paris: Pagnerre, 1857.

———. *L'Enseignement du peuple*. Paris: Chamerot, 1850.

———. *L'Expédition du Mexique*. Veytaux: W. Jeffs, 1862.

———. *Lettres d'exil à Michelet et à divers amis*. 4 vols. Paris: Calmann-Lévy, 1885–86.

Rapports des délégués lyonnais envoyés à l'Exposition universelle de Londres. Lyons: Impr. de Vve. Mougin-Rusand, 1862.

Rapports des membres de la section française du jury international sur l'ensemble de l'Exposition de Londres. 7 vols. Paris: N. Chaix, 1862–64.

Reclus, Elie. "Traité de commerce entre la Chine et les Etats-Unis." *Revue politique* 1 (August 22, 1868): 231–35.

Reclus, Elisée. *Correspondance*. 3 vols. Paris: Schleicher Frères, 1911–25.

———. "Le Coton et la crise américaine." *Revue des Deux Mondes* 37 (January 1, 1862): 176–209.

———. "De l'esclavage aux Etats-Unis. I. Le Code noir et les esclaves." *Revue des Deux Mondes* 30 (December 15, 1860): 868–902.

———. "De l'esclavage aux Etats-Unis. II. Les Planteurs et les abolitionnistes." 31 (January 1, 1861): 118–54.

———. "Un Ecrit américain sur l'esclavage." *Revue des Deux Mondes*. 1 (March 15, 1864): 507–510.

———. "Fragment d'un voyage à la Nouvelle-Orléans." *Tour du monde* (1st semester 1860): 85–92.

———. *La Grève d'Amérique*. N.p., [1877].

———. "Histoire de la guerre civile aux Etats-Unis: Les Deux dernières années de la grande lutte américaine." *Revue des Deux Mondes* 53 (October 1 1864): 555–624.

———. "Histoire des états américains. Etats-Unis." *Annuaire des deux mondes* 13 (1866): 646–788.

———. "L'Insurrection de Cuba." *Revue politique* 2 (December 19, 1869): 270–271.

———. "Les livres sur la crise américaine." *Revue des Deux Mondes* 62 (November 15, 1862): 509.

———. "Le Mississipi, études et souvenirs. II. Le Delta et la Nouvelle-Orléans." *Revue des Deux Mondes* 22 (August 1, 1859): 608–646.

———. "Les Noirs américains depuis la guerre. I." *Revue des Deux Mondes* 44 (March 15, 1863): 364–394.

———. "Les Noirs américains depuis la guerre. II." *Revue des Deux Mondes* 44 (April 1, 1863): 691–672.

——. *Nouvelle géographie universelle. La Terre et les hommes.* Vol. 16, *Les Etats-Unis.* Paris: Hachette, 1892.

Renan, Ernest. "Channing et le mouvement unitaire aux Etats-Unis." *Revue des Deux Mondes* 8 (December 15, 1854): 1085–1107.

Report of the Executive Committee of the Fair for Relief of Suffering in France. Boston: Rand, Avery, 1872.

Ribert, Léonce. "Le Fédéralisme." *Revue politique* 2 (October 24, 1868): 82–85.

Richer, Léon. *La Femme libre.* Paris: E. Dentu, 1877.

——. *Le Livre des femmes.* Paris: Librairie de la Bibliothèque démocratique, 1873.

Rossel, Louis Nathaniel. *Abrégé de l'art de la guerre: Extraits des œuvres de Napoléon, Jomini, d'Archiduc Charles, etc., annotés par L. N. Rossel.* Paris: E. Lachaud, 1871.

——. *Mémoires, procès et correspondance.* Edited by Roger Stéphane. Paris: J.-J. Pauvert, 1960.

Saint-Ferréol, Amedée de. *Les Proscrits français en Belgique, ou la Belgique vue à travers l'exil.* 2 vols. Paris: A. Le Chevalier, 1871.

Sand, George [Amandine Aurore Lucile, baronne Dudevant, née Dupin]. *Agendas.* Edited by Anne Chevereau. Paris: J. Touzot, 1993.

——. *Correspondance, 1812–1876.* 6 vols. 4th ed. Paris: C. Lévy, 1883–95.

——. *Souvenirs et idées.* Paris: C. Lévy, 1904.

Sand, Maurice. *Six mille lieues à toute vapeur.* Paris: Michel-Lévy, 1862.

——. "Six Mille lieues à toute vapeur. II." *Revue des Deux Mondes* 37 (February 1, 1862): 635–686.

——. "'Six Mille lieues à tout vapeur. III." *Revue des Deux Mondes* 37 (February 15, 1862): 903–947.

Savardan, Dr. Augustin. *Un Naufrage au Texas: Observations et impressions receuillies pendant deux ans et demi au Texas et à travers les Etats-Unis.* Paris: Garnier Frères, 1858.

Schoelcher, Victor. "L'Esclavage aux Etats-Unis." *Liberté de penser* 8 (1851): 773–793.

——. "L'Insurrection de Cuba et les Etats-Unis." *Liberté de penser* 8 (1851): 441–463.

——. "Loi du 18 septembre 1850, sur les esclaves fugitifs aux Etats-Unis." *Liberté de penser* 8 (1851): 174–204.

Seauret, P. A. "Souvenirs d'un ouvrier français aux Etats-Unis." *Revue socialiste* 44 (1906): 61–74, 169–93, 339–49.

Senior, Nassau W. *Conversations with Distinguished Persons during the Second Empire from 1860 to 1863.* London: Hurst and Blackett, 1880.

Sibbet, Robert L. *The Siege of Paris by an American Eye-witness.* Harrisburg, Pa.: Meyers, 1892.

Simon, Jules. *L'Ecole.* Paris: A. Lacroix, 1865.

——. *L'Instruction populaire en France, débats parlementaires par MM. Carnot, Havin et Jules Simon, avec une introduction historique par M. Jules Simon.* Paris: Degorce-Cadot, 1869.

———. *La Politique radicale.* Paris: A. Lacroix, Verboeckhoven, 1868.

Simonin, Louis-Laurent. *Le Grand ouest des Etats-Unis.* Paris: Charpentier, 1869.

Special Report of the Anti-Slavery Conference, Held in Paris, August 1867. London: British and Foreign Anti-slavery Society, [1867].

Stowe, Harriet Beecher. *Sunny Memories of Foreign Lands.* 2 vols. London: Routledge, 1854.

Stupuy, Hippolyte. *Fédéralisme. Projet de traité entre Paris et Versailles.* Versailles: Cerf, 1871.

Sue, Eugène. *Lettres sur la question religieuse en 1856.* Brussels: Librairie Internationale, 1857.

Tajan-Rogé, Dominique. *Les Beaux-arts aux Etats-Unis d'Amérique. Deux discours prononcés à New-York les 27 et 31 mai 1856, dans le Clinton-Hall, Astor Palace.* Paris: Bestel, 1857.

Ténot, Eugène. *Paris en décembre 1851, étude historique sur le coup d'État.* Paris: Le Chevalier, 1868.

Thévenin, Evariste. *L'Instruction primaire des deux sexes confiée aux femmes.* Châteauroux: Impr. de Gablin et Dauphin, 1879.

Tocqueville, Alexis, comte de. *De la démocratie en Amérique.* 2 vols. 1835–40. Reprint, edited by J. P. Mayer, Paris: Gallimard, 1961.

———. *Ecrits et discours politiques.* Edited by J. P. Meyer. Paris: Gallimard, 1962.

———. *Souvenirs.* Edited by Luc Monnier. Paris: Gallimard, 1964.

"Transatlantic Tourists." *Blackwood's Edinburgh Magazine* 44 (1851): 545–563.

Vacherot, Etienne. *La Démocratie.* Paris: F. Chamerot, 1860.

Vaïsse, Jean-Louis. *La république universelle de l'avenir: le vote des femmes.* Toulouse: F. Gimet, 1871.

Vésinier, Pierre. *Le Martyr de la liberté des nègres, ou John Brown, le Christ des noirs.* Berlin: J. Abelsdorff. 1864.

Veuillot, Eugène. "Etudes sur les Etats-Unis; l'esprit chrétien; le mariage; le progrès religieux." *Revue du monde catholique* 17 (1867): 75–101.

Vigo-Roussillon, François-Paul. *Puissance militaire des Etats-Unis d'Amérique d'après la guerre de Sécession, 1861–1865.* Paris: H. Dumaine, 1866.

Vuillaume, Maxime. *Mes cahiers rouges au temps de la Commune.* 1909. Reprint, Paris: A. Michel, 1971.

Washburne, Elihu Benjamin. *Elihu Washburne: The Diary and Letters of America's Minister to France during the Siege and Commune of Paris.* Edited by Michael Hill. New York: Simon & Schuster, 2012.

———. *Franco-German War and Insurrection of the Commune: Correspondence of E. B. Washburne.* Washington, D.C.: Government Printing Office, 1878.

———. *Recollections of a Minister to France, 1869–1877.* 2 vols. New York: Charles Scribner's Sons, 1887.

Wellesley, Victor, and R. Sencourt. *Conversations with Napoleon III*. London: E. Benn, 1934.

SECONDARY PRINTED SOURCES

Amat, Roman d', ed. *Dictionnaire de biographie française*. Paris: Letouzey et Ané, 1933–61.
Anderson, Emmet Harvey. "Appraisal of American Life by French Travelers, 1860–1914." Ph.D. diss., University of Virginia, 1953.
Anderson, R. D. *Education in France, 1848–1870*. Oxford: Oxford University Press, 1975.
Antonetti, Guy. *Histoire contemporaine politique et sociale*. 6th ed. Paris: Presses Universitaires de France, 1995.
Bainville, Jacques. *La Troisième République* Paris: Arthème Fayard, 1935.
Barral, Pierre. *Léon Gambetta: tribun et stratège de la République (1838–1882)*. Toulouse, 2008.
Beach, Bert. "La Reconstruction politique aux Etats-Unis vu par les représentants diplomatiques et consulaires de la France (1865–1871)." 3rd cycle thesis, University of Paris, 1958.
Beard, Charles A., and Mary R. Beard. *The Rise of American Civilization*. New York: Macmillan, 1930.
Beckert, Sven. "Emancipation and Empire: Reconstructing the Worldwide Web of Cotton Production in the Age of the American Civil War." *American Historical Review* 109, no. 5 (December 2004): 1405–1438.
———. *Empire of Cotton: A Global History*. New York: Alfred A. Knopf, 2014.
Beecher, Jonathan. *Victor Considérant and the Rise and Fall of French Romantic Socialism*. Berkeley: University of California Press, 2001.
Bell, Daniel. *Marxian Socialism in the United States*. Princeton, N.J.: Princeton University Press, 1967.
Bellanger, Claude, Jacques Godechot, Pierre Guiral, and Fernand Terron, eds. *Histoire générale de la presse française*. 5 vols. Paris: Presses Universitaires de France, 1969.
Belot, Robert, and Daniel Bermond, *Bartholdi*. Paris: Perrin, 2004.
Bemis, Samuel Flagg. *A Diplomatic History of the United States*. New York: H. Holt, 1936.
Berenson, Edward. *Populist Religion and Left-Wing Politics in France, 1830–1852*. Princeton, N.J.: Princeton University Press, 1985.
———. *The Statue of Liberty: A Transatlantic Story*. New Haven, Conn.: Yale University Press, 2012.
Berenson, Edward, Vincent Duclert, and Christophe Prochasson, eds. *The French Republic: History, Values, Debates*. Ithaca, N.Y: Cornel University Press, 2011.
Bernstein, Samuel. *Essays in Political and Intellectual History*. New York: Paine-Whitman, 1955.

———. *The First International in America*. New York: A. M. Kelley, 1962.

Bertier de Sauvigny, Guillaume de. "American Travelers in France, 1814–1848." In *Diplomacy in an Age of Nationalism: Essays in Honor of Lynn Marshall Case,* edited by Nancy N. Barker and Marvin L. Brown, 11–24. The Hague: Martinus Nijhoff, 1971.

Bertrand, Thierry. "Exil et transportation. Sources pour l'étude des proscriptions bonapartistes (1848–1870)." Mémoire de Diplôme D'Etudes Approfondies, Université de Nice, 2002.

Bishop, Morris. "Louis Philippe in America." *American Heritage* 20, no. 3 (April 1969). https://www.americanheritage.com/louis-philippe-america.

Blackburn, George M. *French Newspaper Opinion on the American Civil War.* Westport, Conn.: Greenwood, 1997.

Blumenthal, Henry. *France and the United States: Their Diplomatic Relations, 1789–1914.* Chapel Hill: University of North Carolina Press, 1970.

———. *Reappraisal of Franco-American Relations, 1830–1871.* Chapel Hill: University of North Carolina Press, 1959.

Boorstin, Daniel J., ed. *An American Primer.* Chicago: University of Chicago Press, 1966.

Braka, Florence, *L'honneur perdu du général Cluseret: de l'internationalisme au nationalisme.* Paris: Maisonneuve & Larose-Hémisphères éditions, 2018.

Bressant Marc. *Les Funérailles de Victor Hugo.* Paris: M. de Maule, 2012.

Brinton, Crane. *The Americans and the French.* Cambridge, Mass.: Harvard University Press, 1968.

Brogan, Sir Denis W. *The Price of Revolution.* London: H. Hamilton, 1951.

Brogan, Hugh. *Alexis de Tocqueville: A Life.* New Haven, Conn.: Yale University Press, 2007.

Bunle, Henri. *Etudes démographiques N° 4: Mouvements migratoires entre la France et l'étranger.* Paris: Imprimerie Nationale, 1943.

Calman, Alvin R. *Ledru-Rollin après 1848 et les proscrits français en Angleterre.* Paris: F. Rieder, 1921.

Carlton, Frank T. *History and Problems of Organized Labor.* Boston: D. C. Heath, 1911.

Carwardine, Richard, and Jay Sexton, eds. *The Global Lincoln.* New York: Oxford University Press, 2011.

Case, Lynn M. *French Opinion on the United States and Mexico, 1860–1867: Extracts from the Reports of the Procureurs-Généraux.* New York: Octagon Books, 1969.

———. *French Opinion on War and Diplomacy during the Second Empire.* Hamden, Conn.: Archon Books, 1954.

Case, Lynn M., and Warren F. Spencer. *The United States and France: Civil War Diplomacy.* Philadelphia: University of Pennsylvania Press, 1970.

Castelot, André. *Maximilien et Charlotte du Mexique: la tragédie de l'ambition.* Paris: Perrin, 1977.

Chancerel, Catherine. *L'Homme du grand fleuve*. Paris: CNRS, 2014.

Chardak, Henriette. *Elisée Reclus*. Paris: Stock, 2005.

Chevalier, Louis. "L'Emigration française au XIXe siècle." *Etudes d'histoire moderne et contemporaine* 1 (1947): 127–171.

Chinard, Gilbert. *L'Amérique de Abraham Lincoln et la France*. Washington, D.C.: Institut Français, 1945.

———. "Comment l'Amérique reconnut la République de 48." *French-American Review* 1 (1948): 83–109.

Clark, John P., and Camille Martin, eds. *Anarchy, Geography, Modernity: The Radical Social Thought of Elisée Reclus*. Lanham, Md.: Lexington Books 2004.

Clark, Thomas D. *Travels in the Old South: A Bibliography*. Norman: University of Oklahoma Press, 1959.

Cobban, Alfred. *A History of Modern France*. Baltimore: Penguin, 1975.

Cogniot, Georges, ed. *Le Lyre d'Airain: Poésie populaire et démocratique (1815–1918)*. Paris: Editions Sociales, 1964.

Collins, Irene. *The Government and the Newspaper Press in France, 1814–1881*. London: Oxford University Press, 1959.

Copans, Simon J. "French Opinion of American Democracy, 1852–1860." Ph.D. diss., Brown University, 1942.

Cornut-Gentille, Pierre. *Le 4 septembre 1870: L'invention de la République*. Paris: Perrin, 2017.

Crook, David Paul. *American Democracy in English Politics, 1815–50*. Oxford: Oxford University Press, 1965.

Current, Richard N. *The Lincoln Nobody Knows*. New York: McGraw-Hill, 1958.

Curti, Merle E. "George N. Sanders—American Patriot of the Fifties." *South Atlantic Quarterly* 27 (1928): 79–87.

———. "The Reputation of America Overseas (1776–1860)." *American Quarterly* 1 (1949): 58–82.

———. "Young America." *American Historical Review* 32 (1926): 34–55.

Curti, Merle E., and Kendall Blair. "The Immigrant and the American Image in Europe, 1860–1914." *Mississippi Valley Historical Review* 37 (1950–51): 203–230.

Curtis, Eugene N. "American Opinion of the French Nineteenth-Century Revolutions." *American Historical Review* 29 (1924): 249–270.

———. *The French Assembly of 1848 and American Constitutional Doctrines*. New York: Columbia University Press, 1917.

Dansette, Adrien. *Louis-Napoléon et la conquête du pouvoir*. Paris: Hachette, 1961.

Dean, John, and Olivier Frayssé, eds. "Lincoln in Europe." Special issue, *American Studies Journal* 60 (2016). http://www.asjournal.org/category/60-2016.

Decaux, Alain. *L'Empire, l'amour et l'argent*. Paris: Perrin, 1982.

Delord, Taxile. *Histoire illustrée du Second Empire.* 6 vols. Paris: G. Ballière, 1880–83.

Denholm, Anthony. *France in Revolution, 1848.* New York: John Wiley and Sons, 1972.

Desanti, Dominique. *Les Socialistes de l'Utopie.* Paris: Payot, 1971.

Deschanel, Paul. *Gambetta.* Paris: Hachette, 1919.

Deslandres, Maurice. *L'avènement de la troisième république, la constitution de 1875.* Vol. 3 of *Histoire constitutionnelle de la France.* Paris: A. Colin, 1937.

Dolléans, Edouard. *L'Histoire du mouvement ouvrier.* Paris: A. Colin, 1936.

———. *Proudhon.* Paris: Gallimard, 1948.

Dommanget, Maurice. *Blanqui et l'opposition révolutionnaire à la fin du Second Empire.* Paris: A. Colin, 1960.

———. *Victor Considérant, sa vie, son œuvre.* Paris: Editions sociales internationales, 1929.

Doyle, Don H., ed. *American Civil Wars: The United States, Latin America, Europe, and the Crisis of the 1860s.* Chapel Hill: University of North Carolina Press, 2017.

———. *The Cause of All Nations: An International History of the American Civil War.* New York: Basic Books, 2014.

Dumont-Wilden, Louis. *L'Évolution de l'esprit européen.* Paris: Flammarion, 1937.

Dunham, Arthur Lewis. *The Anglo-French Treaty of Commerce of 1860 and the Progress of the Industrial Revolution in France.* Ann Arbor: University of Michigan Press, 1930.

Dupeux, Georges. *French Society, 1789–1970.* Translated by Peter Wait. New York: Barnes & Noble, 1976.

Dupont, Henry. *L'Amérique dans l'œuvre de Victor Hugo.* New York: Cultural Division of the French Embassy, 1952.

Duveau, Georges. *La Pensée ouvrière sur l'éducation pendant la Seconde République et le Second Empire.* Paris: Domat, 1947.

———. *La Vie ouvrière en France sous le Second Empire.* Paris: Gallimard, 1946.

Echeverria, Durand. "L'Amérique devant l'opinion française, 1734–1870. Questions de méthode et d'interprétation." *Revue d'histoire moderne et contemporaine* 9 (1962): 51–62.

———. *Mirage in the West: A History of the French Image of American Society to 1815.* Princeton, N.J.: Princeton University Press, 1957.

Edwards, Stewart. *Paris Commune, 1871.* Chicago: Quadrange Books, 1973.

Ellison, Mary. *Support for Secession: Lancashire and the American Civil War.* Chicago: University of Chicago Press, 1972.

Erickson, Charlotte. *American Industry and the European Immigrant, 1860–1885.* Cambridge, Mass.: Harvard University Press, 1957.

Ernot, Isabelle. "Olympe Audouard dans l'univers de la presse, (France, 1860–1890)." *Genre & Histoire* 14 (Spring 2014). https://journals.openedition.org/genrehistoire/1990.

Ernst, Robert. *Immigrant Life in New York City, 1825–1863.* New York: King's Crown, 1949.

Ettinger, Amos Aschbach. *The Mission to Spain of Pierre Soulé, 1853–1855: A Study in the Cuban Diplomacy of the United States.* New Haven, Conn.: Yale University Press, 1932.

Eyal, Yonatan. *The Young America Movement and the Transformation of the Democratic Party, 1828–1861.* New York: Cambridge University Press, 2007.

Fauré, Christine, and Tom Bishop, eds. *L'Amérique des Français.* Paris: F. Bourin, 1992.

Featherstonhaugh, G. W., and Germaine-Marie Mason. "Le Départ de Louis-Philippe pour l'Angleterre." *Revue Historique* 200, no. 2 (1948): 202–205.

Fejto, François, ed. *Le printemps des peuples: 1848 dans le monde.* 2 vols. Paris: Amis des Éditions de Minuit, 1948.

Ferris, Norman B. *The Trent Affair: A Diplomatic Crisis.* Knoxville: University of Tennessee Press, 1977.

Field, James A. *America and the Mediterranean World, 1776–1882.* Princeton, N.J.: Princeton University Press, 1969.

Filler, Louis. *The Crusade against Slavery.* New York: Harper, 1960.

Fohlen, Claude. *L'Industrie textile au temps du Second Empire.* Paris: Plon, 1956.

Foner, Eric. *Reconstruction: America's Unfinished Revolution, 1863–1877.* New York: Perennial Classics, 2002.

Foner, Philip S. *A History of Cuba and its Relations with the United States.* New York: International Publishers, 1962–63.

———. *History of the Labor Movement in the United States.* 7 vols. New York: International Publishers, 1947.

Forster, Robert. "France in America." *French Historical Studies* 23, no. 2 (Spring 2000): 239–258.

Frambourg, Guy. *Un Philanthrope et démocrate nantais: le docteur Guépin, 1805–1875.* Nantes: Imp. de l'Atlantique, 1964.

Franklin, John Hope. *The Emancipation Proclamation.* Garden City, N.Y.: Doubleday, 1963.

Frémont, John Charles. *Exposé de la situation de la Compagnie du Memphis, El Paso et Pacific Rail-Road.* Paris: Impr. de Balitout, Questroy, 1869.

Galante Garrone, Alessandro. *Philippe Buonarroti et les révolutionnaires du XIXe siècle, 1828–1837.* Paris: Editions Champs Libre, 1975.

Gavronsky, Serge. *The French Liberal Opposition and the American Civil War.* New York: Humanities, 1968.

Geffroy, Gustave. *Clemenceau, suivi d'une étude de Louis Lumet avec citations de G. Clemenceau sur les Etats-Unis d'Amérique.* Paris: G. Crès, 1918.

Gershman, Sally. "Alexis de Tocqueville and Slavery." *French Historical Studies* 9 (1976): 467–483.

Girard, Louis. *La IIe République.* Paris: Calmann-Lévy, 1968.

———. *Les Elections de 1869*. Paris: M. Rivière, 1960.

———. *Napoléon III*. Paris: Fayard, 1986.

———. *Problèmes politiques et constitutionnels du Second Empire*. Paris: Centre de documentation universitaire, 1964.

Godechot, Jacques. *Les Constitutions de la France depuis 1789*. Paris: Garnier-Flammarion, 1970.

Gray, Walter D. *Interpreting American Democracy in France: The Career of Edouard Laboylaye, 1811–1883*. Newark: University of Delaware Press, 1994.

Green, F. C. *A Comparative View of French and British Civilization, 1850–1870*. London: Dent, 1965.

Green, Jennifer R., and Patrick M. Kirkwood. "Reframing the Antebellum Democratic Mainstream: Transatlantic Diplomacy and the Career of Pierre Soulé." *Civil War History* 61, no. 3 (September 2015): 212–251.

Green, Nancy L. "The Comparative Gaze: Travelers in France before the Era of Mass Tourism." *French Historical Studies* 25, no. 3 (2002): 423–440.

Gregory, Winifred. *International Congresses and Conferences, 1840–1937*. New York: H. W. Wilson, 1938.

Guérard, Albert. *Beyond Hatred: The Democratic Ideal in France and America*. New York, Charles Scribner's Sons, 1925.

———. *French Civilization in the 19th Century*. New York: Charles Scribner's Sons, 1925.

———. *Napoleon III*. Cambridge, Mass.: Harvard University Press, 1943.

Guerlain, Pierre. *Miroirs transatlantiques: la France et les Etats-Unis entre passions et Indifférence*. Paris: Ed. l'Harmattan, 1996.

Guiral, Pierre. *Prévost-Paradol, 1824–1870: Pensée et action d'un libéral sous le Second Empire*. Paris: Presses Universitaires de France, 1955.

———. *La Vie quotidienne en France à l'âge d'or du capitalisme, 1852–1879*. Paris: Hachette, 1976.

Hage, Armand. *Histoire des relations franco-américaines des origines à nos jours*. Paris: Ellipses, 2010.

Hamilton, Maxine T. "The London Times and the American Civil War." Ph.D. diss., University of Leicester, 1988.

Harrison, Royden. *Before the Socialists: Studies in Labour and Politics, 1861–1881*. London: Routledge & K. Paul, 1965.

———. "British Labour and American Slavery." *Science and Society* 25 (1961): 291–319.

———. "British Labour and the Confederacy." *International Review of Social History* 2 (1959): 78–104.

Hawkins, Richmond Laurin. *Auguste Comte and the United States, 1816–1853*. Cambridge, Mass.: Harvard University Press, 1936.

———. *Newly Discovered French Letters of the 17th, 18th and 19th Centuries*. Cambridge, Mass.: Harvard University Press, 1933.

———. "Unpublished Letters of Alexis de Tocqueville." *Romanic Review* 19 (1928): 95–217.

Hayat, Samuel. *1848: Quand la République était révolutionnaire*. Paris: Ed. du Seuil, 2014.

Heath, Richard. *Edgar Quinet: His Early Life and Writings*. London: Trübner, 1881.

Hemmings, F. W. *Culture and Society in France, 1848–1898*. B. T. Batsford, 1971.

Higonnet, Patrice. *Sister Republics: The Origins of French and American Republicanism*. Cambridge, Mass: Harvard University Press, 1988.

Hillquit, Morris. *History of Socialism in the United States*. New York: Funk & Wagnalls, 1903.

Hofstadter, Richard. *The American Political Tradition and the Men Who Made It*. New York: Vintage Books, 1954.

Honor, Hugh, ed. *L'Amérique vue par l'Europe*. Paris: Grand Palais, 1976.

Houbre, Gabrielle. *Le livre des courtisanes: archives secrètes de la police des mœurs, 1861–1876*. Paris: Le Grand livre du mois, 2006.

Hyman, Harold, ed. *Heard Round the World: The Impact Abroad of the Civil War*. New York: Knopf, 1969.

Jeanneney, Jean-Noël. *Victor Hugo et la République*. Paris: Gallimard, 2002.

Jeune, Simon. *De F. T. Graindorge à A. O. Barnabooth: Les Types américains dans le roman et le théâtre français (1861–1917)*. Paris: Didier, 1963.

Jolly, Jean, ed. *Dictionnaire des parlementaires français. Notices biographiques sur les ministres, députés et sénateurs français de 1889 à 1940*. Paris: Presses Universitaires de France, 1960–70.

Jones, Howard. *Abraham Lincoln and a New Birth of Freedom: The Union and Slavery in the Diplomacy of the Civil War*. Lincoln: University of Nebraska Press, 1999.

———. *Blue and Gray Diplomacy: A History of Union and Confederate Foreign Relations*. Chapel Hill: University of North Carolina Press, 2010.

Jones, Howard Mumford. *America and French Culture, 1750–1848*. Chapel Hill: University of North Carolina Press, 1927.

Jordan, Donaldson, and Edwin J. Pratt. *Europe and the American Civil War*. New York: Octagon Books, 1969.

Karsky, Barbara. "L'Influence de Abraham Lincoln sur les libéraux et les démocrates français du Second Empire." University of Paris thesis, 1969.

Katz, Philip Mark. *From Appomattox to Montmartre: Americans and the Paris Commune*. Cambridge, Mass.: Harvard University Press, 1998.

Koht, Halvdan. *The American Spirit in Europe: A Survey of Transatlantic Influences*. Philadelphia: University of Pennsylvania, 1949.

Korner, Axel, Nicola Miller, and Adam I. P. Smith, eds. *America Imagined: Explaining the United States in Nineteenth-Century Europe and Latin America*. New York: Palgrave Macmillan, 2012.

Krebs, Albert. "Lincoln et la France." *Informations et documents* 99 (1959): 36–42.

Landy, A. "A French Adventurer and American Expansionism after the Civil War." *Science and Society* 15 (1951): 313–33.

Larousse, Pierre, ed. *Dictionnaire universel du XIXe siècle.* Paris: Administration du Grand dictionnaire universel, 1865–90.

Lefranc, Georges. *Les Gauches en France: 1789–1972.* Paris: Payot, 1973.

Lejeune, Paule. *La Commune de Paris au jour le jour.* Paris: L'Harmattan, 2002.

Lemaître, Renée. *La Guerre de Sécession en photos, avec un choix de textes de témoins français.* Paris and Brussels: Elsevier Séquoia, 1975.

Lestocquoy, Jean. *Histoire du partiotisme en France.* Paris: Albin Michel, 1968.

Lewis, Edward R. *A History of American Political Thought from the Civil War to the World War.* New York: Octagon Books, 1969.

L'Huilier, Fernand. *La Lutte ouvrière à la fin du Second Empire.* Paris: A. Colin, 1958.

Lichtheim, George. *A Short History of Socialism.* London: Weidenfeld & Nicolson, 1970.

Longmate, Norman. *The Hungry Mills: The Story of the Lancashire Cotton Famine, 1861–5.* London: Temple Smith, 1978.

Lucas, Edith E. *La Littérature anti-esclavagiste au 19e siècle: Etude sur Mme. Beecher Stowe et son influence en France.* Paris: E. de Boccard, 1930.

Mahieu, Robert. *Les Enquêteurs français aux Etats-Unis de 1830 à 1837: L'Influence américaine sur l'évolution démocratique en France.* Paris: H. Champion, 1934.

Maitron, Jean, ed. *Dictionnaire biographique du mouvement ouvrier français.* 44 vols. Paris: Editions ouvrières, 1964–77.

Malone, Dumas, ed. *Dictionary of American Biography.* New York: Charles Scribner's Sons, 1928–37.

Martin, Percy F. *Maximilian in Mexico.* London: Constable, 1914.

May, Arthur J. "Crete and the United States, 1866–1869." *Journal of Modern History* 16 (1944): 286–293.

Mayeur, Jean-Marie. *Les Débuts de la Troisième République.* Paris: Editions du Seuil, 1973.

McClellan, George B. *McClellan's Own Story: The War for the Union.* New York: C. L. Webster, 1887.

McCullough, David. *The Greater Journey: Americans in Paris.* New York: Simon & Schuster, 2011.

McKay, Donald C. *The United States and France.* Cambridge, Mass.: Harvard University Press, 1951.

Meng, John J. "A Century of American Catholicism as Seen through French Eyes." *Catholic Historical Review* 27 (1941): 39–68.

Michelon, Anne. "Les Socialistes français au Texas." Maîtrise essay, University of Paris, 1973.

Miller, Richard Lawrence. *Lincoln and His World: The Early Years, Birth to Illinois Legislature.* Mechanicsburg, Pa.: Stackpole Books, 2006.

Mitterrand, Frédéric. *Napoléon III et Victor Hugo, le duel.* Paris: XO Editions, 2019.

Monaghan, Frank. *French Travelers in the United States, 1765–1932: A Bibliography.* New York: New York Public Library, 1933.

Moore, John Basset, ed. *History and Digest of the International Arbitrations to Which the United States Has Been a Party.* 6 vols. Washington, D.C.: Government Printing Office, 1898.

Morison, Samuel Eliot. *The Oxford History of the American People.* 4 vols. New York: Oxford University Press, 1972.

Nataf, André, ed. *Dictionnaire du mouvement ouvrier.* Paris: Editions Universitaires, 1970.

Noël, Bernard. *Dictionnaire de la Commune.* Paris: F. Hazan, 1971.

Noll, Franklin. "Repudiation: The Crisis of United States Civil War Debt, 1865–1870." MPRA Paper 43540. 2012. University Library of Munich, Germany. https://ideas.repec .org/p/pra/mprapa/43540.html.

Nordmann, Jean-Thomas, ed. *La France radicale.* Paris: Gallimard, 1977.

Novack, George, ed. *America's Revolutionary Heritage: Marxist Essays.* New York: Pathfinder, 1976.

Osgood, Samuel M., ed. *Napoléon III and the Second Empire.* Lexington, Mass.: Heath, 1973.

Owsley, Frank L. *King Cotton Diplomacy: Foreign Relations of the Confederate States of America.* Chicago: University of Chicago Press, 1931.

Palix, Pierre. *Le Goût littéraire et artistique de P. J. Proudhon.* Paris: H. Champion, 1977.

Palmer, Robert. *The Age of the Democratic Revolution.* Princeton, N.J.: Princeton University Press, 1969.

Parrington, Vernon Louis. *The Beginnings of Critical Realism in America.* Vol. 3 of *Main Currents in American Thought.* New York: Harcourt, Brace, & World, 1958.

Peraino, Kevin. *Lincoln in the World: The Making of a Statesman and the Dawn of American Power.* New York: Crown, 2013.

Phalen, William, *The Democratic Soldier: The Life of Gustave Paul Cluseret.* New Delhi: Vij Books India, 2015.

Pierrard, Pierre. *Les Chansons en patois de Lille sous le Second Empire.* Arras: Archives du Pas-de-Calais, 1966.

———. *La Vie ouvrière à Lille sous le Second Empire.* Paris: Bloud et Gay, 1965.

Pincetl, Stanley. "Relations de la France et des Etats-Unis pendant la Seconde République." Thesis, University of Paris, 1950.

Plamenatz, John. *The Revolutionary Movement in France, 1815–1871.* London: Longmans, 1952.

Plessis, Alain. *De la fête impériale au mur des fédérés, 1852–1871.* Paris: Editions du Seuil, 1973.

Portes, Jacques. *Fascination and Misgivings: The United States in French Opinion, 1870–1914.* New York: Cambridge University Press, 2000.

Power, J. Tracy. *Lee's Miserables: Life in the Army of Northern Virginia from the Wilderness to Appomattox.* Chapel Hill: University of North Carolina Press, 2002.

Pradalié, Georges. *Le Second Empire.* Paris: Presses Universitaires de France, 1969.

Price, Roger, ed. *1848 in France.* Ithaca, N.Y.: Cornell University Press, 1975.

Prost, Antoine. *Histoire de l'enseignement en France, 1800–1967.* Paris: A. Colin, 1968.

Prudhommeaux, Jules. *Icarie et son fondateur Etienne Cabet.* Paris: E. Cornély, 1907.

Rémond, René. *Les Etats-Unis devant l'opinion française, 1815–1852.* 2 vols. Paris: Ministère de l'Education, 1962.

Renard, Edouard. *Louis Blanc, sa vie, son œuvre.* Paris: Hachette, 1928.

Reynolds, David S. *John Brown, Abolitionist: The Man Who Killed Slavery, Sparked the Civil War, and Seeded Civil Rights.* New York: Alfred A. Knopf, 2005.

Richardson, James D. *A Compilation of the Messages and Papers of the Presidents, 1789–1897.* 10 vols. Washington, D.C.: Government Printing Office, 1896–99.

Robert, Adolphe, Edgar Bourloton, and Gustave Cougny, eds. *Dictionnaire des parlementaires français, comprenant tous les membres des assemblées françaises depuis le 1er mai 1789 jusqu'au 1er mai 1889.* Paris: Bourloton, 1889–90.

Roger, Philippe. *The American Enemy: A Story of French Anti-Americanism.* Chicago: University of Chicago Press, 2005.

Rossiter, Clinton. *The American Presidency.* New York: Harcourt, Brace, 1956.

Rougerie, Jacques. *Paris libre 1871.* Paris: Editions du Seuil, 1971.

Rude, Fernand, ed. *Voyage en Icarie: Deux Ouvriers viennois aux Etats-Unis en 1855.* Paris: Presses Universitaires de France, 1952.

Sabin, Joseph, Wilberforce Eames, and R. W. G. Vail, eds. *Dictionary of Books Relating to America, from Its Discovery to the Present Time.* New York: Bibliographical Society of America, 1868–1936.

Sainlaude, Stève, *Le gouvernement impérial et la guerre de sécession.* Paris: L'Harmattan, 2011.

Sancton, Thomas A. "The Myth of French Worker Support for the North in the American Civil War." *French Historical Studies* 11, no. 1 (Spring 1979): 58–80.

Santineau, Maurice. *Schœlcher, Héros de l'abolition de l'esclavage dans les possessions françaises.* Paris: Mellottée, 1948.

Schivelbusch, Wolfgang. *The Culture of Defeat: On National Trauma, Mourning, and Recovery.* Translated by Jefferson Chase. New York: Metropolitan Books, 2003.

Sears, Louis Martin. "A Neglected Critic of Our Civil War." *Mississippi Valley Historical Review* 1 (1915): 532–545.

Sibert, Marcel. *La Constitution de la France du 4 septembre 1870 au 9 août 1944.* Paris: A. Pedone, 1946.

Sideman, Belle B., and Lillian Friedman, eds. *Europe Looks at the Civil War: An Anthology.* New York: Orion, 1960.

Sifakis, Stewart. *Who Was Who in the American Civil War.* New York: Facts on File, 1988.

Silberschmidt, Max. *The United States and Europe.* London: Thames and Hudson, 1972.

Skard, Sigmund. *The American Myth and the European Mind: American Studies, 1776–1960.* Philadelphia: University of Pennsylvania Press, 1961.

———. *American Studies in Europe: Their History and Present Organization.* Philadelphia: University of Pennsylvania Press, 1958.

Smith, Theodore C. "Expansion after the Civil War, 1865–1871." *Political Science Quarterly* 16 (1901): 412–436.

Soltau, Roger. *French Political Thought in the Nineteenth Century.* New Haven, Conn.: Yale University Press, 1931.

Squires, Melinda Jane. "The Controversial Career of George Nicholas Sanders." Master's thesis, Western Kentucky University, 2000.

Stampp, Kenneth M. *The Era of Reconstruction.* New York: Knopf, 1967.

Stanton, Theodore. *General Grant and the French.* N.p., [1889].

Sutton Robert. Introduction to *Travels in Icaria,* by Etienne Cabet. Translated by Leslie J. Roberts. Syracuse, N.Y.: Syracuse University Press, 2003.

Tchernoff, Iouda. *Le Parti républicain au coup d'état et sous le Second Empire.* Paris: Pedone, 1906.

Thomas, Edith. *Les Pétroleuses.* Paris: Gallimard, 1963.

Thompson, J. M. *Louis Napoleon and the Second Empire.* Oxford: Oxford University Press, 1954.

Thomson, David, ed. *France: Empire and Republic, 1850–1940.* New York: Walker, 1968.

Tinker, Edward Larocque. *Les Ecrits de langue française en Louisiane au XIXe siècle.* Paris: H. Champion, 1932.

Tombs, Robert. *The Paris Commune 1871.* New York: Longman, 1999.

Trachtenberg, Marvin. *The Statue of Liberty.* New York: Penguin Books, 1986.

Troyat, Henri. *Alexandre Dumas: Le cinquième mousquetaire.* Paris: Grasset, 2005.

Tudesq, A. J. "La décentralisation et la droite en France au XIXe siècle." In *La Décentralisation. IVème Colloque d'histoire organisé par la faculté des Lettres et des Sciences humaines d'Aix-en-Provence.* Aix-en-Provence: Ophrys, 1965.

Vapereau, Gustave. *Dictionnaire universel des contemporains.* Paris: Hachette, 1893.

Vincent, Jean-Didier. *Elisée Reclus: Géographe, anarchiste, écologiste.* Paris: R. Lafont, 2010.

Voyenne, Bernard. *Histoire de l'idée européenne.* Paris: Payot, 1964.

Weill, Georges. *Histoire du mouvement social en France, 1852–1902.* Paris: F. Alcan, 1904.

———. *Histoire du parti républicain en France (1814–1870).* Paris: F. Alcan, 1928.

West, Warren R. *Contemporary French Opinion on the American Civil War.* Baltimore: Johns Hopkins Press, 1924.

White, Elizabeth B. *American Opinion of France from Lafayette to Poincaré.* New York: Knopf, 1927.

Whitridge, Arnold. *Men in Crisis: The Revolutions of 1848.* New York: Charles Scribner's Sons, 1949.

Wilcox, Walter F., ed. *International Migrations.* Vol. 2, *Interpretations.* New York: National Bureau of Economic Research, 1931.

Williams, Roger L. *The French Revolution of 1870–1871.* New York: Norton, 1969.

Williams, William Appleman. *America Confronts a Revolutionary World: 1776–1976.* New York: Morrow, 1976.

Willson, Beckles. *America's Ambassadors to France, 1777–1927.* London: J. Murray, 1927.

———. *John Slidell and the Confederates in Paris, 1862–65.* New York: Minton, Balch, 1932.

Wilson, Edmund. *Patriotic Gore: Studies in the Literature of the American Civil War.* New York: Oxford University Press, 1966.

Woodward, C. Vann. *Reunion and Reaction.* Boston: Little, Brown, 1966.

Wright, Gordon. "Public Opinion and Conscription in France, 1866–1870." *Journal of Modern History* 14 (1942): 26–45.

Zeldin, Theodore. *Emile Ollivier and the Liberal Empire of Napoleon III.* Oxford: Oxford University Press, 1963.

———. *France, 1848–1945.* 2 vols. Oxford: Oxford University Press, 1973–77.

———. *Histoire des passions françaises.* Vol 2, *Orgeuil et intelligence.* Translated by Catherine Ehrel and Odile de Lalène. Paris: Editions du Seuil, 1980.

———. *The Political System of Napoleon III.* London: Macmillan, 1958.

Zvengrowski, Jeffery. *Jefferson Davis, Napoleonic France, and the Nature of Confederate Ideology, 1815–1870.* Baton Rouge: Louisiana State University Press, 2020.

INDEX